THE SEASON OF THE LONG SHADOW

The Red Path Messenger Series

Other Works by the Author

❀

When Spirits Touch the Red Path
Book 1 in the Red Path Messenger Series
ISBN: 0-9786664-0-2

The Message
Book 2 in the Red Path Messenger Series
ISBN: 0-9786664-1-0

The Season of the Long Shadow
Book 3 in the Red Path Messenger Series
ISBN: 0-9786664-2-9

Watchers From the Shadows and The Light
Book 1 in the Watchers Trilogy

The Brotherhood
Book 2 in the Watchers Trilogy

Lumen
Book 3 in the Watchers Trilogy

In Search of Acasia

Desperate Dreams

Keepers of the Beast

More information on Speaking Wind may be found at:
www.dolphinmedia.com

THE SEASON OF THE LONG SHADOW

❁

The End of Separation

Patrick "Speaking Wind" Quirk

Dolphin Media, LLC
Huntsville, Alabama

The Season of the Long Shadow
The End of Separation

Dolphin Media, LLC

For more information:

Dolphin Media, LLC
6275 University Drive, Suite 37
Huntsville, AL 35806

www.dolphinmedia.com

Printed in the United States of America
ISBN: 0-9786664-2-9

In memory of my father, Patrick David Quirk. Thank you for all the wonderful memories you have shared with us.

And in memory of Grandfather, Two Bears, and my best friend, Cheeway. What we have shared together has always been.

It fills my heart with a good feeling knowing that none of us are ever far away.

AND

To my mother, Vi Quirk, for all the support you have given me as no other could have done. My son, Patrick Timothy Quirk, who is my partner in this great adventure that has been set before me by the Ancient Ones. And to Joe Kelly, from our people's cousins, the Cherokee, in Chattanooga, Tennessee, who always had time to share his smile with me when I needed one.

I wish to thank all three of you for sharing with me the path you travel. Know that I hold you in a very special place in my heart.

Contents

❧

Part VII   The End to Separateness

Part VIII 11 Steps to Healing Our Spirit from Within

Part XI   The Journey Begins

Preface

❀

"Grandfather!" I said, sitting on the top of one of the healing stones on our lands of the mesa.

"Yes, Little One, what is it that I may offer you assistance on?" Came his reply.

"I hold a great weight over me on this day. It is a weight that I cannot seem to lift off of me."

Looking at me with the eyes of his silent wisdom, Grandfather reached over and placed his right hand on my left shoulder and said:

"And what is this thing that bothers you so, Speaking Wind? Is it something you have found among the many speaking words that Two Bears and I have shared with you and Cheeway?

"Yes, it is, Grandfather," I repeated looking for some kind of assurance within his penetrating eyes.

"It is from the speaking words that you and Two Bears shared with Cheeway and myself about The Season of the Long Shadow. All of this has given both of us a great weight of uncertainty to carry," I said.

"And you would wish for me to dispel this feeling of uncertainty from you?" was Grandfather's response.

"Yes, Grandfather…yes, I would like for you to do this. But not only for me, but for my brother, Cheeway as well."

For a few moments, a calming silence filled these lands of the mesa where we had been allowed to share our earth walk. It was a silence that was going to be lost in time, for what Grandfather was about to share with me would not allow me to ever hear this silence in the same way again, not in the way I had become used to hearing it before…before he gave me this answer I had asked of him.

"This is not possible, Speaking Wind. This removal of your feeling of uncertainty is something that must be worn by both you and Cheeway."

"Then will it be for a long time, Grandfather?" I asked.

"It will be for as long as it is required, Speaking Wind," was his reply.

Taking a few moments to look deep within me, within me where my spirit resides, he smiled a calming smile over me. And as he shared his face of peace with me, I too was feeling what he had come to know so well, this feeling of complete balance within him, and all life that was around us.

"Little One, you must be willing to hear with truth what I am about to share with you now. For if you will not hear through your ears of spirit, then I am afraid what little assistance I can give to you on this matter will be lost. And once Two Bears and I are gone, there might not be another chance for you to hear us again. That is, if you will not come to understand what I am now willing to share with you.

"Look around you, Little One. Look around you and see all of the wonders of life that is filling these lands.

"All this life that is before you now…it will not always be here. Not in the same way.

"The time for all life in this domain is only a little while longer, and for those who would not prepare themselves from within, I am afraid that they, too, will have to go away, like all of these memories of how life in this domain once was.

"Unless they can come to a place of understanding for themselves and all things that are with them, Speaking Wind, then I would fear from the knowledge of what will happen to them. I would not wish to have this knowledge, were I not prepared, because of what I feel when I only think on it."

Hearing this from Grandfather's speaking words forced all of the blood that was in my face to fall into my feet.

I knew he would be able to see this surprise that was over my face—this surprise that was continuing to fill me with even more uncertainty now.

And as had always been the case, Grandfather knew what to do. He placed both of his hands over my shoulders and said:

"Do not be concerned with those things you have no effect on, Little One. For they are not meant to be controlled by you, or anyone else.

"Always remember that on this path we travel, ours is not to control. Ours is only to understand those things that are presented to us. To understand them so when it becomes time for us to move on to other lessons, we will be ready.

"Listen to me, Speaking Wind. What I have shared with you is also being shared with Cheeway by Two Bears at this same time.

"Both Two Bears and myself went to the lake of tears to see more of this spirit path both of you have come into this domain to travel. And we were shown many things...many things that will require each of you to prepare for the times that are ahead.

"And this feeling of uncertainty that is about both of you now, well it is only a sign of those many things that are yet to be born to you. Those things that you will need to hold a great understanding for before the Old Ones will speak through you. Before the Ancient Ones will share their wisdom and teachings so others may also prepare themselves for what is to come."

"And this ending of time as we know it, Grandfather, will there be nothing remaining of what is now?" I asked.

Looking over me with the love I had always come to know from him...this love of freedom and understanding for all things. He only gave me one word. "No!"

Publisher's Acknowledgements

❀

Cover layout and design by Cliff Collier and Jim King.
Photo on back cover by Bryan Rohbock.
Edited by the author, David and Sharon Dooling, and Jim King, Huntsville, Alabama.
A special thanks and appreciation goes to Sharon "White Wolf Mother" Dooling for her encouragement, support and efforts.

Author's Note

All of the events and occurrences in this book have been presented to you as they have been presented to me. No deletions or additions have been made. Only the names of the lands on which these visions have taken place have been changed. For unless one has been called to them, their location is not to be known by any other.

Prologue

❀

We have all been on a long journey. It has been a journey where each of the four races—the red race, the yellow race, the black race, and the white race—have each been given 10,000 years to cleanse themselves and make their own choice.

This choice we have been given was to follow the path of spirit, the path that leads to the right and is fed by spirit and is led by spirit as well; or, to follow the path of the body, the path that leads to the left and is led by the body and fed by the emotions.

During each race's time for cleansing, the other three would stand aside and give to them the same freedom they found when it was their time for this cleansing. As each of the four races would find themselves in their respective time, they were given complete dominion over all they would see, and unlimited freedom over all that they would do.

This was to allow them the freedom of choice, the same freedom of choice that would allow them to see which of the two paths they would follow.

During this time of the races cleansings, they were given their individual freedom of choosing which of the two paths they would follow, they were given many lessons to gain insight from, lessons that when learned from, would give them another piece of the truth they had been searching for.

However, during this time of cleansing, there were always those who could not find their own way. And they would spend great amounts of time and effort in keeping others from finding theirs as well. And these people would place many obstacles in front of other peoples paths so they could not see where they needed to go…obstacles that would have anyone believe if they would travel on the path of spirit, they would suffer greatly.

But, as it is with all things in an earth walk, no one can determine whether an individual is doing well or poorly on their path. Only their own spirit within has this ability. And to think that one can sit and judge another from their own limited perspective, is not a truth, and leads to a false path. It is a false path that will be seen for what it is, but only when it is close to the end of their journey with the Earth Mother.

This has taken place for all who have entered this domain to travel a life path. These choices and lessons from both paths have been given equally to all.

Now, our time is almost at an end, and the last of the races (the white race), has completed its cleansing.

This last race completed its cleansing in July of 1992. When this took place, the protective hand from all life was removed, and all began to feel the newness of being held accountable for their own actions and deeds once again. All life felt this new accountability come to them but regarded it as a mere inconvenience, like something that would go away if they would not give it much attention.

However, this did not happen, and from July of 1992, many more two legs (people) began feeling this accountability come to them. But as it continues to grow in its intensity, they can only see it through the eyes of fear.

This accountability began many changes in everyone's life. And I say everyone, because no one will be missed. All who are here with you, all who you can see and those you cannot see within this world, are feeling these same things.

People feel they no longer belong where they have spent many of their seasons. They feel as if all they had come to believe in has been taken away from them. And from those many untrue things they once believed in, when they were needed to lean on them for support, they found them not strong at all...for much of their beliefs crumbled under this new weight of their uncertainly.

The groups they once found comfort and safety in no longer hold the same value for them either. And many people are beginning to fall away from the group's guidance and direction and are now coming to place more and more trust in their own decisions, these decisions that must be found from within themselves.

This time we have begun in July of 1992 is called The Season of the Long Shadow. And it has come to remind us that time, as we have known it in the past, is soon to end. All we have come to know and live with will either be changed tremendously, or taken away to another place and another time.

My teachings come to me from Grandfather and Two Bears of the Pueblos in northern New Mexico. We called them Spirit Callers, but today, many people call them **Shaman.**

My best friend, Cheeway, and I were prepared for many years by those things they taught us...those things that had been handed down from the Ancient Ones...the Anasazi.

We were given this knowledge and many spirit visions and told to hold onto them until the time was right, to hold them to ourselves until we had entered this time that is called The Season of the Long Shadow.

We are in this time now. We are living in the time of prophecy that has been spoken of by the generations of the past, and we are living in this time that has been spoken of for more generations than we can count.

The information that is contained in this book is true and its presented to you as it has been presented to me, either from the speaking words of Grandfather and Two Bears, or from the spirit visions I have been given from the Ancient Ones of our people.

I call all of my books novels because I have changed the names of the lands where these events took place. These locations are not meant for any, unless they have been called to them. This is my reason for doing this.

These written words will not be for all who are traveling in this domain. These words are only for those who will have the eyes to see, the ears to hear, the heart to know, and the willingness of spirit to understand. For the ones who will understand this work, I wish for you a good journey as you begin a great adventure.

For those who cannot understand what is being presented, I wish you luck.

The speaking words that are being presented, to those who will understand them, will bring you a great blessing. It will allow you to begin to do those things you have come here to do, those things that will assist you in bringing your spirit to the next higher place...this next higher place that will allow you to see what is waiting ahead, and to understand why this time we know now is soon coming to an end. It is not because of any punishment—it is only because it is time...time to move on.

Read well, those who can see and hear. Read well and know that all is as it should be.

Speaking Wind,
Land of the Pueblos

PART I

THE CALLING SPIRIT

CHAPTER 1

❀

Calls in the Night

I was standing in front of a house when I turned my head to see a man approaching me. I was not sure if I should stay or leave, because he held many strange colors over him, colors that I had always associated with being in a great state of confusion.

"What is your name, fella?" came the first speaking words to me from this man of the white skin. "Why are you here? I haven't seen you before."

"My name is Speaking Wind, and I do not know why I am here," was my response to him.

Looking at this man who had walked very close to me, I could see many small beads of sweat covering his face, and a look of far distance in his eyes.

And each time he would speak to me, he would change his face many times. He would have a face of pain over him one moment to one of pleasure the next. And this would continue for all things he was speaking to me.

"I know you are not from here, you look too different for that," the man said as he ran his eyes over me.

"I know. You're an Indian aren't you."

"I am not Indian, mister. I am part Native American. If that is what you mean," was my rather terse response to him.

"Well, I really don't care what you are. But I will tell you this," he said as his spit rolled out of the sides of his mouth. "If you know what is good for you, you will let me blow your head off right now."

And with that, he pulled a large pistol from under his shirt and pointed it straight at my head and began laughing to himself.

Then, as I was looking into the barrel of the gun, I heard him pull the hammer back and saw the next bullet rotate into the chamber—this next bullet that might find its way into my head if I was not very careful.

As I stood in that place, I could not find any speaking words come to me that would make any sense. I could only utter small sounds from my mouth, and I was sure that if they were not making any sense to me, they would not be doing any good in explaining to this man that what he was about to do was not good for me.

Then, just as I could feel the energy from this man press back on the trigger, he lowered the gun slightly and looked at me.

And looking into his eyes, I could not find anything human about him. All I saw within him was an empty shell, one that did not have any of the attributes of any of the living I had ever seen.

It was then that I knew what he intended to do. He had made his mind up that he was ending his journey with the Earth Mother and did not mind taking others with him.

But why, I kept asking myself! Why would this man do such a thing? And why could I not say anything to him? And why could I not move from this place I was standing?

"I do not know you, so I don't have to take the responsibility for you," the quickened words came out of this man's mouth.

"But if you know what's good for you, you'll will do the same thing I have done for those I am responsible for," he continued.

"You see those bodies that are laying by the windows and door of my house?" the man said, pointing the way with the barrel of the gun.

"They are my family, and they are the ones I have responsibility for. And now…now I have taken care of them and they are all safe."

Looking over to the direction he had pointed to, I could see they had all been shot, some of them once, and others many times.

They were no longer inside the house. It looked as if they had been standing next to windows and doorways when they had been shot. And the force of the bullets threw them to the outside where I was now looking at them.

"If you have any good sense left to you, stranger, you will follow me. For this is the only place left where anyone can be safe and I know the way," the man continued.

"Follow me if you want to find your safety!" The man spurted out his words mixed with his saliva.

Then after his words fell out of his mouth, he turned the barrel of the gun to his mouth and pulled the trigger back. But before he did this, he looked at me with eyes that told me he was sure what he was about to do was the only path left for him to take. And that soon, he would find safety from whatever it was he was running from.

I wanted to ask him what had caused him to have so much fear, but before I could say anything to him, he had pulled the trigger and both he and the gun fell to the earth beneath them.

For the gun, it was over…but for him, there was still time for him to wait. And it was during this waiting that he continued to utter sounds, not just to me, but to many whom he felt were still with him.

"Run!….Run now!" He muttered as he was trying to speak through his fluids that were filling his mouth.

"Run for cover or they will get you!"

And that was the last of his words that I could hear.

Then looking over to the place where the rest of his family was lying, I could only think on one word…Why? Why was this thing taking place?

I did not feel a part of it, but yet…I was here and it was happening.

My attention was suddenly taken away from those thoughts of what had just taken place by the sounds of running feet coming toward me.

Turning my head to see the direction they were coming to me from, I saw a man and a woman running frantically in the street, running with an almost hysterical look about them.

When they saw me standing next to the man who had shot himself, they ran over in my direction as they yelled: "Run!….Run!

"If you do not run to safety they will come and get you. Look! They are closer now.

"They are coming after me now. If you don't find safety, they will soon be coming after you, too!" came their worried-looking expressions as they hollered to me.

When they had arrived within a few feet from where I had been standing, I saw they each had a gun in their hands.

Coming to a complete stop before me, they each raised their guns to their heads and pulled the trigger.

One went off and the woman fell to the ground, but the gun the man was holding only made a clicking sound.

He repeatedly pulled the trigger, as the gun remained pointed to his head several more times—enough for him to make sure that no bullets were left.

Then with this last click, he threw the gun down and looked over to the place I was standing and spoke once again.

"Help me…please!" came his tear wet cry to me. "Help me to get away…they are coming. They are coming and I have to get away!"

Then, looking to the place where the man before had shot himself, he saw his gun lying next to one of his outstretched arms.

He immediately ran over to this place and picked up the gun to examine it. I thought he wanted to make sure that it, too, was not empty of bullets, but he had another reason within himself.

"There is only one more bullet left…is this the one for you?" he asked, panting through each labored breath he was taking.

I could only shake my head so he would know that this last bullet was not for me. And seeing this, he placed a look of relief over his face, then continued.

"Then, you are sure you do not want to use this bullet for yourself?" he asked.

I could only look at him and ask him why he and all these others were doing this.

"If you don't leave now, it will be too late. They are coming…they are coming for everyone. And soon it will be too late to find safety."

Finishing these speaking words, he pointed the gun to the side of his head and released the last bullet, then fell to the ground to lie next to the man who shot himself earlier.

Lifting my eyes from their two bodies, I could see that many more people were running up and down this street. And they, too, were running with guns and shooting themselves as well.

And when one of them would fall to the ground, another would pick up the gun and shoot themselves, too. And this process did not slow down, but it was increasing, increasing in shooting as well as the number of those who were running in the street looking for a gun to shoot themselves with.

I did not understand what was taking place here, and I did not understand why I had been placed where I was standing as if I were being held in some kind of a trap, one that did not allow me to move at all, but one that was forcing me to look at all of this death that was being spread over this land.

All I could do was to place this one word in the front of my thinking mind…Why?….Why?

As this thought was flooding me, I heard a voice come to me. But it was not a voice that was coming to me from any of those whom I could see, but rather from the air that was all around me. And it was then that I realized that this voice was only meant for me to hear and would not be heard by any other.

"Speaking Wind, what you are seeing now will soon be with you. What you are seeing now is soon to be with all who are in the domain of the Earth Mother—for its time is not yet…but it is very close at hand.

"We are coming to share an understanding with you, an understanding of why this is now taking place before you. And when you will hold this understanding with you, then you, too, will be one that these others will fear and run from. That is, unless you will come to know who they are, and why they are doing this.

"We are coming to you, Speaking Wind. We are coming to you very soon now…and so is this time you are looking at.

"Listen well for our call, Little One.

"Listen well and come to us when it is time."

As the voice faded into the air that was around me, I felt a sudden pull on my back. This caused me to take a great and deep breath and look to where this pulling had come from.

As I turned around to see who had done this, I found myself sitting up in my bed…and all alone. But I was also covered with the wetness of sweat that had come to me from the vision I had been shown.

I knew I had only one course of action to follow, only one course of action I could take since I did not understand what I had been presented. And that was to wait until I was called, to wait for the ones who had taken me with them and shown me those thing they did.

As I looked over this room I was in, I was assured that this was my sleeping room in my parent's house. And for this, I was grateful.

But why had I been shown such a terrible thing? Why had this been shared with me when I did not ever mean another any harm? And why did these speaking voices tell me they were coming for me? And when they would, that I, too, would be one of those whom others would fear and try to run and hide from?

Feeling this great weight for all of those things I did not understand come on me, I lay back on my bed and wondered. I wondered on who I was, and who they were. And as I felt myself being taken by the dream spirits, by the dreamer who comes to us from the spirit side of all life paths, I could hear their words come to life for me once again.

"Listen for us, Speaking Wind...we are coming for you... soon...very soon!"

CHAPTER 2

❀

Entering the Lands of the Ancient Ones

It was the beginning of the growing season on the lands of the mesa and the year was 1964. I was still living with Grandfather, Two Bears, and my best friend, Cheeway.

Grandfather and Two Bears were two spirit callers of the Pueblo People. But as I would travel through many more seasons of my earth walk, I would come to know them by another name. This name would be more generally used by those whom I would have contact with, and that name would be—**Shaman.**

Cheeway and I had been together for as many seasons as had been given to us on our life path. And whenever one of us would be seen, the other was not ever far behind.

The majority of our time was spent in the northern part of New Mexico. This is where many of the villages of the Ancient Ones were to be found. And it was at these villages that many of our adventures would have their beginning.

This was to be the case on this day. Grandfather and Two Bears brought Cheeway and me to one of the older villages of the Anasazi. Grandfather and Two Bears were taking this time to make us more familiar with our song legends about the Anasazi. Those song legends have held much of our people's teachings and wisdom.

However, as we arrived on this land in the early part of the day, we saw there had been a very great storm the night before. From the intensity of the storm's move through the valley of the old village, we could see many of the children of the leaf (the plants) were in desperate need of our assistance.

"Look out before you, little ones, and tell what you see," came the speaking words of Grandfather as he stood just to the back of the truck.

Both Cheeway and I were still getting our provisions put together, but managed the time to look out over these lands Grandfather was mentioning.

"We see there are many of the children of the Earth Mother who are no longer in their proper place of growing, Grandfather," came our collective response to his question.

"And what would you do with these children who are in need of such assistance—this assistance that if not provided would not allow them to continue on their own life path?" Two Bears posed to both Cheeway and me.

As Cheeway and I heard these speaking words come to us, first from Grandfather and later from Two Bears, we both knew that this was not going to be a short lesson. It was showing signs of being a lesson that would require both of us to give it our full attention.

And with this in the front of our thinking minds, we both laid our provisions aside and began to look more closely at what was being offered, at those things that were only now coming to each of us as a beginning lesson.

"Would you have us tend to their needs, Two Bears?" I asked.

"Speaking Wind…," Grandfather picked up from where Two Bears left off. "Speaking Wind, one does not answer a question with a question. That is if one has a clear understanding of what is being asked.

"And if one does not hold an understanding of what is being asked, Little One, is it not better to say this to the one who is asking?"

"Yes, Grandfather," I replied, "it is better to do such a thing. But I did not want to appear unwilling to listen to what was being shared with me. And I felt if I would simply say that I did not understand, that I would give this impression."

"And you, Cheeway? Do you also hold this in the front of your thinking mind, Little One?' came the questioning from Grandfather.

"Yes, Grandfather. I, too, hold these same things as my brother, Speaking Wind, does," Cheeway responded. "I did not want to appear as one who would not be willing to listen to what was being shared—things that would bring to me a great lesson. And it was for this reason that I, too, held these same speaking words with me."

Both Grandfather and Two Bears stood in their places looking at Cheeway and me, as well as all of these children of the Earth Mother, all of these children who had been torn from their homes during the night's storm over these lands.

We could tell their thoughts were being equally divided between both of us and that they had taken a very quick journey into the silence. This silence was where not only many of the answers to ones questions could be found. This same silence was also used by our people to share the speaking thoughts with each other.

For the seasons Cheeway and I were with them, we experienced this many times. Many times we would think to ourselves they were doing this to keep us from knowing what they were sharing.

However, in the later seasons, both Cheeway and I had become aware of their reason for this. The reason was not one of not having us know what it was they were sharing between themselves, but one that would allow both of us to see there were other ways of sharing our speaking, ways that had not been completely forgotten between the two-legs (people) who were still traveling within this domain of the Earth Mother.

Holding this in the front of our thinking minds, Cheeway and I went into a silence of our own, not the same kind of silence Grandfather and Two Bears had found, but one that would not interrupt either of them, at least not until they had completed that which they had entered this silence to complete.

Just as these thinking thoughts had come to both of us, we saw from the eyes that were within Grandfather and Two Bears return.

"It is good that both of you have reached this place of understanding, little ones," Grandfather began. "For there will be many of the two-legs who will also observe the both of you doing those things we have shared with you. And when they will see these things taking place between you, they too will begin to feel as if you are attempting to hide something from them.

"Hide from them those things that they can neither see nor hear with the eyes and ears they have become so used to using on this earth walk of theirs.

"But I will tell you both this and I tell you this in truth. Whenever one will see anything they do not hold an understanding for, they will come to believe that something is being hidden from them. And they will spend a great amount of time and effort in trying to discover what it is from another rather than looking within themselves to find their own answers."

"Remember well, little ones…," Two Bears picked up from those speaking words of Grandfather.

"Remember, that when you will see something from or in another, it is only to remind you that you too hold this within you. For what you are seeing in another is being shared with you as a confirmation or answer to the many times you prayed for assistance—from those many prayers you have been requesting assistance for in showing to you where you are now.

"When you will see this something that is within another, it is telling you that you are now at the proper place of doing these same things for yourself—that you have prepared yourself sufficiently to do these same things, too.

"For if you had not prepared yourself properly, and if it was not yet time for you do these things, little ones…you would not have seen them in the first place.

"And you have seen this in Cheeway and me?" was my question.

"Yes, little ones…," Grandfather began once again.

"Both Two Bears and I saw both of you bringing this new level of understanding to the front of your thinking minds…this new level of understanding that what we were doing was not being done to keep you out, but was being done because of a greater need…a need for being in a place where we could share more completely—in the ways that had once been given to all of the two-legs to share with each other.

"But, Grandfather…," Cheeway began. "We were trying to be as quiet as we could so we would not bring to you a disturbance for those things you were working with."

Then looking at Cheeway and me with eyes that were always filled with a kind and understanding love for us, Grandfather continued.

"Neither of you were giving us a disturbance, Little One. For what you were doing was to give to us a new face to be seen by both of you, and this new face was being presented for our benefit.

"You see, it is when one will begin to see those things that are before them for what they are in truth that we will have a good face to wear for them. For this will be a good sign that they are beginning to wake from their own sleep of illusion…this sleep of illusion that only allows them to see things for what they would wish for them to be. And this is to see from a very selfish viewpoint, little ones.

"However, as they begin to waken from their sleep of illusion, they discover there is more to their earth walk than themselves. And there will be many things presented to them that are for the benefit of many…and not just for themselves.

"Very soon, little ones…," Two Bears picked up from Grandfather's speaking words. "Very soon, you, too, will be shown the direction to the Spirit of Silence. And when you will arrive at this place, this place where you will be reintroduced to the way all of us used to share with each other, then you will discover that there are not as many limitations on you as there are in the present—as there are when you will only know one way of sharing…this way of sharing the speaking words of the mouth.

"You see, when one is within the Spirit of Silence, there are no limitations for them. There are not the same limitations that there is on both of you now.

"It is when you are in this place now…this place where the only sharing of speaking words comes through the mouth, that there is a single level path to share with another—a path that does not hold room than to do more than one thing at a time.

"However, when you will have entered and come to know your way through this Spirit of Silence, you will come to see and understand those same things Grandfather and I have come to know and understand. You will see there are many levels of understanding and awareness that will come to you. And you will no longer hold the limitation of doing only one thing at a time.

"Do you hold an understanding for these things we are sharing with you?" Two Bears asked.

"You mean that you can be in many places at the same time, Two Bears?" was my response to his question.

Looking over me with a warm smile on his face, Two Bears nodded his head that shared with me that I was correct in what my response to him was, and I knew this was good.

Looking over to the place where Cheeway was sitting in the back of the truck with me, I could see a good face was being worn by him as well.

"Now, little ones, let us get back to the original question we began with, shall we?" came the speaking words from Grandfather.

"Both of you have shared with me that you do see these many children of the Earth Mother who are in need of our assistance…in need of our assistance because of what the night storm has done to them.

"Is this not correct, little ones?" Grandfather questioned.

"Yes, Grandfather, this is correct. But I do not hold a place of understanding for this question you are asking of us," I returned.

"And what is this place of not understanding, Speaking Wind? Can you share this with us so that we, too, will hold a direction for where you are going?"

"Yes, Grandfather. It is a place that comes from what has been shared with us many times from both you and Two Bears," I said, holding a great tone of respect in my speaking words.

"Many times we have been shown that to interfere with the life path of another is to do a great injustice to them. That when we will attempt to change or control things, we are only making foolish efforts for those things that are going to take place anyway. And that our efforts may possibly stop the learning process for the one that lesson had come to."

"Yes, Little One, and is this the place where you are speaking from now?" Grandfather asked.

"Yes, Grandfather," I answered. "I am not understanding what we are being requested to do because I still see it as doing something that may not be on these little ones' path. I am seeing this as a kind of interfering for those things that are needed by them."

"It is good your eyes are beginning to see, Speaking Wind. But I will share with you that what we are asking of you, this assisting all of these children in finding their way back to their homes. That this is not anything that will take them away from their life path. But it will assist them in maintaining their earth walk because of what has taken place on this land."

When Cheeway and I heard these speaking words of Grandfather's, we held a great look of surprise over our faces, a look that could not help but be seen by both of them.

"These are lands that we have given our word to, little ones," Grandfather continued. "And these words have come to us from those who traveled before. Those who have long since left this domain and returned to the waiting place.

"It was during last night's storm that both Two Bears and I heard these small ones calling to us. And they were calling to us for our assistance.

"As we heard them calling for assistance, we held the knowing that this was a good thing for both of you to see—this wave of destruction that had come to these small ones of the Earth Mother's children.

"Now, when you will look over this land and see how many of these small ones have been uprooted and taken out of the land that gives to them their life, you will see what lies ahead of both of you.

"When you will look on this face of life that is before you, little ones, you will see a picture of those times that are ahead for all of the two-legs. And I say all of them because there will not be any left out of this time that is soon to come to them.

"So what we are assisting you with on this day, this assisting being shared with those who are in need, we would ask both of you to remember this time well, for what you see today in the life path of these small ones of the leaf will soon be replaced by what you will see in the life path of all the two-legs. And I share this with you in truth, this time is not far away.

"And this time that I am speaking of is called The Season of the Long Shadow.

"However, from the looks that are over both of your faces, I can see there needs to be more explanation. Especially for why we are so much in attendance for these lands we now stand in....in these lands where these children of the Earth Mother live.

"Let us take our provisions out of the truck and set them up in one of the stone overhangs that is near. Then after we have provided our assistance in returning many of these children back into the earth, we will share this explanation to both of you over our midday meal.

"Will this be good for both of you?" Grandfather asked.

Both Cheeway and I nodded our heads in a manner that would allow both Grandfather and Two Bears to know that this was indeed good for both of us without breaking our silence with speaking words.

For both of us, I held the knowing that this method of agreeing with them would not only be the polite way of doing such things, but was also a means of practicing for ourselves. Of practicing the way we used to speak…and that is without speaking words, but in speaking pictures.

Also, it was giving us another good exercise to use when it would be time for us to enter the Spirit of Silence, this place we had seen Grandfather and Two Bears enter so many times before.

For the next few moments, all of us busied ourselves with placing our provisions into walking blankets, strapping them over our shoulders, and carrying them to the stone overhang Grandfather had seen earlier. Then after setting them in their proper places, we all entered the valley below us to begin replacing all of the small ones of the Earth Mother back into her earthen arms once again. Back to the places they had come to call their home…back to this place where they had all found the Spirit of Belonging.

CHAPTER 3

❀

The Illusion of Helping Another

After setting our provisions in the sheltering place, we began our entry into the role of assisting. This role of assisting these small ones of the Earth Mother would be explained later to us by both Grandfather and Two Bears.

We held the knowing that whenever Grandfather or Two Bears would be willing to share things with us, it would always bring us the beginning of a great adventure.

And holding this in the front of our thinking minds, we hurried down the small and almost unseen stone trail that would lead us back into the valley below. For we wanted to complete our task quickly so we could hear those things that were soon to be shared with us, those things that would bring both Cheeway and me to a place of understanding why our assistance was so much needed in this place we had been brought to.

From all of the seasons that we had been given to travel with Grandfather and Two Bears, there was never a time that I could remember when they had done anything that was without reason. And all of those things they had shared with both of us held a great impact on both Cheeway and myself, a great impact that allowed us to see more clearly those lessons that were before each of us. We needed to learn those lessons before we could take our next step on this path of the spirit.

And this was not going to be any different, for as I looked over to the face of Cheeway, I could see that he, too, was holding this kind of thinking with him. I could see this because he was just as much in a hurry to enter and complete this task we had been given as I was. He, too, held the knowing that when we had finished, the sharing of speaking words would begin.

Cheeway and I arrived on the floor of this valley well before Grandfather and Two Bears. This made us feel very accomplished in the beginning. Later, we found that we held more time on our hands than we knew what to do with.

So, not wanting to waste our time waiting, we began a conversation.

"What do you think this is all about, Speaking Wind?" came the questioning of Cheeway.

"In truth, I do not hold a knowing for this, my brother," was my reply.

"I only know there have always been great reasons behind all of Grandfather and Two Bears actions, and I believe this is to be no different."

"I guess this is just the mark of the times, Speaking Wind," Cheeway continued. "But do you think you are ready for another adventure…so soon?"

"Where are you speaking to me from, Cheeway?" was my question.

"It has not been two full moons since your last journey into the domain of the Ancient Ones, Speaking Wind. And from all that you have shared with the three of us, this was no small matter," Cheeway continued.

"In truth, my brother, this was not a small matter. But I will share with you that most of it has been taken away from the front of my thinking mind. It is like all of the weight that I had received from the message of the Ancient Ones has been lifted from me...or it has gone to another place.

"Does this cause a concern for you, Cheeway?" I asked, trying to look to his within place as had been done many times on us by Grandfather and Two Bears.

"Sometimes it does, Speaking Wind...but then, sometimes it does not. It is almost like being at a doorway to another understanding for all things that are around me. But I do not yet hold the understanding for what I have been feeling for this concern I have for you...this concern for all of these events that have been placed before you."

Just as Cheeway had finished his speaking words to me on this topic, we both felt familiar hands hold us on the shoulders from behind.

"This is good that you have found the time to think over these things that have been coming to both of you, little ones," was the opening of Two Bears' speaking words.

"And, Cheeway, you have been feeling a blending of those things that you have been prepared with...those things that have allowed you to see this path of the spirit our people have been the keepers of.

"Remember, little ones," Two Bears continued. "Ours is not to control or change...ours is only to understand those things that have been presented to us. And when we will do this, we will hold a clearer understanding for them.

"It is when we will hold our own understanding that we begin to see why it is not possible for us to judge another. And this judgment comes to us in the form of either telling them they are wrong, or caring for them too much...caring for them to the point of telling them what to do because it is for their own good."

"You see, Cheeway," Grandfather picked up from the speaking words of Two Bears. "When one will tell another those things they are doing are wrong, or when they will exercise too much caring for them, well, both of these paths will eventually lead to the same place. And this place will be the one of judging another.

"When one will tell another what they are doing is wrong, they are taking the most direct approach to the place of judging them.

"However, when one will care too much for another, they will be fooled with the illusion they are helping them—that they are assisting them from falling into many pitfalls. But as they will do this, Little One, they only do so from their own limited perspective. They will do this from their own limited perspective because in truth, that is all one has at this point of understanding.

"If they held a greater perspective, they would not attempt doing such a thing to begin with.

"Now, since this other one they are trying to help does not have their same experiences nor their same path to travel, there is a great burden placed over the one who is trying to help them. It is a burden they will carry with them for many seasons…or until the other person will see that this thing they are trying to do for them is not help and will walk away.

"So for the one who is trying to help them, at first they will feel very accomplished when the other will listen to them, when they begin to listen to them and seem to avoid falling into this pitfall that had been seen for them.

"But remember, the one they are trying to help does not have the same path to travel. And their spirit within does not have the same needs and lessons as the one who is trying to help," Grandfather continued.

"So after this first effort of trying to help them has been completed, the one who believes they have been helped sees them as knowing their way better than they do. They look on them as one who is needed by them to see any more dangers that may lie ahead of them and will not do anything on their own with consulting with this person first, this person who tried to help them.

"But from all of the councils they will share together, the person who has begun this helping of the other, they will not see things in the same way. They will only see things in their way, because this is their path. And when the other one will come to them with their concern for what has come to them, they will appear to this person as someone that is very dumb and out of place.

"This causes the one who has begun with what they thought were good intentions to see this other person as one who is just not capable of seeing or doing for themselves. They will see this other person as one who is really in great need of their assistance because they do not hold the ability of seeing those things that are in front of them for what they are.

"But I tell you this in truth, little ones. What they are doing is to look at this other person through the eyes they have been given to travel their own path with. And when they will do this, they will see this other person as very far away from what they perceive as truth—from what they perceive as their own truth.

"For they will not have come to the place of understanding that where there will be two people, there will be two truths. There will be their truth, and there will be the other's truth.

"When there will be three people gathered together, there will be three truths, and they can only be applied to each individual.

"When this first person who began helping the other one looks on them, they will see them as one who is just not capable of seeing things for what they are.

"They will do this because they are looking at them through their own eyes of truth, these eyes of truth that have come to them from working with the many lessons that have been presented to them," Grandfather said.

"But they will not hold the understanding that for all they can see now. For all they hold as their own understanding is only for themselves and not any other. This will be the reason they see this other person as doing so many things that are wrong and just not right to do. Because they are seeing them through their own limited perspective.

"This is when trying to help another will take a very dangerous turn. This will be where helping will turn into telling another what they are supposed to do…what they are supposed to be in order to fit into someone else's way of seeing.

"I tell you this in truth, Little One, what began as a simple way of trying to help, very quickly turns into controlling. And controlling is another word for judging.

"If one will not judge and be aware of when they are beginning to do so, they will not have the need of controlling. Then they will be willing to allow this other one to have the freedom of doing all of those things that have been coming to them. And in this process, they will have been given a great gift, a great gift that will allow each of them to reach this place called understanding for themselves and all things that are around them.

"They will see that not all things can be in the way they would wish for them to be. But they are as they should be. And this will eventually lead them to find their own path of the spirit.

"When they have arrived at this place of understanding, they will understand that all we will do is for a reason—that those things are considered of value only to their spirit…and no one else's.

"For it will be at this time when one will realize there are lessons and need not only for them, but for others spirits who travel near them as well.

"When one will see this, Little One, they will not become so concerned as you have been about the number of events that have come into your brother's life path. You will hold an understanding that all of them are taking place just as they need to. And, if you wish to assist them as he will go through these many events, then it would be so much better if you would hold him in the front of your thinking mind and allow him the freedom to find his own path for understanding them.

"Do you hold an understanding for these things I am sharing with you, Cheeway and Speaking Wind?" was the questioning tone of Grandfather's speaking words to us.

Looking over to the place where Cheeway was standing, I could see he was holding the same face I was wearing.

It was a face completely filled with surprise for all that had been shared with us, by those things that had not only found their way into our within places, this place where each of our spirits reside, but to the outside of ourselves as well.

From all of these lessons that had been shared with us from the speaking words of Grandfather and Two Bears, we could feel the weight of them over us. And this was causing us to wear a face that was not only filled with surprise but one that was also seen with both of our mouths wide open.

Even if we had wanted to, we could not have uttered any speaking words in return to Grandfather's question. And even if we had wanted to, we could not have shook our heads with them when we did not yet hold a clear understanding for those things they were willing to share with us.

So with the ever present gentleness and love that both of them held for us, Grandfather and Two Bears reached over to the places we were standing and calmly closed both of our mouths. After placing our mouths in a position where they would not catch as many of the smaller flying ones, they continued with their sharing—with this sharing that they could see we each held a great need for.

"Look at it in this way, little ones," came the beginning of speaking words from Two Bears. "You both have seen many people with more seasons than either of you have. And you have seen some of them who act as if they do not have half that number.

"You see them as ones who have not grown in their life path, and their actions are still very childish.

"Well, I tell you this in truth. They have not become like this all on their own. The reasons for them acting immature and selfish are not entirely their own doing. For they have been given much help from those who were trying to help them see their way out of the many pitfalls another saw before them.

"However, the part of their own responsibility comes to them from having believed in this other person...from having believed that this other person knew better for them than they did at the time.

"And as they passed through more and more of their seasons on this life path, they became more and more dependent on them to tell them what they should do so they would not fail at anything.

"But these others, the ones who have been telling them what and how to do things, they could only see through the eyes of those who were trying to guide them—eyes that could only see things in their way and no one else's.

"As this dependency became very strong, they began to lose what sight they had gained from their own eyes. And as they would lose this seeing that had been given to them, this seeing that had come to them as they would continue to work through their own lessons and emotions, they slowly gave up their own efforts of understanding and would listen more and more to the others telling them what to do. For this became the safe path for them to follow.

"As we have shared with you both, little ones, there is not ever anything done that does not have a price to pay, especially this.

"The price that was paid by the one who had been given this help was that they would have to give up their own way of seeing. For they would no longer be allowed to see through their own eyes, but would have to see through the eyes of another or others.

"And the benefit, as they would see it, was whenever they would get themselves into trouble by doing those things they were told to do, they would not have to carry the responsibility of their own actions. Because it was not their actions they were doing, it was the actions of those who were telling them what to do.

"When one will do what they are told, by another, they will not carry the responsibility of those actions themselves. But they hold others responsible for them.

"And as this process of believing in those who have been trying to help continues, soon the one who is being helped will no longer have any responsibility for anything they have done, or will do. For they will believe that another is responsible for them. And they will not have any accountability for themselves.

"Now, when you will look at those I have shared with you, the ones who are older than you but do not act in that way, then all you will have to do in order to gain a clearer understanding of them is to look at those who are always close by them. Look on them and you will see who has been responsible for having them act in this way.

"When you will, you will always find one or several around them who will have been spending the greatest part of their time in telling them what to do, how to do it, and always getting them out of the trouble they manage to get themselves into.

"It will be then that you will see who and what they are acting like. You will also see when this first began for them, for when one will give up on their own path and listen to the guidance of another, they stop all of their growth from within.

"Look on the face they carry with them, this face that will be seen by many as selfish, cruel, greedy, and uncaring for another. When you see this face, place it in its proper perspective and in the age group where this behavior is usually expected. And you will understand when it was they made their decision to sell themselves to another who would tell them what to do.

"Now the one who has been telling them all of those things they need to do, they do not hold a good face over themselves either. For they will always be so busy in trying to get this one out of trouble, or trying to make sure they do not fall and hurt themselves, that they will be very tired and short on temper with any others who will come to them.

"For them, they will no longer see their life path as one where they may grow and learn from. But they will see it as a chore for them to do, a chore that does not have an end to it because the one they are trying to help does not seem to listen to them, at least not in the way they want them to. And this is because they are trying to get them to listen and become like someone and something they are not.

"So you see, little ones, in this comparison of what takes place when one will try so hard to help another, the outcome is the same for all who will enter it. And for all of them, there is no longer any growth or freedom.

"For all who would enter this path, theirs is a prison, a prison of their own creating, and one that will not allow them to leave.

"So when either of you see another who is acting in a way that is much younger than the age they carry with them, remember these speaking words that Grandfather and I have been willing to share with you. For when you will do this, you will hold an understanding that this is a person who has been offered this trying kind of help, and has accepted it.

"When these kinds of two-legs will cross your path, then you will have the needed understanding for what it is you must do. When you will hold an understanding for what presents itself, you will be capable of making a good decision, one that will allow you to gain in strength so you may stand strong alone. And once you can stand strong alone, then you may stand with another."

Standing before us, both Grandfather and Two Bears were wearing a face that was meant for both of us to see. It was a face that was sharing a deep love and concern for both of us, but it was also a face that allowed us each to see that all of those things that had come to us had done so only for us. And to have another see through our own eyes…well, this would lead them to the place of those we had discussed.

"Do either of you need further speaking words on this place of learning, little ones? Or do you now hold a clear understanding of what can happen when you are caught in the illusion of trying to help another?" came the questioning of Grandfather.

CHAPTER 4

❀

Assisting the Children of the Earth Mother

After hearing those speaking words come to me from Grandfather and Two Bears, I was holding a question in the front of my thinking mind. But it was a question that I was not sure if I should ask.

I was not sure if this question was truly a part of my needs or if it was only a diversion that I was using to get away from the weight of all of these teachings.

However, as I looked over to the place where Cheeway was standing, I could see that he tool held such a question but had not yet formed it into speaking words.

So, returning my eyes to Grandfather and Two Bears, I decided that unless I would ask my question, I would not find the understanding that would assist me. For without understanding...there can be no seeing of things for what they are. There can only be seeing of them for what one would wish for them to be. And in that, there is no truth.

"Grandfather..." I asked, looking straight to his place of standing.

"Yes, Speaking Wind, do you hold a question over you that I may give assistance to?" was his return.

"Yes, Grandfather, I do hold a question over me from those speaking words that you and Two Bears have been willing to share.

"But it is a question that I am not sure of—a question that I cannot fully see the face of."

"So then, Little One, why do you ask this of me?" Grandfather returned.

"It is as you have shared with my brother and me many times before, Grandfather. That if one will hold a question within themselves and not see the full face of it, then they are made to feel this uncertainty within them as something that would surely bring them great fear. And this is a fear of appearing very silly or without intelligence."

"From what you have been willing to share with me, Speaking Wind, I would say that you have been very attentive in listening to the speaking words Two Bears and I have been willing to share with you. Please continue," was Grandfather's response to me as he held a warm smile over his face that I knew was for my benefit.

"When we will have this feeling of fear for appearing silly or without intelligence, then this is one of the veils the illusion will attempt to pull over us, one of the illusion's tricks to keep us trapped." I continued.

Looking over to the place where Cheeway was standing, I was looking for some kind of reassurance, not a particular kind, but one that would share with me that I was not alone in this endeavor I had begun.

As I saw the face of my best friend, I could see he was nodding his head to all I had been willing to share. And this motion of his was what I had been looking for, for I could see that he was not only keeping up with all that I was sharing…but that he was also in agreement with them as well. And this gave to me the strength that I had been looking for, this strength that would allow me to continue with this question that had been formed in the front of my thinking mind.

"My question comes from those speaking words you were sharing about those who do not ever seem to grow up, Grandfather. Those who remain in the place of their growth when they had sold their eyes and path to another who said they were trying to help them," I began.

"And why does this bring to you a question, Little One? Could it be for these things we are now giving our assistance for, these small ones of the Earth Mother's children who have been pulled from their homes by the passing of the night's storm?" Grandfather asked.

"This is what I have been holding with my question, Grandfather. But I did not want to appear as if I were questioning those things you and Two Bears have been willing to share with us by asking this, Grandfather," I said.

"If one will be afraid of being themselves, Little One, too afraid of calling their uncertainties out in the form of questions for others to hear, then one will truly be trapped in the sleep of illusion, and this spirit of illusion will have won a great battle with you. And by winning this battle, it will have a good place to reside within you and begin to grow," Grandfather said.

"It is only when one will be a part of all things for what they are that they see there cannot be a full understanding for all of it. Only then will they come to realize how limited their own levels of understanding are. And when this is seen, they will not fear asking questions for what they do not hold an understanding for. But they will see these questions are bringing them closer to finding their own path in this domain of the Earth Mother, that all of these questions are bringing them another part of the light of truth, this light that is their own truth.

"Ask your question, Little One, and know that all is as it should be. For to think anything else is to fall back into the sleep of illusion where you will not be allowed to see."

"Then the question to you is this, Grandfather," I said holding as much respect in the tone of my voice as I could. "If it is so wrong to think one is helping another by doing many of their own things for them, then isn't it the same thing we are doing with all of these plants, these small children of the Earth Mother, Grandfather? Are we not doing to them the same thing the others were doing to the person who stopped their growing?" I said.

"First, Little One, you must be willing to keep in the front of your thinking mind that there is no wrong that can be done. There is no wrong because to think like this means you are still within the sleep of illusion," Grandfather began.

"You must be willing to remember there can only be your own right and wrong and be willing to see that I, too, have mine, Two Bears also has his, and Cheeway has his as well.

"Once you will hold this within your own eyes of seeing, then you will know that you and you alone must make all of your own choices for what you will be presented with. But, you will be required to do this work before you can see this choice clearly.

"Then you will be allowed to see clearly those things you need to make your own decision on. And before you have done this work, then all that will have come to you will be the questions, these same kinds of questions you and Cheeway have been putting to yourselves. And this has been the work each of you have been required to do…this work of working your way through the emotion that comes before action, this action of finally arriving at the place where you can ask this question.

"I will share with the both of you that this thing you have done is no different for you than it is for any other, this emotion that you have worked your way through in order to ask your question. Well, it is just a part of the work that is required by any who would wish to travel or even find their own way to the path of the spirit.

"However, for the speaking of clarity, Little Ones, I will rephrase your question so that each of you may hear it in another light, one that may not be as difficult for you to follow.

"Perhaps then you will see this question of yours more clearly. One that will allow you to see why it is necessary to perform this work that I have been willing to share with you."

With these speaking words of Grandfather finished, both he and Two Bears were looking over us. As they were doing this, I could feel their smiles of warmth come to me, feel them more than see them for I was looking to the place of their eyes, looking in this place to see any new light of direction they might provide to me on this day, and for this question.

"Look at this question of yours in this way, Little One," Grandfather continued.

"You saw similarities from the way the others were giving their help to those they were in truth stopping them from their own path. And by stopping them from traveling their own path, they caused them to stop their growth as well.

"Now, we have shared with you that we are willing to assist these small ones of the leaf to find their way back to their homes, and you saw that we might be trying to help them as well and be stopping them from traveling their own path.

"Is this correct to this place, Little Ones?" Grandfather asked.

Without wanting to break our silence of the moment, both Cheeway and I nodded our heads to share with Grandfather that he was correct without having to use any of our speaking words.

"Well then," Grandfather said. "What I can see has brought this question to the front of your thinking minds is that you do not yet hold an understanding of why we are willing to do this assisting for these small ones of the Earth Mother's children when we would not be willing to do such assisting for one of the two-legs," Grandfather continued.

"I will tell you this, Little Ones: these small ones you see before you are very special. But I will go into that in a few moments.

"For now, I would ask you to listen carefully to these things I am willing to share with you, for they will assist you both greatly in those times that have yet to come.

"The reason we do not apply this kind of help to the two-legs is because they have the ability for changing things for themselves. If they find that they are caught up in this help of illusion, they have the ability of leaving their environment or surroundings, for they always have this freedom of choice.

"But these small ones of the leaf, they do not have this same freedom because they do not possess the mobility that the two-legs do. And to see them all uprooted from their homes, well, if it were not for our willingness to assist them in returning, they would surely suffer. They would suffer for they would be like one of the two-legs being buried in the earth and asked to live out their life path in such a way.

"So we are offering our assistance to the ones who do not possess their own ability of righting those things that have come to them. And when these things have been righted for them, then they will have the freedom of choice for this life path they too have entered this domain to travel.

"Does this clear up a part of your question, Little Ones?" Grandfather asked.

"Yes, Grandfather," I returned.

"But you have shared with Cheeway and me that this place is very special, and this has brought a great curiosity into us. Can you share more with us on this?"

"Of course, Little Ones, but only if you and Cheeway will be willing to listen as we continue to work," Grandfather returned, "for if the reflection of the Great Spirit in the sky becomes too hot, then surely all of these little ones will feel harm come to them. So then, while we will do our part in assisting, we can also share those speaking words that will tell both of you more about this place of the Old Ones.

"Is this agreeable to the both of you?" Grandfather asked.

"Yes, Grandfather, this is agreeable to us," was our response.

Without anything further, each of us knew what we needed to do, and that was to begin speaking to these small ones of the Earth Mother in the ways of the Old Ones, as we would replace them into the earthen home they had come to know so well.

As we would walk up to each of them, we would make a trill sound from our throats. This was to call their attention to the fact that we did not hold any bad places within our hearts for them, and that we only held good things for them to feel from us.

With this done, we would then place the pictures of what we were willing to do for them into the front of our thinking minds and show this to each of these small ones…pictures of them resting and growing back in their earthen home, then wait for them to respond. For to do otherwise would be to interfere with their paths, and we had been well prepared by both Grandfather and Two Bears on what the results of doing something like this could do.

As I had found, using this process that had been shared with me by both Grandfather and Two Bears would allow those who were in need of assistance to choose if their time in this domain had come to an end, or if they would remain for more seasons in which they could grow.

While all of us were using our talents in returning these many small ones back into their homes, I was quietly reflecting on the vision that had come to me yesterday morning. I was reflecting on those scenes and voices that had been presented to me and was weighing them within myself, weighing them to see if I would have a need to share them with Grandfather, Two Bears, and my best friend, Cheeway.

For all of the seasons that I had been given to travel with them as one of the members of our council of four, there was not anything that was considered out of place to share. Not with them, for we had become a family.

And as we would travel together, we were always reminded about the purpose of each of our life paths crossing, that Cheeway and I were being prepared for those things that had yet to come into this domain. And we were being prepared to share those things that had been shared with us, to share with the many two-legs that were not yet awake from their own sleep of illusion.

These thought pictures that were crossing the front of my thinking mind were gaining a weight to them that was allowing me to see the value for what I had been prepared for. Those things that had been given to me to share with the many, and this vision that had come to me...well it seemed to be another piece of the picture I was continually being presented.

As I was thinking over these things, I recalled one of the teachings of the Old Ones. It was the teaching of responsibility. It was the teaching that shared with me why it was important for me to do my own work, for then I would arrive at my own decision from what had been presented to me to learn from.

But with the limited number of seasons I had to my life path, I was not sure if I had experienced enough to make sense out of this vision I had been presented.

And that was the reason I was in the presence of Grandfather and Two Bears. It was so they could assist me on those things that I did not understand.

Placing many of these small ones of the leaf back into the earth, I was still wondering if I should share this vision with them or not. And lifting my head to a place where I could see them better, I saw that all of us were working our way back to the center of the valley, to a place where Cheeway and I might be able to hear Grandfather's and Two Bears' speaking words when they would be willing to share them with us.

As I gave one final look into their direction, I could see both Grandfather and Two Bears looking at me with a familiar smile over their faces. It was a smile that shared with me they had been following me as I was thinking over this vision I had been given. That smile also shared with me they would not ever place me in a position of having to do something, but that they knew of this vision already. And if I were to be in need of their assistance, they would be willing to provide it.

This was giving me a good feeling for their presence in this valley of the Ancient Ones' oldest villages, this valley where we were providing our assistance to all of the children of the leaf who had been pulled from the Earth by the passing night's storm.

Just as the last of the children had been placed back into the earth, Grandfather stood up and stretched his back.

"It is good that we have worked so well," Grandfather said looking over the large valley floor.

"Have you heard the approach of the Spirit Wind over these lands, my brother?" Two Bears asked, shaking the dirt that had collected on his hands and pant legs.

"Yes, I have heard this, my brother, and I have been shown the stone overhang will not be sufficient for us to find shelter in," was Grandfather's return.

Pointing his hand to the old Anasazi village, Grandfather continued. "I do not believe the Old Ones will mind if we share this with them. I see some of them waving for us to enter."

"And from the look that is placed over their faces, I would say they want us to hurry," came the return from Two Bears.

Cheeway and I looked at each other very quickly then turned our eyes to the place Grandfather had pointed. We did not see anything that they were speaking of, but only saw what appeared to be shadows on some of the walls.

However, from all that had been shared and shown to us by them, we had come to know that there was nothing they would do or say that was neither without reason, nor without truth as well.

So, without any speaking words, we followed them back to the stone overhang to retrieve our provisions and move them into the sheltering of the Ancient Ones' Village, this village Grandfather and Two Bears said they saw the Old Ones' calling to us from.

"It is as we have shared with you, Little Ones," Grandfather said, picking up our provisions and placing them inside our walking blankets. "Many times there will be things that will call to you. And other times, you will have to let spirit within you lead.

"As you will come to allow your levels of understanding for yourself and all that is around you grow to another level, you will understand there are many eyes within each of us. And as we will grow with this understanding, so will our eyes, those same eyes that will begin to see those things that have always been present—those things that have always been there, but were just not available to you before you were at a proper place of understanding for them."

As always, Grandfather and Two Bears had seen within both Cheeway and me. And when they had looked, they saw what was going through both of our thinking minds, our thoughts of wondering if there were really others inside of the old Anasazi village waving for us to enter.

However, just as we had become used to thinking on this, there was a great clap of thunder in the sky overhead. And as it made its presence known in the sky above, it fell to the face of the valley floor and began its roll.

By the time it reached our place, we could feel its presence of force and knew that the time, this time of relocating from the stone overhang and into the protection of the Ancient Ones' village was very short.

PART II

From the Keepers of the Past

CHAPTER 5

❀

The Passing of an Illusion

We had arrived inside the Old Ones' village just as it had begun to rain. The skies above us went from a pale blue to a very dark gray quickly. This was not unusual on these lands we four had come to call home. For in these mountains, the blessings of the water spirit could come over us very quickly, and this had given all of us the need to listen to the messages that were being carried by the Spirit Wind.

When I was only of a few short seasons, I was told of the need to do this, to listen to the messages of the Spirit Wind. From the time I could remember, whenever the thunder spirit would accompany the water spirit in a storm, I would always feel I was being awakened after a restful sleep. And this is what I had been expecting from the coming of this storm as well.

However, this was not to be the case on this day. A presence over this land was making itself known not only to me, but also to Grandfather, Two Bears, and Cheeway as well.

Looking to where they had found our sitting places, I saw each of them looking in all directions, looking for something Grandfather and Two Bears could not see, but they could feel.

Whenever I would feel a presence and see another of our council looking for it as well, I would feel a sense of relief come over me, a relief that told me I was not alone in this event.

But on this day, even knowing that I was not alone with this feeling of a new presence over this land was not helping me. This presence seemed to be making itself stronger and stronger with the passing of each strike of lightning.

I could not help but place this feeling that was coming over me as one that was similar to the weight of not understanding. It was like the weight of not understanding when the Ancient Ones had called on me to join them so I could hear The Message.

It did not occur to me that this feeling was the same thing. For it had only been two moons since I had my last vision with them. And I did not think they would call on me again so soon.

With this in the front of my thinking mind, I let this thought drop behind me and looked at Grandfather once again.

I saw that he was looking deep into the skies that were over us, into the skies that were now filled with the cloud people as they carried great amounts of the water spirit's blessings to these lands.

"It is going to become very cold as this storm settles over the valley," Grandfather said. "We should use this time that is left to us to gather some wood for a warming fire before the full force of this blessing is on us."

Without further speaking words, all four of us left the protection of the Old Ones' village that had been built into the side of this mountain to gather pieces of the standing people, those pieces of them they had discarded when their earth walk was over.

Cheeway and I ventured into a part of the valley floor that was not too far from the place Grandfather and Two Bears had gone. But it was not close enough for us hear what they were sharing between themselves.

"What do you think they are sharing, Cheeway?" I asked.

"Why are you so concerned with this, Speaking Wind?" was his reply. "You know if it includes us, they will tell us when the time is right."

"Oh yes, Cheeway, for this I am sure. But I was thinking on something else, something else that I thought Grandfather and Two Bears had seen from me," I returned.

Cheeway stopped gathering the small pieces of wood for the warming fire and stood in his place without movement. He was looking over me and placed a look over himself that shared his coming query—his follow-up to my statement.

"Speaking Wind, what gives to you this concern for what Grandfather and Two Bears might have seen from you?" Cheeway began. "Have you been given another vision? Another one so soon after the last one?"

I could only look on the face of my best friend and nod my head to share with him that I had, but without breaking my silence for this question of his.

"Why have you not shared this with us before, my brother? Is it something that is giving to you weight once again?" Cheeway asked, placing a look of concern over his face now.

"I did not hold the believing that I should yet bring this up, Cheeway," was my response. "I was trying to make my way clear without the assistance of another, for this is the direction we have been told would be needed in the seasons that are still unborn to both of us."

"Why would you say this, Speaking Wind?" Cheeway asked. "Grandfather and Two Bears have always been with us, and as long as they are, do you not think they would be willing to assist us in any of those things that are presented to us...in any of those things that are presented to us that we do not hold an understanding for?"

"Yes, my brother," I returned. "But they will not always be with us. One day, they too will have to drop their robes and cross the Great Spirit Waters to enter the waiting place.

"We must all do this when it is time. And, what I was holding in the front of my thinking mind, was that when this time would come for them to do this thing…well I just wanted to practice on finding my own answers."

Looking at me with a caring smile over his face, Cheeway reached over and placed his right hand on my left shoulder, then continued with his speaking words.

"My brother, you have forgotten or have misplaced some of the preparing that has been shared with us, this preparing from the speaking words of Grandfather and Two Bears…as well as from the teachings of the Ancient Ones," Cheeway responded.

"What do you mean, Cheeway? I do not hold an understanding for where your speaking words are traveling," was my immediate response.

I held the knowing that what I was being offered was from a time and a place that had slipped by me, one that had been offered and placed within my spirit, but since it had not come to me for this need as I had expected it to do…then there must have been a need for this understanding to come to me from Cheeway.

And for those things that I did remember, one of them was that when it was time for an understanding to be known—when there was a need, then we would receive this from our own spirit or from another.

And when it would come to us from another, then it was a lesson that was needed by the one who was seeking and the one who was offering. For when we share speaking words with another, it is not only for their benefit that we will do so, but for ours as well.

This reminding was coming to me from the many times it had been shared by both Grandfather and Two Bears.

They would share with Cheeway and me that when we would be willing to share speaking words with another, it was always for our benefit. As we would form speaking words from the thought pictures presented to us by spirit, we would be given another opportunity to practice speaking of those things that we did not yet have a complete understanding for. And if we would be willing to listen to what we had to share with another, in time, we would get it right, and would jump past using the speaking words that we had grown so used to using and remember how to speak in the old way of the speaking pictures.

It was the word speaking pictures that always held my attention to this practice of sharing with another. Grandfather had shared with me this was the original way all of us would speak with each other. That this was the old way of speaking...from spirit to spirit, and did not require the body part to perform this kind of work.

Listening to the speaking words of my best friend come to me over the living air that was between us in this valley floor, I could feel these thinking thoughts filling the front of my thinking mind. These thoughts were sharing with me this answer that I had somehow misplaced, that the reason Cheeway had found and formed the speaking words for this was to allow both of us to gain from the lessons of our past. This lesson was now needed by me to better understand, and this same lesson would allow Cheeway to practice with his own speaking words so he would have another opportunity to get closer to the place we had all been before, this place where we could speak in pictures to one another.

"So, my brother, tell me what it is you are now willing to share with me," was my response to Cheeway.

"It is this, Speaking Wind," Cheeway began. "When we were of younger seasons than we hold to ourselves now, we had been discussing the possibility of Grandfather and Two Bears passing into the waiting place, this waiting place that is across the great spirit waters where everyone goes to wait for the next world to be built.

"And as we shared what we would do when this time would come, we heard a calling voice of eagle over our heads...this call of the spirit of eagle that was to remind us how easy it is to travel with one foot in spirit and one foot in this earth walk.

"When we rose from our sitting position to thank eagle for his assistance, neither of us held a complete understanding of what it was he had been willing to share. That was when we looked down from the spirit caller's ledge and saw how close we were to the edge and could have very easily fallen into the deep valley below us.

"Do you remember this time, my brother?" Cheeway asked.

"Yes, Cheeway," I responded. "I remember this time very well. And it was at this place where we felt the presence of others near us and were relieved to see that it was Grandfather and Two Bears. They had come to this spirit callers ledge as well."

"Yes, Speaking Wind, this is what took place next," Cheeway returned.

"Now, do you remember the speaking words they shared with us? Those speaking words they told us of so we would not have to carry this worry with us any further?

Looking to the place where Cheeway was standing, I used this silence I had found to look within myself to find this answer.

I did remember this time he had been willing to share with me, but I could not find the place where those things that had been shared from Grandfather and Two Bears resided.

Holding this in the front of my thinking mind, I looked back to this place Cheeway was standing and moved my head in a manner that would share with him that I did not remember.

"Then, my brother, I will bring them to life for you once again," Cheeway said looking at me with his face of caring.

"When they had walked over to the place we were sitting, they asked each of us to turn and face them. And placing a warm and caring smile over the face they had been willing to wear for our benefit, they explained why they had come to us when they did.

"They shared that each of the two-legs in this domain will carry a weight with them for all they do not hold an understanding for from their lessons. Then, as they begin to share this in the form of speaking words among themselves and others, they will take on certain colors to themselves.

"Now these colors are not usually seen unless one has traveled a medicine walk for many seasons. And when one who is experienced in this path sees them, they will know which of their colors is truly a need or a want for understanding.

"It has always been the case from both of their teachings, that the needs will always be met, while the wants will be like empty echoes down a long corridor with no one there to hear.

"Next, they told us as these colors would appear over one, the Spirit Wind would also see them.

"And the Spirit Wind is no stranger to any place that is on the top of the Earth Mother's domain, and all he will see, he will hold the understanding for.

"So, when the Spirit Wind saw the colors that had come over both of us from our concern of Grandfather and Two Bears, he picked them up and carried them to the closest ones who would be willing to assist us in finding the understanding we needed. This understanding that was needed by both of us so that we could travel this path we had chosen to follow.

"When he picked them up from us, he placed them on his back and took them to Grandfather and Two Bears who in truth, were not far away from us.

"When he delivered them, they could see that both of us held a great need for understanding what had come to us.

"And sitting down in the front of both of us, they continued with this explanation of why they had come. They told us they had seen this concern of ours about when they would finish with those things they had entered this domain to do and would rejoin our spirit family in the waiting place.

"Then they looked over to both of us and shared a great teaching. One that allowed each of us to drop our concern of what we would be able to do when they were no longer walking with us."

As Cheeway had finished these speaking words, I looked into this face he was wearing for me to see. And from my place of seeing, I could tell that he was reliving this time when all four of us had been sitting on the spirit-calling ledge on the mesa.

And as he was reliving those times, a peace crossed over him, a peace that was so great, it was filling me as well.

Then, without changing this face he had been willing to wear, he continued.

"We had both been very concerned that day about what we would do when it came time for Grandfather and Two Bears to drop their robes and leave this domain.

"Remember, Speaking Wind?" Cheeway said lifting himself from the place he had wandered off to.

"Yes, my brother," I returned. "I remember this time very well."

"When we sat down before the place Grandfather and Two Bears had found for themselves," Cheeway continued, "we were both filled with such a great weight of uncertainty that our eyes were being filled with the tears of the water spirit.

"For it was at that time when we both realized that they would not always be with us. And this new place of knowing was filling us both with a great fear that was not understood by either of us.

"Then Grandfather and Two Bears smiled on us that day and placed their hands over our shoulders and said:

"When it is time for us to leave this domain, little ones, do not be sad for us. You must not try to change those events that will take place regardless of what you will do.

"All of our generations have come here to learn and share. And all of us have entered this earth walk with the same level of understanding that reminds us our time here is not of unlimited seasons, nor was it one that was without learning from lessons.

"If we would choose to learn from lessons given to us, we would be seen as one who had traveled a balanced life path with much accomplished for our seasons.

"And for those who would not wish to learn from lessons offered them, they would be seen as ones who did not walk in balance with the Earth Mother and left with nothing accomplished for themselves or the ones who entered their path to play a part in it.

"But in any case, we all have maintained the understanding that when one enters this domain, they must also leave it, leave it as the way you can see and hear us now.

"However, as we have shared with both of you on many occasions, little ones, this is the domain of the great illusion. And this illusion puts many to sleep unless they are willing to do those things that have come to them as their lessons, those lessons that will lead them out of their sleep of illusion and into the path of spirit, their own path of spirit.

"And this one teaching that we are willing to share with you on this day is from the Ancient Ones of our people. From the ones we have come to know and call The Anasazi.

"We, and others like us, are the keepers of this wisdom and knowledge, little ones. And when you have been prepared, then you, too, will become the keepers of it as well.

"But the path both of you have entered this domain to perform is much different than the one we have entered. For when it is your time to awaken, there will no longer be walls that will cause you to see or to feel separation. And because of this, there will be no restrictions over either of you to share the wisdom and teachings we have been the keepers of.

"Now for this weight that has come over both of you, this weight of uncertainty for what both of you will do when it is time for us to drop our robes and cross the great spirit waters.

"We share with you this, and it is in truth. When it is our time to cross over to the waiting place, the only thing that will keep us separated will be the depth of your own sleep of illusion.

"The stronger this sleep of illusion has its hold over you will determine how well you will know that we are still with you. And we do not mean only with your memories, but just as we are now. For when it is time for both of us to leave this domain, we will not drop our robes (our bodies). But we will keep them and enter the waiting place with them. This is why you will be able to see, feel, and touch us just as you can now.

"When it will be time for each of you to cross the great spirit waters and enter the waiting place, each of you will be given this choice of taking your robes with you or leaving them here. But this is a time and a place we have seen that is still many seasons away. And when this choice is given, only you will be able to say which path you will take, for there are responsibilities located within each of them.

"But more on that later. Let us take some time and share what is expected when one will drop their robe in this domain and enter the lands of the waiting place, this place where all of us will be found waiting for the next world to be created, this next world that will give to us all a new home to live in.

"When one will drop their robe and leave this domain in the usual way, they have done this because they could not see they had a choice. And what one does not see, they cannot understand.

"It is when one is still trapped within their own sleep of illusion that this will happen. This sleep of illusion comes to all and only allows them to see those things for what they would wish for them to be. It keeps their eyes and ears closed and will not allow them to see things for what they are in truth.

"And while they are locked within this sleep of illusion, they will come to believe in many things that do not usually hold their own weight of truth to them. And from those many beliefs, when they will be needed, they find they fall over. For they do not hold any truth to them, but still, they hold onto them because they feel more secure with them than without them.

"So when it comes time for them to drop their robes, little ones, they have with them many things that they believe in, those many things they have heard from others, those who have been exercising their own levels of control over them.

"And from what they had come to believe in, they hold many expectations with them—expectations that tell them what to expect when they will leave this domain and go beyond.

"However, when they drop their robes, they are faced with a great fear. A fear that comes to them in the form of expecting to experience pain, enter a black void, or go to a heaven or a hell where they must atone for all the wrong they have done. All of those things others have told them were wrong, but they did not take the time to understand that this too had been given to them by the trickster, illusion.

"As they experience all of these things, they will carry with them a great weight. But we share with the both of you that even this weight is of illusion. And when they part from their robe, they find none of those things they have been told take place for them.

"Then they will encounter all things for what they are, and as they do, the weight of illusion will fall away from them. But the lack of having those things they once believed in causes them to become confused, and they cannot find their own way…and must be guided.

"You see, little ones, from what has been shown to both of us as well as from what has been kept in the teachings and wisdom of the Ancient Ones, there is no place that is either good or evil, there is no heaven or hell. For in truth, there can be no judgment on you by another. There is only one who will judge you for all that you have done or all that you have not done, and that one is yourself.

"But this judgment is done without the limitations that all of us enter in this domain with. For it is done without the frailties of the body that carries their spirit.

"This is a judgment that can only be done by you. And we share with you that this judgment is good, and it is fair. This is truth that we speak to you.

"For the spirit which is us, little ones, it is from perfection, and it is returning to perfection. For that, you can believe.

"It is this same spirit within all of us that will decide what is needed next, whether from another earth walk, or from another domain in order to return to the source of all creation.

"And this is the only judgment that is made, little ones. When those who remained locked within their own sleep of illusion finally come to see this face of truth, they become very confused. Confused and lost because all that they had spent their seasons here with the Earth Mother trying to learn, they find that there was no truth in any of it. And this gives to them a place of standing in the waiting place where they will have to put all of their pieces of truth together before they can see what more is needed by them to learn from.

"But this is not a long process, little ones, and it will only take from one to five moons before they find the balance they need. This balance they will find as they discover their own truths, this truth that will re-share with them the love of creation, this same love that created them, and this same love we are all striving to understand.

"As they become more and more comfortable in this unconditional love that is living all around them, they begin to stand on their own once again and see those things that are still needed by their spirit to learn from.

"But for this time of their confusion, they will not be able to see or speak to another, for they do not have the ability of seeing or speaking to themselves, and for them to go further, is not possible.

"After this time of waiting has passed, and they have their eyes and ears opened, they will be capable of seeing all of those things they left undone in this domain we are traveling in.

"And for the ones who have successfully completed their lessons—those same lessons they had decided were needed in order for their own spirit to grow and advance itself to the next higher place—they will be given one doorway to enter back into this domain that we are standing in. For each lesson that is successfully learned from, there becomes an opening for them to cross back and forth from the waiting place to this domain and return again.

"But for those who have not found the time nor made the effort of learning from their own lessons, little ones, they can only stand in the waiting place and observe the ones they are still attached to, but without a doorway to reach out to them and let them know that all is as it should be and they are all right.

"For them, this is a place where many tears of sadness are shed. And all of the other members of their spirit family will look on them and know what they are feeling. For in the waiting place, there is no thing that is not understood by all.

"There will not be this waiting period for us, little ones. For each of us has seen the many doorways that will be made available for us to enter back into this domain and be with both of you. However, you must keep in the front of your thinking minds that it is only when you have awakened from your sleep of illusion that you will be able to see, speak, and touch us—and not before.

"These things we share with you are done with the face of truth, for they have been shown to us many times by the ones who have passed into the waiting place before us, and with their robes as well.

"Remember, little ones, there is no separation when one discovers who and what they are in truth. For once this takes place, they leave their sleep of the great illusion. And it is the illusion that will cause us to feel fear or sorrow in this way. But remember: this is not truth."

Looking at the place Cheeway was standing, I could see him once again through the eyes of a wise friend, one who would assist me whenever there was a need.

And this need came to me at the time he was there. I could see from the look that was over his face that he, too, had been reminded of many of those teachings we had been prepared with, those teachings that had been shared with both of us by Grandfather and Two Bears.

"Has this sharing assisted you, Speaking Wind?" came the response from Cheeway. "I know they have reminded me of several lessons that I too had been carrying with me."

"Yes, Cheeway," was my response to him. "But tell me one thing, my brother, why do I feel as if this is a good thing, this thing that you have reminded me of from the speaking words of Grandfather and Two Bears? I do not hold an understanding for this, but I do feel its presence with me as something that should mean more than it does."

"Perhaps I can see with a little better perspective, Speaking Wind," came Cheeway's reply. "I can see what you were trying to do; how you were trying to keep from becoming an added weight to Grandfather and Two Bears by not asking or sharing those things you felt you should work for on your own.

"I can see this place you were standing on. However, from those times that are still fresh among all four of us—those times when the Ancient Ones took you on your spirit vision—I do not hold the believing that you are completely recovered from all that had been shared with you and now...now you have been given another spirit vision. And from what I can see of you, my brother, it is one of equal weight—no, perhaps even stronger than what I had seen of you before the last one.

"But, Cheeway," I responded. "I do not feel this weight over me, not like I did the last time."

"Perhaps, my brother," Cheeway continued, "perhaps you do not feel this weight as much because the last spirit vision left you more awake. And being more awake from the illusion, you would not be as inclined to feel its weight as much.

"But these speaking words I am sharing with you are done with the face of truth. And I tell you that you are showing much more now than you did before.

"And this is why I say to you that it would be a good decision on your part if you were to share this vision with us, to share it with us so there may be more light of understanding shared with you.

"Remember those things we have been told, Speaking Wind," Cheeway continued. "There is not ever any thing that will come to you without a purpose behind it. And the more asleep within the illusion you are, then the less you will be able to see what its purpose is."

"And the purpose of those events that will come to us will always be as a friend—as a friend will come to us to share and not to harm or threaten," I returned. "Yes, Cheeway, I understand and hold an agreeing with it.

"Let us get this wood back to the sheltering of the Old Ones' village, then I will share this vision I have been given with all of you.

"You are correct in your speaking words, Cheeway. I have been searching for those things that are not yet within me. And I do hold a great need for the assistance from Grandfather, Two Bears—and you, my brother."

"Good then, Speaking Wind," Cheeway said picking up the small pieces of wood he had dropped during our conversation in this valley of the Ancient Ones.

"It is time we were moving anyway. Look up at the sky above us and you will hold the same knowing for why as I do."

Looking up at the sky above the valley floor we were on, I could see my best friend was right. For the cloud people were being carried to this land in a very quick way now by the Spirit Wind that has spoken to our ancestors from when time could not be remembered.

And now on this day, it was speaking to the both of us as well. As I looked up at the place where the cloud nation had come to bless this land, I could hear the faint sounds of the thunder spirits being carried to us through this valley by the Spirit Wind.

This was his way of telling all who were near the time of arrival for the water spirit was very close. And if they had not made their provisions yet, the time left to them was very short.

Picking up the rest of my firewood, Cheeway and I headed back to the sheltering place that had been carved inside the stone mountain.

There I knew we would not be badly shaken by the arrival of this storm that was being announced for those who had the ears to listen.

It was not long before we saw Grandfather and Two Bears standing at the edge of the village and they were waiving to us to hurry with our wood. Then turning my head over my right shoulder, I could see a great flash of lightning hit the ground close behind me. It was so bright that it laid a carpet of brilliant white light all over the valley floor, including the places where Cheeway and I were running.

I could feel a tingling run over my body, and looking at the expression that had been placed over Cheeway's face, I knew that he, too, felt this.

This served both of us very well, and we ran at an even faster pace because of this nudging by the storm spirits.

Arriving at the entrance of the sheltered village, we both looked over to Grandfather and Two Bears and sighed a sigh of relief. For we felt as if we had come to a place where no harm could ever come to us, this place that was with them.

"It is good to see that both of you did not get lost in your sharing just now," came the first of the speaking words from Grandfather.

Both of us could only look over to the place Grandfather had been standing and smile back to him. For there was no thing that could be added or taken away from what he would share with us. Nothing else could have been so truthful for both Cheeway and me.

Looking just past where Grandfather was standing, we saw that Two Bears had already begun our warming fire and was speaking to it so that it too might know of our purpose for releasing its life of warmth to us. This had always been the way of our people. For us, all has life. And where there is life, there are many life paths to be traveled.

So it was that when one would need the assistance of another life to meet the needs of theirs, they would always share their need with them. Share this need with them so the one who was giving up their own life path could see that it was not done with an empty purpose.

But that it was done with a full purpose, one that would allow all to grow from.

Cheeway and I placed our pieces of wood on the stack that had been built by Grandfather and Two Bears, then sat in a good place next to the warming fire. This warming fire had been given a good start by Two Bears and was feeling very good to all of us now.

Just as we began to feel the fire's warming, we placed next to it some of the rock people, ones who would carry the warmth into them and release it more slowly than the fire would. This allowed us to have a smaller fire and not use as much wood in keeping the warmth over us.

When all of this had been done, Grandfather took out some of the pinion nuts he had brought and began setting them over the stones next to the fire.

This was to release some of the pitch from them before they would be eaten. If this were not done, then one would end up with a sore throat and a very upset stomach. However, this had to be done only once, then the pinion nuts would not have to be cooked again. As to why we would always carry the uncooked pinion nuts with us, Grandfather would remind us that to cut another's life path short only for the matter of your own convenience was not a good thing to do.

He would remind us that all life is very sacred in this domain of learning. And for one to cut another's life path short was to say that they were greater than another was. And from all that we had been prepared with and had come to the place of understanding for, this was not truth at all. For in this and all other domains, there were none that were higher and there were none that were lower than another. All were of the same and would, in time, return to the same.

However, as was most generally the case with those things that had been shared with us, this was not the only reason for doing this—this act of only preparing the pinion nuts we were going to eat.

The other reason was that as each was allowed to continue with its own life path, there were alternatives that would be presented.

The pinion nuts were used only as one example for Cheeway and me. Grandfather would share with us that as we would travel through out this domain that is the Earth Mother, that some time we might come across a place that had been left without the blessings of the standing people, a place that was truly in great need of having them live on their lands once again.

And if we would come across a place such as this and all we would have been carrying with us were the pinion nuts that had already been cooked, there would be no assisting that we could provide. No assistance because the standing people's seeds we were carrying would no longer be alive and could not find a place of growing their life with this land.

However, if we would not have cooked all that we carried with us, then we could share these living seeds with this land that was crying out to us with her needs. We could then place them into the face of the Earth Mother and allow them to find a new home for themselves one that would bring many more blessings to a land that would have otherwise been without them.

Thinking over this for a time and seeing the pictures form themselves within the warming fire, I could feel the presence of another sharing with me, one that had not yet begun, but one that was about to.

CHAPTER 6

❀

Forming the Council of Five

Grandfather and Two Bears positioned our warming fire at the mouth of the great rock opening. While it was far enough inside to provide shelter from the coming storm, it was close enough to allow one to feel as if they were not trapped within the living stone where the village had been built.

This was a remarkable similarity that had come to me from visiting almost all of the Ancient Ones' villages, whether they had been built in the face of a living stone, or even if they had been built in a cluster out in the open. I do not ever remember a time when I felt as if I was trapped within any of them. I would always feel as if I was living within the balance that had been shared with all life in this domain, as if nothing had been forced.

And this was the same in this oldest of villages that had been cared for by our people. For while I was looking at the warming fire and feeling the blessing it had been willing to share with us, I could still see all the way around to the valley below without having to move. This was allowing me to feel the freedom one receives when they will walk in balance for themselves as well.

What a wonderful reminder this had become to me. And as this had crossed the front of my thinking mind, Grandfather began to speak once again.

"What you and Cheeway are seeing here is not by accident, little ones, nor is it something that has only been discovered by the two of you," he said.

"You are making reference to this feeling of freedom that is present in all of the Old Ones' villages, Grandfather?" Cheeway asked.

"Yes, Little One, this is what I am making reference to," Grandfather said as he turned some of the pinion nuts on the heated rocks.

"What has been left by the Old Ones has been done to serve as a reminder to all of us. And this village we are sharing with them is not different. For there is no greater feeling than freedom, little ones. This does not change for any who are traveling an earth walk. However, many of them only pretend to have found this freedom, this same freedom that surrounds all of the Ancient Ones' villages for us to learn and remember from.

"Many will profess to have found this freedom, but when you will look at the face they wear, and the stoop they carry with them, then you will know they have not found their own freedom, but are only trying to get others to follow their controlling words. And you both will see how silly this is.

"From all of the two-legs I have seen cross my life path who are still trapped within the sleep of illusion, they try to fix the ones who are not as broken as they are. And they will do this by telling them things they should be doing that are so far from any truth they have yet to find, that at first, it is hard for me to believe anyone would be willing to listen to them.

"But I am not surprised to have seen this in my many seasons with the Earth Mother, for I am no longer surprised by what the ones who are still asleep within their own illusion will do or say they know to be truth.

"But in this village where you have found this feeling of freedom, this is a great lesson that has been left for us to remember when it is time for us to return to the ways of the Old Ones. And I can feel this time is not far from us now, little ones, not far at all.

"For I can feel the messages in all of the children we travel close to, as they call for me to be more aware of the times we are in because they are soon to end.

"Pretty much like the vision that is clouding you isn't it, Speaking Wind?" Grandfather said, placing his right hand on my left shoulder.

When Grandfather said these speaking words to me, my first reaction was to look where Cheeway was sitting. At first I thought he had told Grandfather and Two Bears that I had been given another vision because I would be in need of assistance due to the short amount of time that had passed since the last one.

But when I looked at his face, I could see my thought was not founded in truth. For the expression that was over his face was one of surprise as well. Perhaps not as much as mine, but nevertheless, he was, in truth…surprised. I knew when he would allow this face to be shown, it was not ever from his own doing. And it was worn without guilt.

So it was that I knew it was not Cheeway who had shared this with them, just as I knew that it was not I.

"How do you come to have this knowing, Grandfather?" was my surprised response to him.

Looking into me with the eyes of caring and warming, he smiled, then continued: "It was only this morning that Two Bears and I had been told we were to come to this village. But we were also told to bring you and Cheeway with us."

"But I thought you were told to come here in order to give assistance to the small ones of the leaf who were in need, Grandfather," I said sitting very straight now.

"Yes, little one, this is truth. For Two Bears and I did receive a request from the spirits of these lands to do just that," he continued.

This is a task that is not normally done by either one of us, but when this calling came, we did not hold a better understanding for why. Then we traveled into the Spirit of Silence to find direction, a direction for the request being given not only to the both of us, but the request to bring the both of you along as well."

"So this is when you felt that I had been given another spirit vision, Grandfather?" I asked.

"Yes, Little One," responded Two Bears. "For nothing is ever presented to us out of idleness. All is done for a reason. And the answer for it resides within each of us. And this was no different. This request, and I will assure the both of you that it was a very strong one, came to both of us from the dreamers. And they found us as we were traveling with the ones we had become used to being with for these many seasons.

"They told us Speaking Wind had been given another spirit vision of the times that are soon to be with us. And this showed us our direction to travel and why we had received such a strong request from the spirits of these lands. And that is as far as we have been given permission to see, little ones. The rest was to be told to us by Speaking Wind when we would arrive on this land."

"We also saw that there were not four of us on this time we are about to share, Little Ones," Grandfather began. "We have been shown there will be one more among us, that there will be five of us on this day of the great visit."

"What do you mean 'visit', Grandfather?" I said still sitting with a great look of surprise over my face.

"The vision will continue, Speaking Wind, and it will continue with all of us in it," came his response to me.

There was no expression left to either of their faces, and I could not remember a time when this had occurred. For as long as I could hold my memory of both Grandfather and Two bears, there had always been a good face that they would wear over themselves. And this was always for the benefit of Cheeway and me for those many times they would take us into places of the spirit we were not yet familiar with.

This was beginning to wear on me, and not wanting to carry more weight over myself from not having an understanding for so much already, I decided to ask them why this was so.

"Why do you not hold a good face for Cheeway and I to see from you, Grandfather and Two Bears? This is not giving me a good place to see from," I asked.

"It is because of this offering that is coming to all of us, Speaking Wind," Grandfather began. "In the times before, both Two Bears and I were aware of what was needed by you and Cheeway. And perhaps this gave us an advantage of knowing how to assist you, and how to present you with what was needed so you could do the work required by each of you. However, from what is coming to all of us on this day, and on this land, neither of us hold an understanding for what is on its way.

"We do not have any more information than you can see, Speaking Wind, and I believe that you have more with you that you do not understand than we have with us that we do understand at this time.

"But for whatever reason, little ones, we have been called to this land and this place as members of a council. This much Two Bears and I have been shown.

"And now we will have to wait, just like the both of you will have to wait until we see what the rest of this vision will share with us."

I reached over to the place where Grandfather was sitting and placed my right hand on his left shoulder and said: "It fills me greatly to know of these things, Grandfather. And I wish to share this with you. For the longest time, I was afraid that I would have to enter this domain of the Ancient Ones all alone. And I will share with you, this is truly a difficult task to follow, especially since it has not been many moons from the last time I had been taken by them to hear The Message."

With eyes that could only share their love for me, Grandfather said: "Little One, you are not now, nor will you ever be alone. For this, you must hold your believing with."

"I hold this knowing with me, Grandfather, but sometimes one can still feel they are alone, can they not?" I responded.

"In the times when Grandfather and I were of short seasons, Speaking Wind, this was true," Two Bears began from his sitting place that was next to Grandfather and Cheeway. "But we are no longer in those times, and I tell you this with the face of truth, we will not ever see those times among any of us again.

"What lies ahead for all who are within this domain is important. It is so important that the Ancient Ones are calling council with many even now. And they have chosen you for the opening of this message they have given to you to hold until the time is right. And they are returning to you, and in the company of all of us on this day for reasons that are so far known only to them.

"It is like Grandfather has shared with you: we must wait and see what it is they are willing to offer. Once they have done this, Little One, we will be shown our path. And it will be shown to each of us as it has always been, and that is with the light of direction that the Old Ones' always provide."

As these speaking words of sharing completed themselves and fell to our within places, there was a silence that had fallen over all of us. And it was not a light spirit, but one that was filled with the weight of not fully understanding the events that were on their way to us.

Feeling this weight come over me caused me to return my gaze into the small warming fire and be thankful for the presence of those who I had come to travel so closely with. I was feeling the presence of them in my heart and within my spirit, and for me, I knew it was good.

CHAPTER 7

❀

Learning to See
What We Ask For

As we listened to the silence that was being played for us on this day, others were also making their presence known over these lands.

In the far distance, I could hear the rolling thunder spirits as they were calling out their direction to all of the children who had come to call this land their home. I, too, could make out this direction…the approaching storm was headed to this place we were.

But this was another storm that I was hearing, another storm in addition to the one that had already shown itself to us but had not yet begun with its blessings from the water spirit, at least not as much as the cloud people had been showing they would.

This first storm had come to us from the east, and now with the distant calling of the second storm, I could tell that it was coming from the west.

However, just as I had become comfortable with two of these storms coming over us, there were two more distinct callings of the Thunder Spirit as they announced another's approach. One was from the south and the other was from the north.

Looking up to the sky that was over our place of shelter, I could see that the Spirit Wind had brought this first storm and placed it directly over us, but did not wish to move it any further. And as I would line up the cloud people who had formed themselves into this storm with one of the walls of the cave, I could see that there was no longer movement from them. But all remained stationary in the sky nation they had come to call their home.

Feeling this silence all of us had gone into, and the weight of the four approaching storms, I looked at an in-between place, a place that was between the small warming fire, and the opening of the large mouth that had been carved into the side of this mountain, this large cave opening that was sharing itself with our needs.

As I allowed my thinking mind to drift off into the living air that was filling this land, I felt a presence. But it was not a presence that was from the spirit side of this path I had been willing to travel. Rather, it was a presence of one who was walking a life path in this domain.

Cheeway and I had learned to distinguish between these two feelings. Extending myself out to the place this sound was coming from to see the face of who it was, I heard Grandfather's speaking words return to life from within me. From this place where my spirit resides: "There are many occasions when one will request assistance for those thing they have to do, Speaking Wind. And it will be during these times when one will not have the clear seeing that they will be asking many questions of themselves.

"Even though they may look and sound like they are praying, Little One, you would do well to keep in the front of your thinking mind that they are only finding another way of speaking to themselves. And when they will see the light of truth that is over this process, then they will begin to see all things that come to them for what they are, and not for what they would only wish for them to be.

"You see, whether one will pray, or ask for assistance, there is in truth no difference between these two words. And because there is no difference between them, then they will all be answered and in a very quick way.

"Remember, as you will continue to travel through this domain that is the Earth Mother's, there will not ever be a prayer that will not be answered. And it will be answered long before you will have the time to blink your eyes. However, there is another part of this truth that you would do well to keep with you. And that is, not all prayers or asking are understood. And for those things that we ask or pray for that are not understood, well...they will not see the answers when they come to them.

"Look at it in this way, Speaking Wind, when you hold a complete understanding for what it is that you are asking assistance for, then you also hold the knowing if it is a need...or a want.

"And as you have prepared by the teachings of the Old Ones, you will remember that when you ask assistance for a want, it will be like calling out in a long but empty corridor, one that will be without the presence of any to hear you. And this is what will be returned to you. You will not receive an answer to those wants because they are not important, not important enough for you to make any efforts for them.

"But when you will understand what you are asking assistance for—these things you are praying or asking for and see them as being needs by you for what you have to accomplish in this domain, then you will find that before you can get them out in the form of your thinking thoughts, that they have been answered. And they will be answered in the same way that you will ask of them.

"But for those who do not hold an understanding for these things that I am willing to share with you, they will be the ones who always say that their prayers are not answered. And they will be the same ones who will try to convince many others that their prayers are not being answered either.

"However, for the ones who understand that all prayers and asking are returned to them, they will see an immediate response. But for those things they do not understand, they will not see their answers come at all.

"They will see these prayers that they are asking assistance for as something that will not ever come to them. And they will hold the knowing that this, too, may be an answer for them, an answer that is sharing with them that they have not yet reached the place of sufficient understanding for themselves and those things that are around them to see what it is they are requesting.

"They will hold this with them and begin to travel within once again, to travel within themselves and search out more of their own meanings for what they are praying for.

"You see, Speaking Wind, the ones who have found the path to their own understanding, they see the journey they have departed on as one that requires them to travel within in order to see the answers to all they hold a need for, to all of those things they are seeking guidance and understanding for.

"And they will understand that when they have achieved this understanding, they will have the clarity of sight to not only see and understand all that they are praying and asking assistance for, but they will also see the answers when they come to them.

"However, for the ones who have not yet found their path of the spirit, this path that will lead them to the place of their own understanding for themselves and all things that are around them, they will not yet have come to the place of seeing that all journeys must first begin from within. For them, they will only see their within place as something they must run and hide from. For them, they will be looking for all of the answers for what they have been seeking to the outside places of themselves.

"They will believe all of their answers and those things they are seeking, lie in others…or other places. But not within themselves.

"But I say this to you, Little One, and I say this to you with the face of truth.

"All that we seek, whether it is for knowledge, enlightenment, or understanding, all of this is not to be found in any of those things that are on the outside of ourselves, it can only be found within each of us. And this is truth for all who are within this domain.

"The only thing we will see from the outside of ourselves will be the confirmation for those things we have come to discover and understand from within first. And this is truth that I am sharing with you, Little One.

"We see those answers to what we have found within ourselves in the world that is to our outside, in those people, places, and things that will come to us.

"You see, Little One, when one will come to you—or an event is presented to you—it does so because you have been requesting this in the form of your asking or prayers.

"How you see them will follow suit to the answers you have been asking for assistance for. And, as I have been willing to share with you, understanding this must first come to you from within.

"When you will come to place a look of concern for the kinds of people who are crossing your life path and you look on them and wonder why so many with the same kinds of problems are coming to you, then it would be good for you to go within yourself to look for this answer.

"When you do this, you will discover that it is not these people who are having this problem, but it is you. And from those things you have been asking assistance on, they are being confirmed to you in the faces of the ones who have been crossing your life path. They are confirming for you those things you still need to work on before you can see clearly the answers you seek.

"When you will be confronted by people who do not give you a good feeling, Little One, do not become angry at them. Be thankful for them coming into your life path.

"For what they are offering you is another way of looking at those things that are within you that still require work on your part. Those things that are between you and your understanding. This same understanding that is needed by you so you will be able to see clearly what it is you have been praying or asking assistance for.

"Just remember, Speaking Wind. When you arrive at this place of understanding what you have been asking assistance for, then you will see the answer. And you will not be so impatient for things to happen, because you will see how quickly they do come to you.

"So, when you are surrounded by people or events that give you a feeling of anger or bad emotion, do not look away from them, and do not blame them. For these things they do, are being done only for you. They are coming to you as confirmation for what it is you still need to work on within yourself.

"When you have come to work on those things within yourself successfully, they will no longer bother you. For you will have come to understand what you still need to learn from and work on within yourself before traveling further on your path.

"Now when you are surrounded by those people and events that come to you, and you see in them things you wish you could do, then look at them as confirmation as well, not as something that is being shown to you to make you feel bad you do not have it.

"For whenever you will see one who is doing great things, understand this is something you could do as well. If you will only look on them as someone who is greater than you, then you will fall into the illusion that you will not ever be good enough to do something like that. And if you would hold a believing in this, then there will in truth be no thing that will ever be possible for you to do while you are in this domain of the Earth Mother.

"But I share with you that this is not truth, Little One. For when you look on one who is doing something you see as truly great, this is not being shown to make you feel bad. This is being shown so you will understand you also hold this ability within yourself, that is if you will be willing to do your own work to bring this out in yourself.

"So do not look on them with a face of jealousy, Little One, look on them with a face of good feelings. For they are showing you that you have the ability of doing as well. They are showing you a confirmation for those things you can do now.

"And when you will see them succeeding with those many things they have been willing to do the work at accomplishing, then be grateful to them. For they have shown you the way to achieving this for yourself as well.

"But in order to find this path, you must be willing to journey within yourself, journey to your within place where you will hold these questions of yours out to your own spirit.

"This will be the time when you will gain the understanding for all that you are seeking. This will be the time when you will understand for all that is being presented to you is in answer to those many things you have been praying and asking assistance for.

"That will be the time you understand that all answers lie within ourselves, and all confirmation to what we already know lies on the outside of us, either in the form of people, places, events, or spirit family members who come to assist us in finding our own way.

"And that is what I have been willing to share with you—that assistance will always come to us as confirmation from one who is traveling a similar path.

"If you ask for this assistance of confirmation to come to you from the body part, then it would do you well to learn as you listen and hear for the answer when it will come to you. For it will come to you through this same path, this same path that will confirm to you what you have asked for and will be shown to you from one who is close to where you are.

"If you will ask for assistance of confirmation to come to you from the path of the spirit, then it would do you well to learn from the answer when it will come. For it will come to you through the spirit of the other side. It will come from the ones who are watching and assisting you from the waiting place. And they will come to you with their own sounds of approaching, just like the ones who will come to you with their own sounds of approaching from this side of the domain.

"Learn to distinguish between the two of them, Speaking Wind. For if you will do this, then you will be more likely to recognize them when they will arrive for you. And when you will recognize them, you will see them for what they are and no longer fear or try to run from them as most of the two-legs do.

"Most of the two-legs ask for things they do not hold an understanding for, and when they see their answers come to them, they see them as the enemy or as something to fear. Because they do not understand, they try to run and hide, not ever realizing what great opportunities and blessings they are allowing to pass them by.

"Learn to listen, Speaking Wind, and learn to see what is before you. When you will keep this in the front of your thinking mind, you will not see a world filled with problems. You will see one that is filled with blessings and you will see the life of the living."

Hearing these speaking words come to life from my within place gave to me a good understanding, one that I had needed.

As I was listening to what was being presented to me from some place that was on the outside of the opening to the great stone we had been sitting in, I could feel this presence of another Earth Walker getting closer now. And this was filling me with a sense of accomplishment—one that I had not been aware of before this time.

Looking over to the faces of Grandfather, Two Bears, and Cheeway, I could see they too had this feeling that was coming to me. And they were also listening to this presentation...the approach of another.

CHAPTER 8

❀

Night Hawk

This feeling was beginning to grow very quickly now, and I could see the reason for this. Both Cheeway and I had been prepared to know that as one would come closer, one who was looking for you, there would be an increase in this feeling.

But the one who was sending this feeling out was not always aware of what it was they were doing. All they would know was that they were beginning to think more and more of the one, or ones, they were searching for.

Then another rolling thunder came cascading down the valley walls and the lightning lit the sky over us. It was then I saw a shadow of a man standing in the open part of the stone cave we were sitting in.

At first, he looked as if he were bigger than life, but when the light from the sheet of lightning cleared, I could see he was large, but he was not as big as I had imagined at first.

"Heya Hey!" came his echoing voice through the cave.

"I heard that you were around here and thought this would be the right place to look for you," came the speaking words of greeting from the man standing in the opening of the cave to the Old Ones' village.

"Mind if I come in and share the warming fire with you?"

Neither Cheeway nor I recognized this man, but from the face that Grandfather and Two Bears had placed over themselves, they did, and invited him to share this land with us.

As he walked to our warming fire, I could see a look of relief come to the faces of Grandfather and Two Bears. I could only place this look as their being grateful for this fifth member of the council to be one they both knew.

And I was not wrong in my assessment of this.

"It is good to see you again, Night Hawk," came the response from Grandfather. "We had been expecting another among our council on this day, and I am filled with a good knowing that it is you."

Reaching the place where we had been sitting, this one called Night Hawk exchanged the customary greetings among all of us.

"And these must be the two I have heard so much of over the past few moons," Night Hawk said looking over to the places where Cheeway and I were sitting.

"Yes, Night Hawk, these are the two we have spoken of with you. The one closest to you is Cheeway and next to him is Speaking Wind," came the response from Two Bears.

"And they are the ones you have been given to prepare?" Night Hawk asked looking over to us with a penetration that went deep inside me.

"Yes, my brother, these are the two we have discussed with you before," was Grandfather's reply.

Hearing Grandfather call this one called Night Hawk, brother, allowed me to feel a little easier at his presence here. And looking over to the place where Cheeway was sitting, I could see that he shared this feeling with me as well.

Looking to the place where Cheeway was sitting, Night Hawk asked if he could join with us and without any wasted time, Cheeway and I both moved over to make room for him by our warming fire.

"It is good to finally be here, my brothers," Night Hawk remarked. "But tell me, what is it that has called all of us here to this land of the Ancient Ones?"

"It is time," was Grandfather's answer. And after this, there was no need for further speaking words among the three of them. Each went into the Spirit of Silence to continue with their conversations. While neither Cheeway nor I could completely follow them into this within place of spirit, we could observe them from our sitting positions.

As I looked over all of the faces that had gathered around this warming fire, there was a calmness of knowing that was filling the air, a calmness that shared with me that what Grandfather had said was understood by all.

For the next few moments, there was silence among this new council of five, a silence that allowed for only the sounds of the Spirit Wind crossing the vast lands of its home. There was an almost silent cry from this Spirit Wind, this totem that I had come to call my companion, a silent cry that was coming to all who would have the ears to hear that time was coming to an end.

Even though I held little understanding for what this companion I had found was telling all of the children of the Earth Mother, I did not yet have a full understanding for why it was choosing this time and place to remind me of this message.

However, I held the understanding that this was not his only purpose for singing to us on this day. For when I looked at the cloud people who had gathered above us, they had not moved. Even with this message carrier of our people being as strong and loud as he was in this time, I could see that his purpose and presence were not only for us to hear and listen to. For he had come to move the cloud nation that was over head...the cloud nation who would always announce the arrival of great events that was about to be unfolded in this domain.

And this filled me with a feeling that whatever the rest of this spirit vision was going to be, it would be with me soon. And soon, I would gain the understanding of what the voice had shared with me and this was weighing heavy on me.

As I looked up from the place I had been caught into, this place that was to the outside of the opening of the stone cave, I noticed that all eyes were on me. But I did not hold an understanding for why.

Holding a small smile on my face, and looking over all of the faces that were looking at me I asked: "Is there something about me that is calling attention?"

"There was a woman standing next to you, my brother!" came the speaking words from Cheeway. "Did you not see her?"

"No, Cheeway, I did not," I answered, feeling a little inattentive to those things that had been taking place around me.

"Do you not feel as if you have missed something, Little One?" came the speaking words from Night Hawk. "She often comes to many of us who have learned to travel The Path of the Wise. Only this is the first time any of us have seen her in the waking time. Perhaps this is why you have seen such a look fill each of our faces."

"Did you hear any of those things she was willing to share with you, Speaking Wind?" came the questioning from Grandfather.

"Not that I could place a face on, Grandfather," I responded. "Only, I thought it was the Spirit Wind that I was sharing with and not a woman."

"And what did you hear, Little One?" Night Hawk asked, holding a deep look of concern in his eyes.

Looking over to the places where Grandfather and Two Bears were sitting, I silently asked them if I should answer this new one of our council, silently asking them with the voice of my eyes.

Seeing this come over my face, they both nodded their heads in a motion that shared with me that this would be a good thing to do.

"I apologize, Little One," Night Hawk replied to this silence of speaking that was taking place between us. "If you will answer my question, then perhaps you will allow me to share a bit about myself with you and Cheeway. It is worth hearing because there is a part that I have been given to share in this adventure that is about to come to all of us. It is one that I too am not sure of, but one nonetheless that I have been invited to attend, just as all of you have been."

Then, looking back to the place where Night Hawk was sitting, I smiled to him and continued.

"It was more of what I felt rather than anything that I heard," I began, and this seemed to hold everyone's attention to the next set of speaking words I would form.

"It was a silent cry that I was feeling come to me. But as I have shared with all of you, I did not see a lady standing next to me, nor did I hear her. I only held the believing that this message was coming to me from the Spirit Wind of all nations.

"And this feeling I was receiving was indeed a sad message that he was carrying with him on this day, and at this time.

"I felt as if he were telling all of the children of the Earth Mother that this time all of them have known is about to end. That soon it will be time for all that we can see before us to be taken away. And this was filling me with a great weight of sadness, but I do not know why.

"This is what had come to me during this time you speak of, Night Hawk. But that is all I could see. It is my hope that this will assist you in the reason you hold behind your question."

Looking over at the place where Grandfather and Two Bears had been sitting, Night Hawk replied to them: "He speaks well for one of his number of seasons. Spirit has been working well with him."

This brought a great smile over the faces of Grandfather, Two Bears, and Cheeway. For when one of us would receive such gracious speaking words for having done well, it was not to be shared on the one, but was to be shared equally among all of us. The teachings I had been prepared with reminded me that there is not ever an accomplishment where one would be the sole purpose behind it. But it was because of many.

As this flooded the front of my thinking mind, I too joined in this smile I had seen in the ones who I have traveled so many seasons with. For it is always good to know that one is One with the One, and this was yet another confirmation of that for me.

Turning his attention away from Grandfather and Two Bears, Night Hawk then looked over to the place where Cheeway and I were sitting and said: "Now, Little Ones, it is time for me to share with the both of you. This is what I have said, and this is what I am now prepared to do."

Preparing himself a little better on the sitting place he found next to the warming fire, Night Hawk took a deep breath and gazed over this village that had been so kind to allow us to share its home.

I could see a look of recognition that had come over his face as he was doing this. And I could feel that there was a presence of more than himself with him, something that I had always felt from Grandfather and Two Bears.

This gave to me a good feeling for those things that this one called Night Hawk was about to share with us. For it was from this additional presence with him that allowed me to see a similarity, one that I had come to know very well that was also with Grandfather and Two Bears.

This additional presence with Night Hawk was giving me a good feeling because of all I had come to know in the seasons that had been given to me at this time—all I had come to know and feel this additional presence with them. The ones, who seemed to have found their peace and calming manner with it, I would listen to. But, for the ones who did not present a calm over themselves when I would feel this presence, they would not be listened to by me. For I knew them to be ones who were still fighting within themselves and had not yet come to live with the balance that was being offered to them.

I could see that this was not the case with this one called Night Hawk, and looking over to the place where Cheeway was sitting, I could see that he, too, had seen and felt this additional presence with this fifth member of our council. And that he, too, held the same understanding for what was being presented to him as I did.

We had been prepared by the teachings of the Silent Brotherhood as well as by Grandfather and Two Bears that when one will come before you, they will first touch with spirit and all of this takes place within one blink of an eye.

But this is also the most crucial time for coming to the place of knowing who and what this one who has come before you is. For it is not going to be revealed by the speaking words they will be willing to share with you. Rather, it will be shown to you by the meeting of spirit—theirs to yours.

And before anything can be shared, such as speaking words, there will be the touching of spirit. From this touching, you will know whether they will be traveling a path that is close enough to the one you are traveling to be able to share with them without losing focus on the path you travel.

It is when one is not on a path that is close to yours that there will be great effort spent in trying to share because there will be no thing between either of you that can be seen clearly. And when this will take place, then it is best to simply smile at the other and move on. For, to do more will not accomplish anything of value to spirit.

However, when this meeting of spirit will take place and you will see the path this other one is traveling is close to yours. Then spirit will share with you that this is a good person, one that is close to you.

And you will know from this spirit touching that there will indeed be good sharing that will be of value to spirit and both of you will have a good face to wear for each other.

From what was being shared from this spirit touch of Night Hawk, both Cheeway and I could see that there was a closeness of paths that had been shown. And because of this, we held the knowing that there would be good sharing of spirit.

Sitting back in our places next to the warming fire, both of us looked over to the place where Grandfather and Two Bears were sitting. We saw they had already looked within each of us for this understanding that they had been willing to share with us.

And from the face they were both wearing for us, they had seen that Cheeway and I had worked through those things that we had been prepared with. And this brought to both Grandfather and Two Bears a good feeling for what we had been willing to do.

With this accomplished, we turned our attention back to Night Hawk to listen to those speaking words he was now willing to share with both of us.

"Grandfather, Two Bears, and I entered this domain of the Earth Mother in the same season," Night Hawk said. "And the village I am from was very close to the one Two Bears had entered his earth walk from.

"However, even though we had known of each other through many seasons, there was not established a closeness of our paths until much later.

"You see, Little Ones, I had much to travel through before I would be willing to find this path of the spirit, this path of the spirit that Grandfather and Two Bears have been traveling from their earliest seasons.

"For me, there was a much different path. And it would not bring us three close together until much later.

"I had entered this domain to learn my lessons through a family that was not spiritual. Not in the ways of our people, that is. And because of this, there were many pitfalls I needed to understand before I would be able to see myself for who and what I am and the truth I carry within me.

"In the earlier beginnings of my earth walk, there were always many others who would stay at my parents' house. But these were not always the same kinds of people or two-legs that both of you have become used to seeing.

"These were many of the ones who had entered this domain as very disgruntled spirits, ones who were always blaming others for all of the problems they called to them.

"As I grew through more and more of my seasons of this earth walk, and listened to them for many days and nights, soon, I was becoming just as they were.

"Soon, I too, had my head buried in their sand of not seeing things that had been presented to me as anything but another pain to live with.

"There were many nights when there would be those others who would seem to camp at my parents' house for as long as there was alcohol to drink and perhaps some food to eat. And they would spend many long hours of the day and the night talking about how bad the whites had treated us—speaking of how many things we could not share with them because we would have to keep them a secret.

"However, what I did not see until much later was that they did not have any idea of what it was they were speaking of. They did not hold an understanding for any of these secrets they professed they had a knowing and understanding for. And I did not see that they were not working through their lessons that had been offered to them, but were trying to get another to do their own work for them.

"But for me and this earlier time that I had entered into, I did not see this in the beginning. And I had joined in with them thinking that this was the way of all our people, for there were no others near who would have been willing to share anything with me other than what I was living with.

"So I too became one of these drinking ones as I call them now, looking for any one else to blame for those things that I could not find, and seeking this drinking of alcohol to keep me from having to do any of my own work and learn from those lessons that had been presented to me to learn from.

"It did not take me very long as I would live with these drinking ones of our people to believe that this was the way.

"I will share with each of you, Little Ones, that if it is on your life path to be one of these drinking ones, then I would hope for each of you that it will not take you long to learn your way out of this trap. And it is a trap that will keep you locked into the veil of illusion that will be placed over you, just as it has been placed over me.

"In the beginning, it seemed to be a great deal of fun for this thing I was doing. For there were no tasks to perform and all of the money that we needed came to us from the government. This same government that we spoke so badly of would always be there holding out a check and we would accept it from them willingly.

"When we would all get together and put this money into one place, then there would be enough to buy the alcohol we needed to make it through another month. This was the path that I had become stuck on, and it was not until much later that I was to find that it was a trap for me, one that I was not sure if I would be able to leave.

"As I traveled with these other drinking ones, I noticed that our conversations did not change. All of those things we would talk of were those same things that would always be talked of. And when I would raise a question of discussing anything further, I would be told that we did not need to look at anything else.

"I would be told that for us, as a people, there was nothing else for us to do but lay down and die for the white skins, for they had robbed us all of our spirit.

"But I began to look at what was taking place here. For it was the money from the white skins that was allowing us to buy so much alcohol to drink, but we were only speaking badly about them. And this did not make much sense to me.

"However, as I became more and more entrenched into this path of the drinking ones, I found that this kind of thinking, for me, was soon to be a thing of the past. A thing of the past because I was becoming more and more grateful for the money we would get so there would be enough alcohol to drink. And soon, this was all I could think of.

"Soon the having of this alcohol was all that had become important to me and all other things seemed to leave themselves in the far distance to where I was standing.

"Then, there came with one of those who had come to camp at my parents' house, a girl. She was truly not one that was impressive to look on, but she was a girl and for me, that was all I needed.

"Immediately, I began to make a friend of her and began to speak with her of things that I had been living with, those same things that would always condemn the white skins for all they had done to our people.

"And those things that I had been willing to speak to her on held her interest. All of this attention by her was giving me a feeling of being important to someone, and this brought a feeling to me of goodness.

"She did not partake with the drinking ones though, but she would always put up with me.

"So as the seasons passed, the girl and I became very close to each other. She would always be there when I needed to be dragged home but I would continue to follow those others of the path of the drinking ones.

"By this time, she had moved into my room with me and we began having little ones of our own. She would always be the one who would care for them and I would always be the one looking for others to drink with and share in the illusion that we had become trapped in.

"Many seasons came and went, but I did not change my path. By now, we had three children, one boy and two girls and they seemed to be doing well. That is, each time I would look on them, this is how they appeared to me.

"And over the seasons I would travel on this path, there seemed to be less and less that was important to me. For me, there was only one thing that held any great weight of importance and that was to drink with the ones who were like me.

"To me, anyone else did not matter, and I did not want anything to do with them.

"When I returned to my parents' house one day, she and my children were no longer there. For they had become so used to not seeing me at home that they decided to leave. At first I thought this was good because that would be four more people that I would not have to put up with.

"Later, I heard that she had taken up a place on the mesa, one that would allow her to live alone with the three children. And this gave to me a thought of relief; for I believed that I would not have to take care of them anymore and I could be with those I could talk and drink with.

"For a time, I was glad that I had this separation from them, but then…my path began to change. My parents became very ill, and now I know what this illness was from. It was the one that comes when the liver stops working. The doctor that came to visit them told them they should not drink anymore of the alcohol.

"However this was not to be, and when he left, they pulled out another bottle of alcohol and started drinking together once again.

"At first I look at them and held the believing that they had found something good that they could do together. And this might be what I needed…a good woman who would share this drinker's path with me.

"Then, and as the alcohol ran out, all of us slept for another night in this house, but when I woke the next morning, I was to hold a great surprise in front of me. One that would bring me a great shock…a great shock that I was not prepared for at all.

"When I woke up the next morning and looked where my parents had been sleeping, I saw that there was a great amount of blood that had come out of their mouths and noses during the night. By now it had dried and was caked all over their faces.

"At first, I thought that they would wake up and clean themselves off. But as I continued to look over them, I noticed that there was no breathing that was going in them or coming out. And this caused my heart to begin beating very quickly.

"Running over to them, I began shouting at them to wake up. I repeated this shouting to them many times before I arrived next to them. When I had come to the place they were both lying, I began to shake them thinking that this would wake them from this place they had found to sleep, but it did not. And I was feeling a sense of confusion fall on me, one that I would not be able to walk away from.

"While I had been doing all of this shouting, some who had found their sleeping places on the floor began to wake. And looking at me, they told me to be quiet and find them something to drink, for all of this noise had given them a headache and I should not be so concerned with those two because they were dead and could no longer be helped.

"This caused me to fly into the anger of non-seeing. I rose from my position next to my parents and began hollering at all of those who had been living and sleeping in this house for many seasons.

"As I yelled at them, I would also find the closest thing to my hands and would throw it at them as well. And this was giving all of them a great fright. For they had not seen me like this before and neither had I and it was giving me a good scare, too. But there was nothing I could do about it, for this anger was coming to me from a place I had not seen before, and the more I would allow it to surface, the more there was to come out.

"Soon, there were none of the others who had followed the path of the drinking ones left in the house, and looking out of the window and doorway, I could not see any of them in the yard either.

"Then, feeling they had all gone away, I ran to get the village doctor, still hoping that he would be able to wake my parents' from this strange sleep they had fallen into.

"But when the doctor came to look on them, he looked up to me and told me they had died in the night. And from the looks that had come over their faces, he was not sure but he thought they had died because of their drinking.

"Looking down to each of them I asked him why he would have thought this thing of them.

"Then reaching out with his pointing finger, he showed me empty bottles still clutched in both of their hands.

"When the doctor left, I could only sit alone in the middle of the room and cry. And all the while I was crying, I was throwing out all of those bottles that held alcohol in them and breaking them on the ground outside where this poison would be carried back to a place where it would not bother me again.

"During the passing of the first night, I was already beginning to feel the absence of this alcohol in my body, and it was crying out to me that it needed more.

"However, I held the resolve that I would not drink any more of this poison, this same poison that had killed my parents. And it was at this time I began to think over all of those things I had spoken of. Those things that had been taking the blame away from me and placing it onto the ones with the white skins.

"I was beginning to see what I needed to do. And what I needed was to quit this drinking of the alcohol and work with myself and those lessons that had been offered to me. Otherwise, I would end up as my parents did—dead, and with no one to really care.

"I had been successful in keeping this alcohol away from myself for two days, but it was on the third that it happened. And I had found a full bottle of wine that I had missed during this cleaning I had done.

"Looking to what had once been my parents' house, I could not see how bad they had really been. For they always had a roof over their heads and heat in the winter. So keeping this with me, I opened the bottle and began to drink once again.

"And this was the beginning of a long night for me. For I went to get more alcohol and drink more and more until I could not tell how many days and nights had passed me by.

"When the last of what I had with me had been drunk, I found that there was no money to buy more. For what I had become used to having was the money that had been given to me from my parents as well, but they were gone now and that was no longer available to me.

"I remembered thinking over many hours where I could get more money from. More money to buy more alcohol, but there was only one other person I could think of that would do such a thing. And that was the girl I had lived with.

"I decided to travel to their house which was well to the outside of the village. And when I would get there, I would ask her for the money and tell her that if she would do this thing for me, that I would not ever bother them again.

"However, when I had arrived at their house, I found that no one was there. But things that had once been on the inside had been broken and thrown to the outside. Just as I was about to leave, a man walked up to me and told me what had happened."

"He told me, 'It was the group of the ones who travel the path of the drinking ones who had come to this house two nights ago. At first they thought you were there, but when they found out that it was only the girl and the three children, they pounded down the door and forced their way in.

"Once they entered the house, and did not find any alcohol or money, they raped the girl, then killed her as well as the three children who were living with her. But then the sheriff came and took everyone away.'

"Then looking at me with a questioning look that was in his eyes, he asked me where I had been. And all I could do was look back at him and shrug my shoulders.

"This had not been a good time for me, little ones, and the more I would think over these things that had come to me, the more helpless I felt.

"It seemed to me that everything that I had in my life had been taken away, and I was helpless to do anything about it. It seemed as if everything I had touched or been around had been destroyed, and I felt as if I was the one who was responsible for having these things take place.

"I held the knowing that the best thing for me would be to stop following the path of the drinking ones, but I also held the knowing that this was something that I could not do.

"So I decided if all of the ones who had been with me had left, that I might as well leave too. And this was what was in the front of my thinking mind as I journeyed out into the lands of the mesa on that day. I was looking to find a way of ending my life path with the Earth Mother that would not be too painful...that is, if there was such a way.

"And it was not very long that I found my answer. For in the distance, I could see the railroad track that crossed our lands, and I could hear the coming of a train. This train, I thought, would be the answer to all of those bad feelings that I was carrying with me now.

"So, I began running in the direction of the tracks hoping to arrive before the train would. And this would take care of all those things I did not want to live with anymore. However, this was not to be so for me. As I neared the tracks, I began feeling the weight of not drinking come over me once again. And it was not a pleasant feeling at all.

"For when this feeling comes over you, there are no movements of the body you can control. The body will jerk and cause you to lose your breath then make you throw up.

"I wanted to end this earth walk of mine by being hit with the passing train, but this was not to be. For as I lost control of my body, I could only lie on the ground helplessly and look at the train as it passed me by.

"I could only think of another chance that I had missed. Another chance of doing what I wanted to do being missed by me and I could owe it all to this path of the drinking.

"That was the last I remembered of that time. When I opened my eyes once again, I found that I had been laid in the back of a truck and was being taken somewhere, a place I held no idea for where it would be.

"Wanting to look around to see where it was, I sat up in the back of the truck. Not seeing anything that was familiar to me, I looked through the cab's window and wanted to call the driver's attention to me and ask him what had happened.

"As soon as I had knocked on the back window, I saw three faces look to me filled with shock and surprise. At first, I did not know why this was coming to me from them.

"However, I did recognize who they were. It was the doctor who was driving and two men from our village who had come with him.

"Then jerking the truck very poorly on the road, the doctor leaned his head out of the door and told me not to move because I might hurt myself. And this came to me just as one of his sudden moves from the steering wheel jerked the truck and made me hit my head on the side of the truck's bed.

"This must have caused me to go unconscious because this is the last I remember from this truck ride as well. The next thing I remember is waking up in a bed in the hospital.

"Looking up, I saw a nurse sitting next to my bed. I wanted to ask her what all of this was about, but before I could get those speaking words out of my mouth, the doctor came in.

"He was looking at me with a very surprised look over his face and it was then that he told me the story.

"He said that I had been found by one of the two men who had been riding with him that day, and when they came over to the place I was lying, he looked at me very carefully.

"He told me that when he arrived at this place I had been lying, he examined me and found there was no pulse or breathing, and that my body had begun to get stiff in the joints.

"He took this as meaning only one thing—that I was dead. However, before making this final judgment, he used his stethoscope to make one more attempt at finding any sign of life within me, but this was not to be found. After that, they began treating me as if I was another one who had killed themselves from drinking too much alcohol for too long a time.

"And they placed my dead body in the back of the truck and began the drive into town.

"This is why they all held such a look of surprise when I sat up in the back of the truck and knocked on the window.

"Then the doctor looked at me with many more questions over his face, and I could barely hear him because of a terrible ringing in both of my ears. But he told me I no longer had high blood pressure and was no longer underweight like I had been. But all of my body signs had seemed to recover themselves to what they should have been for one who did not drink—to what they should have been for one who had not been drinking as heavily as I had for so many years.

"Then I felt the heaviness of my eyes closing in over me and went to sleep. I was told that I slept for eleven days and nights.

"And it was during this time that I was taken by the dreamers to places I had not ever heard of before, places where I was shown many things and one of them still holds a great place within me now.

"I was being led by two of the dream spirits down a long corridor, and I remember that I could hear my own footsteps on the floor but I could not hear theirs. Through all of this, I would ask each of them just to let me go. For I did not want to continue on this way any longer and did not want to return, even though I did not hold any knowing of where I was going, or where I did not want to return to.

"Suddenly, we entered what appeared to be a large room. And it was filled with many people. Soon, there appeared before me, a man, and he was holding a book with him. He opened it to a place that only he seemed to know of. He began to read out of it. But his reading was not from the book. He seemed to have already memorized what was on these pages, but was reading them to me anyway.

"I do not recall what it was that had been shared with me on this time, but when he had finished, I saw there was another form of myself that had appeared just behind him. And when I saw this other form of myself, I tried to say a greeting to it…but it would only look on me, smile, and do nothing more.

"Then the man who was holding the book stopped his reading and looked over to me, as did the other form of myself. Then my other form walked from behind the man with the book and up to the front of my standing position. It was then that he spoke to me.

"He told me I was the old me and he was the new. That if I wanted to change places, then everything would be all right. But I should not do such a change unless I was truly ready.

"I could feel the weight of truth come over me from his speaking words and I could feel that I was in truth ready to change places with this new me. For I felt the old me had really had it, and could not continue.

"As we stood together I could hear him tell me that I should not worry, for all of those things that were still needing to be done by me would be taken care of—by him.

"And this is the last I remember from those things he had shared with me. Then the next thing I knew, I woke up and was back in my room.

"The doctor once again entered the room to examine me and told me there was absolutely nothing more wrong with me. That I was as healthy a person as he had ever seen but he did not understand what had taken place. But if he could understand it, he too would allow himself to die and come back completely healed from anything that was wrong with him.

"Then I remember the doctor looking into my eyes and asking me who I really was. For while it was nothing that his instruments could tell him, he could feel that I was not the same person he had known for these many years.

"I could only look back at him and tell him that I was my new self. But since I did not have any further information on the subject of me, I had nothing else that I could share with him and left the hospital to return home.

"Arriving at my home, this home that had once been my parents', I did not feel the same way about it as I had once felt. And that was to feel the loss of their not being with me any longer. And that was not all, for there was no longer within me any of the feelings of drinking the alcohol either, and this I could not understand.

"However, instead of mulling over these things that had been presented, I decided that it was time for me to begin my work. And I set out repairing the entire house, then moved on to some of the neighbor's houses to repair them as well. I seemed to be making up for all of the times I had been too drunk to do anything. Each of the neighbors' houses that I would be drawn to and fix were also the ones who had become the most disturbed by me, my parents, and the ones who would always seem to be staying with them.

"After doing all of this work on the houses of those who had been bothered by my old self, I lastly went out to the place where the girl and my three children had lived.

"I looked over to this place and gave to them my thanks for all they had done for me, and then began to repair this house as well. I was surprised to find that I would not lack for any money to do this work. For as I found a need for money to buy new material, it would always be there. Either from one of the other villagers or in the form of having what I needed donated to me by the ones with the white skin.

"In any case, I did not question this good fortune that had been visiting me. I would only give my thanks to all who had been so willing to give me their assistance now that I had become my new self. And for each of these efforts, I could feel something within me begin to grow.

"About the time that I had come to complete all of the needed work on this last house, I knew that I was no longer a part of my past, that all of those things that were needed to be done to repay what had been done by the old me were finished, and I was ready to begin a new path, one that I could not see yet, but one nevertheless I could feel waiting for me to come find it.

"It was then I had come to see Grandfather and Two Bears. And when they walked over to me, they shared that they, too, saw I was no longer the same person they had known, and invited me to sit in one of the Councils of the Wise Ones with them and as their invited guest.

"This filled me with a great feeling of lightness and it was on that first meeting with these Councils of the Wise Ones of our people that I had been invited to remain with them and travel my path by theirs, that is, for as long as our paths would follow close enough.

"And this is my story, Little Ones," Night Hawk concluded. "Are there any questions that you hold with you that I might be willing to answer? After all, it seems as if all five of us have been called together for this event that is about to happen. And it is good if we do not approach it as complete strangers or ones that still hold places among them they are not yet comfortable with from another."

Looking over to this place Night Hawk was sitting, I looked at him very carefully. I could not see any of the markings of the one he had shared he was before, this one that he called his old self. But I could see that the colors he was showing to me as he spoke were in truth the colors of the one he had said he had become, the colors of this new one he spoke of. And this was giving to me a good feeling for him and those things he had been willing to share with us. Looking over to the face that Cheeway was wearing, I could see that he, too, was sharing these same thoughts about Night Hawk. And I felt this too was good.

Turning my attention back to him, I asked: "You have shared with us that you were called to this land for an event that has not yet come to us, Night Hawk." I presented these speaking words to him.

"Yes, Speaking Wind, this is what I have been willing to share with you," was his return.

"When Grandfather and Two Bears heard this calling, they heard it from the children who live in this valley, these children who were in need of assistance for what the night storm had done to them."

"Did you hear this in the same way?" I asked.

"Pretty much, Little One. But since my path travels closely with all who are in this valley of the Old Ones, I did not have as clear an idea of what was waiting here for me. I only held the knowing that my presence was required, not only to assist in the children who were here, but to also join with another council.

"I was also shown that until I would be willing to join with this other council and the event that was on its way, none of it would be able to complete its circle.

"This, then, was what I heard come to me, Speaking Wind and Cheeway. This was my calling...and I came," Night Hawk explained.

There was a cloud over me at this explanation that had been shared by Night Hawk. I did not hold an understanding for his path, and I had found that it was this lack of understanding that was giving to me this feeling of uncomfortableness for him.

I knew that Cheeway was feeling this same way as I was from the look he had been willing to place over his face. But I did not know where to go from here. I only knew there was a great part of something that was missing.

Looking over to the places where Grandfather and Two Bears were sitting, I could see that they had placed a large smile over their faces, one that shared with me that they had already seen this place Cheeway and I found to be stuck in. This smile also shared with me that they would now be willing to lend their assistance and fill in this piece that was giving both of us so much trouble.

"May we assist in what is needed at this time, Night Hawk?" Grandfather asked.

Looking over to see the faces that were being worn on both of them, Night Hawk smiled and nodded his head in a motion that would share with both of them that he did not mind their assistance.

Then looking back to the place where Cheeway and I had been sitting, he smiled and said: "It is good to find such company on this path of the spirit. And seeing the two of you on such a path gives to me a good face to wear for those things that are soon to come, for those things that are even now on their way to all who reside within this domain of the Earth Mother.

"Yes, my brothers, your assistance to these two little ones would be very good at this time."

Then looking over to the place he had come in from, the opening of the large stone cave we were sitting in, he continued.

"But I can see that our time for doing such things is not to be much longer for I can already feel them approaching."

"Yes, Night Hawk," came the reply from Two Bears. "We too have this knowing and will not take very long to share what is needed by Speaking Wind and Cheeway."

From the faces of the three who had come to sit before Cheeway and me, there was a peace that had filled us. It was a peace of knowing that all was as it should be and this was good.

CHAPTER 9

❀

Arriving with the Storm

"When you will look over these lands, little ones, you will see before you many things that you do not yet hold an understanding for," came the speaking words from Two Bears. "For this is a land that has remained in balance to all life. But we have not shared with you how and why this has come to be."

Looking over to the faces that were being worn by Grandfather and Night Hawk, I could see that Two Bears was waiting for their approval for what he was about to do—for it was something that would bear a great weight to it. And if we had not come to the place of understanding for what was about to be shared with us, there would be an even greater weight over both Cheeway and me—a weight that would not complement what was already with us.

While Two Bears was waiting for the confirmation that was coming to him from Grandfather and Night Hawk, I took this time to look to the outside of the great stone cave we were sitting in, to look out and see if the Spirit Wind had decided to move the cloud nation he had brought to us on this day.

But when I placed my seeing eyes to the outside of this sheltered place, I saw the cloud people who had first arrived over these lands had not moved. And looking further into the distance, I could see the two other storms coming closer, and could hear the roll of thunder spirits bringing the fourth one closer as well.

I held the knowing there was not going to be any movement of these cloud people on this day. But there was going to be an increasing of storms over this land as these other three were continuing their movement and direction to this place we were now in.

"It seems funny, my brother," came the speaking words from Cheeway.

"What is that, Cheeway?" I asked, noticing that he too had been looking over the sky that was above us.

"It is as if the Spirit Wind is bringing the storm to us from each of the four directions," Cheeway continued. "And he is not going to move any of them once they have reached this place."

Looking over to the place where Cheeway was sitting, I could see that his eyes were completely fixed on the cloud peoples' lack of movement. And hearing the calling voice of the Spirit Wind, he was not sure how to take such an event.

For him, I could see from the many seasons I had been given to travel with him that there needed to be a calling of order for all things. And to Cheeway, with the Spirit Wind calling over all of the lands as he was, and there not being any movement in the cloud people…well, I could see that this was weighing heavy on him.

"Is it always like this just before a spirit vision, Speaking Wind?" Cheeway asked, still looking deep into the sky.

"No, my brother, not at all," was my return to him.

"So this is pretty powerful stuff then, I guess," Cheeway asked still looking up at the sky.

"Cheeway," I said, placing my right hand on his left shoulder. "I do not believe the spirit vision has begun yet."

Finishing my speaking words to him made him turn his head into my direction very quickly.

"You mean this is not a part of it, Speaking Wind?" he asked with a slight trembling in the tone of his voice.

"No, Cheeway, what you are seeing now is only a calling of the Old Ones to all who are within this domain of the Earth Mother, a calling to all who has ears to hear with, that they are on their way. And this thing that you are seeing, my brother, is only a calling sign from the ones who are soon to arrive and be with us."

Looking at me with his usual face of having his mouth open, Cheeway held a blank look over him for a few moments and then uttered:

"You hold this knowing to be true because you have been through this already, haven't you, Speaking Wind?" Cheeway managed to say.

"Yes, Cheeway, from what I have already seen of the last time I had been called by the Ancient Ones, I can share with you that this is nothing in comparison to what is coming. That this is only a reminding to all of the children in this valley of the Old Ones that there is soon to be an arrival, an arrival of those who are returning now to share great truth with the earth walkers.

"Listen, my brother," I continued with the sharing of my speaking words, "listen to the calling of all of the children who are of the wing. Do you not hear them for what they are saying?"

"I do not hear any of them on this day, Speaking Wind," was Cheeway's puzzled response to me. "And I do not hold an understanding for what it is you are asking of me either."

"When the Old Ones come," I replied, "all of the motion that is usually to be found in this domain will stop. That is, if you are listening with the ears you have come to understand with.

"When there will not be any of the children of the wing traveling through the skies, and you know they should be, then you will hold the knowing for what they are saying to you and all who would be willing to listen.

"They are sharing that soon it will be time to be still and listen. This then is their sharing though the silence with all of us.

"For they do not have to look through the illusion of those things that have been covering us these many seasons. For them, Cheeway, they are not born into this sleep of illusion like we have been."

Looking at me once again, I could see that there was a little more clarity that had come over Cheeway's face. And for this I was glad.

I was glad for this because of what I had been willing to share with him was all that I had come to understand. And I held the knowing that, if I were to tell or allow him to find this out at this time, he would only feel more lost than he was feeling already.

But now, the time of silence that had been achieved by Grandfather, Two Bears, and Night Hawk, was over. And they were calling to us that we should return our attention to those things they were now prepared to share with us, those things that they had each confirmed among themselves.

Both Cheeway and I heard this silent call to both of us. Shifting our weight and position on the sitting stones we had found, we were once again looking on the faces of the three who had come to assist us in finding these small pieces of understanding we had been seeking, these things I had shared with them but were not allowing me to see clearly.

CHAPTER 10

✤

Passageway of the Ancient Ones

"It is time to share the history for this land we have today, little ones," Two Bears began as he sat with a good face to share with both of us.

"We have seen that it is now your time to share in this knowledge that has been given to the three of us for safe keeping through many generations of time."

"I will share with you each that there is much more to learn on this path you have so willingly taken up in this domain that is the Earth Mother," Grandfather picked up on the speaking words from Two Bears.

"Much more of the wisdom and teachings that will be shared with you both once the remainder of this spirit vision has been shared with us.

"But for now, we three would be very grateful if you would give your attention completely to Two Bears. For what he is willing to share with you now is something that will hold great value to both of you when it is your time of waking and all of your preparing has been completed.

"We are sitting in a very sacred place now, little ones, a sacred place that has long been used by us, and the Ancient Ones as well," Two Bears began. "It was a time when our people of the Pueblo

Nation were very young, a time when we were not much more than gathers and hunters. It has not been for all time that we have been living in our villages built of mud and stone.

"However, there had come to us many of the teachings from the Great Spirit on how we were to live among all of this domain that is the Earth Mother. And one of these teachings was to allow for our old ones and wise ones to listen to the calling voices of spirit, to listen and share with the rest of our people those things that had come to them for us to learn from.

"Looking back to those times that are still within our people's memories and song legends, little ones, I cannot help but think that we had become a people who had been left with no memory, left with no memory of our times from the before.

"And it is in seeing these things from all that is still left on the cave walls of our most ancient ancestors that this comes to the front of my thinking mind.

"For there was a significant level of social strata that had been developed by us in those most ancient of times. We had the ones who walked a medicine walk and healed our people in their times of need. We had the ones who would travel the path of the wise ones and learn from those children who lived with us their ways of continuing all life paths. And we had the ones who would travel the warrior's path and would provide the protection that our people needed when it was time.

"But there did not seem to be any memory of where these things had come to us from. So it was that we would wander through all of these lands of the mesa and mountains gathering and sustaining our life paths.

"However, there have been a few of the old records on some of the cave walls that make reference to this. Others among the people felt the same way as I have that there was a great piece of our history missing from us. One of these reasons was in a question asking why our people had become wanderers over these lands, to continue this search for something that would share with us our missing past.

"It was many seasons of wandering and gathering that had passed before our people came to know of the Old Ones, the ones we refer to today as the Anasazi.

"When we came to first look on their villages that they had built, many in the sides of great stone mountains, we were very impressed and thought they were from the spirit world for they held with them many wonders and could speak in ways that we had not yet learned.

"They would make jars and vessels that would hold water and food for long periods of time, and they did not seem to hold a great fear for any who were within this domain with them.

"Once we had become used to seeing them for who and what they were, we would come closer to those villages they had built in order to observe them. But only to watch them from distant places where we would still feel the safety of not being in a place they could see us.

"However, once this had taken place for a few moons, they would come out of their villages and leave us food and water. They would leave them in those same places we would gather to observe them.

"And all through this time, many of our wise ones would often gather to share among themselves. For there was something about these people of the great medicine that was very familiar to all of us, but we could not place it. It seemed to be just beyond our reach.

"It was not long before we had begun to share things back with them. We would leave, in those same places where they had left the food and water for us, those things that we had found to gather on the lands of the mesa and mountains.

"Then before many seasons passed, we found they were waiting for us to come to them. After that, they no longer left things for us to take, but would wait for us to arrive and hand them to us.

"This was the beginning of a great adventure for all of our people, little ones. For this was the beginning time when we would finally be shown all of those things we had been searching for, those things that would allow us to replace those missing pieces in our memories. And it was all because of the Old Ones.

"It was from that time in our people's history that we became very close to the Old Ones. And many of our wise ones as well as some of the young ones would be taken into their villages where they would live with them for awhile.

"All of our people were very impressed with the things they had learned from the Old Ones. And one thing was becoming very clear to us, and that was the direction the Old Ones were leading us into.

"We were being shown many things from living and learning with them—things that would no longer force us to be the wanderers and gatherers we had once been.

"But as I have been willing to share with you, little ones, the reason we had been wanderers and gatherers was only done as part of a search, a search to this missing memory that all of us seemed to be experiencing in this time with the Earth Mother. And it was through our searching for these missing parts of our memory that we had become wanderers and gatherers. This was the reason, because to do anything else would not have allowed us the freedom to go so far and to so many different lands.

"And now we were being shown how to build with mud and stone, how to build dwellings for ourselves that would keep us dry in the wet seasons and warm in the sleeping seasons.

"This was something that was very new to our way of life, and there was a great amount of discussion among the elders of our people in coming to a place of seeing, a place of seeing if this was the path needed by all of us.

"For to follow such a path meant that we would have to leave behind many of those things we had come to know so well. And this was a heavy burden on us, this burden to give up a way of life that had become so much a part of us.

"As the new aspects of this change were being offered, the wise of our peoples' ancestors who decided to remain with the changes and take up these new things that were being offered to us to learn from are the result of we who stand before you. And, as is the case among all things that will come to be shared, there were some of our people who decided that this would not be for them. And they continued with the way of living they had grown so accustomed to before.

"This then was the first recognized split of our people, little ones. While most of them remained with the Old Ones to learn from them, there were a few who did not and took up the wandering and gathering path to them once again.

"In the seasons that were to follow, our people grew increasingly closer to the Old Ones of the great villages. There were many council fires shared with them where there was much revealing of those things of the past, those things that would now be shared with us that we had been seeking for. Those things that would once again allow us all to see clearly our reasons for feeling this strange closeness to these people, to these people who, like us, did not seem to have a known past to themselves either. For if they had a past, then it would have been seen by us from our many wanderings over these lands.

"However, they seemed to appear, villages and all, out of nowhere and in less time than the passing of one generation.

"But now that we were beginning to share these council fires with them, they had become willing to share with us those things that would make all of this clear to us once again.

"And I say once again, little ones, because there is not ever anything that will be presented to you that will not have been with you all of these seasons you have traveled here—not any of those things that are of truth that is.

"You see, it was during these council fires of sharing with the Old Ones that this and many other things were being shared, things like where we had come from and where they had come from—those things that we needed in order to make sense for our own life paths.

"All of us at this time held the knowing that there was much more to our past than any of us could remember but we felt something was there. This allowed us to more readily accept what was being offered to us as truth.

"We held the understanding that when truth is offered by another, then it can be easily understood, and there is no thing about it that is complicated.

"This is because when truth will be shared by another, then this other will hold a clear understanding for it. Then there is nothing that is unclear either to the one who is willing to share this truth or by the one who is willing to receive it. Both will understand all that is being presented when this is present.

"However, when one who is not clear on their own levels of understanding to those things they are trying to explain, then there is created over them a great cloud of non-seeing. And this cloud not only is seen by the one who is trying to explain something they do not understand, but they will add to it by their unsure efforts of explaining to another.

"They will do this in an effort of showing to the one who is receiving how much less they know than they do because they cannot understand. And this will give to them the illusion that they are at a higher place than the other one. But I share with the both of you that this is illusion and not truth. For there is not now, nor has there ever been, another in this domain who is either higher or lower than another...and this is truth.

"These Old Ones whom we have come to call the Anasazi began to explain to us that all of the two-legs who are now in this domain are not a new race—not new by any standard that may be applied to them.

"They are not new, but they are returned. And it was one of the conditions of this returning that had caused them all to lose such a great part of their memory for those things that had once been with them from the before times.

"They shared with all of us that we had all come from places that were beneath the face of the Earth Mother. And the reason was to escape from the great waters of cleansing that had come here.

"There had to be an end to one world before the next one could begin, and this was the cleansing of all that had been, of all those things that had been built and created by the race that had been given this time of making their choices—those choices of traveling on the path that would lead to the left…this path that is led by the body and fed by the emotions, or traveling on the path that leads to the right…this path that is fed by spirit and led by spirit as well. And when this time had finished, all that would have served as a reminder to it had been washed away from all life's memory.

"And when this time came for all of this land that is in this domain of the Earth Mother, there were many of the Old Ones who entered these lands for our purpose. Their purpose was to call to the ones who live in the underworld and ask them for permission for all of us to enter their domain, to enter their domain and explain the purpose and length of its time to them.

"They explained to these dwellers of the underworld that this was an ending to the next-to-last-race. And their domain was now needed in order to allow those who had come to see and travel the path that leads to the right, a place to go, a place where they and theirs could find safety from the cleansing that was about to take place.

"Seeing these Old Ones who had re-entered this domain of the underworld dwellers come do this request, they saw that they were not of the kind who had the emotions of lessons unlearned holding onto them. For the Old Ones who had entered at this time, and at this place of the underworld to see and hear, they had been the same ones who had long ago crossed the Great Spirit Waters with their robes. They were the ones who did not have to go through the pains of death, and for that reason, they retained the ability of entering this domain with their same bodies and without having to go through any more processes of birth and dying ever again.

"When they gained this permission of the ones who resided in the underworld places, little ones, they returned to the top of this domain and lands that you see before you and relayed this welcome that had been extended by the residents of the underworld.

"For along with this welcome from the residents of the under-world, came their willingness to share with all of us who would enter their domain how to live in this new environment, and how to maintain our balance in the domain we were soon to enter.

"But they also shared with all of our people that when the great cleansing waters would wash over this top portion of the Earth Mother, there would no longer be any memory of how things had once been. That as the waters would cleanse the Earth Mother of all memories of what had once been that they would also cleanse our thinking minds as well. And this was needed by all, for to retain any of this memory would be unfair to the last race who would soon emerge to be given their chance at this great cleansing, their chance to cleanse themselves just as all of the other races had been given.

"They were told, when it would come time for them to emerge once again from this underworld, there would be a memory cleansing for them as well. For when they would have taken their first step back into this domain that had been given to them to travel in, they would lose their memory of the ones who had been so willing to share their own domain with them for those many seasons in the underworld.

"So it was, that when our people and those of the other races emerged from the underworld, they had lost all of the memories of those things that had once been with them, as well as all of the memories of the location and entry ways to the underworld itself.

"And this was needed because in order for the last race to begin its cleansing, it would have to be offered the same starting place as all of the other three had been given. And this was only in balance to those things that were needed so there could be growth and freedom of choice made by those who would enter this domain to travel a life path.

"All of our people began to see the beginning of a light that was being formed around all of the Old Ones, around all of these who we had come to call The Anasazi.

"As they would share those many things that would be given for us to relearn from, they began to take on another appearance to us. They were beginning to resemble less and less those who we had first come to see and know as the strangers.

"They were becoming more like the light people we had heard of from the stories they had to share with us. What I share with you now, little ones, is only to be found in the most secret of our places, only in the most kept of song legends that have been carried by a few of our wise ones.

"It seemed that the more we were being prepared with, the more these Old Ones were willing to share with us. As we would achieve the level of understanding for all of those things we held a great need for, they would lose one more feature of themselves.

"They would lose one more feature that had at first come to us as seeing them like we were. And as they would lose one of their features, there would appear from within them, a bright light. Small at first, but as they would spend more time with us in explaining many of those things that we had forgotten, many of those things that we now needed in order to make sense from this earth walk of ours, they would become brighter and brighter until they would all hold with them a great glowing white light over all of their body.

"But this was something that was done at such a gradual pace that not many of our people noticed, and when they finally were aware of it…they became shocked. It had taken such a gradual effort in allowing itself to be that we had only come to see this as something that was natural for these Old Ones to have this glowing light about them. And we continued to listen and learn from their seemingly unlimited fields of understanding, this was also something that we seemed to accept as a part of them, something that would not be without their presence and something that their presence would not be without.

"It was through all of these times of sitting around the council fires and living with the Old Ones that much of what has been shared with us in our song legends remains. For our people, those things that had been shared with us in those olden times hold just as much truth to them today as they did then.

"When you will look at many of these teachings that are being shared with each of you, I would venture to say that neither of you will be able to place a time on them, a time when they had first been shared with our people. This is because what was shared by the Anasazi was truth, and truth does not age nor is it placed into only one time. And this is what has allowed their teachings to live among us for such a long time.

"But I am getting away from the intent of my song legend, this song legend that allows us to hold this place and this land as a sacred place.

"As I had been willing to share with both of you, this was the time when the Anasazi were willing to teach our people of when we re-entered this domain that is the face of the Earth Mother, and why we lost all of our memories—those memories not only of the times that had been before, but of those times that we had gone to live with the beings of the underworld, the ones who had allowed us to share their path and domain until we could once again return to this one we have come to know now.

"They further explained to our people how each of us carries a piece of Great Mystery within us. And this piece is of such perfection, that we only have to go within ourselves to find it, to find it and be shown our place as One within the One.

"As they continued this sharing, they also told us that there would be a day that would end this time that we had all entered into, a time that would be marked by many strange things and occurrences that would be seen by all who travel a life path in this domain. And when this would come to us, that we would do well to remember the path of the spirit, this path that leads to the right and is led and fed by spirit.

"All they had left for us would be a reminding place for those who would still see and hear from the path of their own spirit, this path of their own spirit that resides within each of us.

"They had left many spirit paintings in our sacred places. And for the small ones of the leaf who they would leave in the valley floors of these places, we should always ensure that they would be cared for. And when there would be a need of our assisting them to continue with their life path, that we should be willing to attend to their needs.

"They did not tell us why we should do this; our members of the councils who learned from them did not hold a reason to ask such a question of them. For they held the knowing that they were not being shared anything that was not truth. And if they did not hold the understanding for this truth that had been asked of them, this truth in assisting all of the children of the leaf when there would be a need, that there would soon come a time for them when this would be cleared for them and when the time was right for them to understand, they would be shown.

"In the seasons that remained with the Old Ones to share with our people, there were many things that were taught and understood, things that until this day have not yet come to the place of understanding, for their time is not yet.

"But nevertheless, we still carry them and continue to pass them from one generation to the next, holding the knowing that when it will be their time to be understood, we will see.

"So it is that much of what has been carried with our people from those ancient teachings of the Old Ones is now understood…and this is good. But there is still much that has been left with us that is not yet understood, and we hold this to be good as well.

"This village that we are now sitting in and sharing its protection, well, this is no different. We still do not hold a complete understanding for what they had requested us to do, this request in not only assisting all of the children of the leaf on their valley floors, but this requesting of also maintaining these villages but not living within them. Yet, we have maintained their request.

"And from all of this, little ones, I will share with you that we have only come to understand just a small part of their reasons, a small part of their reasons for there being a need in keeping these villages alive, but without any of the two-legs living in them.

"For we have managed to be shown from those teachings of long ago that when there will come the time and the ending of the last race has been completed, then there will be a great need for those who would search for their inner self, this self that is their spirit part. They will have a great need to look upon these villages and valley floor once again to find those things they seek.

"For within all of these things that are continuing with their life path there are many great mysteries to be shared. But they will not be shared with any of us until this time is right and they will once again see their need among all of us again.

"It will be at this time when all of them will once again rise up and live again—rise up and share with those who would come to them, all of those things that need to be remembered, all of those things of balance that will be greatly needed by all who will be living in these times that are still ahead of us.

"And, Speaking Wind, you have seen this from the last spirit vision you have taken on, this last spirit vision when the Ancient Ones shared with you this time is near and will be seen by you."

When Two Bears had said these speaking words, I could feel the eyes of all that were present look at me. And I could feel eyes of others that were also with us, but did not have with them a robe to travel in, look at me.

All of this gave me chills that were running up and down both of my arms, chills that I had come to the place of understanding that would come over one when those who were traveling only in spirit would touch you to let you know they are with you.

Looking back to the place where Two Bears was sitting, I nodded my head in a motion that allowed him to see that I was still following those things he had been willing to share with me, a motion that would convey these feelings of mine to him and without having to break the silence I had found, this silence that had placed itself over me so that I could see life and understand those things he was willing to present.

Looking over to the place where my best friend, Cheeway was sitting, I could see that he, too, had returned his seeing back to the place of Two Bears and that he, too, was now ready for him to resume with this song legend from our past, this song legend that was new to both of us, but which we could feel very strongly lived within each of us.

Seeing this look from Cheeway and me, this look of being ready to listen to more, Two Bears continued: "It was at this time when the Old Ones with the glowing lights coming from within them stopped teaching our people in such great numbers. For it was from this time on that they would only look over the great numbers of our people who would come to them, and would pick only a few to take and sit around their council fires.

"Once one had been picked by the Ancient Ones, they would always have a place by any of their council fires. For even if they had not returned to the same one they had been sitting at, when they would go to another, they would always be welcomed. And for this reason, once one of our wise ones had been picked, then it was not important for them to return at any given time or to any given place.

All that was important was that they continue on their path and stay focused on their work.

"All of this was understood by our people, and they were given the freedom of doing and learning these things from the Old Ones. For our people held the knowing that all that was being shared with a few was being done for all of them. And that when there would come a time and this sharing would be needed by our people, it would be there for them.

"But for now, the Old Ones had their own reasons to share with only a few. And this reason was not important to be understood at the time as much as was the fact that they were willing to continue to share with all of us through these small groups of our wise ones."

Looking over to the place where Cheeway and I were sitting and listening very attentively, Two Bears raised both of his hands with their palms face down and said: "There are not many who will hold an understanding for what is being presented to them at the time. For there are none of us who hold the knowing of what this sharing will bring until we have crossed through the time that is ahead.

"So it is best to listen to those things that will come to you with the innocence of receiving, and this comes from the child within each of you. In this way, you will not ever have to be concerned with those things and their reasons for being with you. All you will have to hold with you will be to look for the face of truth for those things that are being shared.

"As you will come to see if there is or there is not a face of truth to what is being shared, then you will have all you will need to make your decision. When you will see that there is a face of truth that is within those things that are being offered to you, you will hold the understanding that for you, they are good, that when the time is right, and you have prepared yourself sufficiently, you will come to understand.

"And for those things that you will not see your own face of truth in, then it is good for you to walk away and not argue any of the points that do not fit you.

"You see, little ones, there will be others who will hold a need that you will not. And if you would waste the time of one who is willing to share with others only from your own perspective, then you will not be assisting either yourself or any other in trying to prove to them that there is no truth to what they say.

"Only the ones who will see their own greed and that all others should be like them will do this. The ones who have found the pathway to their own spirit—they will know and understand better. For they will have found their path that will not only allow them to see the face of their own spirit, but this same path that will share with them once again how to become a human being. And becoming a human being allows another to see that there are many who travel in this domain who have needs, needs that may or may not be like theirs.

"When they will come to see this, then they, too, will have found the wisdom in what I have been willing to share with you. That when there will not be a truth in those things that are being offered to you, that there will be another who will find truth in them. And you will have been arguing for those things that you will not, in truth, have any effect on anyway; and that when you would do such a thing, you will only be delaying the inevitable and you are not assisting either yourself or any other.

"Remember, little ones, if something is not for you and the path that you have been willing to travel, do not spend your time foolishly trying to destroy it. For all of your efforts will not change those things that are going to be anyway.

"Rather, walk away from them and hold the knowing that there will, in time, be one who will come to them, one who will have a need for those things that they too have entered this domain to do.

And they, like you, are also looking for those bits and pieces of understanding so they may find their own path.

"Hold this with you, little ones. And then your wisdom will grow within you, this wisdom that will allow you to have a place near the council fires of our Old Ones, a place that will light your path when the night comes, a place that will keep you warm when you feel cold from the loneliness of your journey; and a place that will allow you to always see the point of connection that all of us have been given to remember, this point of connection that allows us to know we are not ever alone."

Once again, Two Bears looked on both Cheeway and me with a warm smile. We could see that the face he was now wearing for us was for a reason that had been shared with both of us many seasons before. This reason that shared with each of us that while we may not now hold the understanding for those things that would be offered to us, there would, in time ahead, be a need for this.

And with this in the front of both of our thinking minds, we returned his smile of warmth and understanding and remained silent so that he would be able to continue with those things he was now willing to share with us.

"Now, as the Ancient Ones would continue to share with our wise ones, there was something that was being noticed. It was a change that was coming over all of the Ancient Ones that could be seen and felt by all of our people.

"As they continued to teach us, the light coming from within them was increasing. There were times when our people could not stand to look at them for long periods of time because of this bright light that was continually growing from within each of them.

"Then, as the Ancient Ones could see this trouble come over the faces of our people, they took the time to share with us what it was that we were seeing on them, what this light was all about.

"They would hold council with the ones they had chosen to share with, and took the time of explaining that the light that was continuing to grow from within them was only a sign, a sign that was coming to them, and us, from their own spirit within.

"It was at this time that they explained to all of us that their path in this domain was one of handing down all of those things that would be needed by the two-legs, those things that would be needed in order to have all earth walks make sense to us.

"They reminded us of all that had been forgotten by those entering this new world, and would explain those feelings of our searching for what we felt had been lost to us, and how by their sharing and teaching our people that we no longer held this feeling of a need to wander over all of these lands, but now felt very good about remaining in one place.

"They further explained how it was not their path to travel with us, but their path was one that only allowed them to stay in this domain only for the time of our need. Once this need of ours had been worked with, there would no longer be a need for them to remain. When this time would come to them, they would all return to their home...this home they called the waiting place.

"And now that this time for their need in this domain was almost complete, there was the light of the spirit from within them that was beginning to call them back, to call to them while giving all of us a sign that this time for us to remain among them was almost at an end.

"When we asked them why this light did not appear among any of our people, they reminded us that for them, all that was needed to be accomplished had been done long ago. And when one will accomplish all that is needed by spirit in this domain, they will be given this robe they wear and be allowed to take it with them.

"When this takes place, there will no longer be any need by them to enter though the birth process, or leave through the death process, because they will hold onto the shell that is needed to carry their spirit around.

"They reminded us that in the times that were far in the distance, there would be an ending even to this world that all of us had entered into. And when this ending of the last world would take place, they would return in great numbers. When they would, they would give to those who could still see and hear with the eyes and ears of their spirit many signs and visions so they would know when this time would be close at hand—signs that would not be mistaken and visions that would be very powerful to behold.

"But the time left to them was not long, and soon they would be leaving. And when they would leave, it would be done before all of the eyes of those who had been chosen to learn and study among them.

"For they would be the ones who would be left with the understanding of what had been offered to them and would enter in their song legends for others to see and later understand.

"It had only been with the passing of one moon before the announcement had come to us. And this was the time when they had called all of those who had been chosen to study with them, as they would do this calling of theirs.

"Even though many of them had been told of these events that were about to take place, not all were willing to believe in it. For when the Ancient Ones would appear in the village and be seen, there were many who would become frightened and run or try to hide from them. And all of this had been told to the ones who remained with the Ancient Ones, and all of this did take place as they said it would.

"Even though they had been told of what this great event that was about to take place meant and that there would be no harm to any of them, there were still many who would not hold this to them as a truth of any kind. And by not holding this as a truth to themselves, they could not understand any of it.

"When any will come across an event they do not understand, little ones, they will always see it through their own eyes of fear, and they will run from it because they will only see something or someone before them who could bring to them great harm. And for those who remain in their sleep of illusion, this is something they do not want to have taken place for themselves.

"At first, they will see this as something that they must only run and hide from. But as time will pass and they continue to see and feel the presence of this near them, they will come to see it as an enemy of theirs, one that must be dealt with in the only way they know how.

"And the Ancient Ones held this understanding for those who had not yet reached their place of understanding. They knew the time left would be very short before the ones who had not yet reached their understanding would begin to attack them as they would an enemy.

"With this in the front of their thinking minds, they reminded those who had been chosen to learn from them that they would have a great need to hurry and observe this last thing they would be willing to share with us.

"For it was when all of the wise ones of our people had been gathered together—in the place that is just to the outside of this village we are sitting in—that they shared with us the last of their lessons, the last of the lessons they would be willing to share with us for the time that they had been given to walk among all of us.

"Then our wise ones took their seated positions in the valley that is below us, and the great adventure began, one that would not be forgotten for all time as we would know it.

"When our wise ones took their sitting places in the valley, the elder of the Anasazi took his place on the outside ledge, this outside ledge of the village where all of us are sitting now. The elder raised both of his hands to the great sky nation and told our wise ones that their time now was over, that they would all be returning to the waiting place and would take their robes with them.

"However, they would leave a few of their numbers as well as the villages that would be needed by us in the time we could not yet see, those times when they would once again return to us. And we would do well to keep them maintained, not only this village and others we would soon find, but also this valley where many of the children of the leaf had been residing.

"For by doing this, we would always be reminded of the balance that is needed in any life path, the balance of spirit which would be a constant reminder to all of us by the presence of this village, and the balance of being rooted in the Earth Mother, which would be seen when we would look on all of the children of the leaf who resided here.

"He reminded us that when it would be time for the beginning signs of their return, this place would be one of many where those signs would be found. And when they would return once again, this would also be one of those places where they would make their entry.

"However, he continued to share with all who had been gathered in this place, that there would be nothing gained by trying to guess at when this time would be. For to do such a thing would be to take away from all of the work we each had to do. If we would waste our time for those things that had already been set into motion, then we would be taking our own eyes away from the lessons that were being presented to each of us. And when this takes place, there is a stopping of one's growth, this growth that leads the way for us to our own understanding.

"Without understanding for oneself and all of those things that are with them, then they will remain blinded to truth, this truth that resides within each of us.

"Then the elder lowered his arms back to his side and made a motion for the rest of the Ancient Ones to join him on this standing place. When they joined with him, there was a sudden burst of light that enclosed all of them, and when it had faded into the air that was around all of us...they were gone, all but a few of them, and they looked over to the places each of our wise ones were sitting and walked to them.

"They told us that they had chosen to remain with us for a short time and during this time, they would continue to teach the ones who would be willing to understand, all of those things that would be needed, all of those things that would be needed by the ones who were with us in this day, as well as all of those things that would be needed by the ones who would follow.

"For the remainder of time that was left to them, they spent with the wise ones of our people in the Great Spirit caves we continue to go into and learn from. When they would enter these places, it was the light that each of these Ancient Ones would carry with them that would allow them to see in the darkness of those places without the need of fire.

"The time that was left to them was spent in transcribing many of their teachings for the time that was, as well as for the time that would be, and all that would be needed in order to remember their prophecy for what would take place.

"It was from these places that are still held as sacred by many of our wise ones now that we continue to travel to, so that we may see what lies ahead.

"However, we are almost at the end of these events that had been foretold by the Ancient Ones. Those spirit paintings and song legends are also near their end, and this is what is bringing to many of us like Grandfather, Night Hawk, and myself, our own weight of not understanding.

"For we were told that when the last spirit painting would live out its time, their return would surely be close at hand. And this has taken place, little ones, this has taken place already. For when we enter many of the caves where these spirit paintings are, we do not see them clearly any longer. It is as if they, too, have realized that their time is over and they are blending into the Earth once again.

Looking over to the place where Cheeway and I were sitting, I could see the face that Two Bears was wearing for us was one of concern, a look of concern for what was lying ahead for all of us.

This had filled me with my own weight of concern and looking at Cheeway from the corner of my eye, I could see that he, too, had been filled with this weight as well. For neither of us remembered a time when either Grandfather or Two Bears had worn this face, at least not where either of us could see it.

"And this brings to you a feeling of being lost, Two Bears?" I asked, looking over to his sitting place across the warming fire that we had built.

"Not a feeling of lost, little one," Two Bears responded to me. "It is rather a feeling of expectation for what will take place next. For this time that had been foretold to all of our wise ones is almost completed. And it is for this reason that none of us hold an understanding for what is to take place next."

"However," came the speaking words of Grandfather, "we do hold the understanding for those things that are coming to us now. Even though they are not contained within our song legends or spirit paintings, we do understand that they are a part of these signs and visions that have been foretold to us by the Ancient Ones from long ago.

"We are very close now to entering the time of prophecy. And this is a time when there will not be anything withheld from those who will seek to find their own truths.

"Remember, little ones, when one will have the opportunity of entering the time of prophecy, they will not ever do such a thing alone. For this is a sacred and special time that will be offered on the back of all those who have ever been.

"It is a time that will either be seen as a great blessing and confirmation to all of those things that have been foretold, or it will be seen as a time when there will be nothing but confusion and darkness that will fall over the ones who would travel with it.

"But in any case, all of us have seen visions of this time that is ahead, but we have not yet seen when it is to take place."

"And does this time have a name to it, Grandfather?" Cheeway asked, sitting in a way of expecting a calming answer come to him.

"Yes, Cheeway," Grandfather continued. "This time does have a name to it. It is called 'The Season of the Long Shadow.'"

CHAPTER 11

❀

The Season of the Long Shadow

Looking over to the place where Grandfather was sitting, Cheeway and I could see that he had placed a warm smile over himself, one that we could see was for our benefit for what could not yet be seen by us, but what we would see…and in a very short time.

"There is a question that has formed in the front of your thinking mind, little ones," was the response to our faces from Grandfather. "Would you care to share it with us?"

"Well, yes we would, Grandfather," was my response to him. "It is for a clearer meaning of this time that you have been willing to share with us, this time that you have named as 'The Season of the Long Shadow'.

"I do not feel as if I hold a good understanding for its name and would be willing to listen to your explanation for what this time is and what it is holding for us."

"Then I will be willing to share this with you, little ones," came the pleased look from Grandfather.

"'The Season of the Long Shadow' has been held within our most ancient song legends and spirit paintings. This is the time when there will come to many, great fears for those things they do not hold an understanding for. For the ones who will hold this understanding, they will see this time holding many great blessings, blessings that will come to them from all they have done, all they will do, and all that they are doing in the present.

"This time is one of great mystery for those who will enter this domain that is the Earth Mother. And they will not be able to ignore it or to even look away from it once it has arrived.

"However, the reasons for this are many, little ones, and I tell you this in truth. That each one who has an earth walk to travel does so to learn their own lessons, and they will be as different from another as day is to night. For no two life paths will ever be the same.

"But for the name of 'The Season of the Long Shadow', this comes to us from truth that has always been, this truth that has been shared with us from the Ancient Ones.

"Think of the ending of one of our days and as you will, you will see how long the shadows of all things become during this time.

"When you will look on this time that I am willing to speak to you about, there is in truth no thing that will come to the front of your thinking minds that will cause you to feel fear.

"For when you will see this time come to all lands, as it does for each day, you will be allowed to travel through. Then you will look on this as just another event in the circle of life you are traveling in—as another event that the time is nearing for the ending of another day for the Earth Mother. And soon, it will be time for the night. This nighttime, when used as it was meant to be used, will allow the body part of yourselves to rest and re-strengthen itself while the spirit part will travel with the dreamers and continue with the lessons of spirit.

"As you look on this time when the shadows become long in this domain, you will feel the need to rest and be still. For you will hold the knowing that soon a new day will arrive and you will need your strength and energy to keep up with all that will be presented, with all of the blessings that are continually offered to all who enter this domain to learn.

"And this is not any different from this time that I am now willing to share with the both of you, this time that our people have come to call 'The Season of the Long Shadow'.

"But it will be seen as something very different by those who would be traveling within this domain of the Earth Mother. It will be seen and felt as something that holds a great fear for all of them. And the reason for this is they have forgotten to remember those things that have always been with them, those things that are carried by each of their spirits within them.

"You see, little ones, when one will enter this domain of the Earth Mother and begin an earth walk with her, they enter a sleep of illusion. And it is this sleep of illusion that will not allow them to see things for what they are. This sleep of illusion only allows them to see things for what they would wish for them to be. And this way of seeing does not hold any part of the face of truth.

"As they continue to travel in this domain and gain more and more seasons over them, they find themselves being comforted more by listening to what others would have them believe rather than finding their own way. And they are led into the false believing that what these others are doing must be right for them as well, because there are so many of them doing this.

"As they continue this path they have made their own free choice to follow, they come to believe this is the only way for them to go, that there is nothing good they could ever do that would not come to them from the direction and decisions of others—others who are just as lost in their own sleep of illusion as they.

"And for them, little ones, because they have given away so much of themselves to these others, they do not see what has become of them. They have been allowed to follow them by selling themselves a piece at a time until there is nothing left. And when one will reach this place on their path, they believe there is no thing they can do for themselves any more.

"They hold the believing that without the acceptance and approval by those who they have been listening to, there can really be no thing they will ever do that can be right.

"But I will share with the both of you that this is not correct. This is as far from their own truth as they could ever be.

"But to the lost, no one will be able to convince them they know their way. For they will be so consumed by their own emotions of fear and uncertainty, they will not allow themselves to listen to any one who would wish to tell them this.

"And when they have arrived at this place, little ones, they will be living on the emotion that is boiling up from within them. For they do not now, nor will they ever, find the peace and comfort that they believe to be out there for them. The more this emotion will eat at them, the more emotion they will find within themselves to drive them, to drive them to where they will also be telling others what to do and how to do it.

"When one arrives at this place of the boiling emotions, they no longer see. They only have the believing in those things that have failed them. Because for them, there can be nothing else. For them, this is all there is. And for them, if you will not agree with them and this path of failure they have chosen to follow, you will become an enemy of theirs, and all of their efforts will be aimed at destroying you and those things you have found on your beginning path.

"For many who have just begun to see they do have a path of their own to travel, they would look at them and say it is not fair. That this is just too much for them to encounter because they will perceive to have so many obstacles to overcome.

"And from their limited point of seeing things, little ones, they hold the believing that what they are saying is truth. But it is not.

"While it is truth that they will indeed encounter many great obstacles that are in front of them, obstacles that must first be overcome by them before they will be allowed to travel on this path they have begun to see, they will not have the fullness of understanding for them, this fullness of understanding that would share with them that all things that will come to them, do so for a great reason. And the greatest of reasons will be to allow them to learn more about themselves. As they come to learn more about themselves, they find this understanding that we have spent so many seasons sharing with the both of you. And they will see how necessary it is to find this before they can see themselves.

"However, those great obstacles that will be seen in front of one who is just beginning their path of the spirit, this same path they have designed for them to travel, they will not see the reasons that are behind them, not until they have come face to face with all they still carry with them, those many things they carry with them that do not hold the face of truth, but they still believe in, believe in because they hold many of their old habits within them.

"You see, little ones, when they will see these obstacles in front of them as great, what they are doing is to look at them in the way they had become used to looking at all things from their seasons past…in a way that was not to look at them with their own eyes, but to look at them through the eyes of others who have been telling them what to do and what is right and wrong for them, those same others that have been standing in the way of them seeing themselves.

"When they see these obstacles as being big, it is because what they are being shown is themselves…and they do not fit into the mold others have created for them. When these obstacles do not fit into a mold, they are perceived as being too big for the space that has been reserved for it.

"However, when they come to the place of having to make their own choice, which only they can do, if they choose to leave behind all of their old habits and ways of seeing things, if they continue to be true to the one who is within them, they will find these obstacles are not big at all. In truth, little ones, they will see these obstacles do not even exist for them.

"Once they will have come to this place of seeing, then they will be well on their way to finding the path to their own spirit.

"But for those who would not see clearly through their own eyes, the ones who would not be willing to see for themselves things as they are, they will be found returning to the path they had tried to leave.

"For them, there is only discomfort on any other path. And they will believe that when they will travel with the many, then they must surely be on the good path, the right path—for this is what they have been told.

"You see, little ones, the difference from those who travel on the path that leads to the left, this path that is led by the body and fed by the emotions and those who would travel on the path that leads to the right, this path that is led by the spirit and fed by it as well, the difference is this.

"For those who are willing to travel the path of the spirit, this path that leads to the right, they will not be concerned about the approval or disapproval of others.

"They will not look to them for their approval for any of those things they will come to do, and they will not look to them for understanding in any of those things that will be presented to them.

"They have come to understand that all of those things they do and say will have to be answered for by themselves. And for all that will come to them, only they will have the accountability or responsibility for it.

"For the ones who will be willing to travel their own path of their spirit, they will hold this believing that it is they who must agree with all things that they will come to do. For only they will be held accountable for them.

"Now for the ones who have been willing to travel on the path that leads to the left, the path that is led by the body and fed by the emotion, they will not make the time of listening to themselves for any of those things they will say or do. They will not do this because they will only have ears to hear others tell them what to say and do…others who are as lost as they are.

"And it is this path that will make one believe that if they are not trying to please everyone, they are not doing good, and they surely must be a bad person.

"Those who come to this place believe that all they will say and do must first win the approval of those who are near to them, for if they would ever go against them, surely they would lose their way.

"But I tell you both, they are as lost as any can be in this place they are at now. And it would not be possible for them to get any more lost. And this is truth.

"So it is that while the ones who travel the path of spirit will look for their approval from within themselves, the ones who would travel the path of the body will look for their approval from another, or others. And this does not change no matter where in this domain you will travel, no matter which of the four races you will find yourself traveling with.

"When the time comes for the beginning of 'The Season of the Long Shadow', there will be more who will be traveling on this path of the body and fewer who will be traveling on the path of the spirit.

"This is because of an imbalance that will exist among so many from the new levels of energy that will come flooding in. But when there is no understanding for what is taking place, there can be no seeing for what it is. And this will cause many to see through fear and run to others for their strengths.

"For it will be those who will not have come to know their spirit within who will feel lost and out of place when this time arrives for them, when 'The Season of the Long Shadow' will share with them that something is ending but they do not know what.

"This season will share that the ending to something is near and they will not be able to see what lies ahead for them. And, it is this uncertainty which causes many of them to lose their way.

"But in truth, little one, all they have to do is see the truth that will relate so well to all that is being presented to them. That for everything that ends is in truth, an illusion to begin with. For there is no thing that can end, because it has always been.

"And this includes spirit as well.

"However it would do both of you well to keep in the front of your thinking minds that while there is no thing that will ever come to its end, there are always those things that will be in a constant state of change, for this is the path of all spirits.

"Understand that without change there will be no growth, and without growth, there will be no understanding. And it is this understanding for ourselves and all things that are with us that we find our way back home."

Finishing these speaking words to all of us, Grandfather began to look deep into our within places, these places where our spirits reside.

Both Cheeway and I knew what he was doing, for this had been done with us many times in the seasons we had been given to travel together, seasons where they had always been presented to both of us many blessings and much growth from those speaking words that Grandfather and Two Bears had been willing to share with us.

And now...now Grandfather was looking to both of our within places to see if we had been able to keep up with those things he had been willing to share with us.

Looking over the face he had placed on himself, I could see he had found what he was looking for. He had seen that both Cheeway and I had been able to keep up with those things that he had been willing to share with us.

And this was giving to him a good feeling, one that was being expressed in the face he was now sharing with both of us.

"I have a question, too," came a sudden remark from Cheeway.

"Yes, Cheeway," was the reply from this one called Night Hawk.

"I could see a quick glance from Cheeway to the place where Grandfather and Two Bears were sitting. And I knew this glance was to ask them if it was good to listen to this one called Night Hawk.

However, when I turned my head to the direction to the place where Grandfather and Two Bears were sitting, I could see them both looking at this one called Night Hawk. And I knew this was their way of telling both Cheeway and me that for what we were asking, there was no need.

For this was their way of telling both of us his speaking words were weighed with the same truth as theirs were, and to think otherwise would not be good.

Seeing this from their faces, I knew that from this place on, there would no longer be a need to see this one called Night Hawk as being separate from Grandfather and Two Bears. For I had seen this sign from the both of them before.

And looking to the place where Cheeway was sitting, I saw that he too had received the same message.

"This question I hold with me is this, Night Hawk," Cheeway continued.

"My brother, Speaking Wind and I have been well prepared by those things Grandfather and Two Bears have been willing to share with us. And one of those things is what this place called the waiting place is.

"But from what Two Bears had been willing to share with us in the song legend of our ancestors holding council with the Ancient Ones, he shared with us that when they left, they left with their robes with them, and went to the waiting place.

"Am I correct in my presentation to this point, Night Hawk?" Cheeway asked sitting in a position that I had come to know meant that he was really leading up to what he had considered to be a great point.

"Yes, Cheeway, this is the clear seeing that has come to you from what has been shared, so far," was Night Hawk's response.

"Well then," Cheeway continued. "If the Ancient Ones are in the waiting place with the rest of our spirit families, then my question is why?

"Why would they wish to be in that place when they could go home? This is my question and I do not hold an understanding for the reasoning of it."

Looking on Cheeway, Night Hawk placed a warm and tender smile over himself and continued:

"Little one, you must first come to the place of understanding about what the waiting place is. It is only a place where all of us are waiting for the next world to be built.

"It is not a place that is any higher or any lower than any other. It is only where one will return to be with their spirit family and reside in spirit until the right time has come.

"And when all has been prepared, then we will leave this waiting place together and enter our new worlds.

"Does this assist you in what you have been seeking, Cheeway?"

"Then are there no other places one could go to?" was Cheeway's question to his question.

"Yes, little one," was Night Hawk's return. "There are many other places one could go. In truth, there are so many places one could go that they are beyond any number you or I could count to.

"However for the ones who would wish to continue to work in this domain that is the Earth Mother's, they are all in the waiting place. And they are waiting there because there is still so much to do here, so much to learn and so much for us to provide assistance for.

"I understand there is much to explain about the waiting place, Cheeway, but for now you will have to wait on those things I have shared with you. To go further would confuse you from the place you are at now.

"There are many things that I would wish to share with you about the waiting place, Cheeway, but now is not the time," Night Hawk concluded.

As I looked over to the place Cheeway was sitting, I could see he was about to ask another of his questions. And it would have been another question about the waiting place...but he did not.

He was stopped in the middle of his forming this question by something that he saw from the place where Grandfather, Two Bears, and Night Hawk had been sitting.

When I turned my head to this same place, what I saw from them would have also made me stop these things I would have asked as well, these questions for further explanation about the waiting place.

For when I saw Grandfather, Two Bears, and Night Hawk in their sitting positions, I did not see the ones who I had come to know, I saw something that I was not prepared for, nor would I have ever been.

Grandfather, Two Bears, and Night Hawk were still sitting in the places they had begun, but they were no longer reflecting the light from the warming fire. They were becoming more brilliant than the light from the flame.

Each of them was holding a glow about them. And this glow was changing colors from yellow, to red, to black, to white. And this whole process was repeating itself over and over again.

"What do you think is happening, Speaking Wind?" Cheeway asked with a noted tremble in the tone of his voice. "Is this a natural process to a spirit vision?"

"I do not know if it is or not, Cheeway," I replied. "From all that I have been prepared with, each of them can be as different from the other as a fish is to eagle," was my response.

"I have seen such things before, Cheeway, but it was through the spirit totems that had come to me. It was eagle, bear, and buffalo who had come to take me to the Ancient Ones to hear their Message," I continued with my response to Cheeway.

"However, from what I can see, there is now only Grandfather, Two Bears, and Night Hawk who are glowing in their colors at this time. And this is not clear to me, for when I had been given my last spirit vision, everything was affected, not just a few.

Finishing my speaking words to Cheeway, I turned my head back to the direction of Grandfather, Two Bears, and Night Hawk. I wanted to continue looking at those colors they were wearing, those colors that were coming to them from their within places.

However, just as I turned my head to look on them, I heard a voice. It was a voice that seemed to live within the air that was around all life in this domain.

"Have them sit with you, Speaking Wind," came the beautiful voice that seemed to weave in and out with the passing of the Spirit Wind. "Have them sit with you but in a straight line, and on the other side of the warming fire you have built."

Just as the calling voice had finished, I could see there were no longer any of the four colors coming from either Grandfather, Two Bears, or Night Hawk. It seemed as if these colors had finished those things they had come to do at the same time the beautiful voice had. Looking over on their faces, I could see that they were once again moving their eyes and were back with Cheeway and myself.

"What has come over you, Speaking Wind?" came the questioning voice of Grandfather. "It looks as if you had seen something that has given to you a great surprise."

For the next few moments, I shared what had taken place among all three of them. And when I would pause from sharing my speaking words, Cheeway would support all that I had said with his own.

All of this gave them a look of great surprise, one that I could tell was genuine.

"We hold these things you both have shared with us as truth, little ones. But we must also share with you that none of us recall these events taking place," came the speaking words of Two Bears. "Tell us then, did all of this take a long time?"

"No, Two Bears." I continued. "It did not take long at all. In truth, I was not counting, but I do not believe that it required more than a few breathing times for Cheeway and me to have seen all of this."

"Yes, Two Bears," Cheeway continued. "It did not take very long for all of this to happen. But while it was taking place it seemed to be very long. Does this make any sense to you, Two Bears?" came the shaken words from Cheeway.

"Yes, little one, this does make sense for all three of us," was Two Bears response. "And it should begin to make sense to Speaking Wind as well. For the process of living within a spirit vision is no longer a complete stranger to him…is it?"

Looking over to the place where all four were sitting, I was taking my time at looking into each of their eyes. I was doing this to see if there were any confirmations within myself that I still needed to share.

For when one will find something within themselves that they cannot see clearly, they will use this process of looking into the eyes of others who are near you and find something that will call to your spirit, something you know will not be of them, but something that is being reminded to you by them.

This is the process of understanding that all that is needed is located within ourselves, in the within places where our spirits reside.

However, there will be many times when we will not have the clarity of seeing which will allow us to know what these things are. And the reasons for this are many.

But when we will open ourselves to ourselves and become no thing, we will look into the eyes of others who are near us, we will be reminded of what we had been trying to see of those things that are needed by us so that we may express them in speaking words.

So, looking into the eyes of Grandfather, Two Bears, Night Hawk, and Cheeway, I was looking for anything I could see within them that would not be from them, something that I would know was being shared with me by their spirits so I could find my own way to what was being presented.

It was then that I found what I had been looking for within each of them. As I continued to look deep into their eyes, I could feel there was something they were not telling me, something that they were holding within themselves that I could not see, and this was the assistance I had been looking for.

Then I could see clearly what had just been presented to me, but had been presented to me at such a time that I did not hold a remembering for any of it.

"That is not all that has taken place, Grandfather," I began with the forming of my speaking words once again.

I could feel all four of them looking on me with eyes of great expectation and questioning. And looking on the place where Cheeway was sitting, I could feel his wonderment growing from his within place.

For he had been with me during this time of the glowing colors that had come over Grandfather, Two Bears, and Night Hawk. But I could see that he was not aware of what had come just to me.

"Did you not hear anything else, Cheeway?" I questioned him expectantly.

"No, Speaking Wind," was his reply. "What was this something else? Was it another part of this spirit vision that is coming to us?"

I could see from the look that was within the eyes of my best friend that he did not hear anything else. I could also see from his face that he was speaking his truth.

Then, turning my eyes back to the places of Grandfather, Two Bears, and Night Hawk, I continued.

"It was a calling voice, Grandfather," I began. "A calling voice that was very beautiful and seemed to bend with the Spirit Wind as he was crossing our lands."

"And what did this calling voice share with you, Speaking Wind?" came the questioning of Grandfather.

"She shared with me that we all needed to sit together and in one line," I returned. "Oh, yes, and that we should be on the side of the warming fire so we could see out to the opening of the mouth of the great stone cave."

"And did this beautiful calling voice share anything else with you, little one?" Grandfather asked.

"No, Grandfather," was my return. "This was all that was shared with me."

"But why was it that no one else heard her, Grandfather? Cheeway did not hear her and he was sitting next to me.

"Speaking Wind," came the beginning of Grandfather's response to me. "When spirit shares, it is usually done with only one at a time. It is not uncommon for one to be in the middle of many and still be the only one who will either hear or see the calling voice from the Old Ones.

"When spirit hears the calling voice of the Old Ones, it is because there is a need only for them to hear. And this is most likely the reason you were the only one to hear them at this time.

"Do not be concerned with those things that you do not hold any control over anyway. For they are going to be, with or without your assistance. Only understand what has been offered. When it is needed by you, little one, it will be made clear.

"Do you hold a clear place of understanding for what I am willing to share with you, Speaking Wind?" Grandfather asked.

"Yes, Grandfather." I responded. "In truth, I do hold this understanding for what you have been willing to share with me."

"But there is something more that you wish to share with us, little one?" Grandfather asked.

"Yes, Grandfather," was my reply. "Why did she say that all five of us should sit in one straight line...and together? If this spirit vision was only coming to me, then why are the rest of us included?"

Looking over to my place of sitting, I could feel the warmth of caring come over me from Grandfather, Two Bears, and Night Hawk.

"Well, little one, I would say that this is not going to be one of those usual spirit visions," Grandfather answered.

"You mean all of us are going to be in Speaking Wind's spirit vision, Grandfather?" Cheeway asked with a trembling note as he formed his speaking words.

"Yes, Cheeway," Grandfather responded. "I would say that all of us are going to be visited on this day by the Ancient Ones. And the reason is as it should be. For within each of our life paths, there will be a need for what is soon to be shared with all of us. So for now, I would suggest that we do as Speaking Wind has been instructed, that all of us sit in a straight line on the far side of the warming fire. Was there any picture given to you, little one, that would assist us in finding our places?"

Hearing these speaking words come to me from Grandfather, I held the knowing that I had been shown an order of sitting. But I did not carry this with me on the outside and knew I would have to travel within to retrieve this information.

So, closing my eyes for a brief period of time, I searched and waited until this picture had found me, this picture that had been shown to me by the beautiful calling voice of the spirit.

"Yes, Grandfather," I finally responded. "I have been shown a picture of all five of us sitting on the far side of the warming fire that is before us. First, there was Night Hawk and he was sitting on the far end of the line we had formed. Then came you, Grandfather, followed by Two Bears, then Cheeway, and finally myself. This is the picture that I have been shown, the picture that shares with me our sitting places for this vision that is coming."

"Very well then, my brothers, let us move to our places and sit in our silence of waiting," Grandfather said.

Rising from our sitting positions, we all ventured into those places that I had seen from the calling voice of the spirit. And arriving in them, we all five sat in our silence, this silence of waiting and listening to what would soon be coming to us.

However, as I looked over to the place where Cheeway had taken his sitting place, I could see that he was wearing a new color over himself. It was one that was white but it was not the same kind of color that we had seen coming out from Grandfather, Two Bears, and Night Hawk. Rather it was one of concern for those things he knew were on their way.

Seeing this feeling cover my best friend, I placed my left hand on his right shoulder to share a comfort with him and said: "It will be all right, my brother, we are with you."

I could see Cheeway's head nodded in an up and down motion, one that would share with me that he had heard what I had been willing to share with him.

Then looking over to me from the small part of his eyes, he said:

"This is a feeling that I have not yet come to know, Speaking Wind. And for this, I am filled with gratefulness for your presence here with me.

"I am also filled with a new respect for you, my brother. And that is for what I am now feeling from this approaching of the spirit vision of the Ancient Ones. I am not sure if I could have gone to them all alone as you had done."

"I am sure that you would have done those things that needed to be done, Cheeway," I responded. "For there is not ever anything presented to any of us in this domain that we are not ready for. That is once we will leave the illusion of emotion and enter the face of truth, this face of truth that shares with all of us that our path does not lie in controlling...but in understanding what is being presented."

I could feel Cheeway calming himself from those speaking words that I had been willing to share with him. And for this, I held a good feeling, one that shared with me we had done what was needed.

PART III

❀

THE ARRIVAL

CHAPTER 12

❊

Calling Voices in the Storm

Looking out of the opening of this great stone cave where the Ancient Ones left their village for us to remember them, I saw the distinct forms of the other three storms, that were being carried to this valley of the Old Ones by the Spirit Wind.

Looking out over the valley floor then up to the far places where the great mountains rose from the land, I could feel the presence of all who had gone before us, those who no longer had an earth walk to travel in this domain.

However, as I was holding these thinking thoughts in the front of myself, I was feeling something else with them. It was that these Old Ones did not have an earth walk to travel in this domain any longer because they did not hold a need for lessons any longer, all of their lessons had been learned by them, and now they were returning to share with us what we forgot to remember.

As these things were crossing the front of my thinking mind, I could hear the sounds of one of my spirit totems calling to all in this domain. The Spirit Wind was rounding all of the seen and unseen places to make sure that all of the children of the Earth Mother were aware of what was about to take place in this valley of the Old Ones.

Then without any warning, the Spirit Wind came rushing into the opening of this stone cave we had come to find shelter in. And as he entered, there was no place he did not touch.

His presence was felt by all of us as he pressed himself against each of us until all our clothes were in disarray. And as each piece of clothing was flying over our heads, I could hear another presence in this place we had come to, this place that, for as long as I could remember, had been maintained by the wise ones of our people.

It was just at the middle of the tossing of all our clothing around us that I heard familiar voices come to me. But they were coming to me from a place that was behind us, this place where most of the Ancient Ones homes had once been.

While my clothes were still gathered around my head and neck, I could not see any of the places where these new sounds were coming to me from. I could only hear and feel those things that had taken on a life of their own, but I could not see them.

These noises were becoming louder and louder, and the Spirit Wind that was over each of us was becoming stronger. All I could think of at this time was if Grandfather, Two Bears, Night Hawk, and Cheeway were hearing these things that I was hearing.

However, as the Spirit Wind was keeping my clothes over my head and neck, I could not find a place to look through. All I could do was sit in my place and wait, wait for him to finish with those things he had come to see a need for.

Then as the Spirit Wind seemed to be the strongest among all of us, I heard conversations come to me through these noises, conversations that I recognized to be from our people…the kinds that would normally be shared between two earth walkers in this domain.

But this could not be because in order for one to be in this place behind all five of us, they would have had to enter at a time when we were still seeing clearly, a time that was before the entry of the Spirit Wind in this valley of the Old Ones.

I was confused by this event that had been presented to me. As I held this thought in the front of my thinking mind, I could only hope that the rest of our council was hearing this same thing. I did not want to be the only one this time to go through this. Not when I was holding the feeling of how wonderful it was going to be to have them with me, these who had been with me for so much of my life path already. For I could still feel the tiredness over me from the last spirit vision when the Ancient Ones allowed me to sit among them and hear The Message.

As this thought was becoming stronger within me, so were the voices I could hear, those voices that were continuing to carry on a conversation behind me.

All of this was weighing very heavy on me as I was being held within the blanket and shirt that I was wearing. It was not allowing me to see if the others of our council were also hearing those things that were coming to me.

For if they too were hearing those things, then I held the knowing I would not be required to travel into this spirit vision alone. And this was something I did not wish for myself. I did not want to travel alone so soon after my last vision.

Then, while trying to pull those things that were over my head away, I yelled from the top part of my speaking voice over the rushing sounds of the calling voice of the Spirit Wind: "It is too soon for me to travel into your domain all alone! I do not wish to have this come to me! I am tired of this loneness over me and I do not wish for it any more…not so soon!"

"You are not now, nor have you ever been alone, Speaking Wind," came the same voice of the beautiful lady I had heard before all of this began this same lady's voice that had shared with me where all of us should sit for their coming.

"And, little one, there will not ever be anything that we will present to you that you will not be ready for. Anything that will be presented to you, Speaking Wind, will be what you have prepared yourself to receive.

"For this is the path of understanding that I share with you. This is the path you have found to travel.

"Do not waste your time on trying to change or alter those things that are, Little One. Understand them, for this is the path that leads back to us.

"It is when one will understand, when one will attain a level of understanding, that they will find there is no longer a need by them to control. For as understanding will increase, the need to control will decrease."

Then as I heard the last of her speaking words fall away, I held the understanding that whatever would be presented to me, I would be ready for.

And this, as well as so many other events that had come to me, I held the knowing was the face of truth. That this was the face of my truth for me, and I decided to stand with it, to stand with it even without the understanding. For too often I had seen how well this face of truth had led me to the places where I could learn to see, learn to see those things that were needed by me.

Just as I was getting comfortable with what had been shared with me by the beautiful lady's voice, I stopped trying to pull away those parts of clothing that had been hiding my eyes from what was taking place around me, those obstacles that had seemed insurmountable to me to get rid of so I could see what was taking place.

As I quit this effort of mine, I heard the conversations that were forming behind me more clearly:

"Do you hold an understanding for what they will do when this time we are about to unfold for them is shown?" came the voice from what sounded like a younger man.

"It is only their time that will share this," came a second voice that sounded like it belonged to one who was much older.

"I can only hope they will come to the place of understanding for those things that are soon to be offered to them. Without it many of them will only find great fear," the older voice continued.

"And it has been fear from those things that have been shared with them that has brought them so much disaster hasn't it?" the younger voice asked.

"Yes, it has. It has always been the fear of those things that are not understood by the two-legs that has brought death and destruction to much of the life that has come to call this domain its home," came a third voice, one that sounded female.

"However, this time that is about to be unfolded for them, there will be no stopping it. For what is soon to arrive in this domain is something that they cannot do away with…and it is certainly something they cannot ignore, either.

"For its time has surely come but are we to be the ones who will release it?" asked the voice that seemed to be coming from the younger person.

"We are not the ones who will release it, Little One," came the quick reply from the one with the voice of the female. "We are only opening the doorway for them to remember what is soon to arrive. For our place in this unfolding is to open the entryway for the Old Ones to return once again. To return to this domain and share with those who would have the eyes and ears of the spirit to see and hear with. To share with them of what is on the way."

"Then it is good what we do now, isn't it?" came the questioning voice of the younger one.

"It is good, Little One. It is good because it is time for this to be once again," returned the voice of the older sounding male.

Then I heard their conversations drop to the silence. I felt a quickening of the movements of the Spirit Wind within this great stone cave we five had found shelter in, this shelter that was being shared with all of us as we waited for that which was already coming, for the ones who had given to me the spirit vision of so many two-legs shooting themselves and trying to run and hide from something that I could not see, nor did I understand.

But just as quickly as the Spirit Wind had entered this place of our shelter, it had left. And as this silence came over these lands all five of us were sitting on, there was a sudden beating of a drum from behind me, from the same place where the voices had come to me from.

And as this silence had come over me, I took the opportunity of clearing the clothes from my face to see what was waiting in this direction.

However, when I cleared my eyes in order to see what was there, I was not prepared for what I saw. Looking over to the place where Grandfather, Two Bears, Cheeway, and Night Hawk were sitting, I could see that they, too, had removed the clothing from their faces and were standing with the same look of surprise about them.

This look that was filling each of us was coming from what had come to not only myself, but to my relief, Grandfather, Two Bears, Night Hawk, and Cheeway as well.

When I look over to the place where these voices had been coming from, I no longer saw the old ruins of the Ancient Ones, those ruins that I had become so used to seeing without anyone living with them. But now there was life in all of them, life that was not as we had become in this domain of the Earth Mother. But it was a life that had lived among all of us very long before, from the times that are only whispered now by the wise ones and carried in our collective memory of time, as we have come to know it.

When I looked to the back of the great stone cave we had come to find our shelter in, there were no longer the shadows of the past living there. But now, there were many people who were walking and sharing their speaking words with each other, and there were many fires that had been built over the top places of roofs.

While I could sense that these who had made their appearance to us did not need the warmth of those warming fires, I could feel what we were being shown was for our own benefit, a benefit that we still needed in order to make some kind of connection to what was being shared with us…and to what was about to be shared with us.

Then with very quick movements, they began to look over to the place where all five of us were sitting, to this place I felt I had been glued to.

And with all of their eyes fixed on us, they began to sing a spirit chant, one that held a great meaning for all five of us, but one nevertheless that held an even greater meaning for them. For these of the old times who had re-entered this day of our present held before them a great gift for each of us to receive, one that would assist us greatly in the times that would soon be born to us.

As I listened to the words formed by the spirit chant, I could feel something very deep within calling, calling to me that these speaking words were something that I remembered, something that I remembered but could not find the place of understanding for them.

So with this in the front of my thinking mind, I listened. But before I did, I took one last look over to the place where the rest of our council was sitting to make sure that I was not the only one hearing this. Seeing that they too were following the same steps, I returned my attention to the ones who had come to share with us on this day those who had been so long ago and were now again.

'We hear you in spirit
And spirit is what we will see.
'We follow the light that guides us,
To travel the path that is.
'Hear us, Great Spirit,
We know our hearts to be true.
'Hear us, Earth Mother,
We who return to you.
'Our journey is almost ended,
For this time is soon to be at its end.
'For those who will travel with us,

Soon they will understand.
'That what is about to enter,
Is time for it to be.'

As their spirit chant ended, I could feel the air around us begin to vibrate. As this vibration continued to make its presence known to all five of us, I could feel another change coming, one that was finding a place of living in the air we were breathing.

As the air was beginning to vibrate, I could feel a weight come over it. It was a weight that I could not hold, but one that I could feel. As this weight began to make its presence known to all five of us, I began to hear a sound from it, a sound that was almost like an announcement for what was about to be shared.

This sound that was living within this air was one that seemed to be very low, much like the sounds I had heard from the electrical power generators that I had seen from the lands north of us, those lands where they used the water to make electricity.

But this sound did not hold to it the same piercing sounds from the machines. Rather it was humming to all who were present that it was a gentle creation to behold. One that would not become intrusive to any other life path...one that would not make its presence known to those who did not hold a need over them for its sharing of presence.

Then, just as the weight of the air and the humming sound made their presence felt and known so much that I could feel as if I could lay on them without falling to the earth below me, I saw another change come. It was a change that was coming from those who had returned to this domain, from the Old Ones who had once again made their presence known to our eyes.

As I looked at them, and in all of the places they were standing, and walking, they all began to show a small but very visible white light from within them.

It was a light that was only drawing my attention to it at first, but as this time that was being shared with all five of us passed, it grew.

And it continued to grow within all of them until there was nothing left of any of the visitors that had been standing before us, nothing left but one brilliant light left in each of their presence. They had once again given to us a great surprise, one that I held the knowing would not leave me for as long as I would have seasons to travel in this domain with the Earth Mother.

As each of these individual glowing and brilliant lights formed, they began another movement among themselves. It was a movement that was calling them all to come to one place in the village, a place where each of them knew the meaning for, a meaning that would allow them to perform what was needed next.

With the swiftness of the eagle's flight, each of them was coming to the place that was called to them. Each was gathering to himself in order to form one great ball of glowing light. And once they arrived at this place, they began to grow.

At first, I held the believing that they would continue to grow until they would fill the entire opening of this great stone cave we had come to find shelter in. But just as this came to the front of my thinking mind, there was another change that came to all of them, one that I had not been ready for.

Just as they seemed to sit in the middle part of the air that was in this great stone cave and grow, it seemed the larger they would become, the more they would radiate, and the less visible they were for us to see. It was almost as if they would grow to a great size and just as they were about to become an intrusion to others who were also sharing this same space with them, they would begin to fade away.

I held this believing that it was coming to me from within this once seen place that had been formed by all of them when they merged into the one. I could not really know for sure, for this voice that I heard also seemed to be coming to me from the air that was around us, the humming sound that had formed within the air, as well as the earth, the buildings, and the rocks that were with us.

It was as if I knew where this voice should have originated, but even with this knowing it was also in every other place as well as every other thing that was with us as well.

Then, just as they were about to disappear from our being able to see them, there was another change that filled the land we had found to sit on, this land that not only had been willing to share its shelter with us, but this land that was allowing all five of us to share those things that were being presented to us.

The glowing ball of light was beginning to disappear from our sight when the Spirit Wind held its position in all places he had been traveling. The weight of the air, and humming sound that had found a need to share its presence of life with us, began to grow so much that I was sure I would soon be forced to the earth beneath me if it were to continue.

It was during this heaviness of silence that a wonderful voice came to our council of five. Even though I could not move my head or body, had I wanted to, I could feel the presence of Grandfather, Two Bears, Night Hawk, and Cheeway.

And it was through this feeling that I was being shown how to see understanding. For it was understanding that was being shown that allowed me to feel the presence of our other four members of this council and was allowing me to understand that they, too, were being shown these same things, that I was not alone in this, but they were with me, and with me they would remain.

Breathing out, I could hear the sounds of relief being carried on the back of my own breath, this sound of relief for not having to travel this path alone.

Hearing this sound reach my ears, I heard another voice come to me. It was a voice of one I remembered, but of one I could not place. It was the same voice that was coming to me from the air and all places that were with us in this great stone cave that held the village of our Ancient Ones.

"We have come to you in the way we have, my brothers, to remind you of what will be needed in the seasons that are yet to be born within this domain that is the Earth Mother," came the beautiful voice from all places and all things.

"We have chosen this place and this time because it is time. But more than that, we have chosen this way because of what it will remind you of, and that is what you have forgotten to remember.

"You have seen many of us who were walking, standing, and sharing our speaking words in this village that have been retained by the wonderful and loving efforts of your wise ones. You have seen many of us enter this place that is the light of all ancestors, this light that has once again been pulled into the Oneness of the One.

"And from this light, we have become that which we have always been, the light that is a reflection of the unconditional love of creation.

"For it is from this love that our spirits have been created, and it is to this love that we will return…when it is time and we have made our own choice to do so.

"However, there are many who travel among you who remain trapped within their own sleep of illusion, this sleep of illusion that shares with them that if they were to become One within the One, they would no longer be the individual.

"But we have come to you, in this time and in this place, to share that this believing does not hold a face of truth to it. For there are none of us who are within this One you have been shown that have been lost.

"There are none of us who do not continue to hold our own identities with us even though we are One with the One.

"For those who would hold such a believing with them, they are truly lost and will remain lost while living in their own shadows of fear for all time that has been given to them. For all of the seasons they will come to pass through while they are within this domain that is the Earth Mother, they will gain no thing. They will only find that in their end...it will end.

"And we share with you that for those who would hold this fear over them—this fear that would have them believe if they were to become One within the One, that their own identity would be lost to them. We share with you that for all that they hold the believing in, that all they hold to believe that this is truth, for them, there will surely be an end to all things.

"But it will only be an ending to those things that are not with them in the first place. For when they eventually come to the place that all of the two-legs will come to, this place where they too must drop their robes from themselves, this will be the time when they will surely see an end to themselves, but it will not be an end to the spirit who is them. For it is not spirit who ends...only the body will.

"When you see them come to you seeking comfort for this fear they have allowed to grow within themselves—this fear they have been carrying around with them for all of these seasons—when they come to you, you will surely see a face over them that will show you their end. But this ending is of the great illusion and this face of illusion is all they had come to know.

"So it is that we have come before all of you on this day, we have done so in order to remind you that each one will have a time set for them to return to spirit once again. And this will come to all, for none will be passed by this event. And when this time will come, you will find yourself as One within the One regardless of the present fears you may hold with you.

"However, when they will find themselves as One within the One on this side of spirit, on this side where they no longer hold a body with them, then there is no learning, there is only a returning to this place they have always been.

"It is when they find their path of the spirit in this domain that each of them will find their own way home, to find their own path to follow that will lead them back to becoming One within the One so there will be growth for them to receive. And it is through this growth of spirit while one is still traveling an earth walk that the greatest gift of all will be presented to them.

"When one will return to the One within the One, they will find the balance for all things that are with them. And they will see the understanding to all of those wonderful lessons that have been offered to them from their own within place, this place where each of you reside in your own spirit with us.

"When they will come to freely choose their own path…a path they were meant to find anyway, then their spirit will feel the growing that is only to be found in this domain of the Earth Mother. Only then will you hold this peace for creation with you, and only then will each of you see your way back home.

"Remember, my brothers, we are not alone, nor have we ever been. Only those who have been misled by their own efforts believe that they are alone in this domain. And for them, they are alone but it is their choice to be so.

"When one feels that they are alone with themselves, they fit in no place and with no other. This is why they fear being lost within the One.

"It is only those things that we do not understand that we will always fear losing. And this comes to all from a false place, anyway. For it comes from the illusion that will make them afraid of ever looking at their own face of truth, fearful of looking at themselves for what they might see.

"Remind them, my brothers, remind them of what has been shared with you on this day.

"We who have always been with you are still ourselves, but we are also One within the One, for in truth, we are not alone.

As these speaking words of truth finished, there was a silence that was around all things with us in this place we had been sitting. A silence that had allowed me to feel the presence of more that was about to be shared.

I could feel the weight of expectation that was filling everything that I could see or feel an expectation for what would next be shared with us. It was living in all of the smallest parts of air, dust, and clothing that was next to each of us. This was not a false feeling that had come over me. And it was not a false feeling that I was understanding from the ones who were with me as well.

For I could feel the understanding of the other four members of our council. And I could tell they too were wearing this weight of expectation for what would be shared next.

None of us, even if we had wanted to, could move from our places as we continued to look into the direction that had been behind us, this place where the once empty village of the Ancient Ones was.

Then the beautiful voice spoke once again, and with the same places of beginning it had been before, from all of the places that were over us, from all of the places that were under us, and from all of the places that were on the outside and inside of us. For this was the place of the beginning of the wonderful voice that was now willing to share with us was coming from. And for this knowing, I was beginning to understand that when one is One within the One, there is no separation. For all that is…has been, and all that is yet to be…is already.

"We who have always been with you are with you still, my brothers," the voice from all things and all places began. "We who are yet to arrive with you, we have always been with you and we are only returning to those places we have not left. We who have been so blessed to share with you, we must leave to open another doorway, one that will allow passage to those who are now on their way.

"For this is a time that has always been for you. And this time is soon to awaken among you once again. Be well, my brothers, and know that we are, and will always be, with you. And when you will call us, we will come.

"We must leave now, but do not lose this place of knowing from the front of your thinking minds."

As these final speaking words of sharing had come to all five of us, there was a sudden movement of the Spirit Wind. This sudden movement of the Spirit Wind came as a surprise to all of us.

For the time of this vision, we had forgotten where we were. And we had forgotten the force that had been over us from the Spirit Wind before these speaking words of reminding had come to us.

But now the time of silence was needed no longer and the movement of the Spirit Wind came to life once again with the same force of movement that had forced our walking blankets and parts of our shirts to be held over our faces.

However, when the Spirit Wind returned to life in this great stone cave, there was another surprise that had come to all of us, one that we did not hold an understanding for. When the Spirit Wind came back to life, it did not return to us from any of the places that were on the outside of the cave opening. Rather, it seemed to birth itself from the places that were behind the Ancient Ones village in the back of the great stone cave. And all of us knew that this should not be. For there was no open air for the Spirit Wind to travel and gain its momentum in that place.

The place where it was coming from was not more than a few feet of open space at best, but this force that was over us from the Spirit Wind was one that we would have expected when he would have had miles of land to travel to gain such force.

From the corner of my eye, I could see that Grandfather, Two Bears, Night Hawk, and Cheeway were doing the same thing as I was. We were all looking to the direction that the Spirit Wind was coming to us from. We were looking in this direction to see if we could tell where it was beginning, and to see if there would be more that would require our presence to see.

However, these thoughts did not hold long for us. For the Spirit Wind crossed our faces with such force that we had to hold our eyes very small to continue to see. But behind this great force, there was another calling voice that made its presence known to us. But this calling voice was not the same as the first one.

This calling voice was much different than before. It was not of a feminine form of sound at all, but a male sounding voice. And it, too, was coming to each of us from all things and all places.

"Listen well, my brothers," came the first of the shared speaking words. "What you are about to behold is something that only comes into this domain once. And its time is close at hand.

"Many of you will not remain on your earth walk when its time for birth comes over all of these lands you have all come to know so well. However, there will be at least one of you who will be given the opportunity of walking through this time that is coming, through this place that is about to unfold for all who will be traveling their life path in the domain of the Earth Mother.

"Listen well, my brothers, for what we are sharing with you is now making its way to this domain you travel in. And it is not only for a few to know of, but it will be for all life that is residing here.

"For those who would have the needed understanding for themselves and all things that are them, there will not be seen a face of fear for the times that are soon to be at hand. For the ones who do not hold this needed level of understanding for themselves and all things that are of them, for them, there will be a great face of fear and it will spread over all of this domain that is of the Earth Mother.

"It will spread to all lands and all people, and there will be none missed.

"And, my brothers, there will be no place that they can go to get away from what is coming…for it is time.

"Look to the other side of where you now sit. Look to the outside of this place you have come to find shelter in and see who we will open the doorway for. For those who are arriving soon are coming to share those things that will be needed for the times that are soon to be with you.

"Turn and look at the arrival of the ones who carry the messages of what is coming...turn and see the beginning of...The Season of the Long Shadow."

Then as the speaking voice finished, there was a loud sound in the voice of the Spirit Wind that was forcing itself over our faces.

We turned from the direction the Spirit Wind had been coming to us and looked to the back of the great stone cave and the Ancient Ones' village...to the direction the voice had shared with us to look into, out of the opening of the great stone cave and into the valley that was below us, this valley that had come to be known as the valley of the Ancient Ones.

As we turned our heads and bodies in the opposite direction, there was an immediate relief each of us felt. For now, instead of feeling the pushing against our faces and bodies by the Spirit Wind, we were feeling its support against our backs and could almost lean and rest against him from our sitting positions.

There was another relief that had come to each of us as well. And this relief was coming to us from not having to squint our eyes in order to see. For now, there was not the need that had once been with us to do such a thing. We were no longer looking directly into the Spirit Wind, which allowed us to clear our eyes from all that had been forcing itself into them.

As we looked over the valley of the Old Ones, there was a seeing that had not been present before, a seeing of those same things that had been seen by us, but not with the clarity as we were seeing them now.

It was as if they were all coming to each of us through an added dimension that shared with me another form of life to the life that was within all things.

Looking at this, I could feel a color being presented to me for this life. And for all of this, I knew it was good.

It was good for me because it was allowing me to see through another dimension for those things that I had been with for all of my life path with the Earth Mother. To see all of the children who were before me through eyes that were close to the ones they would often use to see all of us.

For it was this new dimension that was allowing me to see that they, like all of the two-legs, held many things with them as well.

That for each of them—for all of the children of the leaf, the children of the rock nation, the cloud nation—and all that was within this domain of my seeing, each of them held to them many lessons and many things that they, too, were working their way to understanding, those things that would be presented to them in the form of lessons that were needed by spirit within them.

With this additional dimension that was being shared with me, I could see that they too held a life path to travel, one that carried the same weight as ours. And with this came the understanding that each of them was at a specific place in their path, just as each of the two-legs.

It was this knowing and understanding that allowed me to see that there was, in truth, no difference between any of the children of the Earth Mother and ourselves.

However, there had been many times I held the believing that it was only the two-legs who held the ability of thinking and hurting, a believing I was now being shown was false.

As I continued looking at each of these children of the Earth Mother, I could see where each of them was and the path they held to travel. I could see what they were working on for their own advancement of spirit.

And, I could see those things that were bringing to each of them pain or pleasure, from those things that had come to them, as well as those things they had brought themselves to.

All of this was allowing me to see they were no different from the two-legs.

As this continued to flow into my within place, this place where my spirit resides, I could feel how limited I had been when I had at first held the believing that there was a great separation that existed between all of the children of the Earth Mother and ourselves, a separation that would always exist because we were so much better, a separation that would continue to exist because they were not like us.

With this understanding came the flooding of how all of our people had been treated by the ones with the white skins because we were not like them, because we did not wish to change those things that were with us, for we had come to understand our own truths.

While I was thinking of this, I was placing this kind of thinking over all of the two-legs as well as all of the children of the Earth Mother. And for all of this, I was receiving the understanding that there was in truth, no difference.

The only difference was while each of us was trapped within our own sleep of illusion, it was ego that would keep us trapped from seeing all things for what they are. It was the sleep of illusion that would allow for an ego to stand in our way of seeing that which is…that which is in truth.

This was filling the front of my thinking mind when I felt a great tugging on my shirtsleeve. Turning my head to the direction it was coming to me from, I saw that it was Cheeway. He was sitting at my side with both arms on the sides of his hips, a position that I knew him to always find when he was very concerned with something.

"Is this a part of the spirit vision, Speaking Wind?" Cheeway asked, sounding somewhat annoyed with the sudden turn of events that had come to him. "If it is not, then I am not sure I would wish to go much further. That is, not if I will have my way…"

"Yes, Cheeway," I responded to his speaking words. "This is in truth, a part of the spirit vision. And I, like you, am filled with much that I do not hold an understanding for."

"Then I am confused, my brother," came the beginning of Cheeway's speaking words to me on this subject.

"So am I, Cheeway," I responded. "What is it that brings you this face of confusion, Cheeway? Even though I have not been through as much as Grandfather and Two Bears, perhaps I could be of a small assistance to you."

"I thought you would be able to, Speaking Wind. But now I am not so sure that any would be of assistance to me," began Cheeway's speaking words. "I know it has not been more than two moons since you were last with the Ancient Ones of our people. And I also hold the knowing that you have been willing to share all that had been shared with you to Grandfather, Two Bears, and me. But those events that had taken place in these lands from the last time, well...none of them are making any sense to me."

"What is it that you are trying to share with me, my brother? I do not hold a clear understanding for this," was my response to Cheeway.

"Well, Speaking Wind," Cheeway continued. "I held the believing that from all of the steps you had been requested to perform from the last spirit vision, this last spirit vision when you were given The Message...I thought that if I were to remember what they were, when it would be my time for entering the domain of the Ancient Ones, I would hold at least a partial knowing of what to expect.

"But from all that has been shared with us so far, I cannot say that any of it seems familiar to me, not from what had taken place with you before. Do you think those who are coming to us might not be the same Ancient Ones, Speaking Wind? Do you think that they are someone else because all of these events are so different?"

"No, Cheeway," I responded. "I do not hold the believing that they are someone else. I believe that they are, in truth, the Ancient Ones who are coming to us, and that all of these events are those that each of us hold a need within ourselves to understand. Do you remember the speaking words from Grandfather and Two Bears that shared with us such an occurrence? Those speaking words that shared with each of us there would not ever be an event, a person, a place, or a thing that would come to us in the same way? That is, if we were to learn from its lessons the first time? And when anything would seem as if it were being constantly repeated to us, then the reason for it to do so was only because we had not learned from it the first time?"

"Yes, Speaking Wind, I remember this," was Cheeway's response. "And this is what you hold the believing in that is taking place here and with this spirit vision?"

"Yes, Cheeway, I hold the believing that all things will come to each of us in their own light, and in their own path. That is when they will not have the need to repeat themselves to us anymore.

"When we have taken the time of doing our own work at seeing those things that have been offered to us the first time, then the next lesson or offering will come to us in a much different way than the first one did.

"Do you hold an understanding for what it is that I am willing to share with you?"

Cheeway remained in his place and nodded his head in a motion that would share with me that he did hold an understanding to those things that I had been willing to share with him, and without breaking the silence we had found.

However, before either of us could find any other speaking words to share on this matter, our attention was taken to another place in the great stone cave. Our attention was being drawn to the place where Grandfather, Two Bears, and Night Hawk were standing.

And as we looked over to them, we could see from the faces they each held over themselves, a great look of concern, one that was not as familiar to either Cheeway or me as their other faces, the ones that would always share with each of us that all things we were going through were being understood by both of them.

But now, this was not a face for them to wear. We also held the knowing that this face was on them because it was a part of their face of truth…a face that shared with both Cheeway and me that all of this was new for them as well. And they, too, were looking for their needed levels of understanding for these events that had been presented to us on this day.

They were sharing speaking words between themselves, and if this had been a usual case, both Cheeway and I would not have listened...not unless we had been invited to do so.

However, this was not the usual case, and in the tones that they were speaking, we could both tell that they would not mind if we would eavesdrop on what they were sharing.

So, departing our own efforts of trying to understand what was taking place on this land, and in this place, we turned our complete attention to those things they were sharing.

We did this because there was always much more direction to those things they would share with us than what we could find on our own. Not because they would have any better knowing for those things that we should be doing, but they had come to know their own path so well that we could see more of ours by learning from theirs.

CHAPTER 13

❀

Into The Valley of the Old Ones

"It must be closer than we had come to believe, my brothers," came the speaking words from Grandfather to Two Bears and Night Hawk.

"I can see this holds the face of truth from what you have to share with us," was the reply from Two Bears.

"It has been many generations since there have been any spirit visions that have come to more than one at a time. It would seem that we are close to those times that have been spoken of from long ago, the time of prophecy."

"You are making reference to the times of the living prophecy, Two Bears?" Night Hawk asked, holding a small but warm smile over the face he was wearing.

"Yes, Night Hawk, this is what I am speaking of," Two Bears continued. "We have often sung of those times in the long before when visions such as this one were common among the wise ones of our people. It was during those times when all of our old ones would receive many visions from the Ancient Ones."

"And the young would dream strong dreams," Grandfather picked up on the speaking words. "Yes, my brother, I hold this time as close to me as you do, those times that before now we had only seen in the most distant of memories of our ancestors' records, the records that are still living within the song legends of our lands."

"But in those times when so many would see these visions among them…well, those were the times when we were about to leave one world and enter another, another of the worlds that had been reminded to Speaking Wind by the Ancient Ones," Two Bears picked up the conversation. "So if we were not closer to those times that were shared with not only Speaking Wind, but with us from the teachings of the silent brotherhood, then why would all of this be taking place now? That is if there was still more time left to us to cleanse in."

"I would agree with you, Two Bears," Night Hawk began. "It would seem as if those times that had been sung of in our most ancient song legends are close at hand."

However, before continuing with his speaking words, Night Hawk paused for a brief moment to look around at all who had been standing close to him.

I could feel his entering each of us with the looking to the within place that I had come to know so well from Grandfather and Two Bears. But there was a great difference that I was feeling from him. It was a difference that was also being felt by Cheeway, Two Bears, and Grandfather.

It seemed as if Night Hawk was not requiring himself to look into each of us individually. This was considered to be a usual means.

Rather, he seemed to be able to look into all of us at the same time, and without taking time to pause and see clearly those things that were within each of us, those things he was looking for to make sure if we were in a place of understanding what he was about to share.

Each of those times I would feel this entering my within place by either Grandfather or Two Bears, I would always feel the face they had been given to wear from their own within place. In other words, they did not enter me as anyone different than the one I had come to see before me at the time.

It was not unusual for one to go through many changes in their earth walk. And for Grandfather and Two Bears, this was not any different. For as they would change, both Cheeway and I could feel their face from within change as well, the face that would share with both of us that they were the same ones we were looking at.

But in the case of Night Hawk, there was something different about this entering, this entering our within places to look for something, that was only known to him.

As Night Hawk would enter each of us, there was nothing familiar to him at all. There was no thing that we could feel or see of him within us that seemed to match any of those same qualities he had been presenting to us from the place he had taken, in the place he was now willing to share with us from.

All of this placed a great weight of concern over me.

"Remember, my brothers, those times that have been before, they have not left any of us," Night Hawk said. "They are just as alive in this day as they were when we had shared them before. There is no thing that is ever without life to it. And this includes everything within this domain of the Earth Mother.

"The only great difference from the past to the present is that we have forgotten to look through the illusion that has been placed over it, to look through this illusion because we have been willing to listen to others tell us where we are going rather than seeing our own direction for ourselves.

"I share with you in this time and in this place, what has been shared with us by the Ancient Ones has not been in vain...nor is it a warning for the times you think are near.

"They are close, my brothers, but they are still not allowed to live in this domain yet. For that is a time that will be seen when its time has come to be born. And to think of knowing when this time would come over us…well, this is to take one's mind off from their own path and onto one that does not yet exist.

"When one will take their thinking minds off their own path and place it on other things, then in truth, they are saying that they are not willing to do their own work because it is something that is just too difficult for them to do and they wish to make another working effort for themselves by looking at another life path or event. And they will do this, because to them, it appears to be a much easier task to perform."

"As it is with all things, Night Hawk, there is a time and a place for all," Grandfather returned.

"Yes, my brother," Night Hawk replied.

"And this is the time and place for such an event to take place then?" Two Bears questioned.

"Yes, my brother, and to do anything other than to allow it to be born would be to take away from its own life path. It is only when we will stop our trying that we will allow ourselves to be," Grandfather replied.

"And it is when we will have allowed ourselves to be, that we will find the freedom within us to see our face of truth for all that is," was the return from Night Hawk.

Once again, a silence filled this place we had come to find shelter from the coming storm.

I could see another new face come over both Grandfather and Two Bears, one that neither Cheeway nor I had come to see before.

From this newness, I could feel Cheeway becoming more and more confused. But this feeling was a good companion for me, for I too was lost in all of these events that had come to present themselves as well. And seeing that I was not alone in this, I felt much better.

As I continued to look over the face that Grandfather and Two Bears were wearing, I could see a look of such intensity come over both of them that I could feel the reflection of their efforts come over me as well.

Each of them was looking deep into the place where Night Hawk's spirit resided. As they would do this searching, I could feel from both of them, that they too had become confused by his efforts of looking into all of our within places and not feeling those things of him from the one who was before them.

But more than that, I could feel that they had become very concerned by those things that they had been willing to share with us, those things that had been contained within his speaking words.

I did not know what it was Grandfather and Two Bears were looking for so intently within Night Hawk. But it was something that was being shared with me by my own spirit, something that was allowing me to almost follow them in all of these efforts they were making at looking for whatever it was.

For the time being, Cheeway and I could only stand and observe these events that were taking place before each of us, observe them and hold the believing that when it would be time for us to understand them, that they would be offered.

However, even with this knowing, we were still wanting to know what it was that was taking place from this one called Night Hawk, what it was that had concerned both Grandfather and Two Bears so much that they had been willing to share with each of us a completely new face for this effort they were making…this effort that was requiring both of them to travel within this one they had known for so many seasons of their earth walk.

"You have changed greatly, my brother," came the first speaking words from Two Bears.

"You are not the same as we have come to know you, Night Hawk," was the reply from Grandfather.

Looking back to the place where both Grandfather and Two Bears were standing, Night Hawk only nodded his head in a motion that would allow them to see that he was in agreement with both of them without breaking the silence he had found.

"Is this something that you can share with us, my brother?" Grandfather asked.

"Yes, it is something that I may share with all of you," came Night Hawk's reply. "However, its time is not yet to be among us. But when it is, then I will assure you that there will no longer be any questions that will be formed within any of you."

From the sounds that had come to us from Night Hawk's speaking words, we could tell he had finished with this time of sharing, from sharing anything further for what he had been asked for from Grandfather and Two Bears.

Looking over their faces, I could see this was not something that had set poorly with either of them. For they were holding an understanding of what it was they had found, at least enough that had given them an understanding that what they had found within Night Hawk would be shared with all of us when it was time.

Seeing this face come over the two we had come to know and love so well, both Cheeway and I breathed a little easier. For neither of us could welcome more than what had already been offered to all of us on this day, especially if it was going to cause Grandfather or Two Bears any feeling of uncomfortableness.

Because if this would be the case for what had been seen by both of them, then Cheeway and I would certainly carry a weight that could not be missed. It would be a weight of fear for those things that had come to us that we did not hold an understanding for.

But seeing that Grandfather and Two Bears were all right with this, with not knowing what they had asked Night Hawk for, allowed both of us to see a little easier what had been presented. And seeing this allowed us to let this mystery lie and wait until the time would be right for us to understand.

"It would be a good thing for us to sit where Speaking Wind has been shown, my brothers," Grandfather began. "For I can feel the approach of the Ancient Ones in the air that is around us and we should be where they have requested all of us to be. It would be a wise thing to be ready for the arrival of those who have come such a distance to share with us."

Hearing those speaking words come to us from Grandfather filled me with a knowing that what he had seen within Night Hawk had been a great surprise to him. And from the look that was over Two Bears, I could see that he, too, was of the same mind as Grandfather.

Both of them had seen to his within place, this place where all of our individual spirits reside. But when they had arrived in this place, they were greeted by something that was not this same person they had come to know and travel with.

But I could see what had been shared with them was not completely understood, and this was filling me with another way of looking at both of them, another way that was to become a great blessing for me and all that was still lying before me on this path I had chosen to travel.

I could feel that each of them was filled with the non-understanding for what they had gone in search of. But even with this, I could feel their willingness to allow themselves to be, to allow all things to come to them when it was time for them to be shared.

Looking over this path they had been so willing to share with Cheeway and me, I could feel a new sense of admiration pour into me. For these feelings I held for these two who I had come to know and respect so well had just increased. It had allowed me to see how well both Grandfather and Two Bears had come to live all of the teachings they had been so willing to share with us.

Looking at both of them as they were finding their places of sitting by the warming fire, I could hear the speaking words of Grandfather come to life once again from my within place, this place where my spirit resides.

I could not only hear those speaking words of his come to me, but I could also see the place where he and Two Bears had been so willing to share them with Cheeway and myself. It was a time when we were of few seasons and sitting with both of them on one of the spirit caller's ledges of the mesa.

It was a time when both Cheeway and I had been missing our mothers who were spending so much time in and out of hospitals while our fathers were working two and three jobs trying to pay all of the medical bills.

And it was in this time when both Cheeway and I were feeling as if no one wanted us around them, for there was no one else who would take care of us…that is, had it not been for Grandfather and Two Bears.

"Remember, little ones," began these teachings of Grandfather's that had come to live with my spirit. "Remember that for all things there is a time and a place. But this time and this place for all things to be cannot be known to any unless they have been willing to do their own work in understanding themselves and all things that are around them.

"The reason I share this with both of you is simple. When one will know many things, they are like a walking book, one most anyone can come to and ask to see an answer.

"And for those who hold with them a great amount of knowing, they will be able to give those answers that are being asked by another without much trouble or difficulty.

"However, for the ones who will often come and ask these people who hold so much knowing with them, well, they will not see them in a good light.

"They will not hold them in a good light because there will not be a connection seen by them, a connection from what they are being told by the knowing one, and where it holds its truth in their life path.

"They will look on them as one who knows much, and as one who can show them the answers to many of those things that they will come to them with. But they will also see that if they do not know the right questions for them to answer, all of this knowing they have been collecting to themselves will be of no value to the one asking their questions.

"They will look on them as one who knows much and as one who can show them the answers to many of those things that they will come to them with. But they will also see that if they do not know the right questions for them to answer, all of this knowing they have been collecting to themselves will be of no value to the one asking their questions.

"They will need to know specifically the right question to ask if there is to be any gain in what it is they are looking for. And all of this is because there is a great similarity between this person who holds great amounts of knowing with them and a great book.

"Think of walking up to a great book, little one...a great book that you hold the believing has all of those answers that you require.

"But unless you will know where to look for this answer and how to recognize it when you will come across it, then this great book is of no true value to you. The only value this book will hold for you is that you know where it is located. All that is within this book will not be of value to you because you do not know how to find what it is that you are looking for.

"And for this person who will spend much of those seasons of their earth walk in accumulating as much knowing as they can, well, it will be the same for them as it is for the book.

"Unless you will hold the knowing for exactly what you are seeking, they will not be able to assist you in locating your answer.

"Now, if you were to know what it was you needed to ask of them and understood how to recognize it before you walked to them in need of this assistance, then you would have saved yourself a great amount of time and effort, for you would have already had your answer with you and could have come to them to confirm what you already knew but did not yet understand.

"When this is the case, little one, then the ones who acquire great amounts of knowing will be of assistance to you...but not before.

"However, when one who acquires this knowing and is willing to do their own work for those things they acquire, then they will come to an understanding. And understanding is the result of knowing.

"When one will understand those things they have come to know, you will see them as one who has seen clearly the path they travel. And you will see that for all they have been willing to share with you, they too follow their own advice. They will be the ones you will see who will have with them the ability of following their own wisdom, this wisdom that will be shared with many simply by their presence.

"When you will see one who understands what they know, you will see there is a connection which does not require you to ask so many questions from them.

"There will not be such a need to ask them so many questions, because you will see that they follow their own path. And when you will see this in them, you will know that such a thing is just as possible for you as well.

"Once you will have been successful in finding one who holds this understanding for what it is they have acquired knowing for, there will be many things shared with you which you will hold a need for, things that will be shared with you by this person because you will be willing to listen very well to them.

"You will be willing to listen to them because you can see no distance from those things they have been willing to share with you and the path they are traveling.

"This is what takes place for the ones who will come into your life path, little one, the ones who not only see their path, but understand it as well.

"From them, you will feel this connection they have found and you will know this to be good. And it is from this knowing that you will be able to do much of your own work in finding your own understanding just by being with them...just by being with them and seeing them walk their own life path with understanding.

"Keep in the front of your thinking mind that when one will only have the knowing that they are like the walking book, and when one will have attained the understanding of those things they know, then they will be the ones who will live what is in the book. And by watching them live what is within their own book, you, too, will benefit and this benefit will come to you in knowing that you hold this possibility within you as well.

"So learn to see this connection in those who would come to you, little one. If there is no connection to those things they are telling you, and what you see them living, then it would be much better for you to remain in your own dark, to remain in the place where you are feeling lost or confused.

"For if you would be willing to listen to one who had not found their own connection, then you will become even more lost, more lost because of them, not because of you.

"When you will become lost from another, it requires more effort on your part to find your own way out. For you will not only have to do your own work on finding your own levels of understanding for those things that are confusing you, but you will have to do theirs as well.

"This is because when you have listened to them and took those things they had shared with you within yourself, then their problems became yours as well. And before you will be able to clear yourself of this confusion, you will have to work your way through their own levels of confusion. And this may take a great amount of time and effort, and in this process, you will find yourself tied to them because without them, there will not be the clues you will need to find your way out.

"When you will find one who has found their connection, then what they will be willing to share with you, they will share, but they will not ever force."

Hearing those speaking words of Grandfather fall away from my thinking mind allowed me to remember what had been shared with me those many seasons before.

Looking over to the place he was sitting, I could not help but feel my heart growing for this one I had come to know so well, this one who had once again shared with me in the old ways of seeing that he had come to understand his path…and that by understanding it, he was willing to walk it as well.

I could feel my heart growing for those things I had come to know of from my seasons with him and Two Bears. For there had always come to me many confirmations from both of them that all they had been willing to share with both Cheeway and me were only those things they had connected themselves to, only those things that they had come to understand.

And it was through their understanding that the sharing they had been willing to share with us was good. With this in the front of my thinking mind, I took my sitting place next to Cheeway, this place that I had been shown we should all be in.

Then we waited…waited for the arrival of the Ancient Ones who would soon be with us on this day of the shared spirit vision.

PART IV

❀

FROM SPIRIT WITHIN

CHAPTER 14

⚙

Through the Eyes of Understanding

We all took our seats near the warming fire and were looking over the valley below us.

I could feel the weight of expectation that was coming to me from my best friend, Cheeway, and I could hear his breathing getting very fast now, so fast that I knew he would be in trouble with his body part if he were not to slow down.

"Take time to breathe slowly, my brother," I said to him while placing my left hand on his right shoulder.

"I do not know if I will be able to do this, Speaking Wind," came Cheeway's exhausted sounding reply. "There has been too much taking place on this day for me to sort through. And I am reacting to the emotion of all of it, but I do not know what else to do."

"Cheeway," I continued. "Do you remember what Grandfather and Two Bears have shared with us over these many seasons? Those things they had been willing to prepare us with for times such as these?"

Looking over to the place Cheeway was sitting, I could see there was not a look on his face that was remembering this. There was only a look of emptiness for all he was trying to think of.

And knowing this feeling very well for myself from having been in the same place, I knew that whatever I could share with him at this time would serve a great need, one that would assist him in coming to the place of seeing clearly for himself once again.

"What had been shared with us from those many seasons past, Cheeway, was about what we should do when we would find ourselves in a place where all events around us were moving so fast, when those events would not have the clarity of seeing from us to them.

"They had shared with both of us that when this would happen, it would be for a great reason, a reason that would, in time, be seen and understood by us.

"But while they were taking place, then we should sit and observe, sit and observe all that was being presented to us at the time.

"The reason for their speaking words was because there would not be anything we could do about them anyway, that there would be nothing either of us could do to change or alter any of those events that would be coming to us.

"And when one cannot change or alter events before them, then it is always best to sit and observe them as best as one can."

"But I am observing them, Speaking Wind," Cheeway responded to me. "I am observing all that is taking place and this is the reason for my fear and shortness of breath. All of this has come to me from seeing so much and in such a short time."

"What I am sharing with you, my brother, is this," I continued. "When these events will come to any of us, events such as the ones that have been presenting themselves to all of us on this day, we will have an instinctive effort from within us to try to change or slow them down.

"This is a very usual circumstance for all of the two-legs, Cheeway…a usual circumstance for the ones who are not yet awake from their own sleep of illusion.

"But for us, my brother, we have been well prepared to allow ourselves to drop these events away from us. That is, to drop away all of our own efforts in trying to slow them down or to change them for what we would wish them to be.

"The reason we find for doing such a thing is to allow ourselves to be ourselves, and not the confusion or fear that we are experiencing.

"It is only when we will allow ourselves to become lost in something or someone that we become them, and this is in addition to ourselves. And my brother, this is where I hold the believing that you are now.

"It is with this same believing that I hold that has shown to me the danger of it all, the danger of becoming so lost in the emotion that has come to you because of your own failed efforts of trying to slow these events down and this has given you a face of fear to wear. And this face of fear is coming to you from the shortness of breath you are holding, as well as the sudden urge of getting up from this place and running."

"But what if this is what I need to do, Speaking Wind?" was Cheeway's reply. "What if I was not ever meant to be here in the first place?"

"Cheeway," I continued. "If you were not meant to be here, then you would not have come. Remember, my brother, truth is simple when it is understood. It only becomes difficult when one does not hold a clear seeing for it."

I could see that Cheeway was beginning to slow his breathing from these speaking words that I had been willing to share with him. And this was giving me a good face to wear for him; one that I felt was being shared with him as well.

"It is good that I, too, am not alone in this place and this spirit vision, my brother," Cheeway began once again, but with more of a sense of peace that I could feel from him.

"It is good that we are all here for each other, Cheeway," came the response from Grandfather. "For in truth, there are none of us who are ever alone. But it is only when we will become lost in the illusion of not understanding that we will find ourselves feeling this way."

Then, as the speaking words trailed off, I could see that Cheeway had placed a smile over his face and was looking at me. And for both of us, I knew this to be good. I could feel that he had found his own place of observing these events that were being presented to all of us on this day. And I could feel that he was alright with all that was taking place.

Taking the time to look to the left of myself, I could see that all of us had come to sit in a straight line, one that was the same as I had been shown by the calling voice of the spirit. Next, I looked over to the place where the small warming fire had been built and saw that it was getting very low on fuel. Without any attention to it, there would soon be no fire at all.

Just as this had come to the front of my thinking mind, I saw several small pieces of wood being thrown into this fire. And looking into the direction where they had come from, I was relieved to see that it was Two Bears who had made this effort.

Seeing me look at him, he smiled to me and said: "It will not be long before the Old Ones are here, Little One. And it would be of great assistance to all five of us if there is a light that will show us the way to return, that is, if we will be required to do any traveling with them on this day."

Then looking over to me with a warm smile, I could feel that he had been making reference to the last spirit vision I had been given by the Ancient Ones, and how they required me to build my small fire so I could have a path of returning to this domain.

Holding this in the front of my thinking mind, I returned my eyes to the front of the great stone cave and out into the valley of the Old Ones, this same valley we had spent so much time in returning all of the children of the leaf back to their homes in the Earth Mother. As I was thinking over this event, I was also thinking what life would have been like in the times of the Old Ones, in those times that Night Hawk shared with us from so long ago.

Then, and without any warning, I heard the Spirit Wind begin to move at great speed across the front of the opening of this sheltering cave we had come to sit in. I could hear the many voices that had been given to this spirit totem of mine, and all of them were singing out to me now.

'They are coming for us to see, my brothers,
They are coming for us to know.
They who have always been, will soon be here again.
Listen…listen,
For their footsteps are just behind the wind.'

Then as this singing voice of the Spirit Wind continued, there were other sounds that were filling all of the spaces that were his to roam.

For there began the beating of many spirit drums and the playing of flutes, sounds that were in direct accompaniment with those things the Spirit Wind was now singing of.

As time passed before all five of us, there was an ever-increasing tempo building. A tempo that was sharing with all of us that the time was near, this time we had all been invited to attend.

Looking into the valley that was below us, I could see there were many sudden gusts of wind that had come over these lands, gusts that were more than I had become used to seeing in my seasons on this land of the mesa. For these gusts were great enough to knock a man and horse over if they had been standing in their presence.

But, just as soon as they appeared, they would disappear…and without any warning before…or after them.

Looking into the horizon that was beyond the valley of the Old Ones, I could see what appeared as two giant legs walking toward us, legs that were so big that only from their knees down could be seen below the clouds. They seemed to be formed from columns of clouds.

Each time I would see them take a step, there would be a great clash of lightning and rolling of thunder. It was as if each of these great footsteps that were being taken in our direction was causing this to be a calling of some kind. While these giant legs were coming closer to this place we had come to find shelter in, I looked into the valley below us, this valley where we had given our assistance to so many of the small children of the leaf.

And looking to this place, I could not help but wonder if they had gone through any of this before we had been able to reach this land and this place.

I wondered if they had come to suffer needlessly because we had not been here when we were supposed to be.

Then coming to me through the rushing of the Spirit Wind and all that he had been able to gather to himself, I heard the calming voice of Grandfather come to me.

Even though the powerful sounds of the Spirit Winds and thunder beings were great, I could still make out what it was that Grandfather had to share with me.

"Speaking Wind," came a muffled but audible sound from Grandfather. "Do not hold yourself committed to anything you have not been prepared for, things that you could not have altered in any way.

"For when you will take your time and effort for such things, you will be taking away from what is being presented to you.

"Remember, Little One, when one will arrive at a place, then they will have done all that has been required by them, and they are ready. When one will not arrive at such a place, then there is still much for them to do, much for them to do so they will be able to see clearly when it is their time to do so. All of this is coming to you from finding the freedom all of us have been born into. It is a great freedom that will come to you when you will understand what I have been willing to share with you.

"That when it is time, it is. And when it is not time, it is not.

"To think otherwise is only to fool yourself and not find the freedom that is within you, Little One.

"Look to those small children of the leaf below us and see how they are continuing to live their own life path, to live their own life path and learn from all of the lessons they have entered this domain to learn and understand from.

"Now look at you and where you are sitting. Look at all of those things you have been willing to learn and understand from, those same things that have served you well in allowing you to prepare for what is before you in the present.

"Then consider this: If you had not done all you have done, and when you did, would it have allowed you to prepare so well for what is coming to you now?

"If you had not been willing to perform all that had been done by you, then you would not have been so well prepared for the Ancient Ones of our people. And if you had not prepared yourself for this time, there would not have been shared with you any of the messages that you have come to receive from them.

"Now, when you will think over these things that I have been willing to share with you, look at them with the eyes of seeing. You will find there may yet be another cloud of illusion that is needed to be seen by you.

"It is the cloud of illusion that would tell you if you would not do all that you were supposed to do, then you would have missed out on a great opportunity...an opportunity that would have allowed you to find growth in what had been presented to you...or at a time that is yet to be born to you.

"It is from this kind of thinking that will make one feel very uncomfortable because they will be filled with the thinking of not wanting to do something that is wrong, or out of place to what is needed by them to prepare.

"However, they do not hold any knowing for what it is that is and is not needed by them for this preparing. They do not understand what it is that they should do, and to think on such a thing will only bring them to do what they do not understand. And those things that are not understood will be seen through the eyes of fear.

"When you will do something, then it is time for it to be. Do not be so concerned with not doing any of those things that are not seen by you. For to do this, Speaking Wind, will only allow you to miss that which has come to you, those things that are ready for you to learn from.

"When you will think on those small ones of the leaf in the valley below us, they too are doing all of those things that are needed to be done by them. All of what they have entered this domain of the Earth Mother to learn from is being presented to them as well.

"To think we must always be with them so that they may learn, is to be lost within the illusion. When we will fill our thinking minds with things such as this, there is no longer any more room for us to grow. There is no longer any place left for us to see what is all ready and we will miss much of what we have entered to do.

"So it is, Speaking Wind, that whatever we do, we must hold in the front of our thinking minds that it is time, and it is good. When we will not come to do something, then we must also hold in the front of our thinking minds that this is also time and it too is good.

"When you will be in this place of seeing this, little one, you will know the face of freedom, this face of freedom that only needs to be found once in anyone's earth walk.

"This face of freedom will come to you when you have understood what I have been willing to share with you. When you come to see that all things that are, are for a reason, one which may only be understood by the one who is receiving them. Then there will be a feeling of freedom born within you. And from this birth of freedom, you will hold the understanding that for all you will ever do, it is time. And that which others do, this too is time for them to be done.

"It will be then that you will come to feel the comfort of freedom, this freedom that will not only allow you to know that all you have done, will do, and are doing is what is needed by you to be done. But it will also allow you to understand all that has been done, is being done, and will be done by everyone and everything else in this domain, is being done at the right time and the right place, and for the right reason.

"Then you will not feel the weight of being responsible or countable for those things that are not of you, for those things that have nothing at all to do with you and the path you have before you to travel.

"Remember, Speaking Wind, when you will allow yourself to be, you are already, and there is nothing more that will ever need to be done. But when you will try, then you will always be someone or something that you are not. And this is the path of illusion, the path that will keep you in a constant state of becoming, and not ever arriving.

"So look on those small children of the leaf and be thankful for all that is being shared with you. Do not be sad for those things that were not for you to share, otherwise you would miss what they are willing to offer you.

"Does this assist you in coming to a clearer place of seeing, Little One?" Grandfather asked.

"Yes, Grandfather, I can see more clearly now from your speaking words to me," was my response.

I turned my head back to the opening of the great stone cave we were sitting in and was looking at the giant legs that were walking to our direction. I could hear for each of their footsteps a great crack of thunder that would later roll over all the valley walls.

Then something called my attention to my left, this place where my best friend, Cheeway, was sitting.

"I am not afraid any longer, my brother. Thank you for sharing with me those things you had been willing to," came the peaceful sounding voice of Cheeway.

"It is good to see this face over you, my brother. It is a good place to be," was my response to him.

Then with a reassuring look that was covering his face, Cheeway nodded to me and returned his eyes to look out over the valley below us to observe the giant legs approaching our position.

I followed his look, and could feel such a warming of my spirit for all that had been shared with me on this day.

For all that was presented to me, I could not feel as if it would carry with it the same weight of the love I had come to know and understand with the ones I had been given so many seasons to travel with, even for this one called Night Hawk whom I did not know very well, but felt as if I did.

So I placed a good face over myself and waited, waited for whatever was about to come before us on this land of the Old Ones.

CHAPTER 15

❀

Preparing the Spirit

Watching the giant legs coming closer to our place of sitting was given me a feeling that it would not be much longer before the arrival of the Ancient Ones.

As each of their steps came closer, I could hear and see the lightning and thunder following them. And I felt that both the giant legs and thunder spirits were somehow connected. For one would not seem to travel without the other following in the same place.

Soon the air was filled with what appeared to be an electrical charge, the kind that would give us small shocks when we would reach out and touch something.

Looking to the place where Cheeway was sitting, I could see all of the hair on the top of his head was standing up. It was almost like someone holding each of its ends up into the air that was above him. Then, just as I had seen him and how he looked, he turned to me, and began to laugh.

"You look as if you had been scared by a spirit, Speaking Wind," came the first of his speaking words to me. "Do you know what you look like?"

"Yes, Cheeway," I responded. "I do know what I look like. But you do not have the mirror to see with, my brother; how is it you hold this knowing with you?" Cheeway returned with a small chuckle in his voice.

"All I have to do is to look at you and the other three members of our council," I said. "If you will look on the rest of us, my brother, you will then see what you look like as well."

As Cheeway turned his head, he placed a grin over his face. I knew that he would have broken into laughter for an event such as this. But with all that had been presented to us on this day, I knew that like him, we did not have time to spend on such a thing.

Finishing his looking to the rest of our council, Cheeway immediately returned his eyes to the front of the great stone cave we were sitting in and to the direction the giant legs that were traveling to our position at a very steady pace.

And soon, it was finished. The giant legs of clouds had completed their journey and were standing in the front of the opening of the stone cave we were sitting in. They stood motionless just to the outside of our place of shelter. I could smell them and it was as if they had been carrying the scent of sage and cedar with them, these smells that had always been associated with cleansing or smudging for our people.

For as long as I could remember, Grandfather and Two Bears had shared with Cheeway and me that these two smells were very important to all life. And it was from the combination of the two of them that there would be a restoration to all life within its range.

It was by combining these two smells that many of those things that would not hold the weight of truth would fall away...fall away and find another place to reside.

And this was the case for me on this day. As I continued to breathe in those smells of sage and cedar, I could feel many emotional weights falling away from me, those things I did not hold the understanding for and had been getting in my way seeing on this day.

With the approach of the giant legs of cloud, there was a cleansing for all of us, a cleansing that would always be present when the two healing ones, the sage and cedar, were present.

With this running through the front of my thinking mind, I could feel a lightness come over me, a lightness that was allowing me to see more clearly.

Then looking at the two giant legs once again, I saw they were disappearing. They had begun to dissolve into the air that was around us. And I knew they had done what had been required of them.

However, when they had disappeared, the smells of the sage and cedar did not leave. These smells remained with us and just as strong as they had been when the giant legs of clouds had been standing before us.

Grandfather had shared, with Cheeway and me, that when there would be a balance in the path we would chose to travel, all that would be needed by either of us would be provided and would come to us from places we had not ever thought of before.

As this thought was forming in the front of my thinking mind, I was thinking over those things he had been willing to share with me on how this will come to all of us, this balance that is needed before we can come to the place of seeing through our wants and into our needs.

"When we will allow ourselves to be, little one, then we find our eyes of clear seeing come over us, these eyes that are needed to separate our wants from our needs," came the beginning of those speaking words Grandfather shared with me many seasons before.

"Remember, Speaking Wind, it is to observe all things that are with us, that we will find the learning and understanding we are seeking.

"When we are willing to observe, we will find the answers to all of those questions. This is truth I am willing to share with you, truth that is simple because it is understood.

"However, before we will have the ability of observing and being observant of all that is with us, we will first have to allow ourselves to be. To be…and we are already.

"This is not to be found among many of the two-legs in this domain of the Earth Mother and it is because of another simple truth, one that I will now share with you.

"You will find in the seasons that still lie ahead of you that there will be many who will come to you looking for answers, looking for answers to things they already know.

"But they will not have the ability of seeing this truth that is within them because they have not been able to sit in the silence and observe, because they have not allowed themselves to be observant to all that is them.

"I tell you, in truth, all of our needs of knowing lie within us, but the confirmations for them will always come to us from those we will see and meet on our earth walk…those who will always be found in a praying mind asking for assistance for many things, things like how they are doing, or if what they are doing now is the correct thing for them to do…or what they still need to work on in order to get to the place they wish to arrive. When the answers come to them, they are still blinded by the illusion they have come to live in. And because of this blinding that is over them, they do not see any of those answers as confirmation to what they have been seeking.

"When one is at this place of living, Speaking Wind, they do not hold the believing in many things. They will not hold onto any kind of reasonable believing in much of anything, because they feel no one is listening to them.

"But for all of the seasons they have been given to travel in this domain of the Earth Mother, they have been given all that they have been requesting, and all of those things they have been needing assistance for, but they have repeatedly ignored them.

"They have looked the other way when their prayers have been answered, looked the other way because they did not see this answer come to them as any assistance. They saw it come to them as something to run away from, as something that had come to them as an enemy.

"Remember well, Speaking Wind, there will not ever be a time when any of the prayers you will ask for will not be answered. And they will be answered for everyone in less time than it takes to blink your eyes.

"However, there are many prayers that are not understood. And those things that are not understood will not be seen as answers when they come.

"The reason for this is that when one will not understand what it is that they are asking assistance for, they will not hold the eyes that will see clearly for them. When there is not the clarity of seeing for those things that they are asking for, they will only come to see them for what they would want them to be, and not for what they are.

"They have become so lost in trying to do things, they have lost their way and cannot see any of that which is with them already. They can only see all things in the way they wish for them to be. And with this way of seeing, Little One, there is no longer any room for truth, no longer room for the truth of anything to come to them.

"They will seek you out in order to find their answers to things they already know. And I will share with you that if you will follow these speaking words I have been willing to share with you, you will hold a great gift to present them with, a great gift for those who can see and hear what you will offer them.

"Offer them this, Little One, that all of that which they have been seeking answers to resides within them. And that those answers will come to them when they will allow themselves to be, to be that which they are already and without trying to be anything more…anything at all.

"When they allow themselves to be, they will once again be able to see what is around them. And they will see it as confirmation to all of those things they have been requesting assistance for.

"Remind them when people, places, or things that will cause them to feel very good, come to them, this is confirmation for all of those things they have already done work on within themselves.

"When they will see people, places, or events come to them that will not give them a good feeling, they should not become angered or frightened by them, but they should thank them as well. For what has been delivered has been the answers they have been asking for.

"When you receive what you believe to be a bad feeling from another person, or from another event, be glad for this. For it has been presented to you so you will see what areas within yourself still need to be worked with. And once you have completed this work, they will no longer come to you in a way that will give you a bad face to wear for them.

"But the two-legs who will come to you in those seasons that are still far ahead of where you are now, they will come to you without the ability of allowing themselves to be.

"For them, it will seem an impossible task for them to do anything without trying. But I share with you in truth, there is no effort required in allowing yourself to be, only a need to believe that all that has been done has been done with a specific purpose to it. And that purpose has been to prepare one for the time they are in now.

"The ones who will have a great deal of difficulty in comprehending this, Speaking Wind, offer to them this saying, a saying that says 'When one will ask you what time it is, answer them by saying Where I Am!'

"You will have given them a great deal to think over, a great thing that in time, will show them they are already.

"When you will do this for the two-legs who will enter your life path, Little One, they will come away with something that is far greater than anything else they hold with them. They will leave you with the knowing that all is as it should be—and so are they."

Hearing those speaking words come to me from my within place, this place where my spirit resides, I could feel another confirmation to all that had been presented on this day, on this day of the arriving for the spirit vision of the Ancient Ones.

I held the understanding that there would not ever be a need for me to try for anything that would be presented to me. I would not need to try to be, because I already was. And all that would be presented to me; I was already prepared to receive. Otherwise it would not have presented itself to me in the first place.

Looking to the opening of the great stone cave we were sitting in, I could feel the warming of those speaking words Grandfather had shared with me take form, a form that was allowing me to see when something would be presented, it would always be in the form of a confirmation, a confirmation that all which had been required of me had been completed, and the offering would be the final confirmation.

As these things were streaming across my thinking mind, I could feel a new presence in the air, a presence that had not been there a few moments before, but was now.

CHAPTER 16

❋

Arrival of the Ancient Ones

The new arrival of this presence was filling me with a great curiosity. For the first time since this spirit vision had begun, there were no visible signs for it being with us.

However there was no mistaking its presence. For when I had received the confirmation of it being with us, there was a sudden thickness in the air, a thickness that was not going to be ignored. For when I would lean into the air in front of me, there was a definite pushing against me. And when I would lean against the air with my back, there was a complete supporting of my entire body part, a supporting that would have held against any amount of force that I would have been able to put against it.

It was as if each of us was being held in place and we could not move. I wondered if we had placed ourselves in the correct positions...the correct one that had been shown to me by the calling voice of the spirit.

Then, and as quickly as this thought had entered me, it was replaced with another, one that had quickly reminded me of those things Grandfather had been willing to share with me before:

"When you are prepared, Little One, what is needed will appear. For when you have prepared yourself properly, there will be no thing left for you to do, but wait and observe from the silence within."

Just as these speaking words had cleared themselves from my thinking mind, there was a brilliant flash of lightning over the entire mouth of the stone cave we were sitting in.

When we could see once again, I saw eleven figures standing before us, eleven figures that had found this place we were in and they were observing us.

However, I could not be sure what they were doing because the flash of the white lightning was still not allowing me to see clearly. All I could do was sit in my position and wait, to sit and wait until the darkness would clear from my eyes, and I could see once again.

It did not take long for this to clear. And from what I could see of the other members of our council, I could tell that they too had begun to see clearly. I could tell this by the feelings I was receiving from each of them, these feelings that we had come to understand from each other when our speaking words were not possible.

However, there was still another limitation that was over all of us. I could feel the thickness of the air that was with us and how it was keeping me from moving. And I could feel from the others that they were under the same constraint as I was.

And this life the air around each of us held was making sure that we would continue to look into the place that was before us, this place that was now being filled by eleven new arrivals.

There was no movement from any of these eleven figures as they stood before us. They only seemed to be looking to our within places to see if we were ready for what they had come to offer.

The blindness that had been given to each of us by the brilliance of the flash of white lightning was passing, and as it was doing so, I could see the faces of the ones who had come to stand before us.

When I saw their faces though, I was filled with a great expectation, a great expectation of what would be coming to all of us next.

For each of these eleven who had come to stand before us had also been present in the last spirit vision that I had been given…the last spirit vision where I had been taken to the place of the Ancient Ones to hear 'The Message'.

And now they had returned. They had come to us this time and the reason for this was not within my grasp.

However, I was very thankful for this. I was thankful for this because I remembered all of the work that had been done before I had been allowed to go to them, to the place where they all sat in council with me.

As this thought was crossing my thinking mind, I was wondering why these same ones had come to me again. I was wondering if there was something that I had missed before, something that I did not remember from those things they had been willing to share with me.

However, before I had the time to place another thought with me, the lady who was standing in the middle of the rest of the eleven Ancient Ones raised her head and said:

"Do not be so concerned with those things that are not for you, Little Brother. For we have come among all of you with a new message.

"It is one of equal weight for the times that are soon to be with all of the two-legs in this domain. We come before you so you may know us better, so you will not have a face of uncertainty to wear when the time comes and the rest of us will enter this domain."

As she finished her speaking words, there was a sudden flash of white lightning that fell over these lands once again. However, this time it was not as blinding to us, but was only coming to us so that we might see better the faces of the Old Ones who had just arrived.

As the light came over these Ancient Ones, I could see the ones who had been male just before were now female. And the ones who had been female were now male.

However, there was another change that had come to them. When the first flash of lightning came over them, I could see they were no longer holding the look to them of our own people, but they had changed to the color black. From what I could see, they were now of the black race and there was nothing left of them from the red race.

Then, and without warning, there was a second flash of lightning from the storm that was over us. And when this second flash of lightning came over us, I could see there was another change of equal proportion to all of these eleven Ancient Ones.

Once again, the ones who had just been male turned into female and the ones who had been female turned into male forms.

But this was not all, for when the second flash of lightning had come over them, I could see that there was nothing left of the black race among any of them. But they all held to them all of the features of the yellow race.

As these changes were coming over them, I was beginning to wonder if it was my eyes that were playing tricks on me. I was wondering if what I was seeing was what was being presented.

But as I looked to the other four members of our council from the very corners of my eyes, I could see that they, too, were seeing those same things. And they too were wondering the same things; that is, all but Night Hawk.

For him, there did not seem to be any reaction to these events that were being presented to us. It was as if he had already reached the place of understanding from something that had come to him before.

I did not have long to wait for the next change. And there was no longer time to give any more thought as to why Night Hawk did not hold any surprise over himself for these changes.

The third flash of lightning had come and as it did, there were other changes that had come to these eleven Ancient Ones.

Once again, the ones who had been holding the face of the male changed into the female and the ones who had been holding to them the face of female changed into the face of male.

As this light from the lightning came over all of them, I could see that they no longer held to them any resemblance of the yellow race, but now they all held to them all of the features of the white race. And for this, I held less of an understanding for this than I did before, even though what I held before in the way of understanding was very limited.

There was another flash of lightning and once again the males changed into females and the females changed into males.

And as the last flash of lightning came, I could see they had all returned to the place they had been before, this place where we first saw them enter the opening of the great stone cave.

For now, all of the ones who had first appeared to us as having the male face to them were back to this place, as well as the ones who first appeared to us with the face of the female. And they had the features of the red race and with this face I could more easily see them as the Ancient Ones of our people.

For this last change, I was very grateful. I did not hold an understanding of what it was that was being presented to me on this day, but I held the knowing that I would be much more willing to listen to the Old Ones of our own people than I would have been if they had been of another race...or another people.

But this thought that was coming to me was making me feel uncomfortable. For there was something that had been shared with me that I did not hold an understanding for...something that was allowing me to feel there had been a great hole in my levels of understanding for what was being presented by this changing of appearance.

However, there was not time for this kind of thinking for me, and soon all eleven of the Old Ones began to walk close to the small warming fire we had built.

As they approached our place of sitting, the one that came to walk in front of the rest raised his right hand in a way I had seen both

Grandfather and Two Bears raise theirs when they were about to ask for a blessing.

He raised his hand in an outward motion that allowed all of us to see his palm. Then he made a wide circle with it as if he were including all of these lands and village we had come to sit in and said:

"These are sacred lands, my brothers and sisters. We wish to travel with you in all of these places you have come to know as your home.

"We are the ones who have come to you from the night stars of time. We are the ones who have been with you at your first draw of breath from spirit within you.

"Allow us to bless you, and all who travel with you. Accept this offering from the love of creation and for all living things both great and small, seen and unseen by those who travel a life path with you.

"For we have returned to travel with you for a short time. We have come to you from a land where there is no time and there is no separateness.

"Our time with all of you is short for now, but soon we will all return. And when we will return, all may know of our face.

"But that time is not now, for it has not been allowed to be born to any of you, yet. We only ask that you share with us a short time, a short time so there may be a blessing of sharing, a blessing of sharing for those things that are soon to accompany us when we once again enter this domain that is the Earth Mother."

Following his speaking words, there was a silence of acceptance by all who had come to these lands.

There was a silence not only from our own council of five, but from the rock nation, the tree nation, the cloud nation, the sky nation, the Spirit Wind, and from all of the small ones that could be seen or felt by us as well.

As this silence of acceptance fell over all life that had come to be with us, there was a filling of spirit from deep within me.

It was a feeling of love that I had not yet come to know or experience, but I had no doubt that it was with me, and it was growing very quickly.

Looking where the other members of our council had been sitting, I was surprised because I was no longer being held by the stiffness of the air that had previously kept me from moving.

Now I was able to move very freely and when I looked over to the places where Night Hawk, Grandfather, Two Bears, and Cheeway were sitting, I could see that movement had been returned to them as well.

On each of their faces I could see a look of need, a look of need that had come to each of us for what would soon be shared by these eleven Ancient Ones who had come. For it was these Old Ones that had seen a need for what they were about to begin, a journey they saw, but we did not yet understand.

The one who had spoken the blessings was looking over the places each of us had found to sit. And as he did this, he continued:

"These are sacred lands, my brothers. May we join with you?" came the request of the Ancient One standing in front of the rest.

"Yes, by all means," came the response from Grandfather holding out his right hand in a motion that they should sit where they would wish.

"It is good to see all of you once again," came the voice of the lady who had been standing behind the first.

"And you, Speaking Wind, are you traveling well, Little Brother?"

"Yes, Old One, I am traveling well," was my return.

Watching all eleven Ancient Ones sitting in their places across from us had given to me a good feeling, one that was sharing with me that I had come home after being away for a very long time.

But for understanding this feeling that was coming over me, there was no clear seeing. For even though I could feel its presence and life within me, there was no thing that I could relate it to and no reason from within myself for its being with me here and now.

"There are many things that are being born to not only you, Speaking Wind, but to many of the two-legs traveling within this domain of the Earth Mother," was the lady's reply to those things that had been silently growing within me.

"As there is only that which is," came the reply from Grandfather.

Then all speaking words fell away from the originators, and another silence was born to all of us, a silence that had been placed over all for a specific reason, a reason that I was not sure of, but one that I was more than willing to go along with.

During this time of silence, I noticed that each of the eleven Ancient Ones was wearing a necklace.

The three who had entered this sitting place first had one that was in the color of red, then the next three had one that was the color of black, the third group of three wore the necklace with the color white, and the last two to enter wore the color of yellow on their necklaces.

Looking to them and those necklaces they had chosen to wear, I found myself in a place of wondering once again, a place that caused me to wonder why there were only two out of this group who were wearing the necklace with the yellow color.

Then, as these thoughts had filled my thinking mind, the reassuring voice of the Elder with the white colored necklace began.

"It is for your benefit that we have been willing to wear such things, Little Brother.

"It is for reasons of your relating to us that we have come to you in this way. What we bring with us now is for your benefit of understanding. If we would not wear these necklaces with us, you would most likely lose much of your way with us.

"However, as we continue to share with you those things that will be needed, those things that each of you hold a great need for, then we will no longer have the need to wear these children around our necks and will take them off when you are ready."

"Tell me, Little Brother," came the speaking voice from the lady wearing the black necklace. "You who are called Cheeway. Can you share with me your level of understanding for the meaning of our colored necklaces?"

"Yes, Old One...yes, I can do this...I can do this very well!" was Cheeway's response.

"This is good, Little Brother. For when we are willing to explain things that are asked of us, we will be giving ourselves another chance to see what it is we understand...and what things we do not yet hold an understanding for," was the response of the woman of the black colored necklace.

Looking over to the place where Cheeway was sitting, I could see him taking in a deep breath. One that shared with me that he was now ready to respond to their question.

Without hesitation, Cheeway responded.

I was sitting in a very surprised place because this was something that Cheeway had not ever done before. All of the seasons he and I had been given to travel together, I would always have to wait a great deal of time for an answer to come from him. From the time I would ask him a question, he would require many moments to think over it. And for the time this process could take, I could almost eat an entire meal waiting for his response.

But now...now with this question coming to him from one of the Ancient Ones, he was not only willing to respond...but he was ready. And the look that had come over the faces of Grandfather and Two Bears held this look of surprise over them as well.

Sitting back in my place by the warming fire, I gave all of my attention to my best friend, Cheeway, and to those things he was now willing to share with the Ancient Ones.

I knew, as they had just shared, that for each time we will come to repeat something, it is not for the benefit of another that we will do this. But it is for the benefit of ourselves—that is, if we will be willing to listen to those things that we have to say.

"It is from our people's medicine wheel of life that these colors come," Cheeway began with his explanation and reply to the question that had been asked of him.

"The three who are wearing the necklaces of red...well, this comes from the South portion of the medicine wheel. This is the home of coyote and the place of child. It is from this place that we find our innocence of accepting all that will be presented to us, this innocence of accepting all things that will come to us with the eyes of the child, this child, which is another word for the spirit who resides within all of us.

"It is also the place of the red path. The red path, which is our people and its color, signify all that we have been, will always be, and are in the time that is with us today.

"The color black from the necklaces worn by the next three...well, this is significant of the West position and is home to bear and the energy of female. In this place on the medicine wheel, we are reminded to take all that is presented to our within place, this place where our spirit resides, and think them over.

"This place and the color black reminds us that not all ways are for any of us, and we must be willing to take the traveling road into the spirit of silence to see which are, and which are not.

"In this place that is the home of bear, we are reminded that while our strengths are great at one moment of time, if we will not take the time to care for ourselves, our strength will be gone from us and we will be left without the stamina we once held.

"But there is another reason for this kind of speaking to the west direction and color of black...and that is for spirit within each of us.

"Unless we come to understand that all things presented may not be meant for us, then we can become lost in those things that are of others...from the weight they will bring to us if we choose to carry them and not look into each of them to see if they are for us or not.

"This will create a great weight over all who would not be willing to take the time of understanding that not all things are meant for them. For if they would think that they are, then they will end up walking their life path with a great weight to them. And this weight will come to them from all of the emotions that will be carried by those events that were not theirs to work with in the first place.

"For the ones who are wearing the color of the white necklace, they represent the colors of the Elders in the north position of the medicine wheel.

"It is from their place that we have come to recognize one who has traveled a good life path and has a great amount of understanding for those things they have been willing to learn from.

"When they will hold with them wisdom for those things they have been willing to learn from, they also hold the understanding for whom they are in truth. And they will not be trying to tell others of those things that are not of truth.

"This north place on the medicine wheel of life is with the color of white. And it is by blending all of the other colors of the medicine wheel that allow this color to be.

"This place on the medicine wheel reminds us that it is not until we have come to a place of understanding that we will begin to see. Only when we will have come through all of the other colors on the medicine wheel that we will find our own way. And this way will be in truth, our own path of understanding.

"It is also the home of the Elders because it is through their understanding that we may see the direction to our own problems, those problems that many of them have already seen the face of truth for.

"Also, this place of the north position on the medicine wheel is to remind us of the home of the buffalo. And it is the buffalo who is the bringer of abundance and life to all who will travel close to him.

"Grandfather and Two Bears have shared with my brother and me that wherever buffalo will travel, new life will follow. For all that they are, and I am speaking of the body parts to them, is used by our people. Even their droppings are used by us for many things that we would otherwise not have.

"Next, for the ones who are wearing the color of the yellow necklace, they would represent the medicine wheel's east position. And this position holds to it the color of yellow, which is the reminding of the reflection of the Great Spirit in our daytime sky.

"It is also the home of eagle, and eagle medicine reminds us that it is not a difficult task to find and maintain one's balance in their earth walk.

"That is, when one will understand truth is unto itself. When one will accept truth, they will not have a need to make it confusing, and they will not confuse others when they will speak of it to them.

"For eagle reminds us that in allowing ourselves to be, we will continually walk with one foot in spirit and the other foot on our path in this domain of the Earth Mother.

"This is what I have come to understand from the colors that are on all of the necklaces each of you wear, Old Ones. Has this given to you what you have requested of me?" Cheeway finished.

"Yes, Little Brother," came the speaking words of the lady wearing the colors of the East position of yellow. "You have done yourself a great showing for what you have been so willing to work for, for those things you have been willing to work through the knowing in order to arrive at the understanding for them.

"But tell me, Cheeway," the lady of the east position continued. "Why did you stop in the sharing of your speaking words to us when you did?

Looking over to the place where Cheeway was sitting, I could see that he held a great look of surprise over his face, one that shared with me what had just been said to him was truth. For as long as I could remember, whenever Cheeway would be confronted with something that he was still thinking on by another, those things that had not yet come to the surface, he would always have this same face painted over him, this face that would share with the one who had asked him this question that they were correct in what they had said.

"You did hold a question with you, did you not, Little Brother?" the lady from the East position asked.

"Yes, Old One...yes I did," came the surprised response from Cheeway. "But I did not hold an understanding of how it would be received by all of you."

"And this is the reasoning that had gone through your thinking mind then?" the lady of the East asked.

"Yes, this is the reason that I chose not to ask it," Cheeway replied.

"Then you would have missed out on a great answer, Little Brother, one that would have brought to you a much clearer seeing than you now hold with you," the lady of the east position replied once again.

"Remember, Cheeway, when one will ask a question for something, a question that they feel they hold a great need to know, when they will ask such a question, they must have the understanding with them that it is not another who they are asking this from...but it is themselves.

"Remember, Little Brother, all of those things that we will see on the outside of ourselves are only confirmations for what we already know. And when we feel this need to ask any question, then we are only asking ourselves. We are only asking ourselves what we already know but do not yet have the confirmation for."

"And this is what I would have been doing with my question, Old One?" Cheeway asked with a small and tiny sounding voice that had come to him.

"Yes, Cheeway," the woman from the East position replied. "This is what you would be doing with any question you would ask. And this is not only for this time we have been given, but it will apply to all things that will come to you in the seasons yet to be born."

Hearing these speaking words returned to him from the lady in the East position, Cheeway reached up to the top of his head to scratch. And I knew that this was one of his signs that he had made a decision, one that would soon be known by all who were near him.

"Then I would like to ask this question now, Old One. That is, if I would still be allowed to do so," Cheeway replied.

"Of course you may, Little Brother. What is this question that is growing within you?" the lady of the East position replied.

"It is this," Cheeway began. "As I look over all eleven of you, there are many things I can feel growing from within me. And for this, I hold the understanding that it is your presence near me that is causing such growth to take place.

"For all that you are, Old Ones, I am grateful. I am grateful that you have been willing to include me in this spirit vision of your presence. And I hold the understanding that this is a spirit vision all of us are being included in."

"This does not sound like a question to me, Cheeway," the lady of the East position replied.

"No, Old One, this is not my question." Cheeway replied. "I was only attempting to show all of you how grateful I am by being here with you and in this time of sharing between us."

"In other words, Cheeway, you were covering yourself for any raw feelings that might come to us from this question of yours?" the lady of the East position asked.

As I looked over to Cheeway, I could see that the color of his entire face was red, a red that would often come to both of us when we were caught in attempting something that we knew was not going to work.

"Yes," Cheeway continued. "Perhaps I would do much better if I were to simply ask my question and not take so much time in worrying how it will be taken.

"This is a good place to begin with, Little Brother," was the response from the lady in the east position.

"Then this is my question," came the speaking words of Cheeway with the tone of great determination over them. "As I look over each of you Old Ones, I see that you are in truth representing each of the four colors of direction, these four colors of direction to our medicine wheel of life.

"But as I look on each of you, there seems to be something that is missing. And this is what is giving to me my question, this question that am now ready to ask of you.

"When I see the ones who are wearing the necklaces of red, black, and white, I see there are three of each represented for these colors.

"However, when I look to the ones who are wearing the necklaces of yellow, this color that is for the east part of the medicine wheel of life, I see that there are only two who are representing this place.

"This is for the reason of what this color of yellow in the east place of the medicine wheel shares with me.

"That it is the home of eagle and the place of spiritual growth for all who would have the eyes and ears to see and hear with.

"Is this going to be less for those days that are yet to be with us, Old Ones? Are we not going to have the wisdom of spirit available to us in the same way as we do now?"

When Cheeway had finished his speaking words to the Ancient Ones, there was a small but very distinct silence that had filled this place we had come to sit and share with each other. But it was also a silence of accepting all that had been shared by both sides, by our side of the council of five as well as the council of eleven, this council of the Ancient Ones.

"It is a good question that you have asked of us, Little Brother," came the return from the lady of the East colored necklace. "And it is with good seeing that you have formed well this question you have been willing to ask of us. For this, we are all grateful for your observation. And we will share with you what you have seen among us.

"It is truth that these times that are with you now will not remain unchanged, that they will soon be changed into something that has not yet been seen in this domain of the Earth Mother. We also share with you that there will not be a decrease in the path of the spirit for any of these times ahead. I share with you that all will be included in these times because there will not be any who will be missed.

"As for the amount of wisdom of spirit that will remain in this domain for these times that are about to be revealed to all of you, this will not decrease, Little One, but it will grow.

"It will grow more than you could ever imagine. For what lies ahead of all of the two-legs will be a choice, a great choice that will mark such a difference to all of them that they must have available to them the wisdom of spirit.

"For without this, they could not make such a choice for themselves. And this choice that will soon come to them will be one that will flood them for as long as they continue to be.

"However, from what you have seen from all of us, Little One, there is great weight to what you have asked. For this question that you hold with you is in need of being answered.

"Speaking Wind has shared with all of you what had been given to him from us the last time, hasn't he? Those things that we had been willing to share with him when he had received 'The Message'?"

Looking over the places the other four members of our council had chosen to sit, I could see that each of them had been nodding their heads in a motion that would allow this Old One to know that they had been told of those things from my last spirit vision with them.

However, as I was looking over to the place where Night Hawk was sitting, I could see that he too was nodding his head in a motion that would also share with these Ancient Ones that he too was aware of what had been presented to me, of those things that had been shared with me in my last spirit vision with them.

But how could he have known of this event? I was sure that I had not shared this with him, and from the way that he had been greeted by Grandfather and Two Bears, I knew that they had not seen him in many seasons.

However, these thoughts were not to remain with me for a long time. Just as they had begun to grow within me, there was another event that had been offered to all of us, one that required my attention to the Old Ones who were sitting before us.

"This observation that you have made is very good, Cheeway. It is something that needs to be seen," the lady with the color of yellow on her necklace continued.

"You are correct in seeing that which is, Little Brother, and it is by this action of yours that we will complete this circle, this circle that before now has been incomplete."

Then reaching within her long white robe, the lady who had been addressing all of us reached inside of one of the folds with her right hand. And when she pulled her hand from this fold in her robe, she was holding the same kind of necklace that she and the other male had been wearing…this necklace that had been wonderfully beaded with the colors of the yellow circle on it.

Then looking over to the place I had come to sit, she said: "This is for you, Little Brother. There will be great need for you to have this with you when you find uncertainty gnawing at you.

"For there are to be many seasons before you when you will not yet be awake from this sleep of preparing. And it will be in those times there will come to you many uncertainties, uncertainties that you will not yet hold an understanding for.

"While you are within this sleep of preparing, Speaking Wind, wear this gift of ours to assist you in remembering who and what you are in truth. And learn to listen well for what lies ahead of you."

Then finishing her speaking words, she handed me the yellow necklace and told me it would be good if I were to place it around my neck.

Just as I was about to reach for this, there was a commotion among all of the Ancient Ones, a commotion that caused me to stop short of reaching for this necklace that had been offered to me.

I froze in my place of reaching and looked over to the Old Ones who had seen something which had caused them to make their sounds, the sounds of commotion that were only to be understood among themselves.

"With what hand do you reach for this gift of ours, Speaking Wind?" came the voice of the lady of the yellow color.

Then looking to what had I had been holding in front of me, I replied, "Why, it is my right hand, Old One."

"Is there something improper to this, Little Brother?" asked the lady of the East position.

Looking to my within place, I soon found the answer to this question that had been placed before me.

And when this understanding came to me, I could not hold my head in an upright position any longer, but turned it down so that it would face the earth below me.

"Yes," I responded. "Yes, there is something that is very improper in this motion that I had made before all of you."

"And would you be willing to share what this is, Little Brother?" the lady of the East asked.

"It is from what had been shared with me many times from Grandfather and Two Bears, Old One," I continued to explain in the best speaking words that I could find within me. "What has been with me for many of my seasons, Old One, I seemed to have forgotten."

Then picking myself up from my within place, I looked to the faces of all who had been gathered with me on this land and in this time.

I could see a look of acceptance come to me from all who were seated. And for this, I knew it was good.

CHAPTER 17

❀

Receive with the Left.
Give with the Right.

I held a good feeling over me for this thing I had come to do, a good feeling over me that was sharing with all that I had come to the place of understanding for what I had done.

And as it was with so many things we do in this earth walk, there are always those that are not received from the best course of travel. It is when we will understand what we have done that we will learn. And it is through learning from those things that we do that we find our own way in this domain of the Earth Mother to finally see for ourselves the path our spirit needs to travel.

Holding this in the front of my thinking mind, I once again found a good place for me to continue with what I had begun, with the understanding for what I had first tried to do and why it had not been correct for me.

"It has been shared with me from the teachings of Grandfather, Two Bears and the silent brotherhood that when we will accept something from one who is not close to us, from one who travels a path that is vastly different from the one I have come to travel...when they offer something to us that may not hold our own truth to it, when this happens, we are to reach out for it with the right hand," I continued with my explanation for what my movements to the Old Ones represented.

"It is when we do not wish to receive something that is being offered to us that we will reach for it with this right hand because it is the hand that gives.

"However, for those who are on a path that is close to our own, and we can see that it does hold a truth for us within it, then we will accept this offering of theirs with our left hand.

"And we will return this back to them, though, with the right hand. And this shares with them that we hold an understanding for these things that have come to us. And this process will allow the circle to come to its completion.

"When we hold with us a respect for the one who is offering, we do them a great compliment by accepting this offering of theirs with our left hand. And this has come to us in a way that can be found on the path of the spirit…this path that has been traveled for many generations by the wise ones.

"When we accept with our left hand, what is being offered will immediately come to us. Not only the physical part of this offering, but the spirit that lives within it will come into us as well.

"When we accept with the left hand, we are sharing with the giver that we do not hold them in any place that is not respected…that we present them a trusting that they will not present us anything that will do us harm.

"But when we will accept with the right hand, we are sharing with the giver that we are still a little unsure of what is being presented, that we are still not comfortable with them and what they are offering.

"So when we accept with the right hand, then this allows us to look on the gift a little closer without having it enter us right away."

"And this is what you were looking at when you began to accept with you right hand, Speaking Wind?" the lady of the East place questioned.

"Yes, Old One," I returned. "This is what I had begun to do, that is, before my attention was called to what I was doing.

"I would not ever wish to present any of you with even the slightest disrespect, and for this action on my part...I can only say that I will be more attentive to what I do in the times ahead of me."

"Then it will go well with you, Little Brother," the man of the East position began. "It is when we gain understanding for what has come to us that we are willing to learn. Keep this in the front of your thinking mind, Little Brother, for this is in truth the reason we entered this domain of the Earth Mother. By doing this, you will continue to see your path clearly.

"However, there is yet another part of this action that has not been seen by you, Speaking Wind. And it would be good for you to hear of it now.

"You would do well to keep with you that there will not ever come to you anything that you will not be ready for. And this applies to this time all of us are in.

"However, there have been many events that have been presented to all five of you that have not been understood...many events that have come to each of you on a new path, a path none of you may be familiar with.

"And it has been with this level of uncertainty that you held with you, Speaking Wind, that caused you to do what you did. It was not any of us who you did not hold the trusting in; it was a combination of what was being presented to you. And it was from the uncertainty of these events that had caused you to reach for this offering of ours in a way that was not entirely correct. In a way that was not entirely correct only because you did not hold an understanding for what you were doing at the time.

"However, you must hold in the front of your thinking mind that there will be many such events that will come into your life path that you will not hold an understanding for. Events that will be presented to you that you will have to work through the emotion of them before seeing the face of lesson.

"So it would do you well to learn to see all that you do. To listen well and completely to all that you say. In this way, when these times of uncertainty will come over you again, you will not allow yourself to be blinded by them.

"If you will keep this in the front of your thinking mind, you will always hold with you a good sense of focus. And it is when we are focused on those things that are needed by us that we may begin to see, that we may begin to see not only where we are, but where we are going as well.

"When one is focused on their earth walk, they will begin to see those things they need to work on in order to find their own balance, this balance of the within for what it is rather than trying to look within the emotion of what has been presented."

As the last of the speaking words fell away from me, I turned my eyes to the place where the lady of the East color was sitting. Looking into her right hand, I saw she was still holding the yellow necklace out to me, and I reached over with my left hand to accept it.

Once this had been completed, there was a sounding of gladness that passed into the opening of this great stone cave made by the Spirit Wind. I could hear a sounding of relief come to me from Cheeway as well, and I placed the necklace over my head so that it would rest on me.

Looking over to the faces of the Old Ones, there was a nod of approval for this action I had taken, also a nod of approval for those things I had been willing to share with them on the difference of accepting with the left and giving with the right.

"Remember, Little Brother," came the voice of man Elder in the North place. "When you will give something to another who you hold respect for, it will always be your right hand that will do this. This is a truth for all within this domain of the Earth Mother. And it does not matter which hand they will come to do most of their work with.

"When we will offer something to another with the right hand, this action becomes an extension of our own spirit. And this is all one needs to hold in their thinking mind when they will feel this need of offering something to another.

"Remember, if the other will choose to accept with either the left or right hand, this will be for them to decide, not you. When they will see an offering come to them from you, and they have reached with their right hand rather than their left hand, do not hold the believing they do not know what they are doing. If they have acted so, they will feel the need rise from within them to ask you if what they have done is wrong.

"When they will ask you, you would do well to tell them…but not before. For you must remember that they too have their own life path to travel and not all will be as ready to receive what has been offered by another.

"It is for this reason that we must be patient with them and allow them to find their own way, just as you have been allowed to find yours. You must hold the believing that they will find the way to their path. And this will be done with or without you, Speaking Wind. And you must also hold the believing that they will find their own way even when their path is not similar to the one you have to travel.

"For to think otherwise, you would be lulled back into the sleep of illusion, and this is not the place where one would be advised to be for what is soon to arrive for all life here.

"There will be many things we will share with all of you on this day, my brothers. And one of the most important is this: before you will have the ability of allowing another to be, you must first have allowed yourself to be.

"For we can only share with another those things we hold and understand about ourselves. To think otherwise would catch us up in the sleep of illusion, this sleep that will allow one to only see those things, as you would wish for them to be while being blinded to everything else.

"For what lies ahead of you, my brothers, there will be many questions, questions that will make you wonder if you are in truth, ready for such things.

"But I share with each of you, when you will see something, then you are ready for it. When something will come to you, then you are prepared.

"What we share with all of you on this day, it would do you well to hold this truth in the front of your thinking minds. For to do otherwise would allow you to miss something that was meant for you to hear and know of.

"I share this with all of you from my place of truth."

Once again, there was a silence that had come over all of us. For those things that had been shared allowed us a seeing, a seeing that told us there was going to be a great deal of sharing with us on this day and in this time.

And if we were going to accept those things, we would have to understand that no thing would ever come to us for which we are not ready. Otherwise, we would be too caught up in the illusion and not see a great gift, this great gift that had been brought to all of us by the arrival of the Ancient Ones.

CHAPTER 18

❀

The Rainbow Healing

As the silence continued among us, I could feel the presence of the Ancient Ones' eyes looking into us. But they were not looking with the intent of seeing or finding anything. This was another kind of looking that I was feeling from them.

I could feel what they were doing was not being done to locate any of the knowing or understanding we had come to find; rather it was an effort on their behalf to make sure certain things were left within us, things they had seen each of us held a need for.

For me, this was what had come to the front of my thinking mind. As they continued to sit in their silence, I could see many pictures flowing into my within place, this place where my spirit resides, pictures of things I was familiar with as well as things that I was not. And from the preparing that I had received from Grandfather's and Two Bears' teachings, I held the knowing that when the time would be right, and I would have a need for them, I would understand their meaning and these things would return to me with a complete understanding for what they were all about.

As this was crossing the front of my thinking mind, there came into me a picture of a great rainbow, one that was filled with the most brilliant colors of light I had ever seen. It only lasted for a short time, but I remembered holding onto this picture.

"Do you hold an understanding for what this rainbow is, Speaking Wind?" came the voice from the Elder of the West colored necklace.

"I know that this is a promise that has come to our people, Old One, this promise that shares with us that we are not alone on whatever path we have come to travel," was my response to her.

"This is a good place of beginning, Little Brother," the Ancient One in the West position replied. "However, there is more that is being held within the reminding rainbow…one more reminding for what it brings to all who have the understanding to see that is.

"Do any of you have an understanding for what this is, my brothers?" the Old Ones asked looking over to each of the faces of our council of five.

Following her eyes with my own, I could see there were some looks that had come to Grandfather's and Two Bears' faces, but they were not complete ones, not ones that held a complete understanding for what had been asked of them.

So, along with me, the rest of us continued to sit in our places of silence and waited, to wait for what would soon be shared with us about the significance of the rainbow.

"As it is with so much that had been left in this domain of the Earth Mother, there has been a great deal that the two-legs have forgotten to remember. And the reminding of the rainbow is one of them," the Ancient One of the West position continued.

"When you will look at the colors of the rainbow, there will be many changes come to it, changes that will allow the one observing them to see how wonderful this blending is, for all that is within it.

"But more than that, there is the reminding that all of these wonderful colors within the rainbow are the reflection of all life. And all life holds these constantly changing levels of colors over itself as well.

"There are still many among your people who can read these colors the two-legs carry with them. They hold this need about them because from these colors, they can see what is needed on any one's life path, those things that are missing and can be shared with the one who is feeling this loss of themselves.

"Or, as I am now willing to share with all of you, they will use these colors to see what illness is being carried by one who has come to them for a healing.

"It is the rainbow that reminds all of us there can be a healing on ourselves when we will hold the understanding of how to do this. And this is the reminding that I am now willing to share with all of you on this day. For there are four of you with this need. And for the fifth, it is good for them to hear this once again."

As these speaking words fell to the earth below me, I could not help but think on what had been shared by this Ancient One of the West position. That there was a great need by four of the five of us to learn or re-remember what was about to be shared.

But there was one among us that did not hold a need for this, one who would only be invited to listen. I was thinking over what had just been shared with all of us, and wondering who this Old One had been making reference to.

Then suddenly my eyes were drawn to the place where Night Hawk was sitting and I held the knowing, but not the understanding, that it must be he who had been referred to by those speaking words.

Seeing him sitting in his place next to the warming fire, I could feel a great mystery growing within me once again, this great mystery of wondering why so much uncertainty had been around him, why there was so much about this one that did not seem right when I would use those things that had come to me from the teachings of Grandfather and Two Bears…as well as from the silent brotherhood.

But without having more time to think on this, I was suddenly turned to the speaking words of this Ancient One from the West's position. My attention was drawn there because her next speaking words were addressed to me.

"Speaking Wind," came her speaking voice. "Before this day of sharing is over, there will not be the same level of uncertainty left with you. For when our time with you is over, you will have had most of your questions answered by us.

"But for now, Little Brother, sit and listen. Learn to live with the spirit of belonging for what is with you now. When you will succeed in doing this, then all else will fall into place for you."

Looking back to her, I nodded my head to her in a motion that would share that I did understand, but without having to break this silence of listening that had come to me.

"It is good then," she continued.

"Now we shall discuss the healing rainbow and why it has been left within this domain that is the Earth Mother. If you will observe the rainbow closely, you will see that it will begin from the left and go to the right. This is the natural order for this small child of the Earth Mother because she has been given charge for sharing the direction to all healing that will take place in this domain.

"And the most important face of any healing is when one will be capable of healing themselves. For this healing of oneself, look at the rainbow and you will see the wisdom that lies within her and what is needed to perform such a thing. All that will be required to heal oneself before healing another will be shown by this example I am willing to share with you now.

"The great tree nation is rooted in this domain and for them, there is a continual healing that passes through all of them. However, this is largely due to the fact that they are, in truth, rooted here.

"But the rainbow, just like the two-legs, is not physically rooted. And it is for this difference that the rooting must take place in a completely different way, in a way that is continually being shared with all of you by the rainbow.

"When one of you will need the healing of your body part, it would be well for you to begin this process with both of your shoes off. This will allow you to share a contact with the face of the Earth Mother.

"It is when we are in direct contact with our host that we begin to feel the benefit that will come to us from her. By not having anything between you and her, you will find the path you are seeking.

"There are many things the two-legs cover themselves with that keep them from attaining this contact with the Earth Mother. So by removing those things you wear on your feet, you will be able to feel her in this process that we are now willing to share.

"Take a standing position while having both of your feet bare, and think of the rainbow and how she will begin to take on her life in the skies above you. As you think of this, see how she will begin on the left and end on the right while holding all of the colors that are with her.

"Then remember that all of these colors within her are the same ones you wear on a daily basis. However, when an illness comes over you, there will be at least one of those colors that will not be complete. And you will be in great need of its attributes in order to be healed from whatever has come over you.

"You will need to embody all of those colors you see in the rainbow and allow them to begin growing within, just as you have seen the birth of the rainbow over these lands you have come to travel on.

"When you find a place to stand on the face of the Earth Mother while having both of your feet touch her, see yourself as you are in the present, see yourself as one who is not complete for all that should be with you. And this incompleteness will be seen by you as having only partial colors of the rainbow that is within your body.

"When you have reached this place, my brothers, the next step will be much easier. For the next step is to see those colors that are within the rainbow form just under your left foot from a distance that will be seven feet below you.

"As they form under your left foot, you will know they have come to life on their own, a life of their own that is soon to share with you its healing.

"At first you will think that this is only happening in the front of your thinking mind, but it is not. For whatever is asked for in the ways of our Old Ones is given without delay.

"As you hold this picture of the healing rainbow under the bottom portion of your left foot, there will begin to form a tingling in this same part of the left foot where the life of the healing rainbow is coming into you.

"Once this tingling has begun, and you have accepted all of the colors that are within the rainbow, there will be a warmness that will begin to fill your foot. This warmth that is coming to you is from the unconditional love of creation that so many will seek, but few find during their earth walk.

"But this unconditional love has always been with them. They have just forgotten their own way of seeing it.

"When this warmth fills your foot, allow it to come to you in its many colors of healing and look up to the great sky nation and share with them who and what you are in truth. Share with them, from your within place, who you are and what it is you are in need of, those things that are not in balance within you that have created this need for a healing by the healing rainbow.

"Next, look to the ones who are living with you on this place that you have come to stand on. See all of the nations that are with you at this time, the great tree nation, the rock nation, and all of the other children of the Earth Mother who have come to call this land their home as well.

"And again, from your within place, share with them how grateful you are for having been allowed to share their home with them and you are willing to return to them in the ways of their need when they will show this to you.

"When this gratitude has been completed, look to the earth that is beneath you and do the same thing. Thank these children of the Earth Mother for all they are willing to share with you and for the support they share with you by so often giving up their own life paths so you may continue with yours.

"You see, my brothers, in this domain that we have come to call the Earth Mother, there is nothing that is not living. For if it were not living, it would not be here.

"Think for a moment. All that has been created by Great Spirit has been done by holding a piece of himself within it. And there is no thing that you can ever see or imagine that has not been created by him.

"So it becomes very foolish to think of anything as not being alive. And this is why we have shared with you that all things should be held as sacred, as being sacred because each of them have life with them, and all that lives has a path to travel.

"But until one will come to understand this, it is just not possible to allow or even consider giving this recognition to anyone or anything else, for it is not possible from this path of not understanding. For those who do not understand this, there can only be one person in their earth walk, and that is themselves. And when there is only them, if anything is not done in their way, it cannot ever be correct or good. It will always be bad or wrong.

"This is why we have come to request of all the two-legs to give their thankfulness and gratefulness to all life. For it is in this way that one will come to see more clearly those things that are. And it is through this seeing that they begin to understand that all within this domain is living and has a path of its own to travel.

"And it is the same with balance, this same balance that is being sought through this healing. When there is only a small imbalance among the two-legs, there is the physical need for healing. But when this imbalance will be carried for a long time, then there needs to be a healing of the spirit, a cleansing of their own spirit that can only be done by them. For no other will have the knowledge or understanding for how to do this better than they.

"Once you have given your thanks and gratitude to all life that is sharing with you, there will be a need for you to see this small but living healing rainbow under your left foot begin to grow. But it is not you who is bringing this growing to the healing rainbow; it is this small one itself.

"Once you will accept this truth that we have been willing to share with you, there will be an immediate recognition of your needs by this small one of the healing path. When this is completed, the little rainbow will begin to grow and draw all that is needed by you from the love that is within the Earth Mother.

"As the Earth Mother releases all that has been requested by this healing rainbow, it will travel up your left leg in a manner that is seen when the rainbow will appear in the day time skies over all lands.

"You will feel this healing one travel up your left leg encompassing all the parts of your body then will hold itself at the top part of your head, but only for a short time before it will continue on with its journey down your complete right side where it will once again enter the Earth Mother. It will hold itself about seven feet over your head before it will begin its journey back into the Earth Mother.

"As the healing rainbow continues its healing into you, there will be a flooding of many things into you from the left foot. And this flooding will be all that is needed by the body part to allow for its renewal.

"You will feel yourself becoming fuller with each passing moment, and you will begin to wonder if you will explode from all that is pouring into you. But I tell you in truth, you will not.

"What is taking place is the replacing of all that had been within you that caused you to feel this illness. These are being washed out of your body through your right side.

"As they are washed out of you, they will once again enter the loving embrace of the Earth Mother. And she will heal them and allow them to find their way on the path they too have to travel. But now they will be able to travel as a complete life, not one that is missing so much of what they need.

"For those things that had been making you sick or ill are removed through your right foot, and are returned to the loving arms of the Earth Mother where they are made whole once again. When another will come to you seeking a healing from the healing rainbow, what had once been with you as incomplete will enter another as a completeness. And they, too, will benefit from the gifts of the healing rainbow, one that will allow them to continue their life path just as you will have assisted in doing.

"So it is that in the true path of all life, there is always exchanging from one so another may continue. And when exchanging is done in this way, all life benefits and will continue to grow," the Ancient One from the West position finished her speaking words.

"There is another step in this process that we are willing to share with you, my brothers," came the speaking words from the Elder in the South position.

"It is a step to be found from those you will assist in their own healing…those who come to you for a healing of those things that are not in balance with them, those same ones who have not yet come to know the path to healing themselves.

"When you will come on another who has not yet found their own path to travel, you will see one before you who is like a great water dam and they will be just about ready to explode from holding back so much within them.

"For them, this feeling of being filled with so much within themselves comes from having traveled so many seasons in this domain without ever looking within themselves to discover their own truth, to see who and what they are.

"Because they have not yet taken the time of doing this, or thought that they were not worthy of performing such a task for themselves. I will share with you that they are in truth so locked into their own sleep of illusion that they can only see things as they would wish for them to be.

"Truth does not hold a good face for them. Truth for them will only come wearing a great mask of fear. And they will not feel as if they are strong enough to look at it, to look at their own face of truth.

"As they come to travel many seasons in this domain of the Earth Mother they collect many lessons to themselves, lessons they are not willing to learn from.

"Remember, when a lesson is turned away from, it adds another layer of emotion over it. But this emotion is not to punish or bring harm to the one who is the owner of it. It is only trying to remind them to look at what they have agreed to learn from on this earth walk. It is only bringing them this reminder through the emotion and it will not go away until they will be willing to look at their own work, until they will be willing to learn from those things that had been placed before each of them…by themselves.

"It is from having so many lessons that have not been addressed that causes them to appear as this great dam of water which is about to break. When one of them comes to you in search of a healing, then it is good to remember what we have shared with you about them being like a great dam of water ready to explode.

"From the moment you agree to perform this healing over them, there will be a sudden rush of their waters of emotion flood into you, a sudden rush of these waters that have clouded their own vision for such a long time, and have manifested themselves into their illnesses and pains.

"Once you have come to the place of agreeing to assist them in their healing, there is an immediate transfer of those things that have been making them feel bad into you. But this is nothing they do on a conscious level. Rather, it is because there is more room within you than there is within them for these unresolved emotions, illnesses, and pains.

"If you will keep in the front of your thinking minds that all which is seen and unseen in this domain of the Earth Mother is living, then you will be able to follow these speaking words of sharing.

"When these unresolved emotions, illnesses, and pains see there is more room within you for them to reside, and you are close enough to them physically for them to go from one body to another, then they will make the transfer from their original host and into you.

"They will do this because there is no longer enough room for them in their original body part—the one who has been carrying them so long within them—and these emotions are looking for another place to reside.

"But their intention is to only remain with this new body for a short time. When they can once again see an opportunity of reattaching themselves to the one they first left, they will, and with even more emotion attached to them than before, even more emotion attached to them than there was when they left the first time. But I would have each of you hold in the front of your thinking minds, that none of this is done in a way of punishing. It is only being done in a way of drawing attention to the lesson that is behind all emotion.

"The longer lessons are not looked at and worked with by the one who they have been designed for, the more layers of emotion they will draw to themselves, until they can no longer be ignored.

"However, this is for another time and another place of sharing with all of you. For now, I will return to explaining the need for keeping each foot grounded to the Earth Mother by using the healing rainbow.

"When you will arrive at understanding who and what you are, and have come to know the way into the spirit of silence for yourself, there will be many great truths revealed to you, truths that will allow you to see how well balanced all life is within this domain that you are now traveling.

"However, until you will have found this balance within yourself, then all we are willing to share with you will seem new. It will seem like something that has not ever been known by any other before.

"But in truth, my brothers, there is nothing new that has been shared with any of you. The only reason it seems that way is because you have forgotten to remember what was with you all along.

"Now, when this one who is in need of healing comes to you, this healing that they too forgot they could do for themselves, then you will be caught up in a dilemma. And the dilemma is this: You will feel when these transfers of emotions of the illness and pain enter you. And you will feel their presence within you taking root.

"If you would allow them to remain with you, my brothers, then most assuredly they will make you ill as well. This will not be anything that is only in your minds, but in truth, you have taken over their sickness.

"However, this is a very usual path for these emotions to carry, so do not become angry at them. Do not hold a bad face for them because they are only following their path that will eventually allow them to become healed and returned to the one they have been reminding of their lesson.

"Rather than feeling anything for them that would add to their weight, simply allow them to return to the Earth Mother through your right foot. Give them a weight, once they have entered, so they will become heavier than you. And when they will have gained this weight, this weight they will freely take to themselves, they will be able to follow the path of returning to the Earth Mother. They will see this path that leads through your right foot to re-enter the Earth Mother where there will be found for each of them a healing.

"For you see, my brothers, when you will heal another or come to assist them in their healing, then it is not only the life that has spoken to you with its mouth that will need to be healed. There will always be the silent ones who are also in need of this healing, and they have become so used to not being listened to, they have found it necessary to attach themselves to another so they may continue on their path.

"But when they will see from you this understanding of how to give them weight and a path that will allow them to return to the Earth Mother for their healing, they will not remain with you. They are just as eager to be healed as the one who came to you is and they do not wish to spend any additional time within you that is longer than necessary.

"However, as it is with so much that is within this domain of the Earth Mother, there is very little that any of us are capable of doing on our own. This is where the left foot will come into this time of sharing.

"When the one who has come for this healing stands in front of you, make your grounding to the Earth Mother with both feet at that time.

"When you will do this, then you have allowed for the healing rainbow to travel freely within you. And once it has completed its path of entering you through the left foot and exiting from the right, it will continually reinforce all of these steps that I have been willing to share with you in letting those emotions of pain and illness leave you. And this healing rainbow will also cause you to feel the replacement for all of the trails these things that entered you left by. For they will be wiped clean within you and there will be no trace of anything having been within you at all.

"When the colors of the healing rainbow have come to reside completely within you, then you can touch this one who has come for healing. And as you touch them, all of those colors of healing will also enter them.

"For the rainbow is not limited to only one place, my brothers. All you will need to do is to look at any of them when they are in their places of reminding, those places that have been set for them in the daytime skies over all lands.

"As you look at one of these rainbow children, you see as you move, so will they. As you will remain still, so will they. This is not only for you, my brothers, for when you will see one rainbow and another will look to the same daytime sky and see another rainbow, even though both of you are in completely different places, you will both be looking at the same rainbow.

"This is the same for the healing of another, while this healing rainbow is living within you and you touch them. At first, they will see this rainbow that has come to reside within you for its path of healing. But soon, they will see it within them as well and this will begin their path to understanding that they may do their own healing.

"Keep these things in the front of your thinking minds, my brothers, in all efforts you will be willing to make with healing another.

"When you will do this, there will be a balance within each of you that will allow you to do what you have entered this domain to do."

When these speaking words of sharing had been completed, there was another silence that filled the air. But it was not a heavy silence that was with us this time; rather it was one that was filled with a lightness of its own. And with this lightness came a feeling of freedom for all of us.

As this silence was filling all of the places that were near us, I looked beyond where the Ancient Ones had been sitting and into the valley of the Old Ones, into this valley we had come through in order to reach this place of shelter, this place of shelter and sharing with the Ancient Ones of our people.

And as I looked into the distance at the valley below me, I could see that all of the children of the leaf were being bent and straightened by the passing of the Spirit Wind over them, that all of them seemed to be reaching up to the great sky nation and asking for the release of the blessings of the water spirit from the cloud people who had gathered over us on this day, for this release of their blessings of life-giving water to them so they would be allowed to continue on with their own life path.

Then raising my eyes to the cloud nation that was being held in position over us, I could see many flashes of lightning coming through them, through them and to me as they would find their own way back to the Earth Mother past the darkening gray skies above.

With each of their lighted paths finding its own way home, there was the constant sound of rolling thunder, this rolling of thunder that has always been associated with the calling voices of the thunder spirits who have announced the arrival for the Ancient Ones of our people.

All of this was filling my eyes and I could feel my balance being restored once again.

As my balance was restored, I felt a sense of belonging where I was, here where I had been chosen to once again share with the Ancient Ones and had allowed all five of us entry into this spirit vision they were presenting.

This…I knew…was good.

CHAPTER 19

❀

Proving To Another From What We See

My attention was called back by the speaking voice of the Elder who was wearing the color white from the North position of the medicine wheel.

"As each of you travel this earth walk, many will come to you who would have you prove things to them," he began. "Things that you hold the believing as well as the understanding within you to be truth.

"But for those who have not yet have found their way, they will not have any idea what truth is. They will only have the believing that if something cannot be proven, then it could not exist.

"However, this path of thinking does not hold truth to it. And if you will follow it, then you will end up as locked into the sleep of illusion as they are.

"When you will look closely at this need of proving things to another, you will find that it is filled with a great distortion. And this distortion will reside inside of the illusion that keeps one trapped.

"Think on this as you look to the within place of your spirit, this place where all that will ever be needed by you resides.

"When you look within yourselves, there will be a great truth for what I am now willing to share with you, a truth that will allow you to see how foolish it is to believe there is indeed a need by any to prove anything to another.

"When you enter this domain we have come to know as the Earth Mother, there are many things that will allow you to see and understand what has been placed before you. Some of them will have to be learned, while others will be from the way those small and unseen parts within you have aligned themselves.

"When you are still in your own mother's stomach, you are not yet independent of her. Many of those things that she will experience, you will as well.

"But when you have come to the place of being fully developed and can enter this domain as a separate entity from your mother, you begin your journey down the birth canal and for the first time, in this body part you have come to travel with, you become an individual.

"Once this first breath is drawn, there is the beginning of the end marked for all who travel an earth walk. For once this independent place among the rest of this domain has been felt by you, then you will begin the journey that does indeed end, this journey that is ended for the body part of yourself but not the spirit part, for this is a continual movement of growth and existence.

"Now let us say that there are ten parts to your personality in this earth walk. And where all of the members of the great star nation are at the time of your exit from your mother's belly, this will form four of them.

"This was determined by you, as you sat in council with the Earth Mother determining what you would need before you were allowed to enter her domain.

"For it is the personality that you will carry with you that will determine how you will come to learn. And it is this personality that you will carry with you that will determine how well you will see those things that are placed before you as lessons.

"Keep in the front of your thinking minds, my brothers, that no two life paths are identical—but many will be similar.

"The reason for no two being identical is because spirit has need of many lessons and all of them are extremely individual.

"What you have come to learn in this domain can only be understood by you. There will not ever be another who will have this understanding better than you; and in some cases, this understanding is not ever found by the one holding it. But there will be many who would have you believe they know your life path lessons better than you, and their numbers will be many, especially for those who are beginning to find their own path to travel.

"You will know them when it comes to be your time to cross the great spirit waters. You will know them because you will see them with the tears of sadness falling down their faces and their arms empty of any blessings they could have received during their time with the Earth Mother, for they spent all of their seasons telling others what to do rather than finding their own way.

"When you enter this domain as an independent life, then you will already have the gift from the great star nation who had determined four of the ten parts of your personality.

"The other six parts of this personality, or this other set of eyes, will allow you to see those lessons that come to you. They will be developed by you over time.

"These other six parts of your personality will come to you as you will continue to experience many of those lessons that you had come here to learn. And the result of those many experiences and lessons that have been offered to you...they will assist you in developing these other six parts of what can be called yourself and all that is with you.

"Now, my brothers, think of all those seasons of your own earth walks. And for all of those seasons that you have been given to travel in this domain, think of all that you have done, seen, and experienced.

"Now place all of those events in the front of your thinking minds and see if it would be possible for you to explain to another a complete reason for anything that you do.

"That is if one will ask you why you have done such and such a thing, try to tell them all of your reasons, all of those reasons that have given to you a need to do such and such a thing.

"I share with all of you that if you would attempt to do such a thing, there would no longer be any time left for you to do anything else. For all that is involved in doing only one thing is filled with such an enormous amount of learning from all of your experiences that it would be impossible for any of you to do. It would not be possible for anyone to do such a thing.

"And this is not only because of the time limitation, but there is so much of your learning and experience that do not have speaking words that can relate to it. And this is truth that I am now willing to share with all of you.

"So far, this has only applied to what you have done, and how it has affected how you do one small thing. And you can see how involved and complicated it becomes when you will try to associate speaking words for it.

"Look at the impossible task of sharing with another all of the reasons you have learned that have caused you to do any of the things that you do. You will see when you will answer them with a complete truth, that there are not enough speaking words to describe all of them, not enough speaking words that would even make sense to you if you were to try to answer a question such as why you do something the way you do it.

"But I will tell each of you, in truth, this explaining of why you do any of those things that you do is the easiest part for what I am willing to share with you, this reason that lies behind the illusion of feeling the need of proving anything to another.

"For when you will take this explanation of why you will do any of those things you do—when you will take this process just one more step, you will find that the face it holds to it is the one of how you will see what you see.

"In truth, my brothers, there will not ever be any two who will see the same thing in the same way. And this is not because what they are looking at is not being seen by them, or that they are not looking at the same thing. It all has to do with how they have come to learn and develop their own individual personalities from all that they have been through, from all that they have learned and understood. For this will determine how they will see what is before them.

"Look at this small warming fire that is between us, my brothers. Look at it and you will come to call it by the same name as I have.

"But calling the small warming fire by the same name is where this similarity of seeing ends.

"When you will look at this small child of the Earth Mother, one of you will see a life path being traveled by one of the small ones of the Earth Mother, another will see the collector of dreams, another will see one who will carry with its smoke a prayer of need, while another of you will see something that will burn and cause pain, and yet another will see it as something that will cook food, and another will see this small one as something that will end.

"I share with you that all of these seeing of this small warming fire are correct. But they are only correct to the one who holds them. For only you have been blessed with eyes that will or will not see, and what they will see will only be from what your needs are for this earth walk.

"However, when one will ask you to prove something to them, it will always be from something that you have seen. It will not be from any of those things that you do.

"And look at all of the different ways we have just shown to you that one can see this small warming fire. Look at the different ways of seeing what is before you.

"Then think on these differences for a while and think of how you would go about proving to another that you are seeing the correct thing.

"When one will attempt to do this, then they have indeed fallen into a great sleep of illusion. And the one who is trying to prove will have to give up much in order to get the other one to agree with them. When they will agree with them, then what has been accomplished is that you have given up much of the way you have first come to see this small warming fire. You have given up much of your own way of seeing in order to gain the approval or acceptance from this other one.

"Remember, my brothers, when something is seen by you the first time, this is when the chances of its correctness will be the greatest. If you will attempt to change or alter this seeing, you will increase your chances of losing it completely.

"And then the question comes up once again. What has been gained by trying to prove anything to another? And why will so many spend a great deal of their time in doing this?

"I tell you in truth, that it is a controlling over them that has made them do such a thing. A controlling that comes to many which says:

"IF IT IS NOT DONE MY WAY, IT IS NOT CORRECT.
IF YOU DO NOT SEE THE WAY I SEE, IT IS WRONG.
IF YOU DO NOT BELIEVE WHAT I BELIEVE, YOU ARE LOST…
LISTEN TO ME, I CAN PROVE IT TO YOU!"

"Let us take the example of two who are looking at this small warming fire that is before us. One of them will see it as a collector of dreams, a collector of dreams that when one will look deep into the middle of the flame, they will see those many things that they have a need to see. And with the passing of time, they will come to understand them.

"While the other one who is looking at this small warming fire sees it as something that will cook the food we eat, this food that is so necessary to continue our earth walk in this domain that is the Earth Mother...when the one who sees this small warming fire as something that should only be used for cooking food looks on the other one who sees the need for using this warming fire to look at only for dreaming, they will see this as a very foolish thing to do with the life of the warming fire.

"They will look on those efforts of the one who is recalling their dreams within the flame as one who is simply wasting time and mis-using the fire.

"And for the one who will look on the flame of the warming fire as the collector of dreams, when they will see this other one is only using it for cooking, they too will see a great waste of time in their doing such a thing.

"For to them, this is only wasting the flame of the warming fire for something other than what it should be used for. And they will look on the one who has only come to see it in their way as a cooking fire as one who is foolish and not yet awake to what should be.

"However, both of them are in truth not allowing the other to have the freedom to do those things that are needed by their spirit within. For if they would, then there would not be any need of seeing each other in the way they do now, in those ways that I am using for all of you in this explanation I have chosen to share.

"In their own way of trying to arrive at a place of peace, this peace that will only be for them and not the other, they will ask the other one to prove to them that what they are seeing from this small warming fire is truth. They will ask them to prove their truth to them. But they are really getting them to change the way they are see-ing truth without saying this.

"For when one will have become successful in proving what they are seeing to another is truth, there is a great trade. And this trade will be somewhere between what they see and what this other one will see.

"No matter how good their arguments are for what they have first come to see as their truth, unless the other one will have come to see the same thing, there will be no convincing. There will be no convincing because they do not possess the same eyes. For all of their experiences and personality have come to them for another purpose. And this has been the purpose of seeing those things that are needed by them to learn from.

"And this is not within the possession of the other one. For the other one will have done the same process, but only for what is needed by their spirit.

"Now while the two of them are together and looking at this small warming fire, they will begin their proving to the other one that they are right, that it is their way of seeing that is the correct way.

"And I share with all of you that when one will think in this way, they are truly lost within their own trap of illusion.

"For there is only your truth and there is only mine. When they are close to each other, though they will not ever be the same, we can travel next to each other. But when they are not close to the other's truth, then it is good to travel separately and make no further efforts of trying to change the other.

"When one will ask you to prove something, they are in truth asking you to change your way to theirs. For as you will attempt to prove something to another, you will be selling yourself off a piece at a time. And when the other one will argue with you for those things that you are trying to convince them of, they, too, will be selling themselves off to you a bit at a time.

"So when you both have come to agree on a proof of what it is that you are seeing, you have only come to the same place together. And this place is one that does not allow either of you to see any of those things that are needed by spirit within you.

"You have both arrived at a place where you are only taking another's word for what it is that you see. And you have done this in a way that will not be obvious to either of you until another confronts you and what you believe you see.

"When another will confront you and question this proof you have come to see, then this is all you will have to hold onto. For you will no longer have the ability of seeing those things for what they are. You only see them for what you have agreed with another for what they are.

"From this premise, there will not be anything that you can defend or explain to this other person who has come to question you. All you can do then is to get the other one, the one who has agreed with you before, and confront the new one who has questioned you with how you are now proclaiming to see this small warming fire.

"And let us say that this new person is one who only sees this small warming fire as something that will burn and cause pain to them. For to them, there is a great need by spirit within them to see in this way. And from this seeing, there will come to them many great lessons that are needed by them in order to advance themselves to the next higher place of understanding, to this next higher place of understanding for all that is with them and the life path they travel.

"When the one who once saw the small warming fire as the collector of dreams gathers with the one who once saw this small warming fire as something to cook food on, they feel as if they must be right because they have given each other a proof for what they see.

"But in truth, they no longer see. They have given this up in order to prove to each other that they are right. And in this proving to each other they are right, they have come to agree on something that is acceptable to both of them. But what is agreeable to both of them is no longer what they need; it is something vastly different. For they both have given up their ability of seeing.

"But when they will stand together to confront the one new person who has questioned them, they hold the believing that they are stronger, and more in number, than this one. And because there are two of them, then they must be right and this other one must be wrong.

"So they will not ask this other person, this one who sees this small warming fire as something that will burn and cause pain, to prove anything to them at all. They will simply tell them that to see in any other way than they do is just not right and unless they will see this as they see it, then they must surely be their enemy, an enemy that will destroy all of the good work they have done if they will not agree to see as they see.

"Now this new person has two choices. He can either give up on all that he holds to be true, or he can go away and be considered the enemy if he returns.

"If he chooses to remain with the other two, then he will become just as lost and blinded by this process called proving to another as the first two, and there will no longer be any room for the individual to grow and understand. There will only be the controlling of the group consensus they travel with.

"So you see, my brothers, when one will ask you to prove any of those things that you will see, they are asking you to close your eyes to your own truth. For it is not important what another will come to think of you. In truth, it is only important what you will come to think of yourself.

"Do not hold much weight to how others will come to see you. For all that will come to you in this life path will be what you will be in need of. And what will come to another, will be what is needed by them.

"To prove is to attempt to control another to your own way of thinking, my brothers. But when we understand, there will be less and less of a need to control anything...or anyone," came the end of his speaking words.

Once again there was a silence that fell over us, a silence that was allowing each of us to take all that was being shared to our within places, this place where our spirit resides.

Looking over the faces of the other four members of our council, I could see what had been shared was weighing heavy.

And from what I could feel from the within places of these Ancient Ones who had come to us for this time of sharing, I understood that there was much more to share, much more they had entered this domain of the Earth Mother to share with us, and I could feel it was going to be much stronger.

While I knew this to be good, I was wondering if I was truly ready for more at this time, for I could feel myself filling up very quickly from what had already been shared with us, and I knew there would soon be more...much more.

PART V

⚛

Season of the Long Shadow

CHAPTER 20

❁

The Long Journey

The silence was broken once again by the speaking words of the Elder from the East position, the one who had come to wear the yellow necklace.

"It would be less confusing for you if we were to sit in our places on the medicine wheel of life, my brothers. Let us take the time that is needed to allow us to sit in this manner around this small warming fire that has been built.

"Speaking Wind, you may take the place next to me," the Elder from the East position said. "And because there will be one additional place on this medicine wheel council, Cheeway can take the sitting place next to you."

As she spoke these things to me, I looked over to the place Cheeway was sitting. I could tell that this had set very will with him because he was wearing a broad smile that was covering his entire face.

"Grandfather, it would be good for you to join with me," came the speaking words from the Elder in the North position.

"Two Bears, it would be good for you to sit with us," came the speaking voice from the Elder in the South position.

"Night Hawk, since there is still much for you to think over, it would be good if you would join us," came the collective speaking voices of all three Elders in the West position.

Having followed all of their speaking words, and traveled to our places among the Old Ones, I was sitting and looking to the place where Night Hawk had been asked to sit.

As I looked over to him, his mystery was becoming much stronger within me. Why, I was wondering, was he told to sit in the west position of the medicine wheel, this place of the west is one of consideration for all that has come to you, the place where one will take those things that have been holding them to confusion and think them over?

And all of us, from what I could see and feel from the other members of our council were feeling just as lost as the other was. So why was it that these speaking words were given to Night Hawk and not the rest of us?

All of this was confusing for me and it was causing me to wonder about Night Hawk even more. Then just as these things had come to their place in the front of my thinking mind, I heard an Elder from the North position speak to me.

"Speaking Wind," she began. "I tell you in truth that all will be answered for you on this day of our sharing. For at its end, all answers will be provided. So for now, little one, I would remind you to sit and be with the present."

Looking back to where this Elder of the North was sitting, I nodded my head in a movement to let her know that I understood and would do as I had been asked.

"Good then, my brothers. We shall begin," she said. "We have all been on a long journey. And this journey has brought each of us together many times, for there are none among any who are, in truth, strangers.

"But let me take this time to share with you more of what this long journey is about. Understanding this is critical to seeing clearly what we have come to share with you on this day, this time that we have come to call The Season of the Long Shadow.

"From many of the oldest of old song legends that have been carried by your wise ones, there still remains a memory of this beginning of the journey, a memory of the beginning of this long journey that we have all been traveling.

"For everyone has been involved with it, only some have traveled it in ways that are different than yours, ways that no longer require them to travel an earth walk.

"But I tell you this in truth, they are still on the same journey as you. And this is how all of this began.

"In the beginning, Great Spirit saw there was only himself. As it was then, it is now; there is only The One.

"However, as he looked over Himself and saw all that was Him, there appeared to him a great need for additional understanding, a need for this understanding for all that was Him.

"He looked over all that was Him and said it was time to expand Himself, to expand all that was Him in order to give to all of us, who are of Him, more room to grow and understand from this process.

"As he looked over all he had expanded Himself into being, he said with a speaking voice that was heard by all life—by all that was Him, but no longer with Him, that this was the beginning of a great journey for all. That reason of this expanding of His existence was for them to learn and understand from, to learn as they would find themselves going further and further away from Him, but understand they would all return to the source of all creation at the end of the journey.

"There was a condition made on all of us. And the condition that was made was from the many requests of the ones who were feeling themselves being pulled away from the Creator.

"None of them wanted to feel this separateness from Creator and asked for this not to take place for them.

"But Great Spirit saw the need for doing this and told them that if they would return to him, from this journey with more understanding for all that is, there would not be a need to go through this expanded separation again.

"If all would return to Creator with more of an understanding for what they held with them before, with more appreciation for that which has always been with them, they would complete their circle of this great adventure, and for them, there would no longer be a need to repeat it.

"For the ones who would be willing to learn from their own lessons, as they would continue the great adventure, there would no longer be any separation from Great Spirit. They would be the ones who would have the ability of making this journey without separation. All of this would depend on what was needed by their spirit within and would determine the lessons needed to bring them to this place of understanding themselves and all that is with them.

"However, there are many pieces of Creator that must be understood, my brothers, pieces that will seem as far from you as the great star nation, but they are not far at all. For this distance that you will perceive is only illusion. And this has come to you from having lost your ability of seeing clearly with the eyes of spirit.

"In truth, there is no thing that is far from you. And in truth, there is no separation from Creator. For he is with you and you are with him in all things you will do, and in all places you will travel.

"But keep in the front of your thinking mind that the further away he will seem—the further away all things you would wish to be with will seem as well—then the further into your sleep of illusion you will have traveled. This is only a sign that has been left for you to see how much work still needs to be done by you.

"Now, as this expansion of Creator has taken place, there were created many places where learning would be offered, places where many went in order to learn their own lessons that would bring them out of their sleep of illusion and allow them to see the path that had been left for them to follow, this path that would lead them back home…this home they long for.

"Now in each of the places that had been made available to the two-legs, we have come to call a domain. And the memory of separation was left for those who would leave their path and fall into the illusion, this illusion that would allow them to know separateness.

"This was created so all would have with them this freedom of choosing…this freedom of choice that has always been with us.

"When these adventures will begin in a domain, there is nothing that is placed in their way, for they will have with them the ability of speaking and understanding from all life that is around them.

"This lack of separation had been left with them so they could remember how life was when they were one with Creator, of those times that were once with them before Great Mystery saw a need to acquire understanding by all of us.

"However, in each of these places where the two-legs had come to travel, there was always the same result. This result was what caused all to feel even stronger this separation that existed among them.

"It was their believing in false pride that would bring each of them this same learning lesson over and over again. For when all of the two-legs would stand together and see that they were a part of all that was, this would give them a feeling that they were no better or different from all other life that was around them.

"And in truth, my brothers, I tell you what they were seeing was truth. For there are none higher and none lower than yourself. And this is not only concerning the two-legs in this domain of the Earth Mother, but all of her children as well. This applies to all life that is, and as we have been willing to share with you, there is nothing that can be seen by you that does not have life within it. And it is from the same source as each of you.

"When the two-legs would get together and see this Oneness that was over all life, they began to ask questions among themselves, questions that would bring them to a great place of learning, but this place of learning would not be seen by any of them. For they were looking at this through eyes that were filled with a false pride, and these eyes can see nothing of truth.

"They wanted to see themselves as different from all of the other creations that had been set around them. They saw they had hands that could do work and could speak their thoughts. And they believed these abilities should set them apart from all other life.

"These differences that they first came to see among themselves certainly made them much different than any of these other creations that were now sharing in all things they would think, do, and say.

"And they wanted to be different from all of them. In the front of their thinking minds, they wanted to be in a higher place than all other creations that had been set into this same great journey by Creator as they had.

"They wanted to be different from all other life so they asked Great Spirit to give them a different language, one that would not be the same as all other life spoke.

"And as the song legends of the wise ones have shared with you, there is not ever a prayer that is not answered by Creator, and they are all answered in less time than it takes to blink your eyes.

"However, there are many prayers that are asked which are not understood. And for those things that are not understood, one will not have the ability of seeing the answers when they will come to them.

"And this prayer was not understood, but the answer was seen by all of the two-legs. For this answer came over all of them in a very quick and powerful manner, one that is still carried in many of the song legends of all races and all people.

"For when Great Spirit heard this prayer of the two-legs, he granted them what they had asked and they were given instructions for what they would be required to do. There was not one ear that did not hear this calling voice of Creator when it came to them.

"He told all of them to form into four groups. The first group he told was to face the east and when they did, they all came to wear the color yellow over their skins. As their skins were changed from what they once were, they also received a new language.

"The next group he told to face the south. And when they did this, they wore the color of red over their skins. And when this color of red came over all of them, they, too, received a new language to speak.

"The third group, he told to face west. And when they did this, all of their skin was turned black and they, too, learned a new language.

"And finally, the last group was told to turn to the direction of the north. And when they did this, their color of skin was turned into white and they, too, learned a new language.

"Then while all of the groups of the two-legs were looking over themselves and the great changes that had come to all of them, they turned to the others to find out what they felt about such things that had come to them.

"However, when they tried to speak to the other members, they found they no longer had this ability. For none of the members of the four new groups, or races of the two-legs could speak to each other.

"It was at this point when some of the members of each of the four races tried to ask many of the children of the Earth Mother what they thought of these changes that had come to be with them.

"But when they would try to speak to the children of the Earth Mother, they found this ability was no longer with them either. For they were only able to speak among the other two-legs that were in their race. For none who was on the outside of their race could understand them.

"When they finally arrived at understanding what impact these requests of theirs had brought them, there was a great silence among all of the two-legs, all of the two-legs who were no longer of the one, but were now separated into four separate races and with a language that could only be understood by their own kind, a language that did not allow them to speak to the other races nor to the children of the Earth Mother.

"And as they were sitting in this great silence, each of them had come to understand what had been asked for had been given to them. Now, they were different from all life that was around them, but the cost was great, greater than they had ever come to imagine.

"So, one by one, each of the four races sent another prayer to Great Spirit, a prayer that was requesting assistance in being allowed to return to where they had once been, this place where there was no separation among any of life.

"First came the request of the ones in the east, the wearers of the yellow skin. Secondly came the request of the ones in the south, the wearers of the red skin. Next came the request of the ones in the west, the wearers of the black skin. And finally, came the request of the ones in the north, the ones of the white skin.

"When the last of the races had completed their request of being allowed to return to where they had once been, there was a great cry from all of the nations of the Earth Mother. It was a cry that shared with the two-legs what their actions had brought them, that instead of listening to the voice of their own spirit, they chose to follow the lead of the group, this group that was being fed by emotion and the falseness of pride for wanting to be something they were not.

"And what they were feeling now, this being separated from all life around them, as well as from the other two-legs, was the price for what they had asked for, this price of seeing how poorly any decision made by a group of others can be.

"However, through all of these speaking thoughts that were being shared with the two-legs, there was a willingness of allowing these requests to be heard by Creator, so that he could make a decision on allowing the two-legs to return to where they had once been.

"As this was done, my brothers, it was done in such a way that has allowed all of the four races to have an understanding for those things that would have come to them, but in a different way than was expected.

"Keep in the front of your thinking minds that this result is always the same. The only thing that will change will be the path one will travel to get there. And the more variation there is to the path traveled, the more there is to learn from it.

"So when you will see one who holds to them what appears to you as a very difficult path, do not try to help them. For they have entered this domain to learn from this, and I will share with you that while they are given their freedom of learning from what is being offered to them, there will, in truth, be growth for them.

"This is how we have come to look on the path the two-legs have taken in this domain of the Earth Mother.

"We have seen how much difficulty there has been for all of them, and how much suffering and pain they all have had to endure. But I will share this with you now, had they not gone through so much, there would not have been the blessings that have been offered to them, those blessings that are soon to be covered in the light of understanding for all to see. And it will be this light of understanding that will make all of these truths visible to everyone.

"So when Creator heard all of the requests by the two-legs for a path to return, a path that would allow them to return to the place they had all once been, he saw this request of theirs with a good face.

"It was a face of understanding that they were willing to work through their own lessons now. They would be willing to do this because they still remembered what was on the other side of this great confusion they were all feeling, this great separation that had come over all of them by having many different colored skins and languages to speak.

"Great Spirit told all of the two-legs that they could have a path to travel, one that would allow those who would wish to return to this place of being, One within the One. But there would be many lessons that would have to be worked through in order to complete this path.

"He told each of the four races they would be given ten thousand years to cleanse themselves and each of these ten thousand year periods would be called a world. When one race would be in the process of this cleansing, the other three races would have to stand aside.

"For while each of the races would go through this cleansing, there could not be any interference by another race. And since it was so important for each of the races to begin with the same advantages as well as disadvantages, when one race would complete the world they have been given, there would be a great earth cleansing that would take place, one that would not only clean all of the memories of the things that had been done by the previous race, but one that would completely erase from everyone's thinking mind all that had once been.

"Each of the races were told they would only hold onto a faint memory of what it was to be One within the One. But anything more would not be allowed. For if it were, there would not be the same starting place for the race that would come next.

"Each of the four races, hearing those things that had come to them from Creator, spoke among themselves. They did not fully understand the depth of what was being offered, but they did have the knowing that this was the only path available for them to return to where they had once been, this place where all was One within the One and there was no separateness.

"So they agreed to these four worlds of cleansing and hearing this agreement of theirs, Great Spirit told them of one last condition, this condition that would arrive when the last of the four races had completed their cleansing, there would only be a short time remaining before the Earth Mother would begin her last cleansing as well.

"And when this time would be over, there would be such a great change come over all of the Earth Mother, there would be none who could ever recognize any of her places again. But before this great change would take place, there would be set aside a time for all of the two-legs from all races to make their final decisions.

"And this final decision that would be made by them would determine if they would remain in this domain and continue with the Earth Mother in her fifth world of peace and light; or, if they would go to another place, one where they would have all of this to do over again.

"This time that has been set aside has come to be called The Season of the Long Shadow, my brothers. And its presence is soon to be felt among all of you and when it arrives, there will be less and less of what had been separated before remain in the same way.

"The last race, the white race, will soon finish the time that had been given to it for its cleansing. When this time will come, we will enter this Season of the Long Shadow. And I tell all of you this in truth, that there will be no warning for its coming. All that will be known is one day you will awaken from traveling with the dreamers and it will be here.

"This is what we have come to share with you on this day, my brothers. We have come to share with all of you that this time is close at hand and we have come to share with you those things that will be needed by all of the two-legs who will be traveling within this domain, those things they will need in order for them to understand what is being offered to them.

"For if this understanding is not shared, there will only be fear and panic for what is soon to come. And when one will wear this face over them, their chance for growth is lost. And for them, all will seem to have been for nothing," came the end of her speaking words.

For the next few moments, the Elder from the North position silently looked into each of our council of five.

I knew there was something she was looking for, but what...I could not tell.

"Speaking Wind," she began once again. "It will be for you to carry this understanding with you and into The Season of the Long Shadow. From what I have seen within you, you are to be the one."

Looking back to this place where the Elder of the North was sitting, I nodded my head in a motion that would share with her that I agreed with what had been shared with me.

However, the face that I had been wearing at the time was also filled with running water from my eyes. And they had made a great wet spot on the front of my walking blanket.

"Does this bring you a great sadness, Little One?" came the speaking words of Grandfather.

"No, Grandfather, for this task I feel very honored and accept it with a good face," was my return.

"Then what is it that is bringing to you such a face, Speaking Wind?" Grandfather replied.

"It is what I can see, or rather feel from the Earth Mother, Grandfather. I feel as if I am walking with one of the dying ones and this is bringing to me a sad face to wear," was my return.

"Remember, Little Brother," came the comforting voice from the Elder of the North. "Remember that the Earth Mother cannot put on her new face until she has taken off the old one first. And this is what is soon to take place for all who will be here to see this great event. For it is indeed great, Speaking Wind, greater than any can imagine.

"She is going to be made new once again, and all of the darkness that has covered her domain will no longer be with her. But our time of sharing among you is not much longer, and there is much to do."

PART VI

❀

13 Faces for The Season of the Long Shadow

CHAPTER 21

❀

Entry of the Season of the Long Shadow

"Listen well to these things we have to share with you, my brothers," came the first of the speaking words from the Elder of the East.

"What we have come into this domain to share with you will allow understanding to flow into the within places of all two-legs when the time is right, when this time is right and The Season of the Long Shadow has been born.

"For unless all of the two-legs would come to hear these things we are now willing to share with you, they will only see the face of fear come to them from all of the events that are soon to come to them.

"As we have been willing to share, there is no truth to any face of fear carried to anyone. For in truth, there is no fear that exists within this domain that is the Earth Mother.

"There is, however, that which one does not understand from themselves. And this is what they perceive as their fear.

"When one will allow themselves to see the work they have entered this domain to perform and learn from, then they will have lifted at least a portion of the veil of illusion from themselves.

"For truth is in seeing ourselves, my brothers. And this is truth we are now willing to share with you.

"These things that are soon to be with this domain of the Earth Mother will truly be bad for the ones who have not yet attained the needed understanding of themselves and all that is with them.

"However, for the ones who will have at least begun their own path to understanding spirit that is within them, they will see all that we are about to share with you as something that is good, as something that is good because it is.

"What we bring to you now is what we have come to call the Thirteen Faces for the Season of the Long Shadow. And these thirteen faces are things that will surely come to all who will remain here, for there will be none who will be missed.

"Remember what we are about to share with you has always been. But it is in this time of the Long Shadow that all of the two-legs will be awakened to see that which is. For that which is now has always been with you, but it has just not been seen because of the great illusion that has formed itself over so many.

"For all that we are willing to share with you—these things that are soon to take place for all who are here—in truth, they have always been with you, but most have forgotten how to see what it was they had all been traveling with.

"Speaking Wind," the Elder of the East position continued. "You will be the one who will be told when this Season of the Long Shadow will have its beginning. And we will come to you once again to share this knowing with you.

"You will see, once this time has been allowed its birth and place in this domain, that there will be none who will have any awareness for this time, none but those who have already been willing to travel and find their own path of the spirit.

"They will be the only ones who will have come to know of something that has changed. But even they will not hold to them a complete understanding for what it is.

"However, from the time of entering The Season of the Long Shadow, all will see great changes come over them. No one will be missed.

"For them, this will begin their time of questioning. They will question all that they are. They will look at those places where they have spent many of their seasons and feel they no longer fit. They will look at the ones who are around them, and they will see them as someone else. But in truth, it is they who have changed

"And without an understanding for what has caused this change to come into them, they will not know what to do.

"At first, they will attempt to use all of those things that have been given to them as truth, those things that so many others have been telling them to do if they would want to be good and right through the eyes of the world.

"But when they will come to lean on them, they find themselves falling through them. They will fall through them because there is nothing there that holds any weight of truth to support them.

"This will make them feel more lost for all they had been doing through their life path. For they had been doing these things as if they were building up a bank account for themselves that would bring them comfort in the bad times. But when this time we speak of arrives with them, they quickly discover they do not have anything with them, at all.

"This will cause them to feel alone and lost in the darkest of nights. But in truth, they are only becoming aware of how very little they had with them all the time. But this gives each of them a very sudden awakening, this awakening that will cause many who had always been calm to be angry. But they will not know what to be angry about. For they will not have the understanding for what is being presented to them, and this covers them with a great fear of their unknown.

"In their past seasons, they could always go to another to speak with. And this would bring them a little comfort for living with what had come to them.

"But when The Season of the Long Shadow comes to them, they will find that even when they are with a group of others they have been traveling with for many seasons of their life path, they will find themselves completely alone and have no one who they can share with, for there will be none who will understand them.

"All of these things will come to the two-legs very quickly as this time begins. There will not be a warning period for them to get used to such things.

"And I will tell you this in truth, the more they are lost within their sleep of illusion, the more difficulty they will find in achieving an understanding for what is taking place for them. And the further they will be locked into their own illusion, the more alone they will feel.

"It will be the ones who had always come to depend on the direction from others who will feel this the most, my brothers, they will be the ones who will be the most in need of what we have come to share with you on this day.

"The ones who have always followed in the words of others—those who would tell them what is right and wrong for them to do—it will be they who will suffer greatly during this time.

"They will suffer the greatest because there will not be anyone who they can turn to. There will only be the aloneness for them, and it will cover all that is them.

"For them, without having another to listen to, someone to tell them what is taking place with them, this is very painful. It is very painful for them because this will be the first time in their earth walk that they will have to depend on themselves for their own answers. And this has awakened a frightening thing for them to look at.

"But this comes from another truth that has been stripped away, another truth that has been stripped out from another message that had been left with them.

"Many of the two-legs have been told that if they were to look on their own face of truth, they would surely go crazy. For if they were to look on this face of their own inner self, it would surely be too much for them to handle and they would no longer be able to maintain their own sanity.

"But this is not truth, my brothers, and the ones who have done such a thing, the ones who have stripped away this great truth of finding ones own self, they have done this in order to put their own fear within this teaching.

"They have placed their own fear within this teaching so they could hold the illusion of controlling many and have them do things in their own way.

"When you will come across many of the two-legs who will be in great need of these teachings and wisdom, remind them that this teaching they have been holding onto is not one of truth.

"Share this with them, my brothers. Remind each of them how they will arrive with themselves after they have spent the nighttime with the dreamers. And remind them that this process follows them for each day they are within this domain of the Earth Mother.

"Remind them that they do see their own face of truth each time they look into the mirror and comb their hair, put on their makeup, shave, or the many other things they will do before journeying out of their own home.

"Tell them that if they will run out of their own homes each morning they see their face in the mirror, run out of their homes and into the streets screaming because what they had seen caused them so much fear, then for them, there would truly be a great fear in seeing their own face of truth. For them, it would most surely be a face of fear that would make them insane.

"However, if they can look into the mirror and do those many things that are required by themselves each morning and not become frightened by what they see, share with them that looking into their within place to look on their own face of truth will be no different.

"For what they will see in their own reflection in the mirror will be the doorway to their own within place, this place where their spirit resides. And when they enter this doorway, they will find their own face of truth waiting for them, this face of truth that will share with them who and what they are in truth.

"Give each of those who would come to you at this time an exercise, one that will assist them greatly when it is time for the arrival of The Season of the Long Shadow.

"Have them look into their mirror and begin speaking with themselves. Speak <u>with</u> themselves and not <u>to</u> themselves.

"When they will ask themselves a question, have them answer it as well. In this way, they are breaking away from many of their old habits; those same habits that have kept them locked in their sleep of illusion.

"When they will be able to hold a meaningful conversation with themselves, they will be able to hold a meaningful conversation with another.

"When they will find that part of themselves they truly care for, they will also be able to see a part of another they will truly be able to care for as well.

"When they will find they have a friend within themselves, they will have the ability of finding a friend in another.

"All of this is sharing with the two-legs that there is more to themselves than they have been led to believe…that there are more wonders that are within them than they have ever come to think of and all of them are from, because, and for themselves.

"You see, my brothers, when one believes they do not have anything to offer another, that is when they sell parts of themselves to another, just so they will be allowed to be near them.

"However, when one will understand that they have much to offer, they will not be as likely to sell off any of their parts of themselves. For they will have arrived at the place of seeing that if another does not like them, then they will be better off in walking away and looking for someone who does.

"For they hold themselves in a place of seeing, this place of having gotten acquainted with themselves in the mirror. And it has been through this process that they have come to know they hold much to offer but only to the ones who can see it.

"For the ones who cannot see this, then it is not time for their paths to be close anyway.

"All of this has been shared with each of you so there will be a better understanding of what will be needed during this time we are speaking to you of, this time of The Season of the Long Shadow.

"When it is time and this final season will be allowed entry into this domain, there will be great need for those things of the individual. For it will only be the individual in this domain who will truly understand what is taking place—not any group.

"Only the ones who have found their own individuality will be able to see through the illusion that will be presented to all when all of these events will come to life.

"It will be the illusion that will bring the sleeping ones their greatest fear. But for those who have come to know themselves and have seen their own face of truth, they will be the ones who will have the ability of seeing through the illusion of fear and onto the face of truth.

"This face of truth is saying that it is simply time to move on. It is time to move on because the time of their past is done and it must be dropped away from all things.

"Unless the two-legs have come to see their own individuality, my brothers, we fear they will not see the benefit for all that is soon to be offered to them.

"Unless they have come to see that they can stand strong alone, they will be buried in their own fear. And with fear, my brothers, there can be no growth.

"I share with you that in those times that are soon to be with them, there will be many who will still hold some to be in a place higher than they. And there will be those who will still hold others to be in a place that is lower.

"However, if they continue to do this, they will be the ones who will be causing great shadows to fall over much of these lands. And where there is shadow, there is no light. And where there is no light, there is no growth.

"So when this time comes over them and they feel their aloneness, they will feel as if a terrible punishment has come to them, one that has taken them completely away from all that has ever felt familiar to them. And they will feel this loss as something great.

"But they will only be feeling themselves and all they have not yet come to understand that is of themselves.

"You see, my brothers, when one will enter this domain of the Earth Mother, they will have a continual need from a place they perceive very deep within them. It is a feeling that there is something more for them to do, something, which is very important, they should be doing, but they cannot see it.

"They cannot see this because all of those seasons they have been given to travel their life path, they have been looking to the outside of themselves for those answers, looking to other places, things, and people who might hold answers for them.

"And in the beginning, they believe this feeling is theirs and theirs alone. And when they will first attempt to find it, they do so in all of the ways that are on the outside of themselves.

"They will try to amass great numbers of things to them, such as the riches of this domain, or masses that will be in the number of others who will be willing to listen to them or to follow them.

"But when they have arrived at the place they thought this answer for them was, they are very disappointed when they find nothing there. All they have found in this journey was an empty place where the road ends.

"So they will continue to search to the outside of themselves, and the more they will search in this way, the more lost they become.

"Then there will come an answer to them and it is an answer they have been asking for.

"You see, my brothers, even while these two-legs were looking to those things that were on the outside of themselves for their answers, even then they were asking for assistance from the ones who were still invisible to them, the ones they would spend so much of their time trying to convince others that they did not exist.

"However, when they run out of things to satisfy themselves with, they too will turn to those places they told others did not exist, those places where they will continue to pray or ask assistance for themselves.

"You will see many of them in the seasons that are yet to be born to each of you. And you will see them wondering why so much despair has come to them, why they feel so alone and lost, and why they no longer can make any sense out of what is taking place around them.

"But they will still not see what has come over them. For that which has come to show themselves as solitude and loneliness are just what they have been asking for.

"When you will see one of these two-legs come to you and ask what they have done to bring them so much pain and torture—or when they ask you why they are feeling so lonely and sad for all things, then it would be good to share with them that what is now around them is what they have been asking assistance for. And they should not curse it, but they should thank it for what it has been willing to share with them.

"Explain to them, my brothers, that for all of the seasons of their life path they have been looking to others for advice on what they should do, for what they should do with the life that has come to them.

"Have them remember that they have been asking assistance for this feeling they have been holding and growing within themselves for all of those seasons, the feeling of having something that is very important for them to do.

"Then share with them that they have been looking for this answer in the places that were on the outside of them for so long, that this is the only place that seems real to them anymore, and now, they only believe in those things that they can touch or see as being real.

"But they have truly forgotten their way, this way that will allow them to come home once again.

"All they are feeling and going through, all of these feelings of being completely lost and filled with sadness and despair, has come to them holding before it one of the most beautiful blessings that can ever be presented to another, a blessing that is far beyond any of the speaking words one can know.

"For what has been shared with them is the way to their within place, this place where their spirit resides. And when they come to travel this seemingly lonely path—and understand where they are going—it will be then, that they will no longer see what appears to be isolation and despair, but they will see wonderful beginnings take place all around them.

"You see, my brothers, all that has taken place for them is that their eyes have been taken off from where they had been for a long time. Their eyes have been removed from looking at those things that were on the outside of themselves and were shown how to look within.

"But while in this process of remembering how to look within, they feel as if all they had was taken away, that they have been isolated from all of their friends because they do not feel as if they can speak to them any longer. And they feel as if they no longer belong to those places they have been for most of their lives.

"Share with them that they are now looking at themselves through a new set of eyes, that are showing them this path they have been asking for. This is a path that will allow them to begin their greatest adventure of all…the adventure of finding their own path of spirit…and their way back home.

"However, since all of the references they held in the past were only for those things that were on the outside of themselves, and the references that they are now in need of is from within, there will be a time of great confusion and loneliness felt by them.

"But this is only because they are not used to traveling within themselves and there is nothing that looks familiar to them.

"So as they follow this path of their within place, remind them that these feelings of loneliness and despair will soon pass. And as they do, they will come to understand themselves completely once again.

"It does not take long, but when one is in the middle of this, they will feel as if it is taking an eternity.

"This is why we have chosen to share this with all of you now and in this place. It is to assist those who will come to you in need of this information. This wisdom and this knowledge that so many have forgotten to remember.

"Now these events I have been willing to share with all of you—they have always been with the ones who have been willing to do their own work, this work that is needed in order to find the path of oneself.

"But there is soon to be another event that will enter this domain of the Earth Mother. And this event will accelerate all of that which I have just shared with you.

"For it is during The Season of the Long Shadow that what would have taken years to come about will take place in a matter of months. And this will weigh heavily on all who are within this domain during this time.

"Think of it in this way. When the ending of a day is near, there are long shadows that fall from all of the tree nation's people. And you will have the knowing that this is the marking of the end of another day, the marking of the end of one day and the entering into night.

"But this does not bring fear to you because you also hold the understanding that once the nighttime has finished, there will be another day.

"However during this Season of the Long Shadow, there will not be the understanding for many of the two-legs that will relate this to them. There will not be the recognition because of all the changes that will be around them. And those changes will be accelerated for them each day that will pass.

"They will see this Season of the Long Shadow as something that is marking the end of time as they have come to know it. And for this, they are correct. For the time they have come to know, is soon to end.

"But it does not end for them in any way that is final, for this thinking does not hold any face of truth to it. It only holds a face of fear, and we have shared with you that fear is from the illusion, the illusion that would allow many to be controlled by a few.

"So it is for the reason of understanding that we have come among you at this time. It is to share with all of you what is to come and the path that will allow one to understand from it.

"It is our desire to have as many of the two-legs understand this time rather than to run and hide from it. For to run and hide from what is about to enter will not be possible.

"Now if all of you are ready, we will share with you what lies ahead...for all!

"Do not be frightened, my brothers, we have come to share with you—not to force on you a face of fear.

"We will begin with the thirteen faces for The Season of the Long Shadow, then we will move on to more."

As these speaking words from the Elder faded away, I could feel the heaviness that was filling all five members of our council.

From the looks on their faces, I could see each of us was having to make additional efforts to breathe, for there was already such a heaviness around us that even the air was taking on more weight to itself than it was used to.

Then, looking to the place of the Elder of the North, I saw him wave his right hand horizontally. Then the heaviness was gone.

"Now we may continue, my brothers," came his speaking words to all of us. And the male Elder of the East looked over all of us, holding a warm smile over himself, then continued.

❀

CHAPTER 22

First Face

From the Elder of the East—
The Waiting Place Blends With The
Domain Of The Earth Mother

As the male Elder from the East looked over all of us, there was a spark in both of his eyes, a spark that somehow reminded me of the great star nation.

"What you see, Speaking Wind, is a part of what we share with all of you on this day. But this is not yet the time, my brother," came the beginning of his speaking words.

"I would wish to share with all of you what this first face for The Season of the Long Shadow holds to itself. This will allow each of you to be more prepared for what is yet to take place.

"However, I would remind all of you that unless any of the two-legs will come to understand themselves and all things that are with them, they will only see what we are willing to share as something that will bring to them a great fear that they will want to run and hide from.

"But for the ones who will begin the journey to their within place, they will see what is to be presented as a blessing, a blessing that will allow each of them to advance their spirit to the next higher place of understanding.

"But I would wish for each of you to remember that when they begin this great adventure to their within place, this journey that will allow them to see their own face of truth as well as the face of their own spirit, they will first feel the loneliness come to them.

"And if there are none around them who will be willing to share why this feeling has come, I would say that they will not remain long on their own path, that will allow them to enter their within place and eventually find their own path of spirit to travel.

"They will not remain on this path long because these feelings of loneliness and sadness can appear to them as a warning for what they are doing.

"When they listen to the words of others that tell them they are no longer the same person they remember, that they are no longer the seemingly happy ones they used to see, they will begin to wonder, and feel confused.

"They will wonder if what these feelings and words from the others are telling them is that they have taken another wrong path, one that is not leading them to any place that is good.

"However, when there is one who is near them and reminds them that these feelings of aloneness and sadness are coming to them because of this newness of their path—that they are only being felt by them because this is a journey that has not been traveled by them, and all of it feels new and unreliable—then they will understand what has taken place for them.

"They will understand that what they are now feeling is because they have nothing from their past experiences to relate it to. And without having anything to relate to, they are feeling lost and alone.

"Then, they will understand why the others who have always been near them will address them in such a way. And they will gain understanding for what they will miss if they choose to turn back to the path they had been traveling for all of their seasons in this domain of the Earth Mother.

"You see, my brothers, when one is asleep within their own illusion, then anything they cannot see or understand becomes their enemy.

"However, when one will wake from their sleep of illusion and look at this new face of theirs for what it is, to see that these first encounters of feeling alone and sad are coming to them because they do not have anything to relate it to, then they will hold themselves strong and find the patience to continue traveling on this path to their within place.

"As they travel on this path, they are not as likely to fear what they do not understand...if it will have been presented to them from the beginning of their spirit journey, by one who also understood this process and shared its meaning with them.

"This is the reason for the first lesson, my brothers. It is to share with you that what you do not yet understand will be revealed in its own time. But until it does, and if one will fear it, there will not be any learning for what it is. And without this learning, there will be no understanding, and many will continue to run and hide—from themselves and from all they do not understand.

"Without understanding, there will only be a great face of fear for this first face of The Season of the Long Shadow, and it will be worn by those who remain lost within their own illusion.

"For without understanding themselves, and all that is around them, there cannot be anything but fear for them to see.

"You see, this first face of The Season of the Long Shadow will be one that will mark the beginning of the end, the beginning of the end for the great illusion that has kept so many trapped for many generations.

"Throughout all of the seasons each race has been given to cleanse itself, there has always been a choice offered to all. A free choice to make up their own minds if they would wish to perform the work required by each of them to break out of this sleep of illusion, or to remain trapped within it.

"However, what this Season of the Long Shadow brings with it is the end of this time for all of the two-legs, the end of their time for making their choice of remaining within this illusion or making the efforts required by them to break out of the great illusion...to break out of the great illusion and see that which is...and this includes themselves as well.

"For when it is time, and The Season of the Long Shadow has been born into this domain of the Earth Mother, there will be many who will feel its effects immediately, while others of the two-legs will react to this birth more slowly.

"However, all will begin to see something. And what they will partially see is the first face of this time we speak to you of.

"For within this first face is this, my brothers:

"The waiting place will blend into the domain that all of you are currently traveling in. And when this has happened, there will no longer be any separation for the ones who have passed on before the ones who will be traveling their earth walk.

"The two places become one and all who have passed on before will return. They will return and walk among all of their relations.

"Without the needed levels of understanding by the two-legs, they will not have the strength within to look on this face—this first of thirteen faces that will come to them.

"Keep in the front of your thinking minds, my brothers, the reason we have called this place where one will go after they have completed their life path the waiting place—is because this is where all are waiting, waiting for the time when the new earth will be prepared for them, or the time when the fifth world of this domain will be completed.

"But for whatever their reason, all are waiting for a home to travel to. It is at the middle of this time we have come to share with you that this will take place for all to see.

"From the time when The Season of the Long Shadow will begin, and the calendars will end is in 2011. If you will divide this time by two, you will have the year that this will occur.

"But this does not apply to when this time will begin, for there is no advance clue to any when The Season of the Long Shadow will be allowed entry into this domain.

"However," the Elder of the East paused to look deep into my eyes...then continued. "However, Speaking Wind, you will know when this time has begun. You will have this knowing because we will come for you. We will come to you and tell you that it has begun.

"When you will hear and see us, you will know that these things that we are here to share with all of you today. You will know that they have begun. And this I tell you is with the face of truth.

"Now, when this time has come to enter the domain of the Earth Mother, there will be many who will not understand it. This will also be the time when you, Speaking Wind, will begin to write many of these things we have been willing to share with you into books.

"These books will be necessary in this time because there will be many two-legs who will look on this time and see fear. They will hear those things that will once again be born into this domain, those things that will be a path of understanding to follow, and they will see it as an enemy that will threaten to take away their control over others.

"Even though this perceived feeling of being in control by them is another illusion, they will fear it. But they will also fear those things that will be released into this domain...those things that are truth and presented to all in a very simple way that will cause them to see through many of the illusions that had been held over them and have kept them trapped.

"So these writing books that you will offer to all who will be within this domain, Speaking Wind, they will offer them a powerful tool to be used against their own illusion. They will be presented to them as something they may always keep with them. When times come to them they do not understand, they will have the books to read. Our speaking words that you will enter into these books will assist them greatly when it is their time of need.

"And, little brother, it is much more difficult to change something that has been written than it is to change something that is only spoken.

"This is the reason for you to write these books, but that is not all you will have to do. For you will also be required to travel a walk of faith. And this walk of faith will require you to depend on the ones who are sitting with you now.

"For what we will remind you to write in these books, there will be many who would not wish to have this known, many who would not wish to have this understanding enter this domain of the Earth Mother.

"For as we have shared with you, they will perceive this as a threat to all of those things they believe they control.

"So you must not only write these books, Speaking Wind, but in the beginning, you must have them produced as well. That is until they have gained enough strength to stand on their own. Once this will take place, there will be many who will come to assist you.

"But this journey, this walk of faith for your path, will seem to be very long when you begin. But this time is not long, little brother. It is not long, and for this you must hold the believing in, for what we say to you is truth.

"When the first face for The Season of the Long Shadow has begun, there will be many two-legs who will be sitting alone in their homes and see another, or others, standing in the same room with them, but when they turn their heads to look at them, there will be no one there.

"There will be times when the two-legs will be looking at something in their hands and will see from the top part of their vision someone running through their own homes. But when they will lift their heads to see who or what this is, there will be no one there.

"There will be many times when the two-legs will be lying in their bed and almost asleep. Then there will be a noise that will cause them to open their eyes and when they will, they will see one or many standing by their bed and looking straight at them. They will also be making motions with their mouths as if they were speaking to them, but there will be no sound coming out.

"Then, without sound or warning, they will be gone. And there will be no trace of them having been there.

"There will be many times when the two-legs will hear voices come to them. In the beginning, there will only be occasional words that they will hear. But with the passing of time, there will be more and more of these kinds of words, and these voices will call them by their own name.

"But when they will turn their heads to the direction of these voices, there will be no one there.

"There will be many times when the two-legs will feel the presence of another with them, but when they will take the time to look, there will be no one there.

"And all of this the two-legs will attempt to hold within themselves. And for all of the changes that they will perceive coming to them, they will not be willing to share with another.

"For they will hold the believing that if they were to share this with their friends and family, they would consider them to have lost their sanity. And this is something they do not want to be seen as.

"But as I have been willing to share with you, my brothers, this is only the beginning of The Season of the Long Shadow. This is only the first of thirteen faces that will come to everyone.

"However, even in the early beginnings for this time that is soon to arrive, there will be a great need for those writing words that you have placed in the books, Speaking Wind. Even in these early times, Little Brother, there will be a great need to share that which has been shared with you," came the final sharing from the Elder of the East position.

CHAPTER 23

❀

Second Face

From the Elder of the South—
All Relations From The Other Ten Earth's
Return To Observe

"Now we come to the second face for the Season of the Long Shadow—this season that is soon to be on all who are within this domain of the Earth Mother," came the opening of those things the Elder in the South position was willing to share with us.

"This second face is one that will bring just as much fear to those who do not understand what the first face brought them.

"However, this second face will be of a different kind. It will be one that many have been given time to prepare for, but only a very few will have done the work needed so they may be allowed to pass through the wall of illusion that will face them.

"As we have been willing to share with all of you, when one is stuck in the illusion—this emotion that will not allow them to see anything for what it is—they will always be plagued by their own fears and doubts, those things that have always held them from understanding why they have been allowed entry into this domain at all."

Pausing in his speaking words for a brief time, this Elder from the South took the time to look over all five of us, looking more into each of us rather than over us from what I was feeling.

As his eyes passed by each of us, I could feel the entry take place, this entry that Cheeway and I had become so used to when either Grandfather or Two Bears would do such a thing.

I held the knowing that he was looking into each of our within places to make sure that we were still able to keep up with what was about to be unveiled to all of us. Then, satisfied all of us were still willing and capable of doing this, he smiled over us and continued.

"It has truly been a great and long journey that all of us have begun, my brothers, a journey that has taken us all to many lands, and many domains.

"However, from those things we have come to see among the two-legs, there has been much that has been forgotten…much that will soon be needed if they are to find their way through the valley of illusion that is covering so many of them.

"From the time of beginning when Great Spirit allowed so many parts of himself to be formed into their own, we have been on a continual journey that will, in time, return all of us to him, a journey that will allow all of us to return to the place of our own birth, this place that is within the One who is One.

"It would be good to remind all of you when this first split had taken place for all of us. And by all of us, I do not just limit my speaking words to the two-legs. But I include all life that is.

"When we had first come to split from the source of creation, there was a great message that was given to all of us. And this message is carved into the spirit of each one who holds life to them.

"When Creator looked at himself, he saw that there was a completeness all about him. But it was a completeness that was only of him.

"This completeness did not fill him with a great feeling of accomplishment for all that was of him, for there was so much that he felt was missing, so much that was missing from all of those parts that are of him.

"He looked at these different parts of himself and saw none of them knew anything about the others. And this gave him a sad face to wear.

"This face of sadness came to him because while he saw there was a completeness in all parts that were of him; he saw that these parts knew nothing of their other brothers and sisters.

"And without this knowing, and later understanding, that which would come to all of them when they would begin to perform their own work, there could not be a complete harmony among all that is the One.

"It was then that Creator decided to allow all of his parts to break away from himself, and as they each came to spirit unto themselves, he said to each of them:

'From This Time On, Each Of You Will Begin A Great Journey.
It will Be A Journey That will Take You To Many Places,
And Will Put Each Of You Through Many Tests,
Tests That All Of You Will See As Great
And Almost Insurmountable Obstacles.
But I Share This With Each Of You,
For Each Test That You Will Successfully Pass,
There Will Be One Vision Given.
And Each Of These Visions Will Allow You
To See Another Part Of The Path
You Have Been Given To Travel.
This Path That Has Been Set Before You
Will Require You To Go Far From Me,
But In Time, You Will Return To Me.
And When You Return, Once Again,
There Will Be A Complete Awareness

And Understanding For All That I Am.
For You Will Have Passed All Of Those Tests
That I Have Placed Before You.
Tests That Will Share With Each Of You All That I Am.
Test That Will Share With Each Of You
That You Are I, And I Am You.
Travel Well On This Path, My Children, And Know
That None May Return Before They Have
Completed That Which I Require Of Them.'

"As each of us began this great adventure that would return us to Creator, we looked ahead at what had been shown.

"We looked to those places that had been marked for our arrival and saw there was always the same process of growth and choosing our own path to travel, this path that would lead us to the path of returning and being One with Creator. For this was to remain as a constant, my brothers, no matter how many domains we were to travel through.

"As it has been from the beginning, it continues even now.

"However, for many of the two-legs, there has come over them another great illusion. It is the illusion of pride and ego that has been blinding them.

"And if this illusion is not allowed to be seen through, then I fear for what will happen to them when it is time for this second face for The Season of the Long Shadow to appear to them.

"This illusion that I speak of is the one that allows them to think that they are the only worthy form of life, the only form of living spirit not only within this domain of the Earth Mother but through all of the great star nation.

"But I will share with each of you that this is not so. And there have been many who have seen them. They are the ones who are no longer required to travel the journey's circle and have come to be among you even now.

"I am making reference to the ones who do not live on this eleventh earth you call the Earth Mother."

When these speaking words came to us from the Elder of the South, I felt my mouth drop open. Even though I had heard some of the old song legends of our people make reference to what was being shared with us, I still felt very uncomfortable with what I was hearing—this truth that this was not the first land our people had journeyed to.

Looking over the faces of the other four members of our council, I saw that they too were holding a great look of surprise as well.

"Do not look so surprised, my brothers," the Elder of the South continued. "For what I am sharing with you is not new, it has long been left with all of you in the spirit paintings and song legends of all people.

"However, this is another reason for our sharing with all of you. There has been so much truth stripped away from so many of the messages we left, that there is not more than an empty shell left for most of them.

"And this is the same for the great star nation, my brothers. This truth has been left many times within this domain but the few who would wish to continue to live in their illusion of having control over others have stripped away this truth and replaced it with their own fear that has allowed them to maintain control over many in this domain.

"There are those among you who would wish to have you believe that this is the beginning for all life, this place we have come to know as the domain of the Earth Mother.

"And for them, this has to be true. For to even think otherwise would mean they would have to embrace something they could not control. And for the ones who wish to control all things, this would simply not do.

"For if they were to come to believe in such things, they would surely lose what control they believe they now have. But there is no

control, my brothers; there is only fear. And as long as these controllers of others can get another to believe that anything which is not
like them must be evil or could do them harm, then they will continue to hold them to their own bidding. And in the process, there
will be no growth of spirit.

"However, this is not the first earth we have come to, and it will
not be the last. For the next one is almost finished now and will soon
be ready for those who will not be allowed to remain on this one.

"But this is something we will share with you later. Now, allow me
to return to where I was, this place of sharing with you the second
face for the Season of the Long Shadow.

"There is with you now, as there has always been, a memory of
where each of you has come from. And this memory includes all of
the places you have traveled through.

"If you will keep in the front of your thinking minds, this process
has been done by all of you many times before. And for every
domain we have traveled through, there have been those who have
gained greatly from their experiences, just as there have been those
who did not come to the place of understanding who and what they
are.

"However, as it is with all things, there is always the freedom of
choice. And for the ones who have chosen not to learn yet, this is
good. And for the ones who have chosen to learn from all of the
places we have been given to travel through, this is also good.

"Also, we remind you that during this long journey back to Creator, none will be lost or destroyed along the way. All will return
when they have completed their circle, only some will advance more
quickly than others because of the nature of their lessons. But this is
another lesson, one that we will not go into now.

"Remember, my brothers, there is no overall good or bad for
everyone. There is only your good and my good, your bad and my
bad. And if you hold this with you for the seasons that are still yours
to travel here, there will come to you a great understanding, one that

will allow you to share this same freedom you have been willing to see within yourself with another.

"For if you have not found this freedom within you first, then it is not likely that you will understand how to allow another to have theirs. This is because you will not have understood that which is you and that which is another.

"When one will not understand, all one will see is the face of fear come to them for all truth that is of themselves.

"As I have shared with each of you, my brothers, all that has taken place within this domain of the Earth Mother has taken place many times before. This is not the first place our spirit families have come to learn lessons as we continue our way back to Creator.

"This is the eleventh earth we have been given to travel through, my brothers. And this means that there are ten other earth's that we have passed through. And the next earth that is almost ready for entry into is the twelfth earth.

"All that has been done in this eleventh earth has been done in the other ten. And it will all be repeated on the twelfth, and so on.

"For the purpose to our existence is not to remain in one location or domain for all time. It is to travel within these domains so that we will attain our needed levels of understanding in order to find our way back to Creator and once again become One within the One," was the final speaking words about this face by the Elder in the South position.

CHAPTER 24

❀

Third Face

From the Elder of the South—
They Come To See What Decision You Are
Willing To Make

"However, as this third face for The Season of the Long Shadow will approach, there will be many signs from the great star nation of their presence and existence to all who are here," the Elder in the South began.

"There will be many of the stars that reside within the night sky who will come closer for all to see. And they are doing this as a warning for those things that are soon to come.

"When this third face will come to be, my brothers, there will be members of all the previous ten Earths who will travel into this domain that is the Earth Mother. They will return to travel among all of the earth walkers and as they will walk among them, they will observe.

"The two-legs who do not have the needed levels of understanding for what is being presented to them—they will most surely take it in the wrong way. They will not see those who are now walking among them as members of their own spirit family who have come into this domain to observe what direction their relations will take.

"They will not see, nor will they be willing to understand, that they have come here to see if their relations will take the path that will lead them to the left, this path that is led by the body and fed by the emotions, or if they will choose the path that leads to the right, this path that is led by spirit and fed by spirit as well.

"For the path that leads to the left will lead into the twelfth earth. And the ones who will be willing to travel on the path that will lead them to the right, they will be allowed entry into the fifth world of peace and light with this Earth Mother.

"However, all who have entered from the other ten domains will hold the understanding with them that each of their relations must make their own choice, that each of them has a spirit within them to know which path they are ready to travel. And because of this, there is a willingness by them to allow each individual the freedom of choosing their own path to follow.

"These other members of our spirit families have been coming to this domain of the Earth Mother for many generations. They have been doing this in an attempt of preparing the two-legs for what is soon to be with them, this time when they and all of the other members of their spirit families will return from the great star nation to walk among you.

"But from all of their attempts, there have always been those who would not have any know of them. These are the ones who continue to live in the illusion of believing they are controlling others and in this process of not telling them of those who have come among them from the great star nation. They believe that holding this information away from them is for their own good.

"However, for this time that is soon to come to all in this domain of the Earth Mother, there will be nothing that can be done to hide this truth from any. For there will be so many of our relations from the star nation arriving in this domain that they will be seen by all who are here.

"And the preparing that has been done by our relations from the star nation—this has also taken place under the face of the Earth Mother as well.

"For within the underworld of this domain, there are many members of the great star nation who reside here. But their purpose in this domain is only that of observers and to prepare for this time we are now willing to share with you.

"In the many seasons of your past, there have been some who have heard them in their underworld places of living. But only a very few have ever seen them. And those who have seen them were either not believed by other two-legs, or were considered to be crazy and were put into places where they could not speak to anyone else.

"The forms that have been taken by our other spirit family members do not always look like the body parts you have been given to travel in. And this also brings a great confusion to the two-legs when it is time for them to enter this domain and be seen.

"But there is another event that it would be well to share with all of you on this day, my brothers. And it is this:

"When it is time for this third face for the Season of the Long Shadow to be born into this domain, the second face will have arrived at almost the same time.

"So there will not only be the ones who are of our spirit families from the great star nation who will be seen and heard within all of this domain, but those who have been in the waiting place will have blended completely in this domain as well.

"And without the understanding for why this has all taken place, there would surely be great panic and fear among all of the two-legs who will still be here to travel their life path with the Earth Mother.

"This is one of the reasons we have chosen all of you to share with on this day. These are things all of you need to find your own level of understanding for. And as each of you will find your own individual understanding for these events, you will see what you must do. You will see a path to travel that will allow you to share with others who will also have a great need to understand that these times do not come in punishment for them, but they are coming because it is time—time for all life to move on.

"Remember, my brothers, there is no thing that will come to you which is capable of being bad or evil. However, there are those who would wish to have you believe this. They are the ones who would wish to control you through the fear they have gotten you to believe in.

"But there is no evil or bad, my brothers, there are only those things that we do not have an understanding for. And what we do not understand we see as the enemy, an enemy that must be destroyed or taken away from where we are.

"When the time will come, as it will, remind the two-legs who would come to you saying how evil or bad things are of what I have just been willing to share with you.

"Think of all that has been destroyed in this domain simply because it was not understood. There is life in all things, and because of this, my brothers, it too, has a path to travel.

"None of those things we do will be either good or bad. There are only those things we do, and we do them because spirit within has a need to teach us something from them.

"So when the two-legs come to see this third face for The Season of the Long Shadow, remind them there is no thing that has come to them that is evil, good, or bad. But these things have presented themselves to them because it is time for them to be. And they will be, with or without their permission. Just as day will follow night.

"When they see this truth, they will truly see that this time has brought all of their family together once again. However, for the ones who will not see this truth, they will make every effort possible to run and hide from that which has come to be with them.

"But I share with all of you, there will be no place to run, and there will be no place to hide. For all must go through this time that is soon to be with you," came the end of the speaking words from the Elder of the South.

CHAPTER 25

❀

Fourth Face

From the Elder of the West—
The Path To The Left, And The Path To
The Right

After the sharing of speaking words that had come to us from the Elder of the South there was a brief silence that filled all of this land we had come to be on.

It was a sharing that was allowing each of our spirits to reach out and understand there was still room for more of what was now willing to be shared by these Ancient Ones of our people.

Then, and without any further breaking of silence in this place, the Elder from the West made a motion. It was a motion of the hand much like the ones Cheeway and I had come to see from Grandfather and Two Bears…one that they would make when giving thanks and honor to all life that was with us.

This Elder of the West placed a good smile over her face as she continued, and holding her right hand with the palm stretched out and over all of our heads, she sang a spirit caller's song. It was one that I held a remembering for, but not from this earth walk.

This would have placed me in a wondering mind had it not been for the many times these Old Ones had recalled me to the present by reminding me that those things that I did not have a complete understanding for would come to me at a later time when there would be a great need by me to hear them once again.

Holding this in the front of my thinking mind, I continued to observe the elder from the west and listened as she sang this beautiful spirit caller's song that I seemed to recall from a time before, a time that was not with me now.

> "I Hold Myself Open To You, My Brothers And Sisters,
> So All May See My Own Face Of Truth.
>
> From One We Have Begun,
> And Returned To The One, We Soon Will Be.
>
> Our Journey Has Been Long And Filled With Lessons,
> Lessons That Have Been Filled With Emotions,
> Some Of Learning, Some Of Missing,
> But Through Them All,
> Our Hearts Have Grown Strong
> And Our Spirit Has Learned To Fly
>
> Be With Us Now, My Brothers And Sisters,
> Be With Us And Share With Us Your Love.
>
> For It Is Through This Love Of Understanding
> That We May See Our Path Has Not Been Lost
>
> It Is Through This Love Of Understanding
> That We Will See Our Path To Travel
> The Path That Is Within, The Path That Is For Us,
> The Path That Will Bring Us All Home Once Again."

When she had finished her spirit caller's song, there was a brief silence, but I could feel it was for another reason from the others.

For this silence was now being filled with the lightness of sharing…this lightness that is felt when one would accept the presence of another with them. And for all of the life that was with us on this day, I could feel the sharing and love of creation, a love that is completely unconditional.

I could feel the love that was within the rock nation who had come to share these sitting places with us, from the great tree nation who was weaving to and fro with the passing of the Spirit Wind over them, and from the small warming fire that was before us.

I could feel the love being shared with us by the great cloud nation who has brought the blessings of the water spirit over our lands, and from the Spirit Wind, who has always been in such great attendance to all of the needs of the children of the Earth Mother.

And for all of this, I could feel myself returning this same love that was within me to them. It was pouring out of me and into all places at the same time.

During this time, I could feel the same love coming out of Grandfather, Two Bears, Night Hawk, and Cheeway, as well as all of the Ancient Ones.

And for all of this, I knew it was good.

"It is time to begin, my brothers," came the speaking words from the Elder in the West. "As it has been shared with you before, we have all been on a very long journey. A long journey that has taken us to many places where we have walked many paths with one another.

"However, we are soon to be at a time when there will be asked a question of all who hold a spirit with them, not only to the ones who you will see walking a path in this domain, but for all who have ever been as well.

"This is soon to be the time of the great question, my brothers. The great question that will ask each one if they would be willing to remain in this domain, or if they require yet another earth to travel through to learn lessons."

Hearing these speaking words come to us from this Elder in the West was a great surprise to me. Looking over the faces of the others, I could see that this surprise had come to them as unexpectedly as it had come to me.

This surprise had come to each of us from hearing those things that had just been shared, that soon there would be a great question asked of all who hold the spirit of life within them.

I had heard of this question that will be asked of all who travel in this domain that is the Earth Mother. But I had somehow only come to see it as something that would not ever take place while I was on my earth walk, that it would take place long after I had left this domain and reentered the waiting place with all of the other ancestors.

And now this Elder from the West had filled all of us with a great surprise. Although it was not as great as the rest of those things that would be shared later with us on this day, I knew that this was great enough for me to wear a look of surprise over my face.

I knew, from having heard the speaking words of preparing from Grandfather and Two Bears, that when the Ancient Ones would come and sit among us, they would always begin with sharing those things that held the smallest impact first. And as the time of the visions would continue, they would share more and more of those things that held even more weight to them.

When I had asked Grandfather why this was always so, he smiled at me and reminded me that there will always be freedom of choice for all spirits.

"And this will be in the domain of the Earth Mother's or in any other domain where there is life," came Grandfather's speaking words to me. "When the Old Ones share with us, they will always take the least important things to share first. In this way, there will always be left with the one who is sitting in council with them their freedom of choice, to choose to continue with what they have come to share with them, or to stop."

Hearing these speaking words from Grandfather come to live with me once again confirmed my first thought...that there was still much more to come to us from them. And when this time would come, I would know how much more there would be to understand from this spirit vision, and from all that the Ancient Ones had entered this domain to prepare us with.

"It has been from the beginning that there have always been the two paths to choose from," the Elder from the West position began once again. "And it has been from these two paths that we find the lessons needed by spirit that is within all life.

"As I am sharing these things with you, it would be good to keep in the front of your thinking minds that there is no right and there is no wrong choice to make; there is only your choice. To think otherwise would cause you to become lost within the illusion of trying and controlling those things that you have no influence on anyway.

"When this journey was shown to all life as they were split from Creator, there were the two paths. And, at the final path of our long journey, my brothers, there will remain the same two paths to choose from, these same two paths that are so important, even the ones who no longer hold a body part to them will return to participate in it.

"They will return to choose because of the great importance this time called The Season of the Long Shadow has on all of us.

"There have been many earth walks done by all of our spirit families, my brothers, and for the ones that have come to travel within this domain, it has taken 40,000 years to complete this process of preparing...of preparing to make this choice that will soon be with all life.

"I hold the understanding that each of you has seen the identification of these two paths, this path that leads to the left as well as the one that leads to the right.

"However, I would wish to share them with you once again. For it is in repeating that we may hear those things we still need to understand.

"The path that leads to the left is led by the body and fed by the emotion. And on this path, we find the ones who will continually try to be someone or something they are not.

"When one will try, they will always be in the state of becoming, this state of becoming that will not ever allow them to be, but will give the illusion of movement.

"But this movement they will find on this path to the left, will only be in small circles. They will seem to be traveling quickly but not ever arriving at any of those places they wish to get to, and this will cause them to become frustrated.

"The more frustrated they will become, the harder they will try. And the harder they try, the longer they will be in this state of always becoming and not ever arriving.

"This path is one that keeps them locked in the circle of illusion that tells them that if they were not to try, they would not be anything at all.

"And this path that leads to the left, my brothers, it holds many lessons for those who have come to travel on it. For if this were not so, they would not be on it. Now the path that leads to the right is led by spirit and fed by spirit as well.

"For the nature of this path to the right is when one will allow themselves to be, they are. For all of the preparation that has been needed by any of them has already been done. And because they have allowed themselves to be, they will see with eyes of clarity.

"All of the events and emotions that come to those who have chosen this path to the right will be seen for what they are. For if there was not a need for them to do this, they would not have been done.

"And for this way of seeing, they hold the knowing that there has been nothing done by them that is wrong or bad. They have only done that which was needed. And on this path, there is only the need to understand what it was they have done—are doing, or will do—and not to carry the illusion of guilt for any of it.

"When one is on this path that leads to the right, they will see a truth that will come to them in this way.

"It is not important to see anything you will do through any eyes other than your own. When you will see your life path through your own eyes, then you will see how much work there is for you to do. And when you will see what needs to be done by you to learn from, there will no longer be any time to look at another's life path. For it is in looking at another's life path that will take our attention away from the one we are traveling. And when we will do this, my brothers, we slip away from this path that is on the right and fall into the path that is on the left.

"But there is another truth that will come to the ones who will be ready to travel on this path that leads to the right. And it is a truth that has been within them all the time.

"They will see how useless it is for them to try to assist another in finding those things they need to find on their own. For when they will do this, they see that for all their efforts in trying to assist this other one are not long lived.

"Once they are away from them, the ones who had come to them for this assistance are back to the same old place they had been before. And all of this effort that had been placed on them had been done for no long lasting result at all.

"When they have gone through this several times and found the only thing they had accomplished was to remove themselves from their own path, then they will see this truth I am speaking to you of.

"They will see it is only by walking their own truth that another may see what they have come to find. And when another will see that you have found your own path to travel, then they will understand that this is possible for them to do as well.

"For when one will see that this is possible for them to do as well, they will be willing to do their own work to get there. And those things that are worked for, they are always held with more value than something that is given. For to give anything to another, no matter what your reason may be, gives them permission to throw it away.

"You will give them permission to throw this away because they have done nothing for it. But when they will have done their own work for it, then it will hold a value to them. And those things that hold a value to any will not ever be taken lightly and they will be used and not ignored.

"However, as I had shared with each of you, there is no right or wrong way to choose these two paths. There is only a need to understand what is on each of them.

"The reason I am willing to share this with you now is so you will be able to see clearly what is taking place with these two paths, these two paths that will represent this great question that is soon to be asked of all life just before The Season of the Long Shadow has come to its completion.

"For the ones who continue to travel on this path that leads to the left, they are not yet ready to travel on the path that leads to the right. For them, there are still many lessons for them to work through that reside there. And to attempt to travel on the path that leads to the right before they have prepared themselves would not succeed at all. For them, there is still much that needs to be learned on this path of the left.

"For the ones who are ready to travel on this path that leads to the right, they have already learned those things that were to be found on the path of the left. They no longer have need of learning from living within the illusion.

"It is spirit within each of us who will know what we are, and are not ready for, my brothers. This is why it is so important to see your path through your own eyes of truth and not try to see another's path for them. This will only result in wasting your time...and theirs as well. For nothing will ever be accomplished before they are ready.

"It is like being in a great hallway that has many rooms of learning in it. And you will find one who is traveling with you who will need to learn from one room, while your learning is to be found in another. If you will attempt to hold onto another, you will only be keeping them from entering their own room of learning. But in this process, you will be stopping yourself from entering your room as well, and neither of you will have learned anything.

"So live with the freedom of seeing, my brothers, and allow this same freedom to all who will cross your path. Only be concerned with the path you have come into this domain to learn from and allow all others this same freedom as well.

"Trust in spirit who is within you to know your way. Trust in spirit who is within all others to know their way as well.

"When you will be willing to do this, there will be seen clearly what I will now share with you. That another cannot choose wrong. This does not happen, for this kind of thinking is not truth.

"Those who choose the path on the left do so because they continue to hold a need for what they will find there. And the ones, who will choose the path on the right, they do this because they have already accomplished this.

"Now, at the close of The Season of the Long Shadow, there will come before all a Great Messenger. This messenger will be one who all will know, for they have always been with them in ways that are not describable at this time. But rest assured, all will know this one.

"The Great Messenger will enter this domain from the great star nation and will come to rest among all life on the back of the great cloud nation. He will enter this domain to present a final question to all who will be here, and as I have shared with you, there will not be any who will be missed for this event, for this choosing will remain with everyone for a very long time.

"All will gather before this Great Messenger and as they see him standing on the back of a great cloud over these lands we have come to call the domain of the Earth Mother, and from all they have been, they will be asked to review all of their earth walks and see what they have come to understand from them as well as those things that are still needed to be learned.

"Then they will be asked to make their own decision for what path they see their needs on, whether it will be this path that will lead to the left, or this path that will lead to the right.

"At this time, they will see two great paths formed on each side of the Great Messenger. One leads to the left, and the other to the right. And between them there will be the Great Messenger holding both hands down and open for all to see.

"This is a sign of spirit that only truth may pass through this place where these two paths have their beginnings.

"When all see this sign, they understand they must find their own truth for what is still needed by them. They must see these needs through their own face of truth.

"For the ones who would follow the path that leads to the right without having learned all that is needed from the path that is on the left, they will be stopped and not be allowed to continue on their way.

"For the ones who no longer have a need for the path that leads to the left of the Great Messenger, they too will be stopped if they will try to enter this path. For their need on this path is no longer.

"All will be told that this is the ending of all time as they have come to know it. For the ones who need to travel on this path to the left, it will cause them to have a great fear. And for the ones, who will be allowed to travel on the path that leads to the right, they will know this as good.

"When all life will come to the place of understanding that they will not be allowed on any path they do not have a need for, they will enter a review for all they have come to understand from their earth walks, and will see it with the face of truth and sincerity. Only then will they understand that there can only be one course for them, and that will be to follow the path they continue to hold a need from.

"Once all of this has been completed, there will be a great movement by all life. For the ones who will have gained entry onto the path that leads to the right, they will be allowed to enter this fifth world of the Earth Mother. This will be the world of peace and light.

"For the ones who still need to travel the path to the left, they will follow this path as it will lead them into the twelfth earth. This twelfth earth where all that has been done here, will have to be done again, all over again.

Then pausing for a brief moment, the Elder from the West looked over all of us then said:

"There will be none missed, my brothers. This is a time that comes for all!"

CHAPTER 26

❀

Fifth Face

From the Elder of the North—
Many Try to Run And Hide, But There Is
No Place For Them to Go

When the Elder from the West position had finished, there was another silence that had fallen over us. It was a silence of understanding from what had been shared.

Looking over to the faces of the other four members of our council, I could see these events that had come to us from the Ancient Ones were filling them with a great weight. And it was a great weight of truth. For this truth was what had been sung of in the many of our song legends for as long as they have been.

The Ancient Ones were now sharing with us that soon it would be time for The Season of the Long Shadow, and we would be living in the time of prophecy.

Holding this in the front of my thinking mind, I was beginning to wonder how it would be seen by the two-legs…how it would be perceived when it would begin its entry into this domain that is the Earth Mother.

For all that I had seen from the two-legs in the past, I knew they took great efforts in not seeing what was being presented, great effort at covering up truth so there would not be the discomfort of seeing.

As this was clouding the front of my thinking mind, the speaking voice from the Elder of the North position began:

"When it is time for The Season of the Long Shadow to enter this domain, Speaking Wind, there will not be any who are not aware of its presence.

"There will be many who will not recognize it, but that is because they have been away from their own face of truth for so long, they have forgotten what it looks like.

"When this time comes to all who are here in this domain of the Earth Mother, the effects of The Season of the Long Shadow will be immediate. And for those who have been prepared for its entry, will know what has taken place. But I tell all of you in truth, the numbers of those who will have this awareness will be very small. So I explain for this reason.

"At the first moment of entry for this time that is soon to be with you, there will be a feeling of something missing, something missing among each and every one who has a life path to travel.

"At first, this will worry the two-legs. But as time will pass, they will make many efforts at putting this feeling behind them, much in the same way they have done with the many lessons that had come to them time and time again.

"Remember, when you will turn away from a lesson, it will return to you with another layer of emotion over it, that is only to call your attention to something you need to learn from.

"When these feelings of something missing comes to the two-legs, they will try to ignore it just as they have done in their past with the emotions they did not understand or want with them.

"However, just as it is with lessons, these feelings of something missing within them will also return. But when it will return, it will do so in a much different way than the emotions of lesson have done.

It will return to them in a much different way because of what it is telling them and its weight of importance.

"In the beginning, this feeling of something missing within them may be put away, but it will return in a way that may not be ignored by any.

"The second time this feeling of something missing will come to them, just when they believed they were successful in putting this behind them, they will begin to see pictures come to them. Pictures of people and places they have not seen before...people and places that they feel they know, but not in the times of this earth walk.

"In the past, they only had this come to them from the dreamers, when they walked into the night sleep with them and were taken to many places and shown many things, places and people they had known of long before they entered this domain.

"What they will not yet understand is that these places and people are from a time of their past they must now review. They are being asked to look at all they have done, and all they have not done in order to reach a conclusion for themselves.

"They are being asked to review all of those earth walks they have done before and see what is still needed by them. During this process, they will come to see what they might do with the time left to them in order to finish what was not done by them before.

"And when they wake from their sleeping times with the dreamers, they will recall only a very small portion of those things that had been shown to them. But this is only because they do not yet have a full understanding for what is soon to take place among all of them.

"Until they have complete understanding for what is being shown to them, they will only have a part of the picture they are feeling. They will have a feeling that there is something they need to do, something they must do in order to reach a place of completion...but a completion for what, they do not know.

"So once again, they have this feeling of something missing, and once again they will try to put it behind them because they do not understand what had been shown to them is what they still needed to learn from. Those things they need to complete so they will be prepared when the time comes for them to choose from the path that will lead to the left, or the path that will lead to the right. For when this choice will be given to all of them, then it is truth the time that this domain is at its end. For nothing will remain the same as any see it now.

"But they will not understand this and try to put this second calling of theirs away, to put it out of their thinking minds so they will not have to work with it.

"Then this feeling will come to them again, though. And when it does for the third time, they will believe they have been placed into a great room with nothing in it but them.

"They will feel as if someone or something has taken all of what they had work so hard at attaining, for it is no longer with them. At first they become very angry and look for another they can blame for what has happened to them.

"But this will not work because there will not be anyone they can do this to. Next, they feel alone and will find themselves standing in a great room with nothing else with them…not even a light.

"Once again, this feeling of something missing within them has returned. And it has returned to them for the third time, and still they have not understood why it has come.

"However, with this third calling, there will be no other choice for them but to work with it or to ignore their own life.

"But whichever they decide to do, they will not ever be the same. For this event has come to them in this time we call The Season of the Long Shadow.

"And when this time will enter and find them, as it will find its way to all, there will be great changes in the way everyone will come to look and work with themselves, ways that will not allow them to remain the same.

"When the ones who are standing within this large and dark room look around them, they eventually see many of their own friends with them, but not as they have become used to seeing them. They will feel as though they cannot speak to any of them. And they will carry this feeling of being alone in the presence of many for the remainder of their seasons.

"They will look to the places they once thought they belonged and this will have changed for them. For they will feel as if something great has changed within them and no longer feel comfortable in those places and doing the things they have been doing for most of their life.

"For the ones who will understand what is taking place, they will know it to be good. For the ones who will not understand, they will first come to wear a sad face, but this face will soon be replaced with one of fear, a fear of the unknown, a fear of being with something that will not go away from them no matter what they do.

"When they reach this place—and I share with all of you this is only the beginning of these times that are soon to be—they will reach out to all of those things they once held a believing in, those things they had listened to from the ones who would lead them. And they will reach out to them for support.

"But they will find many of those things they have been told are not true, that they do not have the weight of truth to them. When they will try and use them to support themselves during this time of their great uncertainty, they find nothing to support them, for there is nothing of truth within them that will hold them up and keep them from falling down.

"And this, too, will cause the ones who do not yet understand what is taking place to feel fearful, and not know what to do.

"When this time comes to them, they will initially do those things they have always done. They will look to another for their answers, for those things that another would tell them to do in order to feel better about themselves.

"But I share with all of you that this, too, will not work. For the answers they need are only to be found within themselves. And unless they come to understand how to work through the emotions to see their own face of lesson, then they will end up running very fast, but with no place to go.

"However, what is happening to all of them is very simple. They are being shown the path that will lead them to their within place where their own spirit resides. But since they have not ever been on this path, they do not see it as anything that is good for them.

"They believe what they do not understand is certainly evil and bad. But I share with all of you that this is not so, for there is no thing within this domain or any other, that is either bad or evil. There are only those things that are not understood. And this is no different for the path that is soon to be shown to all of the two-legs.

"For the ones who would not be willing to listen to the calling voice of their own spirit, and see the path that is being shown, they will continue to run and look to another who would get them out of this place they are in, out of this place they have come to regard as being bad and evil.

"They will attempt to hide from themselves even more by going deeper into the illusion, but they will only be fooling themselves, once again.

"When they go to others in hopes of them taking these feeling away from them, those they will find will be the ones who have become very good at using emotion to cover up truth. When those who would feel the loss of something within them and see this as their problem, they will have done this out of eyes that do not see.

"And without eyes that see, they will be lulled into the trap of illusion.

"For the others are telling them this is happening because of the great evil and bad things they have done in their past. And until they will be willing to make up for all of those bad things they have done, they will continue to feel lost and without anyone or anything, that all of this has come to them as a punishment for all the wrong they have performed.

"But in truth, my brothers, those who are telling them this are doing nothing more than allowing them to cover up what they are feeling with something that is stronger. They are getting them to cover up what is being shown to them first through fear, then by cultivating their own feelings of hate. For they will use this emotion of hate to get them to cover up what is within them as truth.

"It would do well to hold in the front of your thinking minds that hate is love which is not understood. While love that is understood will be a healing force, hate is just the opposite. Hate will destroy all that it does not understand.

"And it is this hate that will be used on the two-legs who will come to these others looking for relief from what they are feeling within them. And these others will cause them to use this hate to see those who have been willing to do their own work and find their own way as their enemy.

"While this hate will initially cover up those things that are still missing within them, it will also blind them to what has been presented, and they will not see what they have been missing from within. They will not see they have been offered an opportunity of understanding the unconditional love they have been created with.

"They will not see this until it is time for the Great Messenger to arrive and ask them to make their choice.

"Only then will they see they have been closing their eyes to what had been presented to them.

"Only then will they see what they have missed out on by not doing their own work. For by not doing those things that still needed to be done by them, they have not completed their lessons that would have allowed them to choose the path that leads to the right and into the fifth world of the Earth Mother, this fifth world of peace and light.

"For now they must choose the path that will lead them to the left, and into the twelfth earth where they will have to do all of this all over again.

"But for now, let us look at what is taking place for the ones who are not willing to do their own work in this time that will soon be with them, for those who will not understand but will go to others who will teach them how to cover up those feelings from within with hate.

"As I have been willing to share with you, hate is love that is not understood. And this is why it holds such a strong place among those emotions that have come to you.

"The lessons that are about love are many, so it is only right to say that the emotions from those lessons that have not yet been understood are very strong too.

"However, as these feelings of something missing within them gets stronger, they will go to those who have always taken away such things. Because it is the time for The Season of the Long Shadow, what they had been feeling will not go away. It will continue to grow stronger within them. And when they see this, their fears will grow stronger as well.

"So when they will come to these others whom they believe will help them get rid of these feelings, they have come to see this great fear. And because their fears are so great, they will be willing to do most anything they are told to get rid of them. This begins their falling away from this path that has been shown to them, from this path that leads to their own within place.

"However, there will always be the freedom of choice and for this time, it is no different.

"For the ones who will go to others to get away from these feelings, they have their own choice. And this choice is that they are not yet ready to follow this path to their within place. They still need to learn from those lessons that are to be found on the path that leads into the illusion.

"But before they will be able to get out of this place that has been shown to them—this path that would have led them to their within place and to see their own face of spirit and truth—they will have to give up what they have been shown. They will have to give up all of those things they understand and know as good about themselves before they can follow the lead of the others who would be willing to help them through learning to hate.

"Remember, my brothers, hate can only begin after all that is good about yourself has been dropped away. For while there are still things within you that you see as good, there will be no room for hate to take root.

"However, once all of those things that were good within you are left behind, then hate will begin to grow. And as it does, there will be a consuming of yourself, then of all who are around you. Even the ones you are closest to will be blamed for what has held you in this fear.

"Without understanding what has been missed, all who will be traveling in this domain will only feel for what they do not have. And they will feel what they do not have even more when they will look upon another who has been successful in finding and traveling to their within place. For they will see a peace and understanding come over them and will see that this is something they, too, could have had. But for them, they will not believe it is possible for them any longer because of all they have done, not only to themselves, but to others as well.

"You see, my brothers, hate will grow within anyone until it completely consumes them. And to be consumed in hate is to be held within the trap of illusion, this illusion that will only allow you to see all things for what you would wish for them to be, this same illusion that will not allow you to see anything for what it is in truth.

"For the ones who have not been willing to do their own work and find the path to their within place, they will first be asked to perform a few steps by the ones they have gone to, by the ones who would have them believe they can assist them in getting away from those feelings of there being something missing within them.

"First, they will be told that what they are going through is a direct result of all the bad and wrong things they have done in their past. And until they believe this, there will be no further help they can give them.

"But what they are being asked to do, my brothers, is this. They are being asked to look at all of the things they have ever done, and all of the experiences they have had, and see them as being something that is inherently bad, to see that there is no thing they can ever do on their own that is good.

"And when they accept covering those feelings that are within them with hate, they will soon find there is no thing left within them that they feel is good. When this takes place for them, they believe there can be no thing in any other that could be good. And this is where they will begin to use this hate to cover up those things they once felt within themselves that were being presented to them so they could find their way to the within place, where they could see the face of their own spirit, and their own truth.

"In the beginning, all of their hatred is based on themselves. But this does not last long. For as soon as they see the advantage of pointing to another and convincing others to see they are worse than they, they find another way to escape their own feelings of something within them missing. They have found that when they will point out another, then all of the attention will be taken away from them and put on this other person. And soon, no one will be looking at them to see what they are like, but they will be looking at the ones who have been pointed out.

"And this becomes the natural process for those who have learned to hate in order to cover up their feelings, but they do not understand what they have done. They only see how successful they have become in calling attention to others and saying how bad these other people are which causes many to gather around them and listen. And as others will gather around them and listen to what they have to say, they will feel as if they have attained a certain status in this group they have found for themselves.

"However, from those who would listen to them, they are not with them because they feel any loyalty for them. They are with them so they will not have to look at themselves because they have new targets to point at. And as long as there will be others around whom they can point at and use this hate they have found, they will remain together, stuck in the illusion of not having to work with those feelings within themselves they do not understand.

"From this place, they will look at groups of people who will either be different from them, or have been willing to do their own work and find their path to the within place.

"When they see those who are different from them, they attack them with all of the strength they can come up with.

"They increase their efforts at not only calling these others who are different bad, but they will begin killing them. And this they will do, for I have been shown.

"However, it does not last long. As soon as this domain reaches the middle place for The Season of the Long Shadow, there will be such a great event take place for all to see, that those who had been gathered in their groups will no longer see life in the same way ever again.

"This event is when the waiting place blends with this domain and all of the relations from the past ten earth's return to observe the great decision that is soon to be given.

"When the waiting place blends with this domain of the Earth Mother, all who have passed before will return. They will not return as an apparition or vision, but they will be seen just as clearly as you can see each other.

"They will walk among all who are remaining in this domain and will share their speaking words to remind the ones who have been hiding behind their hate of what they are doing and where it is taking them.

"This will set into all of them a great fear. It will be a fear of having to feel and see all of those things they had been trying to run away from.

"No matter where they will look, they will be reminded of them. And for them, there will be no place left to run or hide.

"Some of them will become so fearful that they will find a gun and shoot themselves hoping for a relief from what they are seeing and being reminded of, those things that they still need to work on. However this will not work for them, for there will, in truth, be no place left for them to go.

"As we have traveled through each of these eleven earth's, there has only been one place for any to go. And that place has always been the waiting place, where all will remain until the time of the great decision is asked for and we will either go to the next earth or into the next world on the earth we have come to share a life path with.

"But when the waiting place has blended into this domain of the Earth Mother, and those who wish to run and hide from all that is being reminded to them attempt to end their life, they will find themselves standing and looking at their body as it falls to the earth below their feet, but their spirit will remain standing.

"At first, they believe the gun they used to shoot themselves did not work and will try again. But there will be no change; for there is nothing more for them to shoot at, nothing but the spirit who is them, and a bullet cannot bring harm to spirit.

"This will leave them standing in the middle of their fears for all that is around them. And they will see that there is, in truth, no place left for them to run and hide.

"They will look for assistance from the ones who had been with them, and they will not find any. For all who had been with them in those many seasons of their hating will be just as lost and frightened as they are. And they will not want to help another; they will only want to be helped.

"You will know them because they will be running to many places screaming and crying to anyone and no one at the same time. For they are truly the ones to be sorry for. They are the ones who will remind many of what takes place when one is not willing to do their own work.

And when they will look and see the faces of those who have been willing to do their own work, they will feel a great weight come over them, a weight that will cause them to feel even worse.

"For they see whom they had come to fear the most, was themselves. Had they been willing to do the work they needed in order to find their own within place, none of this would have happened to them. And they, too, could have been walking with the ones who have in truth, found their own way.

"However, when you look on them, my brothers, do not feel sad for them, at least not for any period of time that would be long.

"What they have chosen for themselves is what they need. And what they need is to enter the twelfth earth and do all of this over again. This is necessary because it is the only place where they will find the opportunity of learning those things they still need to learn from."

CHAPTER 27

❀

Sixth Face

From the Elder of the East—
One Disappears And One Remains

There was no need for any silence to follow the speaking words that had been shared with us from the Elder in the North position. As soon as those speaking words had finished, the Elder from the East began. And as she did this, she placed her left hand on my right shoulder and said:

"It is for you to know that all is as it should be, Speaking Wind. If it were not so, it would not be."

Hearing those speaking words come to me answered many of my questions I was holding within myself not only for why so much was now being shared with all of us, but also for the true nature of identity of the one called Night Hawk, this friend of Grandfather and Two Bears who had joined us on this day we were to be with the Old Ones.

From the sharing of the Elder in the East, I again allowed those things that had been gaining weight within me to lose life, or at least allow them to rest until I would hold an understanding for them.

"It is the sixth face for The Season of the Long Shadow that I am now willing to share with you. For it will be in this time when one of the signs will be presented for all to see. It will be a sign that none may disregard or hide away from.

"Keep in the front of your thinking minds that up to this time, there have been great efforts by those groups that have formed to call many away from their own path by instilling fear into them. For fear will keep one from understanding. And where there is no understanding, there is only illusion, the same illusion that will only allow one to see things, as they would wish for them to be.

"The ones who will have begun their own path to the within place but have not yet come to understand it—they will be seen by the groups as someone who may still be won over to them by having them learn to hide from their events behind the emotion of hate and anger, to hide from those things that will have been calling them to look at the work that is still needed by them to do before understanding may be attained and see their own face of lesson.

"When these groups see those who have just begun to travel within themselves, they will see an opportunity of getting them to leave this path to their within place and win them over to their way of living.

"They will see them as being vulnerable at this time, and I share with all of you that when one will begin the journey to the within place, they will be vulnerable indeed.

"For this is the time when one feels alone and rejected. However, the aloneness and rejection only comes to them from within themselves. For in the times that were before this awakening had come to them, they were content to stand at the very outside edge of their circle and look out. As they would do this, they would find great comfort in either judging others, or pointing fingers at them in a way of telling them all of the things they were doing wrong.

"But when their awakening comes to them, they find themselves turned around from all that had been with them before. They no longer stand at the outer edge of their circle of life and look out, but they will be turned around and looking into the path that will lead them not only to the inside of their life circle, but to discover the place where their spirit resides. And it is in this place where they will come to know and understand themselves in truth.

"However, once this journey has begun, there will be many strange and new events come to them. For once they turn to look to the inside of their own circle of life, they will find all of those emotions they once believed were no longer with them are still there. And when they look on them, there will be a great face of fear and concern fall over them. But this will not last long either, for there will be an understanding that will soon come, one that will share with them that all they are now seeing and remembering is needed to be seen and remembered.

"It is needed so they may pass through this emotion that has been attached to them for such a long time. And when they will pass through this, they will find a new freedom for all they once held a fear from, for all they once held with them and saw as being bad.

"But when they first come to look on those things, they will not understand that this will soon pass them. They will only see something that will appear very great and scary. And this is the time when they will be the most vulnerable. And this is the time when those groups who are using this hate emotion to hide behind, will see them as someone who can be easily led back to them.

"They will come to those who are in this beginning of their path and remind them of all the times they had with them before, of the times when they would stand on the outside of their circle of life and be content to only look to the outside…to look at others and see how many things wrong or right they would come to do.

"They will remind them that while they were in this place that there were no bad feelings or emotions that would come to them, at least none they could not handle.

"They will give them many things to think on, and ask them to return to the times they once knew by following them. And they will tell them that if they will be willing to do this, they will no longer be in the position of seeing so much bad in themselves. But they will be returned to where they once were, to those places where they felt the most comfortable in.

"However, there is a great lesson that has come from this, my brothers. It is one that holds to it a great weight of truth.

"When someone will wish for you to speak through their own mouth, there will be one who will fall away from the path they have chosen to travel. And this one will be you.

"For it is when one will not use their own mouth to speak through that they become lost. They will become lost in the other's path and will no longer be able to see their own.

"However, for the ones who would be willing to listen to these speaking truths, we are willing to share with you, they will come to see the face of their own truth. They will have the willingness to perform their own work and will not look away from those things they do not understand.

"They understand that while they may be going through a great and dark night within themselves, they will soon understand these emotions have always been with them, but had been placed behind them. And until they begin to work their way through them, they will remain trapped within the illusion. And they will also understand that no other may do this work, but them.

"When they have come to this place of understanding, my brothers, they will be willing to look past all of the fear and emotions that have come to them, past those emotions that there will be no escape from, regardless of their decision of what to do with them.

"And they will look on them and see their face of truth for who and what they are.

"They will see them as a great opportunity for them to learn from. And once the beginning has been attained by them, they discover their best friend and wisest teacher has been within themselves all the time.

"One of the teachings that has been stripped from its own truth, my brothers, is the one that tells the two-legs that if they were to look on their own face of truth that they would surely go crazy. But I share with all of you this is not so.

"If you will look at your own reflection in the mirror each morning you awake from the dream time without running out of the house yelling like a crazy person because of what you have seen, then when you will come to see your own face of truth, you will see the most wonderful blessing that can ever be given to another. For you will see yourself for what you are…in truth. And I share with all of you, there will only be seen the wonder of creation itself within your presence.

"When one will come to this place, my brothers, they wear a good face for all to see. It will be a face of knowing and understanding that no thing will ever come to them that is filled with bad, evil, or vengeance for what they have done.

"They understand that all comes in answer to their own prayers. They begin to see what they had feared and tried to run from were only those things they did not understand, those things that only had to do with them and the lessons they had entered this domain to learn.

"Remind the two-legs, when it is time for this to be with all of you, that when they will have reached this place on their path, then all who would have tried to get them to fall away from this path will no longer be able to.

"This time will be behind them, for they will have seen their way to where they have been. And this knowing will not only give to them a great peace, but it will give them focus. And one who is in focus and balanced cannot be moved from where they need to be.

"So it is when the time will come for all who will be in the middle part of The Season of the Long Shadow that the sixth step will come over them.

"It will also be the middle of this time that you will be walking next to another. And one moment you will see them, and the next they will be gone.

"But they will not be gone for long, my brothers; they will return in three to eleven days and all who had known them before, will see them when they return.

"They will return in this time to become used to their new path, this path of spirit that has allowed them to leave this domain of the Earth Mother with their own body. And I tell you this, many in the past have performed and been blessed with this, but this information has been kept secret by those who would not have you learn of it.

"For the ones who will be given this blessing of leaving with their own body part will not have to endure the pains of birth and death of the body any longer. They have succeeded from what their lessons had to offer them. And they have the ability of entering this domain, with their body, at will.

"However, when they will return in these three to eleven days, they will not do this re-entry as anything that is meant for them to show off to you, by showing something they have been allowed to do that you have not.

"They will return in this time to share with all who will have the eyes to see and the ears to listen of what has taken place for them, and to tell of those things they have been shown and who they have walked with.

"They will return to share with all who will be willing to listen to those things they have to share so you will know that this is possible for you to do as well, so they will hear those things that are presented and take them within their own life path to learn from.

"As they hear those things that will be shared, they will be reminded of a great truth, one that will share with them the light that is needed for the path they have come to travel.

"They will hear how it is possible for one to have wisdom with them, this wisdom that will allow them to see clearly all choices that are being presented to them while they remain in this domain of the Earth Mother. For these times are the mark of the ending of all times they have come to know," continued the elder from the east.

CHAPTER 28

✣

The Four Steps to Leaving This Domain with Your Robe

The Ascension Process

"They will be reminded of the steps that they will need to follow in order to find the wisdom that resides within each of them.

"First comes the event.

"The event comes to you from all the people, places, and things that come to you. And all comes in perfect timing. They will cause them to feel anger, fear, love, hate, anxiety, and uncertainty for themselves and all that is around them.

"But these events will come to share a great lesson with them. And this lesson leads us into the second step.

"The second step that comes is the knowing.

"Knowing is a result of first having the event present itself. Now, there is a very important lesson to this event that will have presented itself to all of the two-legs. And this lesson has been missed by many of them time and time again.

"Remember when we shared with you that there is not ever a prayer for assistance that will be asked which will not be answered. Then remember how we have shared with you that most prayers are not understood by the one who is asking them? And for those prayers of assistance that are not understood, the answers that come are not easily seen by them for what they are?

"This is the same for these events that continually come to the two-legs. They are in answer to what they have been asking. But since they do not understand what they have been requesting assistance for, they cannot see the events that will come to them as being of benefit to them, or it being an answer to what they have been attempting to see.

"For example, let us say there is one who is continually asking how well they are doing on their path. This one has been asking to see what it is they still need to work on in order to be better at whatever it is they are doing.

"Now, let us say they do not fully understand what it is they are asking for, that they do not see through the face of illusion to this request they are making of those who are with them, who have come into this domain to offer their assistance to them.

"So, when the answer comes to them, they see it as something that is completely incorrect for what it is. They see this answer as something that is bad or as an enemy that needs to be dealt with. But they will not see it as their answer.

"For when this answer will come to them, it will be placed in an environment which they can relate to but may not understand.

"They will most likely see either a bad work situation come to them, the boss will no longer be their friend, their lover will be untrue to them, their family will disown them, or they will have circumstances come to them they do not perceive as being pleasant for them to be in.

"But I share with you, in truth, this is the answer they have been asking for. For what they are seeing in others are those situations that are making them feel very bad, but they are only a confirmation for what they still need to work on from within themselves.

"For all of those miserable feelings they are experiencing from others around them are a confirmation to what is still within them that is not yet understood. And these people, places, and events, that are causing them so much misery, are a reflection of themselves that is coming to them from another, or others.

"However, instead of thanking them for showing what they still need to work on, they look at them as the enemy and will do most anything to get away from them.

"Now this is what I am making reference to as an event. And when one will not see this for what it is in truth, they will turn away from it, and will not come to the place of seeing the next step we call the knowing.

"The knowing is a direct result of the event, when it is not turned away from, when it is looked on for what it is and seen as a part of oneself that still needs work.

"Then there will be a knowing that will show them it is not the one who has come to them that is making them feel very bad. But it is their friends and family who are sharing with them what is still needed by them to work on from the unseen part of themselves.

"When they will see this, they have come to the knowing and will be ready for the third step, understanding.

"Remember, my brothers, first came the event, then came the knowing, and next comes the understanding. However there can be knowing without having understanding, but there cannot be understanding without first having gone through the knowing.

"What understanding shares is how all of the events, and the knowing, relate to each other. You see, when one is trapped within the sleep of illusion, they cannot see how any of this fits into their personal life path. All they see is that it is either being done by someone else or it is for another. But at no time will they see that it is they whom all things are done for.

"They will not see this until they have come to understand their way out of their own sleep of illusion.

"For all that will happen to any who will be traveling their earth walk, there is but one specific reason for its presence. And the reason anything will take place is to assist them in learning those things they have entered this domain to learn from, and later to understand.

"One will attain their understanding for all things that will happen to them when they understand that everything they see or do or which has been done to them, is for their benefit. That there is not ever anything that will happen to them that is not for them to learn from. And it is for their learning that this takes place.

"Many will walk to you and say that they have always been the target for others through their whole life path, but I share with you they are still asleep in the illusion. For if they were even partially awake, they would see that all of this was for them, and for them alone to learn from.

"For the ones who remain locked within their own sleep of illusion, my brothers, they will not find this knowing on the path they are traveling. For those who will find the understanding on their paths, they will see there is nothing that comes to them that has not been designed for them to learn and later to understand from.

"When this is seen by the two-legs who will come to you in this Season of the Long Shadow, they will find understanding for all that has taken place to them, and the reason for what is happening to them in their earth walk.

"When they see how truly personal life is to them, they begin to understand. And understanding will allow them to see all of the people, places, things, and events that will ever come to them and say:

'What Have You Brought to Me to Learn From You, My Brothers And Sisters Of Life?
What Have You Brought Me So I May See Myself More Clearly From All That Is With Me?'

"When they will have come to understand this face of their own truth, they will have surely found their beginnings on their path to understanding, this understanding that will assist them greatly in all they will see and do.

"When they will have completed this third step, they will be ready to begin the fourth step. And this is the step of wisdom.

"This last step in the process I have been willing to share with all of you is the most important. For without wisdom, my brothers, there can be no using of either the understanding or the knowing that have come to you from the event that you have been willing to work your way through its emotion it carried to you.

"Wisdom that is gained from understanding, will allow you to see how well suited each event that comes to you really is. And it is through understanding that there will not ever be anything come to you out of punishment. Follow these speaking words I am now willing to share."

The Elder took a few moments to look over the faces of our council of five. I could tell that there was something she was looking for, something that was within each of us. But the time she spent looking into each of us was not long before she continued.

"Unless the two-legs reach their own place of wisdom for all that has come to them, my brothers, they will not have the eyes nor the ears to understand this next part I am willing to share with you.

"For when they witness the event that is soon to be with them, they will have such a great fear, they will no longer hold a desire to understand it. They will be so filled with fear that they will no longer be able to see what is in front of them anymore.

"And this next face of The Season of the Long Shadow is where there will be two walking next to each other and one of them will disappear and the other one will remain. The one who will have disappeared will leave without a trace of where they have gone, but they will not be gone long.

"In three to eleven days, they will return to be seen and heard by those who have known them before. They will do this in a way of telling others where they have gone. And this place they have gone to will be the waiting place.

"When they return to this domain, they will share with those who are willing to see and hear them that they, too, can do this. And they will also share that once they will be willing to do the necessary work of learning their own lessons, they, too, will no longer have to go through the pains of birth or death. For there will no longer be a need of this for them.

"You see, my brothers, when this time comes, the two-legs will be asked to make their great choice. There will be another piece of truth that will be shared with all life. And this truth will be that when this Earth Mother enters her fifth world of peace and light, there will no longer be the same lessons that are with her now for any to learn from.

"Those lessons will have been moved into the twelfth earth. And for the ones who are still in need of learning from them, they too will have to leave this Earth Mother and go into the next one where they will do all of this…All Over Again.

"The only ones who will be allowed to return here, from that time on, will be those who have left with their robes, the ones who no longer have to go through the pains of birth and death. They will be all who will remain in this domain, for nothing else will be allowed entry.

"This Earth Mother is tired, my brothers. She can no longer continue to offer all of the lessons she once held for us to learn from.

"So in the final times of The Season of the Long Shadow, there will be great fires above and below her and there will be nothing left of what once was. For her cleansing must be complete for her to enter this fifth world of peace and light.

"When she has been completely engulfed in flames, the great star nation will send their comets into her great bodies of water. This will be their effort in putting out all of her flames. And from this effort, there will rise a great white mist over all this domain that you see before you. Then as the clouds of the white mist begin to rise back into the sky nation to find a home for themselves, the ones who had left with their robes, or bodies, will enter once again. And when they do this, life will continue. But it will be a life where only peace and light will be allowed to exist.

"This then is the sixth face for The Season of the Long Shadow, my brothers. Be assured that it is on its way, for there is no thing that may stand in its way, it will soon be time for its birth to be felt by all."

CHAPTER 29

❀

Seventh Face

From the Elder of the South—
Fear Comes From What We Do Not
Understand

There was a brief period of silence that covered this place we had all come to find shelter in after hearing the speaking words from the Elder in the East.

It had come for me at a very good time. For this time was giving me a chance to sort through all that had been shared on this day. There had been many things come to us from this sharing of the Ancient Ones, and I knew much of it would take time to be understood.

However, from those things that had been shared with Cheeway and me from Grandfather and Two Bears, I held the knowing that all of this was being given directly to my spirit. And all things that are touched to our spirit within us are not ever forgotten. They remain in the within place until the time is right, then they will come into our thinking minds. They will resurface once again showing no difference on them from the time they were first shared.

For all of this, I was grateful. For I knew that I could not have held so much within my thinking mind, not as much as these Ancient Ones' of our people had been willing to share with us.

And from the look that had come over the Elder in the South, I could tell he had much more to share on this time that is called The Season of the Long Shadow, this time we were being told was already on its way into this domain of the Earth Mother.

But he was holding his silence for a while longer, and I knew this was to give all of us a short rest, a rest that was needed very badly from all that had taken place.

Looking past the opening of the great stone cave we had all come to find shelter in, I let my thought venture into the valley below, that was still being washed by the tears of the water spirit and blown by the Spirit Wind that was keeping its presence known to all of us.

As I looked at the swaying of the children of the leaf, this swaying of their reminding how to give way to those things which were stronger than they are, I felt a time coming to me from my within place, a time that until now I had thought was behind me.

"Grandfather," came the first sounds from my within place's memory.

"Yes, Little One," was his return. "What is it that brings to you a concerned face to wear?"

"It is what I feel from the people, Grandfather. I do not hold a knowing of why I felt such differences," I returned.

"What people are you making reference to, Speaking Wind?" Grandfather asked with a look of understanding over his face.

"It is the difference that I feel between you and Two Bears and the black robes, those who go to the big churches that are close to our lands.

"When it comes time for Cheeway and me to receive our lessons from you and Two Bears, there is always a great feeling of warmth that comes to us from both of you. And when we forget those things that you have been willing to share with us, you do not get angry with us and tell us how bad we have been. You look on us and say that each of us have a path to follow and those things we have done—those things that have been contrary to the teachings you have been willing to share with us, well—they have only allowed us to see our path a little more clearly.

"But when the black robes who teach in the great church near our lands, when they teach, it is like they are only pretending to teach those things they do not understand. Because when Cheeway and I do something that is wrong in their eyes, they punish us very hard and make us hurt.

"They do not see us as people, but they only see us as ones who are not following their way of living."

"And you are wondering why there is such a great difference from what they tell you to do, and those things they do?" Grandfather asked.

"Yes, Grandfather, this is my question," I returned.

"The answer is very simple, Speaking Wind. All you will have to do is see the difference from where they stand, and where we are standing," Grandfather began.

"You see, little one, those things that Two Bears and I have been willing to share with you and Cheeway, they are from the path of the spirit. And on the path of spirit, there is no separation from anyone or anything.

"For when one will follow spirit, they will see that all is within the One—and the One is a part of all that is.

"However, the ones who teach in the great church near our lands, they do not teach so much from the spirit path, but they teach more from the religious path. And it is religion that keeps them separated from themselves. Separated so much that they no longer see what they are looking for resides within all life, not in a set way of living.

"The Great Messenger that had begun their teachings, the one they call The Christ, he was truly one of the Great Messengers who had come to deliver a message for all who would be willing to hear.

"And he, too, traveled this path of the spirit, not one of religion.

"However, as has been the case with all of the messengers that have been willing to enter this domain of the Earth Mother with a message, they were seen as a threat by the few who would wish to live in the illusion of controlling others through their fear. And this resulted in those few taking the truth out of his message and replacing it with their fear so they could control others, or live in the illusion of controlling others through their fear.

"You see, little one, when one will travel the path of spirit, there is no one who will ever be in control of another. But when one will travel the path of illusion, there must always be one, or a few, who feel they must be in control. For them, there is no other way to be seen or believed in.

"The path of religion is on the path of illusion. For when you look at the Messenger who began their own teachings, you will see that he did not curse or judge another—but the religion people do.

"When you will look at the teachings of their own Messenger, you will not find him holding himself above another—but the religion path does.

"When you will hear those things he was willing to share, you will not find anything in his speaking words that would tell you that anyone is better than another. But when you will listen to what those who are on the path with religion tell you, there will always be one that is better than another—and we have prepared you to know that this is not a truth."

"So why are there so many groups of them, Grandfather? Can they not see?" I asked.

"In truth, Speaking Wind, there are many who still need to learn these lessons of looking past the fear another would place over them, before they can see themselves for who and what they are in truth," Grandfather returned.

"Then their presence will continue to be with us?" I asked.

"For as long as there are those who would need to learn from those lessons, Speaking Wind," was Grandfather reply.

"And when there will no longer be any who would fear seeing themselves for who and what they are, Grandfather?" I asked.

"Then there will no longer be a need for this path of religion, Speaking Wind. There will only be the path of spirit where everyone will be free to follow their own needs without fear," Grandfather replied.

Listening to those speaking words of my past seasons come to life within me brought me to a new place of seeing, one that assisted me greatly in listening to all that was being shared with me from the Ancient Ones of our people. It was when there would no longer be any need of fear that we would all be free to see.

But why would any of us need fear, I wondered. Why would anyone wish for such a thing to come to them?

"It is good to hear you so well, Speaking Wind," came the speaking words from the Elder in the South.

"For you have seen a part of this seventh face for The Season of the Long Shadow, Little One, this face that shares with you fear will only come to you from those things you do not yet understand.

"We have long known of many truths that once held their place within this domain of the Earth Mother, Speaking Wind. And we have seen many of them disappear, one by one, through the efforts of the controlling ones who force others to live in their own controlled image.

"For as many generations as there are stars in the great nations of the night sky, there have been as many messengers sent into this domain to share these truths with those who would have the eyes to see and the ears to hear them with.

"However, as we get closer to the ending of time as it is now known, there are many fears that are being grown in the lives of all, fears that are coming to them with the face of concern, fears that are being held over them by those who even now are feeling their controlling power over many beginning to ebb.

"And this is causing the fear brokers to hand out in greater quantities that which they have been giving to others—fear. But for them, they fear losing what they perceive as the control they have held over many in the past. And this is the fear they will live with until the end of their time.

"But let us go back to what has caused this face of fear to live with so many, and for such a long time. Then we will come to understand what it will mean for them when it is time for The Season of the Long Shadow to arrive.

"Keep in the front of your thinking minds, my brothers, that when truth is understood, it is very simple and able to be seen easily by all who would wish to do so. It is only when truth is not complete nor understood that it takes on a face of confusion and travels on a path that seems to be just beyond one's reach.

"As I have been willing to share with you, there have been many messengers who have entered this domain to deliver their messages. This is not anything new, my brothers; it has been done for all generations.

"Not one generation has been without at least one messenger. And when they woke from their sleep of preparing and saw the path they had to travel, they began to see the truths they brought with them, these truths they willingly and openly shared with those who held a need for them.

"And it is as I have shared with all of you, when they had delivered their messages and the truths that were within them, they were simple and easy to understand, for there were no distortions about them. Because of this, each one who would listen to their messages understood what it meant to them.

"However, from such simplicity of understanding, there came a great fear over those who lived with the illusion that they held control over others…a fear that if everyone would know of such truths that were held in the teachings of the messengers, they would no longer have a hold over those who were around them. If truth were known to all, there would not be any place for leaders, and they would most surely lose their position and status.

"You see, my brothers, truth can be a great enemy to those who do not wish to see change come to anything they have grown used to. It can be a great enemy because when one understands their truth, they no longer see themselves as holding a blind allegiance to another. They understand there is only one Creator, one journey, and one inevitable path of returning. And all of this is done by them, and for them, and without the assistance of another who would tell them what is right and wrong.

"So in each generation, there have been those who would exercise control over many. And it has been these few who have looked very closely at those messages that have been delivered into this domain and seen them as a threat to the positions they held.

"While they have numbered few, their influence over those who were near them was great. And when the messengers would come into this domain of the Earth Mother to deliver their messages of truth, those who were in control would look very carefully at those things the messenger had brought with them.

"It would not take them long to see the simplicity of what was being shared, and because of the simplicity of the messages' truth, they found many ways of distorting and changing what everyone was hearing. They would take the truth out of the messages and replace it with fear.

"This was not difficult for them to do because when a messenger will deliver their truths, there will be nothing confusing about it. For what they will share, will be understood by all.

"So, the controlling ones would take what was being shared and make it more complicated. They would take something very simple and easy to understand and separate it into so many pieces, there would soon be nothing left of what had originally been shared, nothing left of the simplicity of truth that had once been presented by the messenger.

"However, the ones who were doing this, the ones who wanted to control others—they did not see what they were doing as being anything particularly bad. They saw a need to keep this truth away from the others. They perceived them as not being ready to embrace such a thing and had come to believe they were doing this for the good of those who were being led by them.

"You see, my brothers, one of the prices of controlling others is that they will always come to you looking for answers they should be looking for within themselves but they choose another instead. And this brings the perception of a great responsibility with it, one that is locked within the illusion, but one they see as being very real.

"For when these controlling ones see anything that they perceive as being bad for themselves, they believe it would have to be as bad for everyone else around them. To them, there is no other path to follow.

"So when they hear these simple truths that have been delivered by the messengers, they will regard them as something that will take away their authority over others, and see them as something that would rob them of their place in the community.

"Because they see this simplicity of truth as a threat to their own position, they also see it as a potential for great harm to those who follow them…or to those who would listen to them.

"This, then, is the reason they will begin to separate these simple truths into something that is so complicated that no one can follow. They will do this, in their way of thinking, to protect the masses from doing harm to themselves. But in truth, they have done this so they will not lose any of the perceived power they hold over others.

"In the beginning, they will see many that will attempt to understand this complicated mess, but none will succeed at understanding it. And this will bring to them a good face to wear. But it will not last long.

"For they will have come to see that there might be one among the many who could stumble on this truth that had been delivered by the messenger. And this makes them very uncomfortable.

"So they busy themselves in removing all semblance of truth that had once been within the message and replace it with their own fear that will not allow any of those they hold a control over to look for this truth without feeling they are doing something very bad.

"Once this has been achieved, they believe they can rest and continue on with their own business as usual. For they believe they have succeeded in keeping anyone from understanding there is more meaning to their life than they want them to know.

"When one will take a message and strip the truth out of it, there will only be the empty shell left of what it once was, an empty shell that will serve no purpose to anyone.

"When this has taken place, no one will look to the messages for answers, these messages that would have shared what was needed could always be found within themselves. Rather, they will look to those who would tell them what to do, those who have been telling them what is right from wrong, and good from bad.

"And by their doing this, they continue to buy into their own illusion that keeps them from understanding themselves for who and what they are in truth.

"This has been taking place in this domain for all generations and has resulted in many pieces of life being seen, but not understood. And those pieces of life that are not understood are labeled evil or bad by the ones who have followed the path of being controlled by others.

"Once again I share with you there is no thing in this or any of the domains of life that is bad or evil. There are only those things that will come to you, which reminds you of a lesson or lessons you have not yet worked on.

"Rather than look on something or someone as being bad or evil, look at them as an extension of yourself, as a part of yourself that is still in need of work, as a reflection of the you within that is not yet understood.

"For when the time comes and The Season of the Long Shadow is upon all in this domain, there will be a great need by the two-legs to see that all which is presented to them is done with them in mind. This is done for them to see what it is about themselves that still needs work on so they may come to understand themselves for who and what they are in truth.

"Unless they will have come to the place of understanding themselves completely, when the time will come for them to make their great decision, there will be none for them to make.

"For those who have not yet come to understand themselves and all that is around them—completely—they will have only one option available. They will be the ones who will have to do all of this over again. And I share with you that this will bring a great sadness to them when they see they could have made a choice that could have given them another possible outcome to the one they now have to make.

"So remember, my brothers, all prayers are answered. And since each of the two-legs is continually asking how well they are doing in this earth walk of theirs, they are continually given answers.

"And one of the answers is while they continue to see fear before them, there will be many places within themselves that require more work to be done, places that will be directly related to what it is they fear at the time.

"This will be their guidance, then. What they will fear will be exactly what they need to work on—within themselves," came the end of the speaking words of the Elder of the South.

CHAPTER 30

❀

Eighth Face

From the Elder of the West—
We Will Be Drawn To Our Most Successful
Earth Walk

(Author's note: The Season of the Long Shadow began in July 1992 and the first doorway opened. At the writing of this book, the second doorway opened on June 11, 1995.)

When the speaking words from the Elder of the South had finished, she closed her eyes and remained silent. For there was more to be shared with all of us on this day and she was allowing the next part of it to come to life.

Looking over our council of five, the next part of sharing was taking form. And this was to come to us from the Elder of the West.

As he took a few moments to look over us as we were still sitting in our original positions, he shared a large and warm smile, one that we could feel more than one we could see.

"Look well into your hearts, my brothers, for this time of The Season of the Long Shadow is soon to be at hand," the Elder of the West began.

"For when this time is entered, there will be a great doorway opened and all will feel its presence. There are seven great doorways to be opened, and eleven steps with each of them to be passed through before this time will be over.

"The first doorway to be opened will be the one which allows all of the two-legs the opportunity of seeing all lessons they have not learned from. And they will see them as emotions that are very unpleasant to look at.

"At first, they will attempt to blame others for what they are feeling. But as time will pass, they will see that all of those feelings they are receiving are from themselves.

"This will be the time they will either work their way through these emotions that have confronted them in order to find their own lessons and gain understanding from them; or, they will turn back around and look the other way thinking that if they will ignore them, they will go away—but they will not, for the time of doing such things will have passed.

"The second doorway to open will be one similar to the first, but not entirely.

"When the first doorway opened, it offered the opportunity of settling all of the old debts (karma) for all the lessons that had gone unlearned during this earth walk. But when the second doorway will open, it will offer everyone the opportunity of settling their accounts for all lessons missed from all of the earth walks.

"As each doorway will open, there will be a feeling of anticipation that something great is going to happen. And this will be felt by all life. For in front of each doorway, there is a great energy that will present itself before the doorway is cracked open. And this will be felt by all life.

"This presence of energy among the two-legs will make them feel vulnerable and overly sensitive, and creates the possibility of increased anger for all, anger that will get out of hand if they do not understand what is feeding it.

"During these times, each emotion that will be felt and seen within each of you will be like another log that is placed on a hot fire. And when one will begin to express their anger at anything or anyone they do not understand, they will feel their anger grow to not-seen-before levels.

"In these times, the smallest thing will cause the non-understanding person to fall over the edge. For when they get angry at something, at first this anger is small. But if they will allow it to grow within them, then all of those emotional logs they have allowed to gather within them begin to feed their fire of anger. And this will cause them to become like a raving mad person, striking out at any one and all things near them.

"Even they will not understand why they become so angry. But during this time of the Season of the Long Shadow, if anger is left to one in a non-understood state, it can become disastrous for themselves and anyone who is near them.

"From the opening of the first great doorway to the opening of the seventh, there will be an acceleration of this energy that will come pouring into this domain that is the Earth Mother. And as this energy will increase, the likelihood of these outbursts of uncontrollable anger will increase as well.

"So it is important that the two-legs come to a place of understanding what will be presented to them during this time of cleansing, my brothers. For during this eighth face, they will all be drawn to their most successful earth walks.

"They will be drawn to them in order to rediscover all of the talents and wisdom they had attained during those times of their past when they walked with the Earth Mother. They will be drawn to them because they will need them. They will need them if they are to understand this time that is soon to arrive and the choice they will soon be asked to make.

"The drawing to their most successful past earth walks will take place in this manner. And I share this with you so you may share with those who will have a great need as well.

"Once the first gate opens at the beginning of The Season of the Long Shadow, there will be an increased awareness by all of the two-legs for those things that will come before them. Those things that will be from another culture or race, other than the one they had entered this domain in.

"They will have their eyes opened for them during this time, and this opening of their eyes will not close for the remainder of this time we speak to you of.

"At first, they will feel sorry for a people's race or culture that they are looking at. But this will pass by them because after a short time of seeing what is before them, they begin to realize that they are not feeling anything of the sort. They are not feeling sorrow or pity for these people and their way of life, but they feel something familiar with them, something within them they no longer have. And this is the reason they first come to mistake what they are feeling as a sorrow or pity.

"Next, they will begin to look at those things these people are doing, these things that have to do with their ceremony or their way of asking assistance from the One Source of all creation. Or they will look at the remains of certain objects that have been left behind from those cultures or races that no longer live within this domain of the Earth Mother.

"When they will first come to see these things, they will find themselves glued to them in a way they will not be able to take their eyes away from what they are looking at.

"When they have reached this point in their discovery, there will be many pictures begin to form within them, that will present them with an understanding for those objects or things these people were doing, these people and ceremonies they have not been associated with during this earth walk.

"From these silent pictures that begin to take form within them, there will be an understanding for them, that will share what the meaning of what all of this means, an understanding for those objects they are looking at from the people who are no longer residing in this domain.

"As it finds its place to reside within their thinking minds, there will come to them additional pictures from their within place, this place where spirit resides within all of us. These pictures will be of people and lands they have not seen before. But they will recognize them as ones they once knew, but not in this earth walk.

"Through all of this, there will come to them a feeling of belonging, my brothers, a feeling they belong with these people they are looking at, and they will begin to wonder if their earth parents fooled them by not telling them what their real identity is. They will believe this very strongly in the beginning because of how they feel toward this race or culture of people they are looking at.

"However, this does not last long either, because soon thereafter there will be other people, races, and cultures that will be presented to them. And they will go through this same set of circumstances for them, as they had gone through with the first ones.

"When this takes place, they realize it is just not possible for them to have all of these races and cultures within them for this earth walk. For if this were to be the case, they would have had more than one set of parents. And they understand this is not possible.

"So they will content themselves in wondering what all of this means to them, why they have so many ties and feelings to people, places, cultures, and races.

"They begin to look for these answers in the people they have seen, in those cultures they have not been a part of, and those races that are completely different from who had what they are in this earth walk.

"But when they will approach these other people and places, they find they are not welcomed by them in many cases. For the place they come from is so different, they are looked on through eyes of disbelief and are not given any room or place among those they have come to, those they have come to in an effort of understanding why they are feeling such a draw to them.

"There will be many two-legs who will go through this, my brothers. And there will be many who will give up on their searching from what they have experienced from those they have gone to. But they find there will not be a way for them to leave this behind, for the time when that could be done is over, too.

"They will continue to see and feel things from races and cultures other than their own, and they will not understand why.

"It is for what is being brought into this domain by the opening of the great doorways that they are going through this. For when these doorways will open, there will be so much revealed to all of the two-legs—without having come to the place of understanding for who and what they are in truth. There will be no way they can keep up with what will be presented to them during this time for The Season of the Long Shadow.

"You see, when the two-legs will come to feel this drawing to all of these other cultures and races, they are feeling a drawing from within themselves. But it is not a drawing that would have them go and live among those people again, it is one that is calling their attention to whom and what they had once been from one of their many other earth walks with the Earth Mother. These feelings of being drawn to these different cultures, races, and times…they are only reminding them of the places they have traveled before.

"When they understand this, there will be a new level of awareness come to life from within them that will allow them to see all of the talents and wisdom they had attained before. This is what will be needed by them during this time of The Season of the Long Shadow. And this is what is being presented to them from the eighth face for this time that even now is on its way to all," came the end of the speaking words from the Elder of the South.

❀

CHAPTER 31

Ninth Face

From the Elder of the North—
Fear Of Height, Fire, Falling, Etc., Are
From Your Last Journey

"There will be much fear that will come into the life paths of all earth walkers, my brothers—fears that will bring important lessons to all in this time of The Season of the Long Shadow," began the speaking words from the Elder in the North.

"However, they will not have the talents nor the wisdom of understanding their way through this fear until they have come to see what still needs to be worked on by them, those things they have brought with them to understand from.

"There are many fears that are brought back with each earth walker, my brothers, fears that are from falling, fire, suffocating, heights, loneliness, sadness, drowning, being closed in, not seeing, cold, heat, hunger, loud noises, being yelled at, and pain. These are only a few that each one will bring with them when they return into this domain of the Earth Mother. And these fears come with them because there is still much for them to work their own way through.

"You see, my brothers, these fears I speak to you of have come with these earth walkers from another earth walk they have had in the past, one which ended very abruptly for them.

"And it was this sudden ending of their earth walk that has brought them this feeling of fear we are speaking of, for there was no time for them to prepare before their time in this domain was ended.

"Whenever one will come to the end of their path and is not prepared for it, there will be an emotion that will accompany him. And this emotion comes to him from the way they have ended their journey.

"When one will enter this domain that is the Earth Mother, they do so in order to learn. And the only way they can learn to overcome this lesson that has been left with them—this lesson that had come as a quick ending to their last life path—it can only come to them through the emotion of what took place for them.

"It can only come to them from this emotion because there is nothing left they can recognize. They do not return with the memory of their past earth walks, nor do they remember their journey.

"They do not remember any of this because when they return they are submerged into the sleep of illusion that will not allow them to see or understand such things until they have worked their way through many lessons in order to wake from the illusion.

"However, they must work through these ordeals they had gone through, and they can only be worked through while they have a shell to travel in and are within this domain. For this learning cannot be achieved in any other place.

"So, they will enter with the emotion of these events that had brought them to a quick and unprepared end for their last journey.

"Now keep in the front of your thinking minds how the two-legs deal with all they do not have an understanding for. They will either attempt to destroy it, or if they cannot destroy it, they will fear it. And since they cannot destroy it, they must fear it.

"This is why you will see so many carry such a great face of fear on them, my brothers. Much of it comes from something that has nothing at all to do with this earth walk. Most of it has come from another place and another time that they do not hold a remembering of any longer.

"But this fear for them is real, and is with all who enter this domain to walk a life path.

"Now this truth that I am willing to share with all of you has been delivered by many messengers throughout all generations. And it has always been the few who would wish to live in the illusion of controlling others who have stripped away this truth and replaced it with their own fear that would not allow another to know truth, but to fear what they had returned to this domain with.

"It is through fear that another will be controlled, my brothers. And everyone will carry a fear with them until they reach a place that is within themselves to understand their way through it.

"It is like anticipating cutting yourself with a sharp object. When you get a cut, but will not be aware of its coming, there is not the same kind of fear as when you will know the inevitable—that this cut is coming to you.

"When you will not have the awareness of this time that is inevitable, you will not carry with you anything to think on or worry about. And when it will happen, then it happens.

"However, if one were to tell you that you must sit still and wait for this sharp object to cut you and let you observe the process, you would be filled with a great fear that would make this cut hurt more than it would under other circumstances, because you have imposed your fear through emotion over it.

"This is what those few who would wish to control you with this fear will do when you will not understand what they are doing. They would tell you that all you hold with you through this emotion of fear has come to you because you have done something wrong, or you are not doing something right. But in truth, they are saying that you are not doing it their way. And because you are not doing it their way, it has to be wrong.

"The two-legs will listen to them and believe this must be truth. For why else would they know so much of those things they fear, those things they do not have an understanding for. If they follow them and the direction they are told to follow, they will lose their way on this earth walk they have come to learn from.

"Do not take this controlling by these few for anything more than what it is, my brothers. These few do not do this because they are evil or bad, for the teachings that have been shared with us say this is not a truth at all.

"These teachings remind us that there is no thing in this or any other domain that is bad or evil. It is only when we do not understand something within ourselves that we perceive it in this way.

"For those who would follow this illusionary path of controlling others, think of them in the same way one would call themselves to be the owners of lands or animals. And I tell you in truth, there is no difference between them and the ones who would wish to control another by using the fear they have with them. For they do not understand what it is, in truth.

"Let us take the land for this example, this will be the easiest to follow, my brothers.

"When one will come to a place they want to be only theirs, they will say…'This is my land because I have paid for it.'

"They will see this land as something that belongs to them and them alone. All that will be produced by this land will also belong to them and they will be free to do with it as they please.

"They will put fences around it so that others will see it as being different from all of the other lands that are near. And this difference will separate their lands from another's.

"To them, this is very important. For without this separation, in their thinking minds, their lands might be confused with another's and this is something else they fear happening to them. For it could take away the perceived control they hold over these lands.

"They will separate the land by marking it with fences so that all who would pass by it will say that this land belongs to this person or another. But how foolish it is to say such a thing.

"For the land itself has a life to it, and its life path cannot be separated from its other brothers and sisters. For it travels a path that belongs to the One within the One.

"However, the land will follow its own life path. And when you see many people fighting over their small bits and pieces of it, there is a great reason that comes from the land itself.

"When lessons the land needs to learn from do not coincide with the separation the two-legs have put over it with their fences, there comes a cry from the land that is heard by all life around it.

"It is a cry that is calling for assistance to put an end to what has come over it, an end to the separateness that has come over it by those who would wish to claim ownership to something that is not theirs to begin with.

"This assistance comes in a way that makes the one who claimed ownership over the land wish they had not ever had it.

"This assistance will come either through the natural order of having this person let go of their control over the land, or there will come many natural catastrophes that will eventually make it undesirable for the two-legs to remain. But in either case, there will no longer be the controlling aspects that were once there and the land will have the freedom to travel its own life path once again, its own life path where it may learn those lessons that are needed by it.

"It is the same with the ones who are being controlled, my brothers. They will have this controlling come over them until they too will reach out and ask for assistance that will allow them to no longer be owned by being controlled through their fears.

"And the ones who would control through fear, they see everyone as something they own. To them there is no difference in owning a piece of land or one they exercise control over. For both is a possession to them, and both hold equal value.

"But I share with you once again, the only things we have ownership over is what we will take with us to the waiting place when it is time for us to leave. Everything else is only borrowed and it would be good if we would return it when we are finished with it.

"So it is, my brothers, that when this ninth face for The Season of the Long Shadow will arrive in this domain of the Earth Mother, there will be a great need to once again hear this truth that shares these things I have been willing to share with all of you.

"For there will be great acceleration to all that is with the two-legs. And this acceleration will be with them because the time they have all been given to learn from is soon coming to an end.

"When this time is over, there will appear the Great Messenger before them and he will ask them their great question. Will they take the path to the left or will they take the path to the right?

"But in either case, none will be allowed to remain where they are now."

CHAPTER 32

❀

Tenth Face

From the Elder of the East—
From One We Have Come, To One
We Will Return

"We are all in this long journey together, my brothers," began the speaking words from the Elder in the East position.

"But there are those who continue to reside within this domain who do not wish this to be known by any. And they are the same ones who would rather see the great separation before them rather than allowing another to see there is nothing, in truth, that separates any of us.

"In truth, there are none who are greater nor are there any who are lesser. This kind of separation does not exist, for all are equal with the other.

"There is only one difference from one to another—and this does not have anything at all to do with one being higher or lower—and that is that no two paths of learning will ever be the same.

"But when one will not understand this, they are caught in the illusion that another is different than themselves from what they see them doing on the path they have chosen to travel. They are fooled into seeing them as being either higher or lower than they are. However, this has nothing at all to do with truth, this only has to do with the kinds of lessons that are needed by one's spirit.

"When one will see another as being higher than they are, then they will be standing in their shadow. And where there is a shadow, there is no light. And where there is no light, there can be no growth.

"When one will see themselves as being higher than another, they will have caused this other to stand in their shadow. And where there is a shadow, there can be no light. And where there is no light, there can be no growth.

"However, when one will be willing to see through the illusion and see things for what they are in truth, they will see there is no difference from themselves to another, that there is only the difference in what lessons are needed by them for this earth walk and what lessons are needed by another. And this does not create one as being more or less than anyone else. It means that you are here to learn your lessons and they are here to learn theirs.

"Look at it this way, my brothers. When you will see one who has a great deal of wealth to them, do not envy them. For chances are that in their last life path, they were without any wealth at all. And the reason they have entered this domain of the Earth Mother with so much wealth is that they have a need to learn the many lessons that are available to them from this setting.

"When you will look at another as having more or less than you do, then you will be placing them higher or lower than you are. And this does not hold truth to it.

"Look at what you have with you in this life path you are traveling. And when you will, then you will begin to see what lessons there are for you to learn from, those lessons that are needed by your spirit in order to advance yourself to the next higher place of understanding for all things presented.

"Remember, there can be no thing done by you that will be right or wrong. There are only those things you do that are not understood, and what you will not understand, you will not learn from.

"So keep in the front of your thinking minds that while we do all of those things we do, when we will understand them, we will learn. Do not get caught up in the illusion of wondering what you are doing is right or wrong. For if you do this, you will be looking at yourself through the eyes of another. And no other will ever know what is needed by you.

"When it is time and The Season of the Long Shadow has begun, share with the two-legs who come to you with great fear and confusion in their eyes, what would be best for them to do. And that is to sit in their silence and observe a great story that has come to them.

"Tell them this is much like their own flower of life unfolding before them. And as it will begin to unfold, they will be shown all of those events and lessons that have been following them. They will see them through their eyes of clarity for what they are in truth.

"When they do this, my brothers, they will see what needs to be done by them. They will have come to the place of understanding why events come to all of us. And I share with you that they are just as prominent for you as they are for another, just as prominent and just as great in their strength. Then the only difference will be in how they look at them.

"When one will see their lessons as being much harder for them than they appear to be for another, it is only because they are having to go through them. If you would ask another if their events and lessons were harder on them than they seem to be for another, they would tell you they are.

"So remind the two-legs who will come to you that all they are going through is no greater or lesser than what another is going through. For all are only given those things they are ready for, and all are given the lessons they have determined for themselves as needing while they were still in spirit with us.

"However, when the two-legs look at themselves as being the only ones who are going through such lessons and events, they will always see themselves as being alone. And this will make them see all life as being completely unfair to them.

"When the time of the great cleansing has begun, you will see many of the two-legs come to you showing this look of great fear and confusion over themselves. Remind them they are not alone, that everyone is going through the same kind of learning. And when they see that you are sharing with them a truth, they will be more likely to sit back in their silence and observe what is being shown to them—all of it.

"You see, my brothers, when one will enter this domain of the Earth Mother, they design a great story for themselves to hear. It is a story that is filled with adventure, sorrow, happiness, and most important of all, learning.

"When they take their first breath of life into them, they will have taken their first step on this great adventure. They will have begun to have their storytellers speak to them.

"But this story does not come to them in the way their parents read to them, for this is not the natural course of anyone's path. It comes to them in the animated process of having people, places, and things come into your life path. As each of them enters this path you have come to travel, they will bring with them an emotion that will be your friend, a friend that is most often mistaken as the enemy.

"Behind each of these emotions, there lies a piece of your purpose, a piece of the great story you have created and have aligned each event to come into your life path to tell you.

"But when you search for this purpose, my brothers, you will not see it. And when you will try to find it, it does not come.

"In order to find these pieces of the story that you have designed for yourself to learn from, you must be willing to sit in your silence and observe them. When there will be an emotion carried to you by any of these people, places, or things that you have contracted with but do not understand them, look at them for what they are and repeat three times to yourself:

"Thank You For Coming To Me, My Friend. What Have You Brought Me To Learn From You Today?"

"When the two-legs see the truth that is carried in these speaking words, they will find the peace and purpose they have been looking for. They will no longer be filled with the great fear and confusion that comes to all who are still locked into their own sleep of illusion. They will no longer be in a group of many who are all striving to achieve their own individuality; they will be themselves. They will begin the journey to discover who and what they are in truth.

"With this knowing and understanding, there will come a great acceptance to them. It will be the acceptance that will no longer cause them to fear who and what they are, an acceptance that will share with them that who and what they are is needed by them. And for this knowing of understanding, they will be very surprised to find a feeling of completeness and belonging—a feeling of being complete with themselves, and a feeling of belonging as One within the One, of all life."

Then the Elder from the East paused in her speaking words and looked over to the place I was sitting, this place I had been given that was next to her.

Placing her right hand over my head, she continued:

"Listen well to what I am willing to share with you, Speaking Wind. For it is being placed deep within your spirit as I touch you, deep within your spirit to be awakened for you when the time will be right.

"You are one of the messengers who will do a great work in the time that is soon to be here, this time we have come to call The Season of the Long Shadow.

"When this time comes, Little One, you will see all of us once again. When we come to you, there will be no mistaking of who we are, or our purpose with you.

"Then it will be time for you to awaken from your sleep of preparing and the time of doing will be at hand. This will also mark the time when we will remind you all of these things we have been willing to share with you now…and more…much more.

"As I have shared with you, Little One, you are a messenger in this domain. And that which is before you to perform is great and there will be much assistance that you will be given.

"But keep in the front of your thinking mind that you will not be the only messenger. There will be three others, and they are receiving the same messages we are sharing with you.

"However, there is a great lesson for the messengers in the time of The Season of the Long Shadow, and great learning for them to go through.

"For the messengers will not be here to call great numbers to them, but they are here to remind the two-legs to stand strong on their own. And there will not be many who will hear these truths that will remain with you for long periods of time.

"However, as you share with those who would be willing to listen, there will be a great tendency for those who have gathered themselves to you to see you as one who has more knowledge than they. But I share with you that this is not truth. In truth, when anyone will see you as being in this way, they are not yet awake to themselves. It would be good for you to remind them that this is why they will see you in this light.

"For the ones who would see you in this light, Little One, I tell you this. It will be all right for them to do this but only for as long as it does not get in their way of learning those things they need.

"When it gets in their way, you must leave them and go to another place…or you must have them leave. Only by this process will they grow, Speaking Wind. For growth does not come from another…it only comes from within one's self. And if the time will come and they can only see you and no longer see themselves, then either you or they must leave and not return until balance has been regained by all.

"When the time has come and you have been awakened to be one of the messengers in this time we are speaking of, little one, and many come to see you as one who has more knowing than they do, then explain this to them and in this same way we are now willing to explain it to you.

"Remind them that we are all from the same spirit family and began from the same source, from the same Creator of all life.

"When you see they have a place of understanding for these things, share this parable with them, this story that will allow them to understand how you are in the place you are in, and how they, too, may arrive in this same place as well.

"Have them see a great open field where there is soft grass growing and the warmth of a loving sun. And share with them that all who will enter this domain of the Earth Mother are placed into a sleep of illusion which does not allow them to see the great number of others lying on the soft grass sleeping close to them. While they are locked within their own sleep of illusion, they only have eyes for themselves.

"However, as the ones who will first awaken from this sleep of illusion that will not allow another to see anything for what it is, but only for what they would wish for it to be, they sit up from their lying position on the soft grass.

"But they will only be in a sitting position, and not able to move on their own yet.

"However, they will see things around them for what they are. And as they look in all directions that are around them, they see great numbers of others who are also sleeping in this illusion. And they recognize them as being in the same place they just were.

"When one first wakes from their sleep of illusion, there is much for them to do. For they are not completely awake yet even though they can see all things that are around them for what they are in truth. They can see but they do not yet hold with them the understanding that will allow them to know what to do with what they see.

"So it is that when one will first wake from the sleep of illusion, they sit up and see much that has always been around them, but they will not yet know what to do with it.

"This is the place we have come to call the sleep of preparing, for it is a place that is on the outside of the illusion, but not yet within the place of being fully awake.

"As they sit in their sleep of preparing, they can see all that is around them, and all that is being presented to them, and others as well. But there is still much preparing for them to do before they can stand up and walk on their own.

"When they first sit up from lying in the sleep of illusion, they see many others who have also sat up and are looking around, just like they are doing.

"As they see these others who also were sitting, there will be a recognition of each other. And they will understand there is something very familiar about them, but they will not know what.

"As they continue to look around themselves, they see others who have not only sat up, but have been successful in standing up and walking around in this great land they are in.

"At first, they think they hold a great secret for things they do not yet know. And they will call out to them for assistance, assistance they believe will allow them to stand up too.

"However, when the ones who have been standing will hear their calls of help, they only look on them and smile. For they have passed through the sleep of preparing and now are awake. And it is from this awake place that they hold the understanding that they cannot do this work for them. For the ones who are still sitting and calling on them to help must be willing to do this work for themselves.

"When one will awaken, they understand that unless one will take the opportunity of doing their own work, any assistance will be short lived.

"In other words, if another were to go over to the ones who were in their sitting places and help them stand up, the minute they would leave them, they would fall back down. And sometimes when one will fall back down, they become so lost, their chances of falling back into their sleep of illusion would be very high.

"So they will look at all of the sitting ones and smile on them. And what will come from their smiles to these sitting ones is that this is possible for them as well. They, too, can stand up and walk with the rest of those who have awakened from the sleep of illusion as well as from the sleep of preparing.

"However, if those who would wish to join and walk with them are not willing to do their own work, they will look away from them, for there is still much that is required for them to do.

"Those who are in the standing places will soon find others who are standing. But in the beginning, neither of them can walk.

"However, when they will see another who is standing like them, they will feel a great urge to go to each other. And this is what will finally allow them to reach within themselves to find their answers of how to walk on their own in this domain that is the Earth Mother.

"When the ones who will have found their standing places discover they can walk, there will be a great meeting of all of them in special places. When this meeting will come to them, there will exist among all of them a great sharing of talents that will allow them to discover what they are to do in this domain.

"This is the beginning of the gathering of our family. The beginning of the gathering so that all who see will understand they, too, have a place to belong in, a place that has come to them from what they have seen other members of their spirit families succeed at doing for those who have awakened themselves and walked to others who are awake.

"So when another will come to you, Speaking Wind, and ask for your assistance in this Season of the Long Shadow, look deep into them and see if they are standing, sitting, or sleeping. For when you will, you will hold a better understanding for what it is they need to see for themselves, a better place of knowing what they are capable of understanding from that which you will be willing to share with them.

"When they come to you in these times that are soon to be among all life here, share this parable with them. The ones who will have eyes to see with and ears to hear with will understand, and it will be good. For the ones who do not yet have the eyes to see with or the ears to hear with, then understand there is still much they need to work on, and walk away. For there will not be time for you to remain with those who are not yet ready, Speaking Wind; there is far too much for you to do for the ones who are ready.

"For those who are ready to see and listen, they will see there is no thing that keeps them separated from any of life that is around them. They will see how much a part of them all life is and how much a part of all life they are. And for them, there will begin to be seen a balance, a balance that will allow them to understand there is in truth, no religion, country, race, or separation that exists anywhere but within the great sleep of illusion.

"They will understand where they belong is in the place of no separation, in the understanding where all life is a part of One with the One. This will be when they see clearly that we have begun from the One, and are in a long journey of learning and understanding so that we may return to the One. To the One we call Creator—for we are His children—and He is our home."

CHAPTER 33

❀

Eleventh Face

From the Elder of the South—
All That Does Not Hold Truth
Will Fall Away

"It is the eleventh face of The Season of the Long Shadow that will bring many of the two-legs their greatest fear," began the speaking words from the Elder in the South position.

"It is time when there will be many strange events that will present themselves to all who will continue to reside within this domain that is the Earth Mother, this domain where spirit comes to learn its many needed lessons.

"You see, my brothers, it will be during this time when many will come to lean or depend on what they had been led to believe in, on those things they have been told by others was truth. But when they lean on them during their time of great need, they will fall through them. For what they had been told was not truth. What was told to them were the empty shells where truth was once, but now holds nothing within it.

"Entry for The Season of the Long Shadow will be very soon. There will come to all a great feeling of hurriedness, and a mounting level of emotion that will comfort them with each passing day of this time.

"Throughout this time, there will be seven doorways that will open. And within these seven great doorways, there will be eleven steps.

"We will share with you what these doorways and steps mean, my brothers, but you will not be allowed to share this information with anyone until just before they will appear. The reason for this is very simple.

"When the two-legs know too far in advance what is about to happen, their eyes are fixed on those things that are yet to be. And they will not remember to look at what is being offered to them in the present.

"You can share with them that when each doorway opens during this Season of the Long Shadow, there will come to all of them many emotions that will make them feel vulnerable and out of sorts with all they have been close to.

"It is because of this layering of emotions that they will need to lean on those things they had been told were truth, for this is what they will have the most familiarity with. These will be the things they have felt most comfortable with as they searched for themselves through their earth walk.

"It would be good to remind the two-legs of this, my brothers. When they will have an emotion—any emotion come to them—they would do well to stand strong and face it and not attempt to run away from it.

"For what has come to them has done so out of friendship and well-being for their own spirit. This emotion has not come to them as an enemy, but has come to them as a reminder of something that is very important for them to learn from, as a reminder of a lesson they need to understand.

"Remind them, once again, that it is good to stand and face these emotions and say three times to themselves:

'Thank You For Coming To Me, My Friend. What Have You Brought For Me To Learn From You Today?'

"When they do this, my brothers, the emotions that have come to them will be seen as a friend, and not an enemy. They will be seen as a reminder of something that is within them that needs to be worked on. Worked on so there will be an understanding of themselves and all that is with them.

"For the ones who will not have the eyes and ears to see and hear with, they will be seen attempting to lean on those truths that are empty. They will be the ones who will lean on them and fall on their face. For what was once within these truths has been taken out and there is nothing left for any who would come to depend on them.

"Think of it in this way. When each of you were little and had gotten yourself into trouble with some of your friends, what would you do when you knew that there was trouble brewing for you?

"You would run away from it as fast as you could and go to your parents' or grandparents' house where you held the believing you would be safe from those who had brought you this face of trouble.

"When you would get home and enter the first available door, you would look behind yourself and see that those who had been chasing you would not come any further. They would remain out of your house and would pursue you no further, for there was an understanding in all of them that if they were to enter your house, they would have to deal with either your parents or grandparents. And they knew this would not be good for them to do.

"Now this is a truth that you have come to believe in, and because it held truth, you had come to lean on it because it gave you the support you needed at that time.

"But let us say that you did not understand this truth and instead of running into your parents' or grandparents' house, you believed you could run into any house and have the same results.

"Now, when the other kids would run and chase you, let us say you came to an old and unlived in house believing you would find the same protection as you had found in your parents' house.

"However, when you ran into this vacant house, you found the other kids did not wait for you outside. Rather, they followed you into this house and you were given your share of trouble.

"After this trouble had been delivered to you and the others left, you felt deserted for what you once believed in, a believing that would keep you safe when danger would approach you. But it did not and you would react in a most predictable way.

"You would pick yourself up from the floor and began to kick and break down this house that did not protect you as you once believed it would. And if you could have, you would have destroyed it completely, thinking that it was the house's fault for not having provided you what you had been seeking.

"It will be the same way for all of the two-legs who will not learn to see and listen from their own spirit in these times that are soon to be with them. They will encounter many emotions come pouring over them and look to the safety of what they had been taught to believe in, those many things they had been told were truth.

"However, since the emotions are from them, they will find when they enter these places they once believed would protect them—those same places and teachings they had been given to live with, for so much of their life—there will not be the protection in them they had been led to believe, and this will initially cause them to feel frightened. And later they will feel angered, so angered that they will attempt to destroy those places, those teachings, and those who had misled them with things that were not of truth.

"This will be the process that will come over this domain during the eleventh face for the Season of the Long Shadow, my brothers. For you will see that all which does not hold truth to it begin to fall away."

❀

CHAPTER 34

Twelfth Face

From the Elder of the West— Groups Begin to Fall Away, And From What Is Left, They Form One

"But there is another step in this process that would do well for all of you to hold in the front of your thinking minds. It will be when many of the groups who have been living off others will see a great danger come to them, a danger that will come to them from those who have seen their words as not being true," began the speaking words from the Elder in the West.

"It is during this time when you will see the once-great numbers in those groups begin to fall away, and the ones who had been an important part of them, walk away looking for their own truth...their truth that will assist them in understanding what they are feeling and why they wear a face of fear.

"And as these groups, who have come to live off of those they once controlled become smaller and smaller, they find there is not the same amount of money for them to continue. And they will see that they must either change or perish.

"This will be the time for the gathering of all their parts into one. They will gather unto themselves one great group that will believe its strength resides in its large number of those who would follow.

"In the beginning, there will appear to be a gathering of all separate groups into what appears to be the beginning of one. And there will be a call from those who would head this group for an end to separateness, a call that there will not be any difference for those who would walk with them.

"But if you will look on their words closely, my brothers, you will find nothing has changed, the same controlling procedures that were used to hold people before still remains with them. But there are not many who will see this until later.

"So in the beginning, this one group will lead its followers into believing that they are their answer, that if they will join with them, they will be doing a great good because they will be ending the long period of time of separateness.

"And they will tell those who would come to them their reason for doing this is that there is only one Creator, and he has only one way of living if there is to be any peace and happiness at all. And these secrets have been revealed to them so they might share with all.

"But I tell you in truth, my brothers, this is not truth. For what they are telling those who would listen to them now is no different from what they told them those many seasons past. The only difference is that now, the few who would wish to maintain control over the many—they have become a little wiser. And they have seen what had caused the falling away from all of the groups before.

"So they have made a great effort in now allowing this to occur again. And those who would be willing to listen closely to their words would hear this. Those who would be willing to open their eyes would see this as well.

"For the falling away from those things that did not hold truth was to allow the two-legs to see that until they will be willing to walk their own life path—until they are willing to be accountable for their own life—and until they will be willing to do their own work—there cannot be anything of value for them to hold onto. For all that is of value in life resides within ourselves.

"There will be many who will not see, nor will they listen, to those words that are being placed into them from the few who are still controlling. For they are telling others they are different from the groups of the past because they know the way, this way that has been shown to them by Creator, this way they are now ready to share with others who will follow them.

"However, I share this with you in truth: they have not been shown anything by Creator. For if they had, there would not be any groups at all, for this is not the path that is to be shown in this time of The Season of the Long Shadow.

"What they are saying is they have been told this is the way from their own illusion, from the part of themselves that has not been willing to let go of controlling others. And this way they are speaking of will allow them to hold their place within the illusion of controlling others for a short time longer. But I tell you; it will not be for long.

"You see, my brothers, during The Season of the Long Shadow, there is only one path to travel for all life. And this is the path of one's self. There cannot be any who would tell another what to do, for this will be the time of review and understanding for all those things that have been turned away from before...all of those lessons they thought they had buried within them or behind them long ago. And there is no room, nor is there any time, to look or listen to one who would tell you how to do this. For they are only telling you where they are, and this has nothing to do with you and where you need to travel for your own learning.

"But the ones who have called this one group to be formed and have called to the many who are still without eyes and ears to see or hear with, they see the dangers from what had been the cause of them losing so much power before, those dangers of allowing others too much time to think for themselves. And because of their way of seeing this mistake of the past, they will control with even more fear any who are not doing their will.

"It will be then that the ones who follow this group will be so fearful of doing anything wrong or having consequences come to them that they fear not being forceful to any who do not think as the group does. And from this fear, many will suffer, and many will have their time ended by them.

"When those who are in control of these groups see their efforts have not brought everyone back to them, they will perceive those traveling outside of their control as a threat to their existence, and could cause another breaking away of their group.

"In the beginning, there are great efforts made to bring back all who were once in the group. But this will not work for many, for those who have come to see and hear those things of spirit will not have anything to do with them because they will see the same control being used over those who still cannot see or hear.

"Next, there will be a great cry from all of the leaders of this one group for more control over those who are not willing to follow them, control over those who would not be willing to follow their way. For in their minds, there can only be one right, and this right is how they see all things. For any who would not do those things they say must surely be wrong. And they cannot allow such imperfection to remain in existence. After all, they see this as a holy war, and they see the ones who are not of their group as an enemy that must be destroyed.

"This will be what they will tell those who follow them. And they will listen to them—and they will believe in them.

"But I tell you in truth, this is not at all what is behind their words. What is behind them is this.

"They hold the understanding that if those who are under their control have enough time to think for themselves, they, too, would see their way clear of their group. They, too, would see through this controlling that has come over them, and they would leave.

"But the ones in control over this group know that in order for them to keep their followers away from thinking on their own, they must provide them with a diversion that is truly worthwhile. And what they tell them keeps them from finding their own path is this.

"They say that all who are not a part of the one group are bad and do not deserve to share in any of those things that are theirs to eat, drink, or live with. It will be in these times when there will not be much of the food, water, or shelter that had once been with all of the two-legs. This is what we have shared with you already in The Message.

"They will say that to share with any of the outsiders is to take away from the true people that have been led to believe they are the only ones who know the way.

"And, they tell them, if they are to see an outsider come among them, they would not be doing anything wrong if they were to kill them and take away those things they had. For this is only bringing back to the true believers that which is theirs to begin with. That this is their inheritance and they are justified in getting it back from others who are not deserving of it.

"While they keep their followers busy with this killing and robbing of others who are not like them, they will not have to worry about them thinking for themselves. For they will be far too busy in doing the right thing by getting rid of everyone who does not deserve to live, like they do in this domain. And this will indeed keep them busy, for it will require much time on their part.

"They will have cleared the way for this killing and robbing of others who are not like them through all of the governments that are over them. They have done this by saying if they are not allowed to cleanse this land, these governments will soon fall away, and all of their seats and positions among the people would surely be lost.

"This will have completed all of the preparing they need. When this has been done, they will be free to kill and rob as many of those who refuse to follow them, as they will need. And this will keep their members from thinking on their own.

"But I share this with all of you, for those who would follow this group, they are surely locked into the path that leads to the left, this path that requires one to always try, this path that does not allow anything to be accomplished, this path that leads into the twelfth earth where all of this will have to be done all over again by the ones who will follow it.

"They have seen the ones who have found the path that leads to the right, this path of spirit that allows one to understand that when they allow themselves to be, they are. And they see them as the enemy. They have come to see them as the ones they no longer wish to be with. And I tell you in truth; they will not be with them long. For soon after this time, the Great Messenger arrives and shows all the two paths to travel, the one to the left leading into the twelfth earth, and the one to the right which will lead into the fifth world of this Earth Mother—this fifth world of peace and light.

"There will be many tears of the water spirit running down the faces of those who chose to follow the path of the controlling groups. It will be then that you will see all of them crying and hear their sounds of pain from within. For they will hold the understanding that where they are going, all of their history will be repeated. And they will go through all of this again.

"It is this understanding that brings to them this great fear, this great fear that will be hard in all domains that are from the One.

"All will feel their sorrow and misery, my brothers. All will see their tears of the water spirit fall from their eyes as they look upon them. But all will know that until lessons are learned, they must be repeated. And until all will have come to work their own way through them, they will not be allowed to return to Creator, to this place we know as our home.

CHAPTER 35

❀

Thirteenth Face

From the Elder of the North—
Preparing For The Safe Lands

"Now when the tine of forming the one group has come into this domain, not all who are traveling their own path of the spirit will remain," began the speaking words from the Elder in the North position.

"The ones who choose to remain will do so because for them, there is a reason. They, too, will have seen the places where they are to go, they, too, will have been shown the safe lands that will have been prepared for them during this time of the last cleansing of the Earth Mother.

"There will be none who has found their own path of the spirit who will not see where they may go. Each of them will have seen a place that will provide them with the safety they need during this time of the final cleansing. But not all will choose to travel there, for there will be many who are still locked within the sleep of illusion. And because of this, some will remain in the midst of all that is taking place during this final phase of cleansing rather than leave for the safe lands.

"But this will be for those who will begin to wake from the illusion so they may understand what it is they should do.

"The time of preparing for the safe lands will have entered this domain through the confusion of the lost, my brothers. For those who remain locked within their own sleep of illusion will see only the face of fear on all that is near them. And this includes the one group we have shared with you before, as well. For this one group will hold itself together through fear, through the fear that if they would ever break away from it, they would be destroyed.

"All of this has come into this domain through the fear of not knowing those things that are a part of each of us. It is during The Season of the Long Shadow that all life has been given the opportunity of paying off all their old debts, all of those debts that have been with them from the many lessons they had turned away from before, from all of the emotions that have been with them, emotions that have only been reminding them of those same lessons they have not yet learned from.

"As these emotions become more prevalent, they believe a great evil force is coming after them, an evil force that will destroy them if they do not do what others tell them to do.

"I tell you this in truth, my brothers, there is no evil in this or any other domain that has been created, for to conceive of such a thing is to admit being locked within the sleep of illusion.

"Creator has not been responsible for any of the misery that has come to live among any of the two-legs; they have brought this to themselves. And it has come to them from the many lessons they have not been willing to learn and from those emotions that have been coming to them as a reminder for what they still need to learn from—but they have not been willing.

"When a lesson is first encountered, there is only a small layer of emotion in the front of it. However, for each time we will turn away from a lesson, another layer of emotion is added. As time will pass and you still do not look on the face of the lesson, the emotion will gain in its strength until it becomes so insurmountable that you cannot see past it.

"When this time will come to you, then the emotion that is reminding you of what you have entered this domain to learn from is seen as something that is evil and bad, for its size and impact on your personal life has become so great that you can see nothing else.

"When it is time for The Season of the Long Shadow, all of the lessons that have been with you will be accelerated. And this process will cause many to believe their time is surely over, for if it were to continue at this accelerated pace, they do not hold the believing that they could take it any longer.

"To look at the two-legs during this time is to see many small children swinging their arms at the air around them, and in all directions, for they do not understand what is taking place. They do not understand this is being offered to them so they might advance their spirit to the next higher place, this next higher place they are looking for.

"But they cannot see this, and perceive an evil that is all around them, a evil that has come to consume them. And for them, nothing else is real.

"So they gather into the group and the ones who lead them will use this fear they have been feeling to control them into believing they can only escape their own feelings by attacking others who do not share their way of believing.

"When the group has formed, there will have been many changes that will have entered this domain of the Earth Mother. There will be places that will lose the waters of life, and others will have far too much.

"There will have been many great earth shakings and much of what is now known as the outside face of the Earth Mother will have been changed for all time. These changes will not allow her to remain the same.

"From these earth shakes, all of the fuels will have been taken deep within her. And they will no longer be found for transportation, heating, or cooling. And all of the two-legs will find themselves stuck in the lands they are in when this happens.

"When the last of the fuels have been taken into the depths of the Earth Mother, there will prevail a thought in all of the two-legs who are not yet awake to themselves. They will not believe they would be safe to journey more than one hundred miles from their locations.

"They will be in fear of other groups, like theirs, who would destroy any who are not like them. And this fear they hold is real, and they will remain in their locations as if they have been locked into them.

"They will look out over the lands they have ended up on and see a great invisible wall around them. One that is not holding others out but is holding them in.

"When they look up into the night sky, they will see the great circle of the thirteen stars in the west southwest sky and be reminded of that which has been told to them before, those things that had been shared with them before all of this had taken place from the messengers who had awakened.

"They will see this circle of stars in the west southwest sky and be reminded that this is the final time of the cleansing for all life. And soon there will appear to them the Great Messenger who will ask them to make their own choice, this choice of going on the path to the left, or the path to the right. All of this will fill them with a great fear, but this fear will be of themselves and all they have not yet done.

"It is this choice for those who have begun seeing through their illusion that the ones who remain behind stay for. For they see they are ready to see that which is, and no longer require to be locked into the sleep of illusion by those who had been controlling their lives from the one group that had formed.

"You see, my brothers, when this forming of the one group has come to pass, it will have come to place a great blindness over all who would follow its path of controlling, a blindness that will not allow them to see any of the ones who chose to remain behind.

"This blindness will not allow them to see them because they are not living within their illusion. And they will not see them until they begin to awaken and see their own need of truth for what will be shared with them during these last times of the cleansing.

"The ones who chose to remain for the benefit of those who begin their awakening, will not be without any of those things that are needed to maintain their life path. For they will have been shown how to create all they need out of nothing. And as others who begin to awaken from their sleep of illusion see them, they, too, will be given all that they need.

"They will be given food and water, and will be shown how to be invisible to those who would seek them out and destroy them because they are no longer a part of the group.

"They will be shown that they may return to those places they have come from at any time, and will be reminded that their own freedom of choice will not be taken from them.

"Next, they will be shown the lands they have left. But they will see them through eyes that are theirs and not through the eyes of others. They will see that which is before them for what it is in truth.

"They will be taken to the groups that had been controlling them and be shown many things that are not pleasant, such as the places where many will be taken and killed so that the others would have something to eat. Places where the ones who have been infected with diseases carried on the back of the Spirit Wind will be taken and the places on their skin that are infected will be cut away from them. But with no antiseptic—they die, and their unaffected parts will be eaten.

"They will be shown why there are no longer any burials and will see that all of the old, weak, and young who are not useful to the group will be killed for food.

"They will be shown places where the leaders of the one group will be sitting and will hear how they have planned the number of those who would be allowed to reproduce during this time. For there will be great numbers of those who would follow their leadership that will have their reproductive parts cut off, or cut out of them. They will be told this is for the good of the group.

"They will be shown all of these places where this is taking place, and they will be allowed to hear the ones who are in the position of leadership speak.

"When all of this has been shown, they will be led to another place by the ones who chose to remain behind for them. They will be led to a place where they and many like them, will be allowed to work their own way through all of the emotion that has been following them, these emotions that have been holding them back and causing them great pain.

"They will be told that once they have completed their own work on their lessons, they will be returned to the ones who have allowed them to become invisible and provide them with their food and water.

"And when they will return for them, they will each be given a spirit picture, one that will show them the safe lands they may go to that will allow them to continue to grow and understand those things that are needed by them. The safe lands that will give to them great blessings for all they would be willing to understand from, the safe lands that will nurture them until the Great Messenger arrives.

"And for the ones who are still not completely out of their own sleep of illusion, there will be a confusion come to them. They will ask how these safe lands have not been seen by the group. And they will be told the group members have not seen them because they could not be seen by them, much like the way they have been allowed to pass among them without being seen.

"And for those who are not completely out of their own sleep of illusion, they will ask them why they did not go to the safe lands themselves, if they truly exist. And they will be told that if they did not choose to remain in these places, then who could have come to their assistance to show them what is still possible.

"And this will be enough for them to believe in themselves and begin their own work to find the path they designed for themselves to follow.

"Remember, my brothers, from the time of the opening of the first great doorway to the closing of the seventh, there will be a preparing that each one will have to do. And when this preparing is completed, they will be shown a picture of where they may travel—this place that will be the safe lands for them.

"When the time is right, this safe land will be shown to them in the way of seeing a picture in the front of their thinking minds. They will know this place and these lands, and they will understand how to get there. For these lands have been prepared for them, and will call to them when the time is right.

"This is the last of the thirteen faces for The Season of the Long Shadow, my brothers," came the speaking words from the Elder in the North.

"It is time to move on."

PART VII

❀

THE END TO SEPARATENESS
11 Lessons to Be Re-remembered

CHAPTER 36

❀

Lesson 1

Why There Is Hatred
—From An Elder In The East

There was a brief moment of silence that had come over our council of five. And during this time of silence, there were many faces being worn by Grandfather, Two Bears, Cheeway, and me. However, as I looked over to the place where Night Hawk was sitting, I did not see any change come to the face he had begun with. And this was making me feel something different for him.

However, from those things that had been shared with me by the Elder of the North position, I was willing to allow it to be and waited, for the right time when I would understand.

I turned my attention from the group to the place of the small warming fire. Looking at this small and giving child of the Earth Mother sitting before me, I could feel the ever-present blessings he was willing to share with us on this day.

I could hear and feel the whistling of the Spirit Wind as it was making its presence known just to the outside of the opening of the cave we had come to sit in. And within its hands, I could feel the presence of the water spirit's blessings as it would occasionally find its way into parts of the stone cave we had come to sit in.

As it would do this, I could feel its cold penetrate my body. However, just as this cold would make its presence known to me, the small warming fire would dispel its presence quickly. It was as if this spirit of the flame could sense what was needed by me during this time of sharing with the Ancient Ones and would rush to provide its needed blessings.

As I looked at the size of the flames and the amount of wood that was needed to keep this small one alive, I noticed there had not been any wood added during what seemed to be a very long time of sharing. But each time I would look into the flames of the small warming fire, I would not see any more wood being burned by it. It was like a flame that would come out of our gas stove, one that would continue to burn even though there was no wood to feed it.

"There is food for all of you to eat if you desire," came the speaking words from the Elder in the East. "It is warm now and is sitting on the stones near the warming fire."

I had only lifted my eyes for a moment to look at the Elder of the East and hearing what was said filled me with a great surprise. For when I had been looking at the small warming fire only moments before, there was no food there. However, when I returned my eyes to the same place, I saw there were now four stacks of food and water.

This filled me with a great surprise and looking over to the faces of Grandfather, Two Bears, and Cheeway, I saw they, too, were holding the same kind of face as I was. But when I looked over to the place where Night Hawk was sitting, there was still no change over him. And this continued to fill me with a wondering for him...one that I held the knowing would have to be answered at a later time.

"What we have done for all of you, my brothers, you can do for yourselves," began the speaking words from the Elder in the East position. "We are only a reminding to you for who and what you are in truth. But you have forgotten to remember this."

Next, the elder looked over all of the faces of our counsel and, seeing us busy chewing what had been presented, she placed a warm smile over her face, then continued.

"We will now share with you the eleven lessons to be re-remembered, my brothers. These eleven lessons will allow you to see an end to separateness and see the One within the One.

"In truth, there can be no oneness where separateness exists within anyone. And these lessons we are now willing to share will cause you to see your way through the illusion of not seeing and into the path, this path that holds no illusion over it at all.

"The face of this first lesson is hate. And we have seen much of this as we have traveled through this domain that is the Earth Mother.

"We have seen much of this hate for things that are not understood. And it has been this lack of understanding that has fueled their fires for as many generations as have been allowed entry here.

"But soon the time for this will come to an end. And its presence among life will be over.

"However, these things must also be shared with the two-legs who will come to you during this time we speak of. For it will be during The Season of the Long Shadow that these lessons will be needed most because of the acceleration process that is soon to be born into this domain. And without understanding themselves, there will be no growth. For the ones who have remained lost within their own sleep of illusion will only know pain, suffering, and sorrow. And this is why we have come before all of you on this day. For the time to share these truths will soon be with you, and your work will be great.

"In the times that are soon to be born into this domain, there will be many two-legs who will question why they are feeling those things that are coming to them, those things that are bringing with them feelings of self denial, doubt, pity, and most of all…hate.

"When one will come to you with this question, my brothers, share with them what I am now willing to share with you.

"Hate is the reverse of love. It is the reverse of the love we feel for ourselves but do not understand. And because we do not understand it, our hate is simply being placed on another who is convenient for us to blame.

"Have the two-legs remember that all which comes to them is an answer to their asking of assistance through prayer, for all of those things that are yet to be seen and understood within them are being shown to them by this process so they may advance their spirit to the next higher place.

"And have them remember there is not ever a prayer or request for assistance that is not answered in less time than it takes to blink your eyes.

"However, it would be good to remind them they pray many prayers that they do not understand completely. And for those things that are not understood, the answers can be deceiving when they will arrive. And arrive they will most assuredly do for all who ask for this assistance.

"Have them look deep within themselves to see what they have been asking assistance on. And have them come to a place of understanding that when they are standing alone and wondering why they are feeling so alone, so desperate, so persecuted, so rejected, that these are also answers they have asked for.

"For when one will have even a thought enter the front of their thinking mind, it will be heard. And what is heard is answered.

"And this is the most true form of prayer. For what comes to us through our thinking minds from the silence is the true nature of praying. And what we pray for will come to us in the form of our need and understanding.

"And the answers will come in ways that cannot be missed, but will often be misunderstood.

"We all enter this domain of the Earth Mother with but one purpose. And that purpose is to understand from all lessons that are presented to us.

"There are many who know their own name, but do not understand it. There are many who know they are feeling sorrow, but do not understand it. There are many who know they are feeling fear, but do not understand it either.

"However for all of these things they know, there is still no growth, not until they come to understand them from their within place, this place where spirit resides.

"Remember to keep in the front of your thinking minds that we do not come here to know and learn. For when you will look at all of those things you have learned from and all of those things you know, there is not yet growth from within you. For it is not until you understand what you have learned and known that you will see your growth. But before you gain the understanding from those lessons, you become like the walking book, holding great amounts of knowing and learning, but not understanding what you are to do with it.

"It is the same way with prayer or asking for assistance, my brothers. The answers that are needed by you are with you already. But since you cannot see them yet, they will come to you in a stronger way, and that will be through the confirmation by another person, place, or thing.

"When you are confronted by either a person, place, or thing that makes you feel uncomfortable, understand the reason for this. For what you are feeling from this person, place, or thing is a confirmation of all those parts of yourself that you have not yet come to understand.

"Even though you initially see them as something that is bad, remember that what you are seeing is a part of yourself in another that you have not yet been willing to work on, a part of yourself that is still needed to be understood. Until you will come to understand that part of yourself, then everyone and everything that will come to you as a confirmation will be seen as bad, evil, or negative. And what is perceived by you in this way must surely be done away with.

"Now, instead of seeing these people, places, and things as an offering to understanding—or a confirmation for those things you have been asking assistance for—you will see them as something or someone that is bad and convince yourself that until they are out of your way, they will only contaminate you and your surroundings.

"When this kind of thinking and seeing are allowed to prevail, my brothers, it has but one child. And this child is called hate.

"It will hate everything that is not understood as well as what has been touched by this person, this place, and this thing which brought them these feelings.

"At first, they will attempt to ignore what they are receiving, but in time it cannot be ignored, or hidden from. For what they are trying to hide from is themselves, and they will be continually reminded of those things within them that are still not understood. They will continually repeat their own kind of prayer and asking of assistance for what is needed by them, and they will have another one come to confirm for them what it is. But it will be this same thing they have been trying to run and hide from, this part of themselves that is not understood. And because it is not understood, it is seen as ugly and they will hate it.

"But the more times they will repeat their prayers, the more times this confirmation will come to them as their answer. And their hatred will grow, but they still do not see what it is they are doing to themselves.

"Their hatred is growing for something that is a part of themselves. But they believe they are hating another person, place, or thing. They are in truth coming to hate a part of themselves. And this will cause them to lose sight of their own purpose in this domain. This hate will cause them to lose all they thought they had gained up to this point. But anything that one will come to lose was not theirs in the beginning, and if one will fear losing something, then it would be better for them to let it go and be done with it. And as they let it go, do it with dignity and part as friends, not as enemies.

"So when one will hate, they become blinded to all that is of themselves. Until they come to understand that hate is love, which is not understood, they will not see anything that is presented to them as good. For they will not have the sight that is needed to show them this truth, and until they can see this face of truth, they will continue to pray for assistance that will make them into a better person and will be presented with the same answers. And each time those answers will come to them, they will grow in their hatred for it.

"In truth, my brothers, one does not hate the confirmer, the one who has come to present them with what they need to understand. They will be hating themselves. Until they can look on the face of these answers that are coming to them and say, '*Thank you for coming to me, my friend, what have you brought me to learn from you today?*' there will be a continued growth of hatred build up within them. And it will build within them until it consumes their every waking moment. For them, there will be no growth or understanding from all that has been presented to them.

"Remind them that where there is hate, there can be no growth. That where there is hate, there can be no seeing. And where there is hate...there can be no room for understanding what you have been asking for."

CHAPTER 37

Lesson 2

Why There Is Racial Bias —From an Elder in the South

"When The Season of the Long Shadow is born among you," came the beginning of the Elder in the South's speaking words. "There will be many two-legs who would do well to understand this second lesson, that shares with all why there is racial bias.

"This, too, is a form of hatred, but unlike hatred it has a specific target, one that does not allow just anyone to fit into it.

"Unless the two-legs will be willing to understand these things we are willing to share with you, they will not be able to see what is being offered to them. They will be the ones who will only see fear from what has come to them, and the dying for those who are left standing with them.

"It would be well for you to remind the two-legs that to think they have only walked on this Earth once is to live in the illusion that will keep them from seeing themselves as part of the One if they continue to hold onto those things that have no truth for them.

"And for the ones who would not see this truth, that each of you have walked many paths before, and have traveled in all races and cultures, they will be the ones who are in truth blinded by their own ego and foolishness. And they will be the ones who will continue to live in the dark places of their own spirit.

"However, for the ones who would be willing to listen to the speaking words we are willing to share, they will eventually wake from their own sleep of illusion, that would hold all in fear for these times that are soon to be with you, these times we have come to call The Season of the Long Shadow.

"So it is that when the last of their hatred and racial bias has left, they will see themselves as a part of the One, as an integral part of life where all are considered sacred because all have life within them.

"Creator has not created anything that does not live, and all that is living has spirit within it. So is it not right to see all life in this way, to see all life as your brothers and sisters who are all on this long journey back to Creator with you?

"When the ones who have the eyes and ears to see and hear with come to you with these questions that grow out of racial biases for others, it would be well to share what they are feeling for another race or culture has not been born to them because of those they see. Rather it has come to them from a recalling of who and what they once were. And for the ones who have bad feeling for these other races and cultures, share with them that those feelings are from the lessons they did not learn while they were walking in that race.

"And those who have bad feelings for the cultures they see, remind them they are not feeling this from them, but they are remembering another time when they were in this domain and had been offered lessons to learn from, but chose to turn away from them, to turn away from those things that were needed by their spirit to grow in understanding.

"When they tell you they hold within them a great emotional feeling of dislike for these other cultures and races, share this with them:

"When a lesson is turned away from in any earth walk, there is one more layer of emotion that will come over it. However this emotion is not something that is meant to punish you. Rather it is to remind you of something that is still needed to be learned.

"As one continues to look away from their own lessons, the emotions they bring with them get stronger until the two-legs discover that they cannot escape them. For these lessons are laced with the emotions of non-understanding and will follow them wherever they go. They will follow them through an entire earth walk and into many others as well. For these lessons are a part of them and without learning from them, their spirit will not grow.

"So when one will drop their robe and leave this domain through the pains of death, the lessons they turned away from and the emotions that carry them will wait for their return. And when they return, those emotions will attach themselves to them once they draw their first breath. And they will continually remind them of those things they have forgotten to remember...those things they still need to learn.

"But this reminding to them will come in an emotional way. When they will see the race or culture they could have learned their lessons from but turned away, they will be reminded of their past failures. Because they still have not learned their lessons, the emotions over them will be so great they will cause them to look on those other cultures and races as being something evil and bad.

"Because they see them as evil and bad, they attempt to destroy them, or get rid of them so they will not have to look on them any more. But still, they are trying to turn away from the same lessons they have not learned from yet. And when they will return to them, the lesson's emotions will be even stronger.

"For those who will look on another culture or race as being bad and evil, share this truth with them. Since they were not willing to learn their lessons the first time, when they traveled in that particular race or culture, they are being reminded of what they still need to learn from and later understand.

"Have them look on those feelings of emotion and see them for what they are...to understand what they feel is bad and evil in them. When they will do this, there will be a great clue given to them by their spirit within, a clue that will cause them to find the strength to work their own way through these feelings of emotion so that they may look on the face of their own lesson.

"When they will do this, my brothers, they will find those emotions that had once filled them with the racial bias and hate will fall away and will no longer need to return to them, for their time with them is over and their lessons have been learned.

"When they will do this, they will have one more part of themselves that they may call their own, one more piece of understanding that will allow them to continue this long journey back to Creator with eyes that will see and ears that will hear."

CHAPTER 38

❀

Lesson 3

Why There Is Fear Of Falling, Flying, Fire, Etc. —From An Elder in the West

"It may be sad to see what I am now willing to share with you, my brothers, but it is truth," began the speaking words from the Elder in the West position.

"When The Season of the Long Shadow has been born into this domain of the Earth Mother, the two-legs will have become so lost within their own illusion that they will no longer be able to see what is before them.

"It will be this lack of seeing that will cause them to hold onto their own believing that only what they can hold with their hands or see with their eyes is real. For anything else will be too much for them to accept.

"They will not have the willingness to see more because they will no longer be willing to open their eyes to anything other than what has been shown to them by those they have chosen to follow.

"During this time, all feelings and emotions will be accelerated. But it is not to punish or confuse; it is done because time will have grown very short for all. And at the end of this time, there will be the great question asked of all life, this great question that will determine if they are to remain with this Earth Mother and enter her fifth world of peace and light, or if they continue to need the lessons that will leave this earth and enter the twelfth earth where all of the history that has been done here will be repeated all over again.

"It is the accelerated process of feelings and emotions that is coming to all life during this time and allows them to see the lessons of their present and past earth walks they had turned away from. These lessons will be presented to the two-legs in a very quick manner because the time remaining is short. If they are to make a clear decision, they must be willing to learn from them, for each of those lessons has been designed and planned for by themselves.

"But if they will not have their eyes and ears opened, they will not hold an understanding of what is being offered to them, they will only see fear and danger for these times that are soon to be with them. But these times are their last chance of paying off their old debts by learning their lessons.

"We have shared with all of you how emotion precedes lesson. And how each time lesson will be turned away from there will be another layer of emotion that will come over it. This emotion will grow until it will no longer be able to be ignored but will be seen as something that is evil or from the dark side of life.

"However, there are other emotions that are with the two-legs. And they have been brought back with them to assist them in coming to a place of understanding how to look through the emotions of lessons.

"These emotions have been brought back with them so they may have something simple to begin their work with, something that will allow them to see how easy a process it is to work through emotion and see these lessons…and having done this, seeing the emotion leave them so they will be free to go onto their next one.

"You see, my brothers, for the ones who will do their own work through these lessons, they will come to understand how to walk their life path one step at a time, taking each step in a measurable way that allows them to gain understanding for themselves and all that is around them while maintaining their balance. These are the ones who will be seen standing strong on their own and not latching onto another's guidance or direction from their fear.

"But the ones who have not come to this place of understanding, they will be seen trying to take their earth walk in one great step, and will always be seen falling down from their own efforts and wondering why this has happened to them. They will be the ones who will perceive themselves as not ever being strong enough to do it on their own, and will be in a continual search to find another or others, who will do this work for them.

"For they are always looking at another's path and mimicking it. They do not gain insight to their own path, but would rather copy another's until they find one they can follow easily, and without much work.

"They will always be out of balance in their earth walk. They will be out of balance because their attention is on another rather than on themselves.

"This is shared with all of you so your eyes may remember to see what you look at during these times that are soon to be with you, so when this time will arrive, you may have this understanding to work with.

"But let me get back to the emotions that returned to the two-legs, these emotions they brought back to assist them in seeing how to work their own way through emotion to see the face of lesson.

"These emotions that I am now willing to share with you are ones of fear, and it would be well to keep in the front of your thinking minds that fear is seen by those who do not yet have the understanding for that part of themselves being presented to them.

"These are the fears of falling, flying, burning, drowning, choking, being closed in small places, being chased by others, and other fears in the same line.

"These are fears that are the most easy to work through and will make it much easier to do the same with emotions that have become attached to lessons. They hold a great need to learn from these lessons, but do not yet possess the ability of understanding how to work their way through them.

"Let us take one example of these emotions that are seen as fear, the one emotion that has been brought back with you as the fear of falling.

"When one will have a fear of falling, for them, it will be great. But the reason it is great is because this is a clue in learning how to work their way past their emotions to lessons.

"However, until they will open their eyes to see with, they will see this fear of falling is something they must avoid at any cost, and will not see how easy it is for them to walk through fear and into a place of understanding where their fear of falling will no longer be needed by them, and will fall silently away from them.

"Remind them that this fear they carry with them is an emotional memory of the ending to one of their many past earth walks, a memory of an ending they were not ready for, but an ending that did come to them when it was time.

"These feelings they are now in possession of are only recalling for them on how they ended a previous earth walk. And if this fear is in the form of falling, then this is how the path they once walked ended.

"Have them look into themselves and see if there is anything they can relate this fear of falling to. And they will see there is nothing they can remember that would have given them cause to fear this falling—nothing that is in this life path that is.

"Next, share with them this is a memory of an ending of one of their past earth walks. And it was ended in a way that they were not prepared for, which is the reason this fear is so strong with them now.

"Then have them go to a high place, but one that is not so high it would be a danger to them if they were to fall. It must be one that will bring out this fear that is being carried within them, a place where they will feel this fear of falling come to them.

"And as they stand in this place, have them silently say to themselves: 'This is a feeling from another time and another earth walk, a memory of an ending I was not ready for. But now, it is alright and I can see through the illusion.'

"And the reason this feeling of fear has come with them into this life path is to share a very important lesson, one that will be greatly needed by them once they enter The Season of the Long Shadow.

"This fear is only to share how easy it is to look through the emotion of any situation, or any lesson that will be presented to them, to look through the emotion without getting caught up in it. Once they will see through the emotion of a situation, they will see the face of lesson, the face of their own personal lesson. And this lesson comes to them by their own request so they may advance their spirit to the next higher place of understanding for themselves and all that is around them.

"As they will stand on this high place and repeat these speaking words we have shared with you, there will come a great peace to them. It will be a peace that will bring with it an understanding for what they are doing.

"As they repeat the speaking words we have been willing to share with you, they will begin to see a great weight lift from them, a weight that had been placed over them from the illusion of fear. They will begin to see there is no thing that will ever come to them that will have on it a face of fear, not in truth.

"From repeating these speaking words silently to themselves, they will feel less and less of a threat from their original fear of falling. And they will be experiencing this lack of fear because they have been listening to what they have been saying. When one will listen to what they have to say, they begin to believe in themselves again. Once this believing has begun, they will see what a silly thing it was to fear this falling at all.

"But it does not stop there, for once this first hurdle has been crossed, they will see the blessings of using this same procedure for all of the other situations that come to them, that also hold the face of fear—anger, hurt, loss, rejection, and the many other non-understood lessons that had come to them from other people, places, and things…all they do, but do not have a reason to, feel this way for.

"It will be then that the two-legs will come to understand why it is important to say to these emotions they consider to be bad, evil, or from the dark side:

'Thank You For Coming To Me, My Friend. What Have You Brought For Me To Learn From You Today?'

"When they come to understand why they are saying this, they will see there is in truth no evil, bad, or dark side to any thing in this or any other domain that has been created by Creator. They will see this because they have been willing to do their own work on themselves, and as a result of their willingness, their eyes are beginning to be opened for them once again.

"When one with open eyes is seen by another, they will be seen as one who cannot be controlled, as one who will not control, and as one who is in truth free.

"So when the two-legs come to you and ask you why they fear such things as falling, share with them this is only a clue for them to follow. A very simple clue, but it is simple because it is the beginning to their own path of understanding, this path that will eventually show them how to work through the emotions of all events presented to them and see the face of lesson, this face of their own lesson that is greatly needed by spirit within them to learn from."

❀

CHAPTER 39

Lesson 4

There Are No Accidents
—From An Elder in the North

When the Elder from the West finished, I took a moment to look over the faces that were being worn by Grandfather, Two Bears, and Cheeway. I could see that they, like me, were very tried from all that had been presented to us. However, looking over to the faces of the eleven Ancient Ones who were also with us, I could not see a place on any of them that would allow us to have a rest.

I did not know how much time had passed on this day of sharing, for time is not something that held a place in a spirit vision. When one would be with the Ancient Ones, the illusion of time would not be allowed to sit with any of us. For this was a place of truth and anything that was not of truth, there was no place for.

"Speaking Wind," came the opening of the Elder in the North position. "We are well aware of all that has been shared with you on this day. And we are also aware of the tiredness that you only think you feel. For like the illusion of time, this is only a past habit you are feeling. And like any illusion, it will remain with you until you will be willing to see your way through it."

As she spoke to me, I could feel the blood rush to my face. And without looking to Cheeway, I held the knowing that he was doing the same thing, for each of us were not ever far from the other when it came to such things.

"Our time to be among you is running short now," the Elder continued. "But it is not a time that is easily understood by any who are in this domain of the great illusion, for in truth there is time for all things. And the time that has been given to us to share with you will not close before we have shared that which is needed to be heard.

"Another lesson to share with the two-legs is this: there are no accidents or events that come to any by chance. All events and occurrences have been designed by the one who has the most to gain from them; that is when they are understood.

"Long before any life is allowed to set foot within this domain, there is a great council that is held between spirit who is them and the Earth Mother.

"It is during this council that spirit, who is you, presents all that is needed to be learned, all of the learning that will lead to understanding when they will allow themselves to walk in balance here.

"When the Earth Mother hears what needs spirit has to learn from in order to complete its circle of life on the long journey back to Creator, she will look over all who have been given permission to walk a life path with her and make as many matches as are possible.

"After making her determination for which of the needed lessons will be made available for you, she will inform you of the ones which are possible and which ones can not be met for this time you have come to petition her for.

"If this is agreeable to your spirit and the lessons available are valuable enough to go through this domain of the great illusion, you inform the Earth Mother that this is good and you wish to gain entry into her domain.

"Hearing this, she informs you there is still much work needed by you, work that involves asking all of those who will be involved with you in this life path for their permission as well.

"They will be all those who will cross your life path for brief encounters or for long ones. She will inform you that until they agree to bring to you those lessons you have requested you will not be allowed entry.

"However, keep in the front of your thinking minds that while you are still in spirit, there are not the long and arduous tasks that are to be found once you enter the body you now travel in. For spirit does not hold these limitations to it, nor does it recognize the illusion that is so prevalent in this domain.

"So it is your spirit who encounters each person that will be involved in your life path, those people who will cross your life path in your play time, personal life, professional life, family life, spiritual life, and so on.

"These people will be the ones who will make up all of the experiences that will come to you, the ones you will understand, will make you happy, and the ones you do not understand and will not make you happy.

"But in any case, all will be precisely what is needed by you to learn from. To learn from so that later there will be understanding.

"Now it is wise to keep in the front of your thinking minds that there is always the freedom of choice. Not only for this domain that you are in, but it is for all of the domains that have been created by Creator.

"It is through this freedom of choice the most valuable lessons are to be found, and these others who have agreed to assist you in learning those things that are needed so you will understand this. When they come to you with the lesson you have requested of them, it will still be up to you what will be done with them.

"If you will choose to learn from them, you will see them come to you with a good face to wear. However, if you will choose not to learn from them, you will see them as the enemy and will wish to get away from them or attempt to destroy them.

"But in any case, once you return to the Earth Mother and tell that all has been prepared, she allows you entry into this domain of hers. This is when the learning potential begins.

"From the beginning, we choose to call this a potential because it is up to you on how you will see those events you have prepared for yourself to learn from.

"So when the two-legs come to you, my brothers, and say that their path is filled with all of the bad things, remind them the only bad things that will ever come to them will be those they do not yet understand. And then remind them of what has just been shared with you on this day.

"For it is within this fourth lesson that there will be a great re-remembering for them that it is they who designed this for themselves and only they can make any sense out of it.

"There will be no other who will be able to interpret those events they have designed to come to them. For the learning is needed by them and because of this, there are no other eyes that can see its purpose.

"When they come to you in The Season of the Long Shadow, remind them while all lessons will be increased greatly, they are also being offered an opportunity of growing ten times more than they have ever been allowed before. For these times will be moving ten times faster for all life, but is doing so for their benefit. And this knowing was given to all life before they were allowed entry, and all life you see before you made their own choice to accept these opportunities of learning.

"Remind them that they have designed all of these events and situations. If they choose to turn away from them, or to fight them as an enemy, they will come back. And they will come back in another face and another time, but they will continue to return until their lesson has been learned. For this is the path of truth that I am willing to share with all of you, and truth does not change no matter which of Creator's many domains you travel in.

"Share with them that nothing has come to them by chance or accident, but all is as it should be. And if they are willing to listen and understand, then they will grow."

CHAPTER 40

❀

Lesson 5

All Things Come When We Are Ready To Learn From Them
—From An Elder in the East

"This time that is called The Season of the Long Shadow is soon to be with all life," began the speaking words from the Elder in the East. "And its arrival will bring great changes with it. Changes that will accelerate for each day that passes. These accelerations will continue to grow on each other until this time is over, and the great choice will be called for all life to make.

"However, there will be many of the two-legs who will have forgotten to remember many things during this time, for they will have surely lost their way because of these great changes that are around them.

"They will see new diseases come over all of the lands they are in. Diseases for which there is no cure, or protection from. They will see their own homes being torn apart from the inside and what was once a great haven of safety for them, will no longer offer any place of comfort.

"They will see all of the fuels taken deep into the belly of the Earth Mother to a place where no one may reach them. And when this happens, there will be no transportation available. And with the disappearing of transportation, the abundance of food will be taken away from them as well.

"They will look to the outside of their own homes and no longer feel safe. They will have had all of their freedom taken away from them because those who will be in control during this time will also be confused and lost. And will attempt to restore things to what they once were by asserting their control. But they will only be chasing after shadows in the dark, for none of their efforts will have an effect on these times that have come to them. For this time must surely come to them and when it does, it must travel its path to completion.

"It will be through these times that the two-legs will believe there is too much coming for them to learn from. But this will only be another bad habit they have come to learn from their sleep of illusion. And to think in such a way does not hold truth to it at all.

"While these times that are soon to be move very fast, there will be no thing presented to any which they will not be ready for. For what they will see, they will have done all the preparing that is necessary to learn from it.

"That is if they will not still be locked within their own sleep of illusion. If they are locked within the sleep of illusion, they will remain buried in their own past, a past that does not exist for them any longer, but the illusion will cause them to see all things for what they would wish for them to be.

"They will believe the times of their past are the only place they will feel secure in. But like all things they hold onto, there will be an event take place for them that will take even this away. For as this domain continues to move through The Season of the Long Shadow, all that does not hold truth to it will be torn away and shown for the nothingness that it is, torn away from those who would desire to hold onto something that is not.

"However, for the ones who will not be locked so tightly into the sleep of illusion, they will have the ability of understanding and will remain in the present. For those who are willing to remain in the present, then all that we have been willing to share with you will be seen by them, for what it is in truth. And they will see it through their own eyes of understanding.

"For they will be the ones who understand that while all of these events are coming at them at great speed, there is still the most basic of truth to them.

And this truth is one that I have been willing to share with all of you on this day we have been given.

"There will be nothing come to you during this time or any other time that you will not be ready to learn from. But in order to learn from them, you must be willing to remain in the present."

CHAPTER 41

❀

Lesson 6

We Have Done No Wrong
—From An Elder in the South

"There have been many who have allowed themselves to be held back," began the speaking words from the Elder in the South position of the medicine wheel we had formed.

"They are the ones who have listened to those who would wish to control their life paths. And for those, of whom I speak, when the time comes for The Season of the Long Shadow, they will see an acceleration of all those things they have been carrying with them. For all of those things that have been good for them, they will be increased. For all of those things that have been bad for them, they will be increased as well. And for all of those things they had been carrying with them which have been making them feel guilty, they too will be increased. And this is the face of the sixth lesson.

"It is about those feelings of guilt the two-legs have allowed themselves to hold onto and the illusion it creates for them.

"I share this with you in truth. If the two-legs carry their guilt into The Season of the Long Shadow, they will find themselves in a place where the emotions from this guilt will be more than they can handle.

"They will be in a place where they can no longer look away from those things they have considered too unpleasant to work with. And when they reach this point, there will be an unleashing of their anger to any who will be near them.

"They will be the ones who do great harm and cause injury to many, but they will not see themselves as doing anything that is wrong. They will see themselves as paying others back for what has been done to them.

"However, they are not entirely wrong with this kind of thinking. While it is true they have these feelings of guilt because of those who would wish to control them; it is not true that it is only the controlling one's fault. For the only one who is responsible for anything that has taken place within their own life path is them. No other can be blamed for this.

"Remember to keep in the front of your thinking minds that freedom of choice is to be found in all domains, my brothers. And it is through this freedom of choosing our own directions that we will find our greatest lessons that will allow us to learn that it is we who must take responsibility for our thoughts, actions, and deeds, and to see there can not ever be another who will ever have this responsibility for who and what we are or do.

"When one will come to see this truth, they will have come to a place of seeing their own individual freedom. And once they have seen this freedom, they will no longer be in a position of being controlled by another, for they have passed this by and will not be willing to return there, ever again.

"It is the threat of losing control that has caused this freedom to be seen as a great threat by those who live within the illusion of controlling others. For they have seen how losing their control over others has led them away from their power place among those they had come to live with. And this was not good in their eyes.

"For as many generations as have been in this domain of the Earth Mother, there have been those few who would wish to exercise their control over many. And this has resulted in having many rules and procedures for how one is to live their life.

"In some of the lands, it is considered to be good to have many wives. And in others, it is considered good to have many children. While in other lands, it is considered good to live alone.

"This list goes well beyond what I am willing to share with all of you and to go further with it would not benefit us that much.

"However, in all of those lands where one way of living has been set as being good, there will be other lands where just the opposite will apply. And this will lead us to explain the face of this sixth lesson, which states: '*We Have Done No Wrong.*'

"From the first entry of the two-legs in this domain of the Earth Mother, there has always been a great need to set rules for living. And in the beginning, this was good. For it set rules that included no killing of another, no stealing, and so on.

"However, when these rules were seen by those who were intent on controlling others, they took these good rules that would allow others to live close to each other and expanded them in ways that were not good for anyone but themselves.

"They took the rules that allowed people to live with each other and find a balance for their basic needs, not spiritual, and caused them to center their thinking minds on the physical sides of these rules. When they did this, there was no longer time for the two-legs to think on the spiritual sides of issues any longer.

"It was the controlling ones who had taken the spirituality out of the rules and replaced it with their own fear, this fear they knew would keep many trapped within the illusion. And as long as they remained trapped within the illusion, they would be easy to control for they would not ever find their balance.

"It was at this time when the controlling ones began to tell those who would listen how good their way was. And in the beginning, there was no great harm in this. For in the beginning of our generations, when another would tell us that their way is very good, we had only to look at them to see what they were saying, that they have found their own way to live and to them, this was the only way.

"When one will first discover their own path to travel, this often takes place. And with this in the front of one's thinking mind, it is acceptable. However, for the ones who have not yet found their way, they will look on those who have said they know what it is for everyone and they will believe them—believe in them. And this is where the confusion began.

"When one will claim to know the way for themselves, my brothers, this is good and they will have a good face to wear for what they have found. However, when one will say they know the way for all, this is not good and does not hold any truth to it. For there is my way, and there is your way. Each one who is traveling a life path within this domain is so individualized that there cannot ever be one way for two people, much less one way for all people.

"But this is what has taken place for those who have entered this domain and left it without ever having wakened from their own sleep of illusion, without ever having come to see their own face of truth, and without ever coming to see through their emotions and feelings of doubt, greed, and anger.

"When one will come among those who have yet to find their own path and tell them that they have found the way, those they speak to will look on them and believe in their truth rather than working to find their own. They will do this because they are unwilling to do their own work, and this is what begins the guilt that holds them within the sleep of illusion.

"For those who will say they have found the way, they will hold a control over the others who would come to them. For they know those who would follow them will not be willing to do their own work, this individual work that is required before any may find their own path to travel.

"They will keep them in control by making them feel guilty for not doing those things they have told them to do, guilty for doing and saying anything that is not in complete agreement with what the controlling ones would have them say and do.

"This is the beginning and will be followed by more dangerous things that will be seen in time, things such as keeping everyone separated from themselves, by telling them this way being shown to them is the only way, and if another would come among them telling them of another, then surely they must be lost and different from anything that is of their truth.

"As those who have been willing to follow the words of others, the ones who wish to control them—they will tell them all of the actions and deeds they have done which are not in agreement with what is being told to them are bad. And because they had done them, they will be told they each carry a great weight of guilt for having done so many things that are wrong.

"When they will come to believe this, they will feel guilty for all things they have done in their past seasons of life. And this guilt will follow them until they can no longer see through its illusion. For they will have been made to feel so guilty for doing those things of their past, they will fear doing anything they are not told to do by another.

"They will be made to feel fear for doing anything that will not be right in the eyes of those who exercise this control over them. And this fear will be so great they will no longer be willing to look on themselves for what they are. They will only look to the ones who are controlling them for approval of all they will think, do, and say.

"For you see, my brothers, when the two-legs come to this place of being, they will no longer have eyes that will see or ears that will hear. They will be placed in such fear of doing anything that is wrong, they will only look to the controlling ones for their guidance. They will no longer be in a place of believing in themselves any longer, for they have given this away.

"But I share with all of you that when it is their time to cross the great spirit waters and enter the waiting place, the face that will be over them will carry a great sadness for all they had been presented to learn from in this earth walk and had passed it by just so they could listen to the words of the controlling ones who kept them locked within their own fears for doing anything that might be considered wrong by another.

"I share with you in truth, there is not ever anything we do which is wrong. There is only that which we do because spirit within us had a need to learn from it. And from the learning, understanding is born to each of us. It is from those things we do that we find our understanding.

"So it is better to do those things that we are going to do anyway. But do them with understanding for what they are. As you will, you will begin to see the path that is yours to travel, this path that will lead you to the place of being one who will disappear with their body when it is time. This time is not far away. Already it is making its entry known to those who can still see and hear with the eyes and ears of their own spirit."

❀

CHAPTER 42

Lesson 7

There Is No Judging, There Is No Hell
—From An Elder in the West

"To arrive at the place of understanding for this final decision all will have to make, one will have to look on the face of this seventh lesson of re-remembering, my brothers," the Elder in the West began.

"In this seventh face, you will find a great truth, one that has been forgotten many generations before, but one that will soon enter this domain once again through one of you."

When the Elder in the West said these speaking words, I could feel my eyes fall on all of the members of our council. I did not know which one of us was being referred to, but I held the knowing that whatever was said, from these Ancient Ones of our people, it was shared in truth.

As I looked over the face of Grandfather and Two Bears, I could see a face of understanding for what had been shared with all of us. A face of understanding that allowed them to sit in a place of knowing rather than one of wondering.

However, when I looked over the face of my best friend, Cheeway, I could see that he, too, held the same wondering that was with me, wondering who was being referred to.

Then, looking over to the last and newest member of our council, I noticed the face Night Hawk was wearing had not changed. There did not seem to be anything at all that had changed his face even though there were many new things shared that had been given to each of us on this day, things that were so new that even Grandfather and Two Bears had placed a look of surprise over themselves from time to time. But these things did not seem to have an effect on this one called Night Hawk.

"I will tell you this in truth, my brothers," the Elder in the West began once again.

"*There Is No Judging And There Is No Hell.* For these things only have a place within the great illusion, within this great illusion that all must pass through before seeing with their own eyes.

"Where there is no judging, there can be no hell. For one cannot live without the other, even while one is still locked within their own sleep of illusion.

"But there are reasons why these two ideas have been left with the two-legs, my brothers. They have been left with those who are still in need of seeing these lessons for a great purpose. And that is to allow them to see a quick ending for such things, seeing the end of their path within the circle of illusion and how it travels nowhere—nowhere at all while they will hold onto such things as truth.

"When the controlling ones wish to exercise their control over those who are willing to listen, they will have one thing in the front of their thinking minds. If they are to hold these others who have come to them within their control, they will have to give something to them so they can feel as if they too have some kind of control over others. However, keep in the front of your thinking minds that all of this is illusionary and does not exist in the face of truth.

"But I am now willing to share with all of you the reasons why this takes place. And this will assist you greatly in seeing through these emotions that the illusion has brought over all of them.

"When the controlling ones create their own way of seeing things, this alone does not hold any power over another. It only allows them to be separated from those they do not yet control.

"However, when they will begin to tell those others that their way of seeing and living is the only correct way, they begin gaining their attention. For the ones who will listen to them cannot see anything either, so whoever will come before them saying they have seen truth, they will believe.

"It is almost like holding bait out to a fish but not showing them the hook that is just underneath it.

"These controlling ones will offer many empty shells of their truth to others and when they look at them and see nothing inside, they will be told they are not seeing because they have not yet come to believe in them completely, that they are still holding onto those parts of themselves that are sinful and those parts of themselves that are bad.

"That until they will be willing to give up themselves completely, they will not be able to see anything within these truths the controlling ones have shown them. They will not be able to see anything within them because they still believe in themselves and this is getting in their way.

"And in truth, this is what is taking place, my brothers. The more one will believe in themselves, and accept their lessons, the less they will be in a place of being controlled by another. This is why the controlling ones will wish to have them give up themselves and all those things they have come to believe in. They know that until they will do this, they cannot be fully controlled by them or another like them.

"So the ones who are still willing to listen to what the controlling ones are telling them—even after they have not seen anything within their empty shells of truth—they begin their path of giving up themselves and follow what they are told. And in this process, they become even more lost within the great illusion that does not allow them to see anything for what it is, but only allows them to see things for what they would wish for them to be. And in this case, as the controlling ones would wish for them to see.

"The next step in this process is once they have begun this journey with the controlling ones, they need to have something to hold onto. The controlling ones will see that none will remain long with them if there is even one small thing they can hold onto.

"And this is where judging comes into play, my brothers. This judging is given to those who have been willing to follow the controlling ones completely. For they are told that they are now within the seeing eyes of the correct path. This correct path the controlling ones wish to have all of them travel.

"And because they are now on this path of the controllers, when they see others who do not believe as they do, they may learn to use their powers to judge them, because if they are not like them, they are surely going to go to a bad place and could take them with them. This place is called hell within the illusion and keeps a great cloud of fear over all who would believe in such a place.

"And the worse this hell can be made to sound, the more control there will be over another. And the more control, the more judging of others will take place.

"You see, my brothers, all of this resides within the great illusion. For even to think that it is possible to judge another, one would be lost, and the ones who would believe that there is such a place as hell—surely they are the most lost of all.

"In truth, anything that takes focus away from your own path is from the illusion. When one remains focused on their path, they will not have the time or the desire to look at another's path. Their time will be completely filled with all of those things they have to do, with all of the work that is needed by them in order to learn their own lessons, do their own work, and advance their own spirit to the next higher place.

"For those who would be seeking to control others, the greatest gift you can offer to them is to be yourself, to be yourself for who and what you are in truth.

"Think of it in this way, my brothers. Let us say that you have asked a man to add another room to your house, and this man has agreed to do this work for you. And let us say that you wish to exercise control over this man in order to make sure he will accomplish what he has agreed to do for you.

"First, the both of you will sit in a place and reach an agreement for the price as well as the time it will take to complete this project. Once both of you have agreed to these things, you begin to exercise your control over this man for those things you wish him to do.

"You begin this process by telling him the price that has been agreed to is acceptable, but you are not willing to have him take more time to perform this service than has been agreed to. And you will put an additional part to your agreement, another part to this agreement that will say for each day he will take past the agreed time, there will be a daily charge for him to pay.

"Let us say that you have agreed to pay him one hundred dollars but will charge him five dollars for each day he is late.

"This gives you a feeling of being in control of the situation, a kind of control that tells you this man will fear losing money and will do everything in his power to keep all that he can for himself. This will also give you the feeling of power over this man for all his actions that he will make while performing this service of adding another room to your house.

"When this man is locked into the sleep of illusion, he will see these events in the same way. He will not see money as being a vehicle that allows us to do those things we have come into this domain to do, but sees it as an ends to the lack of abundance he is feeling. He will see money as being the answer to all of those things he feels is missing within himself. And with money, he can satisfy all of his desires.

"When both of you are locked into this great illusion, there will not be any problems. For both of you will have given up yourselves for this way of thinking, this way of seeing, and this path you believe is the right one for both of you to travel.

"However, let us say that you are the only one who is locked within your illusion and the man is not.

"When this is the case, there will be no means of control you may exercise over this man. When he agrees to the terms of your late penalty, he will have done this because he believes it is necessary for you to learn from. It does not have any real bearing or weight on him.

"He will do those things that allow themselves to be done. And his actions will not be governed out of the fear of losing money for being late. If he is late in this service, he will understand there are lessons being carried by these events. And for each lesson carried to him, there is a great opportunity of learning.

"When all goes as needed and the room is completed, both of you will wear a good face. However, when things that are not taking place in the desired time, and there is nothing that can be done to change them, this too must be looked at for what it is as well as for what is being offered.

"Let us say that the thunder beings look down on your house and see from you that it is not good for you to have another room at this time. And they decide to make it rain for many days causing the work on this room to stop.

"You will look at this and become angry, but you will not come to see these events as a sign telling you that this is not the time for this room to be completed. You will focus your anger on the man and his inability of completing this room on time.

"If the man is locked with the great illusion, he will do all that he can to complete this room. Even if it means his work will not be good, at least he has done what he said he would do and has not suffered the penalty for being late.

"However, the man who is not locked within the great illusion will see that it is not yet time for the room to be completed and there are lessons being offered. He will not attempt to change those things that are beyond his control, nor will he listen to you blaming him for being late with the work.

"He will look at you through eyes that see and tell you it is not time for the room to be added. When you tell him that he will be charged five dollars for each day he is going to be late, he will look at you and say nothing. For he will understand that when the penalty has become equal to the price he was going to receive for building the room, there will be no need to continue his efforts on your behalf. For his work at this point will be for nothing.

"When this time comes, he walks away from this project and leaves you with much work to be done. And this confuses you because you cannot understand how anyone could do such a thing like turning their back on money that would bring them great happiness.

"However, as this man walks away from this promise of money you had made to him, he has the understanding that he has left you with a great gift, one that has allowed you to see there may be more to this issue than the control of another using the promise of something you do not understand.

"This man will have the knowing that this gift has been left with you and what you will do with it will be up to you. He has not judged you nor has he caused you to feel the fear of things that are not truth. He has simply seen things for what they are and left it at that.

"Listen well, my brothers: we can only judge ourselves, not any other. For when we will attempt to judge another, we must surely give ourselves over to the illusion of there being a hell. For it is only then that the concept of hell can come into one's life path. It is only then that one must use the threat of something terrible happening to them when they do not do what they are told.

"I share this with all of you in truth, in the truth that is to be found when one is no longer trapped within their own sleep of illusion," the elder from the west position finished.

CHAPTER 43

❀

Lesson 8

We Are Who And What We Attract To Us
—From An Elder in the North

"When The Season of the Long Shadow has come into this domain of the Earth Mother, there will be such an acceleration of emotional reminding that many will perceive themselves being lost in it," began the sharing from the Elder in the North position.

"But now is not the time for this, for the waters are relatively calm. But when this time we speak of enters this domain, the waters will be churned as if a great storm has come over them and many will lose their way because of their ferocity.

"They will see increases in poisonings among the food that is eaten by the old and young alike. They will see many of them dropping dead at their own dinner tables, and see many who would drink of the waters of life which flow over the face of the Earth Mother fall dead as well. For it will be in this time that there will be many who will add such poisons to these waters that it will kill any who will drink from them.

"All of this will be seen as evil by the two-legs because they will have become lost within the accelerated emotion that will be over them. And there is no memory of so much having taken place before.

"I tell you in truth, this is only to be the beginning of such events that will enter this domain during the Season of the Long Shadow. For what they will see before them will seem very small in comparison to what is to follow.

"Those who do not possess the understanding of what is taking place will truly be the ones who will be lost. Many will not see until it is time to make their great decision of whether they need lessons that will be located on the twelfth earth, or if they no longer have need of them and will be allowed to remain with this Earth Mother and enter into her fifth world of peace and light.

"When The Season of the Long Shadow will enter this domain, my brothers, we will return. We will return and remind you that it is time to share those many things that have been shared with you, with all people. And this sharing will know no boundaries such as race, culture, or anything that keeps life separated now.

"And this brings us to the sharing of the eighth lesson to be re-remembered. This lesson that will allow the two-legs to take one more step into the direction of their own light that will allow them to leave this domain with their body so they will not ever have to go through the pains of birth and death again, not only in this domain, but for all domains that have been and will be created.

"When The Season of the Long Shadow has entered this domain, there will come to you many of the people who will be lost. They are the ones who have forgotten to remember who and what they are in truth, and how to see the answers to those things they have been praying and asking assistance for.

"They will come before you with their faces filled with fear and confusion from all they have seen, and for all they have been involved in. And they will come to you looking for answers to their own questions.

"But I share this with all of you, if you will be willing to do their own work for them, they will have nothing. For they will come to depend on you for their guidance and understanding. And you must hold in the front of your thinking mind that this is not possible. They are the only ones who can do this work, and they are the only ones who may see their own answers to all that will be confronting them during these times.

"This will not be easy, for those who will come to you will have lost a loved one in the bombing of a building or plane, or will have lost a loved one from the poisoning of food or water, or will have lost a loved one through a gang-related shooting. As you look on them, you will see their freedoms being taken away piece by piece until there is very little left for them to do, until there are very few places left where they can go. But I share this with you, this has not only come to them, but has come to all within this domain, and all of this has taken place for a reason.

"Remember the history of this Earth Mother and think of how many people have taken a life without being conscious of what they had done.

"I tell you this number has been great. When one will take such an action in one of their earth walks, they will have to see the results from the victim's side in order to understand what they have done. And this will come to them in another earth walk. The Season of the Long Shadow will be the time for many of these old lessons to be learned from.

"And those who need to see in order to learn will have these events come to them at a very accelerated rate.

"When one will come to you and say they are truly lost, share this with them:

"Remind them that who and what they are in truth can only be found within each of them. And the path to this place may only be found through the spirit of silence.

"However, before this can happen, there will have to be a preparing, preparing each of them must do on their own, for no other may assist them with this.

"Have them look at all the ones who are near them, the ones they have attracted. Then share that those who are near them, the ones they have a great liking for as well as those they do not have this feeling of good for, that each of them are in their life for a reason. And the reason is to show them where they are on their own earth walk, to show each of them where they are on their own path.

"When the ones who travel with them have found their own path, this becomes a confirmation that they, too, have found their own path to travel, and now is the time to remain focused on it and follow it to its own end.

"However, for those who are surrounded by others who have not found their own path to travel—and see many with them who are vindictive, jealous, envious, and so on—share with them that they are not seeing these others for who and what they are. But they are seeing a reflection of themselves in them. They are looking at a mirror image of those parts of themselves, which they either do not wish to look at, or they cannot see.

"When one will enter their own silence and find their path to travel, the confirmation for who and what they are will come to them from those they attract. As they continue their path of understanding and doing their own work to find their way, the ones they had seen so much bad in will go away. They will disappear out of their life path and find another who is in need of seeing those same things.

"So when one feels lost and trapped by the events that are soon to be in this domain of the Earth Mother, share this with them. Share with them that they are who and what they attract to themselves. Then allow them to do the rest of their own work themselves," came the end of the speaking words.

CHAPTER 44

Lesson 9

Do Not See An Enemy Before You.
See One Who Is An Answer To What You
Have Been Asking For.
—From An Elder in the East

"In this time of The Season of the Long Shadow, there will be many two-legs come before you with a great concern, one that has come to them in particular about those who have entered their life path," began the Elder in the East position.

"They will come to you wearing a face of fear or confusion and will wear a face of believing they must surely be doing something wrong in their life, otherwise there would not be so many who would come to them with these feelings of badness.

"They will tell you that no matter what they have come to do and say, it has not made any difference in their life path. The ones who continue to give them bad feelings are still with them, and when one leaves, another takes their place.

"All of this will concern them greatly. Not because it is there, but because they cannot get away from it.

"When the two-legs come to you and say these things, ask them this question. Ask them if they have been doing and praying or asking for assistance for themselves, prayers or assistance that would allow them to see what they still need in order to find their own way back home, this home all of us are going to when we will complete the long journey back to Creator.

"The ones who will tell you they have been praying for this kind of assistance will be speaking their own words of truth, and you may offer your assistance. However, for the ones who will not admit to this, they are not ready to hear these things we are about to share with you and they should be walked away from. Walk away from them for there will be another who will follow you and will make this offer to them again.

"Remember, my brothers, for the time that is left in this domain, there will not be a great amount of time but the work will be great. So do not waste your time on those who will not see or listen. Spend your time only among those who are ready for what is being shared with you now.

"For those who were willing to admit they have been praying for assistance, share this with them: Remind them there is not ever a prayer, which is not answered, and in less time than it takes to blink your eyes.

"However, there are many prayers that are not understood by the one who is asking them. And the requests we make that are not understood result in their perception of being bothered by so many bad people and events in their life.

"For those things we ask assistance for that we do not understand, the answers will not be recognized by us when they arrive. And the more assistance we will ask for—this assistance we do not understand—the more answers will come to us.

"Within each of these answers lies a great offering, my brothers, and we may find the face of the ninth lesson to be re-remembered, a lesson that will bring the two-legs another step closer to being allowed to leave with their body when the time is right, one step closer to not ever having to go through the pains of birth and death again.

"For the ones who would come to you with their own words of truth, share this with them.

"Have them consider a circle that represents their circle of life. Share with them that each earth walker they encounter will be a reminder for themselves. And for those parts of themselves they have worked to understand from, they will see these others as good people, for they will be showing them those parts of their circle of life they have gained understanding for.

"But remind them there are always parts of their circle of life they will not have seen nor worked on yet. And when another will remind them of this, there will be much that will not be understood and they will see them as bad people.

"This takes place because the emotions that will surface will not have been seen as a part of themselves. They will not have been recognized as a part of themselves because they have yet to see it is their reflection on them they are looking at.

"You see, my brothers, when one will enter this domain of the Earth Mother and begin their earth walk, their vision is very limited. They will only see what is in front of them. It is not until they begin to travel their own path that they will see wider and more completely. For while they are sleeping within the illusion, they can only see those things that will make a direct impact on them. And the greatest of these will be the emotions that will come on to them from another.

"When one will encounter something they do not understand, they will consider it to be their enemy. And when they will encounter emotions that will be presented to them from another—emotions that they do not hold an understanding for—they will consider this person to be bad, and will eventually see them as someone they must get rid of.

"While one is locked within the sleep of illusion, they will handle these enemies in one of two ways. They will either try to run or hide from them, or if they cannot do this, they will attempt to destroy them. But neither of these two avenues will be available to them, for what they see before them is themselves, and from this, there can be no hiding or running away from.

"All that has been presented to them, they have asked for. They have forgotten to remember that no one has any enemies before them, they only have answers that have come from these other people, and the answers they have asked for through their prayers and requests for assistance.

"Remind them these people have entered their life path for a reason. And the reason has been to offer them something they can see and work on to leave the sleep of illusion.

"And the reason these kinds of people have come to them, over and over again is because they are trapped within their own circle of illusion, this circle of illusion I will explain to all of you.

"Each earth walker has a circle around them. And within this circle are the many places that make up our life path, this life path that holds all of the needed lessons we have entered this domain to learn from—then to understand.

"However, not all parts of this circle of life can be easily seen. Even though it is close to us at all times, there are portions of it that are unseen because one has not yet found their own path to travel. They have been held within their sleep of illusion and are looking at all things for what they would wish for them to be.

"Now, when one is in this domain and no matter what their background is, they feel a connection to something which cannot be seen or touched. Some call this God, others call this Jehovah, others call this Great Spirit, and others call it Life Force.

"But for whatever name is used, Creator does not change. For all is from the One, and to the One, all will return.

"Those who feel this connection but do not understand it, always look up to the skies above them, or down to the earth below their feet. They will do this because they do not yet understand where Creator resides and the relationship that exists among all life.

"For those who have yet to awaken from their sleep of illusion, they will be found in a continual state of asking for things to be shown them, but only in a way that will fit their own perception of life.

"And they will come before you saying there cannot be a God because he does not answer them. However, keep in the front of your thinking mind when one will say this to another, they are not making a statement; they are asking for help. Help to show them how wrong they are. But there cannot ever be another who will do this work for them, this must be done for themselves.

"Listen to them when they will come to you with sayings such as this. Listen and understand they are asking for proof to all of those things they are feeling but do not understand. And, to prove to another any of those things that have come to you, leads you away from your path, and will lead them away from theirs as well.

"As you listen to them asking for proof that Creator exists, you will see many scars on each of their faces. Scars that will be from all of the times they have fought with themselves and the illusion that has not allowed them to see what is in truth, but has kept them trapped by only showing them what they would wish to see, to see only those lives for what they would wish for them to be.

"There will be many people come to them and they will feel hostility, anger, fear, resentment, suppression, and control. There will be others who will bring them good feelings as well, but they will not have difficulty working with them so we will not discuss them in depth at this time.

"When you encounter things from people, places, and things as being bad or evil, they will at first appear to you as ones who have been through many battles in this earth walk. And when you listen to them speak, you hear within their words sounds of great frustration. But I share with you, this frustration has not come to them from events that have crossed their life path; this frustration has come to them from not having found another who would be willing to do their work for them.

"So keep this in the front of your thinking mind while you listen to them. It will assist you greatly in keeping your focus on the path you have come to travel. If you will not remain focused, my brothers, you will find yourself falling away from your path and onto theirs in a very short time.

"When these who have yet to awaken from their own illusion come before you and begin to ask questions, questions that I have already discussed, look at them with a good face to wear for them and share this.

"There is not ever a prayer or request for assistance that will be asked that will not be answered. And it will always be answered in less time that it will take you to blink your eyes.

"However, there are many things we ask for that we do not understand. And when one will not understand what is being asked for, there can be no recognizing the answer when it is presented.

"Remind them when one will ask for assistance and not understand what they are asking for, it will come to them in the form of another person, place, or thing. And it will come to them in a way that will cause them to feel emotion from it. But this emotion is nothing more than a reflection of what they need to work on within themselves. Once they understand this, they can see the answers to those things they have requested assistance for.

"When they see these other people, places, or things as a reflection of themselves for areas they need to work on, they will understand they have no need to blame another for what they feel. They will see what has been coming to them has been a messenger for what they have been asking for. Then they will see more of themselves for who and what they are in truth. And when they will encounter another person, place, or thing that will enter their life path and bring them these feelings of bad, they will understand the blessing of saying to themselves, three times: '*Thank You For Coming to Me, My Friend. What Have You Brought For Me To Learn From You Today?*'

"For those who have the eyes and ears to see and listen to you, my brothers, be glad for them. They will be the ones who will see through the illusion and into the face of truth for these great events that are soon to be with all life in this domain, those things that will be born when The Season of the Long Shadow enters.

"For the ones who are not willing to see or listen to those things we have shared with you, walk away from them and do not look back. They are not your concern, and there will be another messenger who will pass by them in time. All life, during this time we speak of, will be given three more opportunities of listening to those things that are of themselves, three more opportunities of hearing these truths that will be presented to them, three more opportunities of finding themselves once again so they will be able to make their great decision with the clarity of sight.

"This then is the face of the ninth lesson to be re-remembered, my brothers, this ninth lesson that has always been with all life but has been forgotten because the illusion has not allowed them to see what has always been," the elder's speaking words finished.

❁

CHAPTER 45

Lesson 10

Look Through Your Own Eyes, Not Through The Eyes Of Others. —From An Elder in the South

"There are many two-legs who carry great disappointment with them, my brothers," came the sharing from the Elder in the South position.

"They have yet to open their eyes and ears of spirit and will see life as a great pounding on them that reminds them they are not good enough nor will they ever complete anything worthwhile.

"However, I share with all of you that this is not truth. For there is no truth within the great illusion, but all must pass through it before they can find their way past the emotions that keep them trapped there. All that they are told is truth—while they are trapped within the illusion—will hold a great disappointment for them when it is time for them to lean or depend on it. For when they will do this, they will fall onto the earth below them. This will happen because there will be nothing of truth that will support them from what others have told them.

"They will look at themselves lying on the earth beneath them and say that this is another disappointment they have found. In truth, they have been shown where they are and this in itself is a great blessing to anyone who will see it. But for those who are locked within the sleep of illusion, they will see this as just another of those disappointing events that has come into their life path, another event which they will stack up with all the others that have let them down as well.

"This then brings us to the face of the tenth lesson to be re-remembered. And this lesson reminds us to look through our own eyes and not the eyes of another.

"The two-legs are in such a great hurry to find peace for themselves, they search for it in others and in distant lands. They are in such a hurry to find this peace, they place themselves in a continual state of trying, and we have shared with all of you what trying will bring to anyone.

"When one will try, they are always becoming something and someone they are not. And the harder they will try, the more difficult their path to understanding will be.

"Truth is very simple, my brothers, when one will understand it. However, when one does not understand truth, it becomes a great and confusing thing for them to look on. And when they attempt to explain truth they do not understand, it even becomes more complicated.

"And in truth, this peace the two-legs will attempt to find in the faces and places that are not of themselves, will not be found. For what they seek resides within them, and its path is simple to follow, once discovered.

"However, as it is with all things, one must be willing to allow themselves to be, before they can see this path I am willing to share with you, this path that is the face of the tenth lesson that needs to be re-remembered.

"There will be many who will cross your life path and ask for the meaning of this tenth lesson. There will be many that will listen but will not hear, and there will be many that will listen and not understand.

"For those who would be willing to make this time that is needed for themselves, share this example of how one will look through the eyes of another or others.

"Remind them there have been many events that have come into their life path. And each of those events has touched them for a specific reason that will assist them in coming to understand themselves for who and what they are in truth.

"However, before they can see the wonderful blessings that are being presented, they must be willing to look at themselves through their own eyes, and not through the eyes of others.

"When one will look through the eyes of others, they will hesitate in doing anything without thinking how it would make another feel first. One will also be looking through the eyes of others when they will not do something they need to do because they fear how it would make someone else feel if they were to do it.

"One will be looking through the eyes of others when they do things to please another and not themselves. They will be looking through the eyes of others when they see themselves as someone else has told them they should be. And one will be looking through the eyes of others when they fear being who they are or saying what they believe.

"There have been many controls exerted over those who have come to look at themselves through the eyes of others, controls that do not allow them to see themselves for who and what they are, controls that keep them in a place of not ever being good enough no matter what or how much they have done in their life path, controls that do not allow them to come up to the standards that have been put on them because these standards are not of themselves, they are from another who has nothing at all to do with them or their lessons.

"Those who would look at themselves through the eyes of another or others will always be disappointed, or filled with despair, hurt, sorrow, and many other emotions that keep them locked into the illusion of seeing themselves as not good enough. And the longer they will see themselves through those imposed standards, the longer they will remain lost within this sleep of illusion which tells them they are not good enough at anything they do.

"The longer they remain trapped within this illusion, the harder they try to be better. And the more they will try, the less they will be of themselves. Soon, they will only be an echo of someone or something they are not and this gives them a feeling of being lost in a world that can no longer see or hear them. This places them into a direct line of seeing themselves as having nothing of value to offer another. And, they come to believe there is nothing good to see in themselves or anyone else.

"For those who wish to remain locked within this illusion by looking at themselves through the eyes of others, their path is one of great sadness. For those who would remain within this illusion, their path is one that leads no place...no place at all. For the path they follow is one that is false, but they will not see it for what it is until the time of the great decision is upon them and the light from the Great Messenger shines through all illusion.

"When it is time, and their journey is at its end, you will see great tears of regret falling over their faces, tears of regret for all they could have done with this earth walk but did not do, tears of regret for not having taken the time and effort of seeing through their own eyes that would have allowed them to see past all of the pain and sorrow, their own eyes that would have allowed them to see that all things which had come to them were blessings and opportunities of learning so they could understand the lessons that were greatly needed by their own spirit.

"And these tears of regret will not be shed for anyone other than themselves, for in truth, my brothers, there cannot be any other who can come before your own needs. And this is the beginning of the path to seeing through your own eyes.

"One of the greatest illusions we have come to see in this domain is the one that says it is good to put another before you, that until you will have come to put another or others before your own needs, you will not find the peace that is within you.

"But I share with you, this does not hold any truth to it at all. When one will place another before them, they are not doing any justice to themselves or another. They are not doing anything for anyone but stopping the progress of their spirit and its path to finding and understanding.

"Ask yourself this, who feels what you feel, and who sees what you see?

"In truth, there is none but you, and there is none but you who possess the understanding that is needed to interpret that which will be presented to you during this time of your earth walk. So why put this impossible burden on another? Why make another responsible for your own thoughts, actions, and deeds by claiming to see all things through their eyes instead of your own?

"Remember this, my brothers, when one will come to you for assistance, look to see whose eyes they are looking through. If they are looking at you through the eyes of others, they will wish to be led. And yours is not to lead but to walk your own path, so others may see it is possible to walk theirs as well.

"When one will come before you has seen how to look through their own eyes, then this will be a good thing, for they will have the ability of seeing themselves for who and what they are. And with this ability, they will see that you walk your own path and this will share with them a strength that will allow them to do the same.

"Remember, there is no thing we do which is right, wrong, or indifferent. There are only those things we do because we have a need to do them. Only when we will take the time to understand all we will do, will we find ourselves looking through our own eyes.

"So do not be concerned with how another will see your thoughts, actions, or deeds. Only be concerned with how you are seeing them, and understand them. For they will be a clue to how you may find the path you need to travel, and discover the work that is needed to be done by you on this journey.

"This then is the face of the tenth lesson of re-remembering, my brothers. Remember to keep it in the front of your thinking minds for it will serve all of you well in this time that is soon to be with you, this time we have come to call The Season of the Long Shadow," came the ending of the speaking words.

❀

CHAPTER 46

Lesson 11

There Are No Strangers Among Us. They Are Our Spirit Family.
—From An Elder in the West

"The two-legs who are trapped within the illusion will see themselves as being alone," came the opening of the speaking words from the Elder in the West position. "They see themselves alone because they do not see another they can trust.

"There will be many they will outwardly call friend and relation, but in the back of their minds they will wonder just how far they will be safe in trusting them, just how much of a friend they will be to them when they will have need of them. And they will always wonder why they are with them, if they are with them for something they have, or if they are with them for something they can do for them.

"But in any case, the two-legs who are trapped within this illusion will not see their friends as someone who is with them just to be with them. They will believe that in order to have friends, they must have something they want.

"This leads them into a place of thinking if their friends would ever see them for what they were, if they would see them for having weak places within them, or they are not who they have showed them they were, they would surely go away from them. And this kind of being alone carries a great weight of fear to any who would travel with it.

"They will go through many efforts of keeping anyone from seeing them for who they believe they are. They will make many efforts at pointing their fingers at another or others to keep their friends' attentions away from them.

"They will make their efforts of making another or others look bad so there will be no danger of being seen themselves. But this gives them a false sense of security, and it is this false sense of security that will veil them with the mask of secrecy, a mask of their own secrecy so others will not be able to see through it.

"But all of this is done with one thing in mind. While they point out how bad others are, their friends will stay with them because they do not seem as bad. And they give the illusion of having something to offer, so their friends will remain with them hoping to get a part of it as well.

"And all the while, they are closing themselves into a place where only they may go, a place where they are truly alone.

"However, for the ones who will come to awaken and see their own way out of the great illusion, they will see the oneness that exists in all life. They will be the ones who will see they are a member of a great spirit family, a great spirit family that will continue to travel the great adventure as One.

"You see, my brothers, before one awakens from their sleep of illusion, they only see strangers before them. They only see those who are around them as just another number, and not much more. Or they see them as an opportunity for them to use them in some way or another.

"However, as one will begin their awakening from the sleep of illusion, they begin to feel something from a few of these other people. They begin to feel something either of comfort or familiarity, and this will be the beginning for their waking process.

"As time passes them, there will be more of these kinds of feelings come to them, and as this feeling grows with them, so does the acceptance of themselves.

"But in the beginning, they will believe they are only believing in others once again. But I tell you this in truth, it is the believing in themselves that is growing.

"For unless one can believe in themselves, there can be no believing in another. And this process will begin to grow in them when they will begin to feel something good from those who will enter their life path.

"As their seasons continue, they feel more of this comfortable feeling. And soon, they will begin to ask themselves a great question of awakening, this great questioning of their awakening of what they are seeing.

"Remind them that while one is trapped within their own illusion, they can only see themselves as one who is alone. While they are lost within this illusion, there will only be that which they will wish to see and nothing more. They will only see those things they wish to see because there have been so many others telling them what is and is not their own truth that this is all they had seen. They could only see they were lost and unless they had something to offer another, they were of no worth.

"While they listened to the path that was placed over them by another, they could not see anything for what it was in truth—not even their own brothers and sisters.

"So when they begin to wake from their sleep of illusion, they began seeing their own light of truth, this light of truth that shared with them all that is for what it is—and in truth, in this truth that has always been within them, but they forgot to remember.

"What they are waking up to is what has always been, and they are beginning to see this. They are seeing there is a great relationship among all of our spirit family, and as they come to increase their seeing of this, they feel the belonging that is theirs, this belonging to all life and all life belonging to the One.

"When Creator began all of us as separate spirits, He did this so that we could find our own way home. But this path that leads us to home once again cannot be seen by an individual who is asleep or locked in the great illusion of being led by another or others. This path can only be seen by those who have awakened to their own truth and are willing to do their own work that will allow their spirit to learn the lessons it needs, to gain understanding, which leads to wisdom and will show them the peace they seek.

"When Creator gave each of us a path to travel, He did this so we could find our way back to Him through understanding and as a family. When those who begin to awaken from their sleep of illusion see there are no strangers among us—but there is only our own spirit family—they begin to see we are all in this great and long journey together, that we have begun together and will continue to travel as a family...together.

"When the two-legs will see this face of truth, they will no longer see an enemy before them when someone will cause them to feel bad. They will see them as one who has delivered this message as one of their brothers or sisters who has been kind enough to carry an answer for something they have been asking, an answer to how they can be more balanced on the path they have chosen to travel.

"But since they did not hold a complete understanding for what they had been asking for, the answer must come to them from another as a mirror reflection to someplace within them that is still in need of work, a place they cannot see on their own. But with the help of one of their spirit family members, they can see a reflection of this in them.

"When the two-legs come to see this truth we have been willing to share with you, my brothers, they will look on the face of this eleventh lesson of re-remembering. And when they will have come to see this eleventh lesson, they will have another layer of fear lifted from them. And each of these layers of fear will hold a greater weight to them during this Season of the Long Shadow than they ever had in the past.

"Keep this with you, my brothers. There will be great need of the wisdom that is held within these speaking words we have been willing to share with you," the Elder in the West position finished.

PART VIII

❀

11 Steps to Healing Our Spirit from Within

It does not matter, nor is it important, what another will think of us.
It is only important what we think of ourselves.

CHAPTER 47

❀

Step 1

We Are What We Attract To Us
—From An Elder in the North

"When The Season of the Long Shadow has been born into this domain, there will be great opportunities for the two-legs, my brothers. That is, if they will be willing to look through the illusion which has been placed over them, this great illusion that can only show us the face of fear and punishment for all that it will bring," began the speaking words from the Elder in the North position.

As these speaking words came to a close, there was a sudden flash of lightning from the storm outside, and the light from this flash showed something I had not been aware of before.

For as the flash of light hit on the sides of the stone walls around us, I could see many others standing and sitting with this council, others who were dressed like the eleven Ancient Ones sitting around the warming fire we had come to use as a council fire.

However, they had none of the markings from the four points of the medicine wheel on them. They did not have the colors of red, black, white, or yellow on them, but were all dressed in white.

I did not hold a knowing for why they were here, nor what their purpose was to be. But as I looked over to the faces of Grandfather, Two Bears, and Cheeway, I saw they, too, had seen these others standing and sitting next to the great cave walls. And they, too, were surprised at their presence among us.

However, as I looked over to the face of the one called Night Hawk, I could see that he had a knowing and understanding with him for this event. And once again, there was a new layer of mystery to this old friend of Grandfather's and Two Bears', one that I knew would be shared with me in time, and one I would have to be content to wait on. For this was not the time, and this was not to be the place where I would be shown the answer to these questions I held about him.

"Remember what we have shared with you, my brothers," the Elder in the North position continued. "You are not ever alone. However, for those things we do not hold an understanding for, you cannot see them. And the less we understand of ourselves and all that is around us, the more blind we will travel this earth walk of ours.

"It is good that each of you have seen our other brothers and sisters sitting and standing next to these walls. For it is by this that you will come to hold an even clearer understanding of how far each of you have come in the waking process of yours.

"When one is asleep within the illusion, they can neither see nor hear any of those things that are with them. And this is why so many have not seen through their own emotions, for they will not see that which is, and they will not hear those things that are being spoken to them.

"The ones who remain asleep within their illusion will always be lost in the emotion. They will be in a continual battle with themselves believing they are fighting with someone else.

"Those who will stand before you and tell you that they have no answers to anything they have been asking assistance for will be the ones who tell others that no one could be listening to them either.

And they will be the ones who will tell you and others like you this path of the spirit is one that surely must be false.

"They will say these things because of what they have found while they were still trapped within the illusion.

"They will stand before you and say there is no truth to this thing called the path of the spirit. They will say that every time they have asked for assistance, they received nothing but trouble and bad feelings. But I share this with all of you, what they received was exactly what they have been asking for. But their eyes and ears have not yet been opened for them, and they could not see. All they saw was trouble finding them around every corner.

"And this brings us to the first of the eleven steps needed to heal our own spirit. These steps, when understood, will allow one to see the blessings that continue to pour into this domain of the Earth Mother, these blessings that are in response to all that has been asked for.

"This first step toward healing tells us we are all that we attract to us. There will be many that will say we are attracted to many things and not the other way around, but this way of seeing is only found within the illusion. For we are the attracting spirit for what we are in need of.

"When those who remain within the illusion come before you, remind them they have been asking and praying for many things to come into their life path. But in order to see this, they must be willing to do their own work and not depend on another to do it for them.

"Share with them the process they need to embark on; it is a very simple one. When truth is understood, it is very simple to explain. However, when truth is not understood, it becomes complicated and no other will see their way to it.

"Ask them why they are feeling so miserable and wearing such a bad face for all things that have come to them. When they answer themselves truthfully, they begin seeing through the emotion they have been caught up in. And when they argue or wrestle with their own emotions, they will not win.

"It is only by going beyond their emotions that they will find their way. When they will be willing to drop away all of the emotional drive they have, they will begin to see past the emotion and look on the beginning of their lesson's face.

"Remind them also, my brothers, that all they encounter of this path is only for them. It does not apply to any other, for these lessons are theirs and theirs alone to learn from.

"Have them sit in a quiet place next to one of the standing people and review all of those things that are bothering them, when they see someone who has more than they do, or as someone who has come to them as a very irritating person.

"Have them review all of those things they have been asking assistance for, from the prayers they have sent to Creator. But have them do this in a way that they will listen to what they say, for within their own words are to be found the answer to this question, this question that must be held in the front of their thinking minds as they look through the emotions they have been flooded with.

"Next, have them look at their own life path and only see themselves. In this way, they will not be so worried of what another would think of them and will see how they can do things for themselves without needing the approval of another.

"Have them look at their life, where they are, and where they need to go. Then share with them that where they are now, and where they wish to get to, there is a great valley between these two points. And this valley must be filled with lessons that have to be learned by them before they can cross.

"Once they have crossed this valley, they will find all they have been seeking. They will find themselves in the place they need to be in. And I share this with all of you in truth; there are not ever any places one needs to get to that are not in complete agreement with one's spirit. And there is not ever a picture of anything one needs to accomplish that they will not have the talents and abilities to perform it well. For all of these things were brought with them when they entered this domain of the Earth Mother. But they must first cross this great valley before they can understand all they have within them, all that has been brought with them in order to do those things they need to do.

"As they look through these emotional issues that have come to them, they see those who have come to them are one of their spirit family members, one who has been willing to bring them the answer to what they could not see, but needed to work on, those things they cannot see other than through the face of another.

"Remind them this is the process of assistance they have been asking for. That whenever they will ask what they need to work on, the answer will come to them through another, through those who will be seen by us as a mirror image of what we need to work on within ourselves before we can see the answer to our requests.

"When this is understood by the two-legs, there will be a peace that will blanket them, one that will show them they are on the path they need to be on. And that all is as it should be as long as they are willing to understand how they relate and not react to them.

"When the two-legs ask for a sign that will mark their progress, remind them that who and what they attract to themselves will be their mark. That all they will attract to them, but not feel good about, will be a sign of what is still needed to be worked on within them. That when they become upset or angered by the actions of another, it is not this other person they should be upset at—it is themselves. For what they see in another is exactly what is needed to be worked on within them and they are upset in seeing this in another because they have not yet been willing to see this in themselves.

"As we understand, our desire to control falls away from us. It is when we will desire to control that we will be in a constant state of altering another's life path so we will not have to work on our own."

❀

CHAPTER 48

Step 2

How To Hear The Calling Voice Of Your Own Spirit
—From An Elder in the East

"The second step to healing resides in the ability of hearing the calling voice of our own spirit. For it is this calling voice that shares with us those things we need to do, and why," came the immediate reply from the Elder in the East position.

"During this time of The Season of the Long Shadow, many will feel an accelerated level of emotion come to them. And it is the emotion that is reminding them of lessons that still need to be learned by them so their spirit may advance itself to the next higher place of understanding.

"However, from what we have seen in the times that have been set aside for the cleansing of the four races, there have not been many who were willing to look through their own emotions to see the face of their own truth from within, this place that exists within each earth walker, where their spirit is to be found.

"While it is truth, there is no thing that will ever come to another that is an accident or coincidence, there are many who remain lost within their own illusion and get caught up in wrestling or arguing with this emotion—or get trapped into listening to another's words instead of their own.

"And it is for those to whom this second step of healing will apply. For they will be the ones who have found that many of the paths they have traveled have led them no place and have left them with less than they began with.

"It will be those who are tired of spinning in their own circles of illusion that will come to you seeking assistance. And they will be willing to hear what is shared with them, these things that will uncover many great mysteries within themselves so they may see the path they need to travel, and not the path that is popular among those who are with them at the time.

"The ones who will come before you at this time will have found there has been no truth in those things they have been told by others, those who would continue to have them live their life path ruled by the fear of doing anything wrong, or something that will not be approved of by them.

"They will have spent many of their seasons searching for answers in others and following those things they have been told were right for them to do. And they will be the ones who will have not been willing to do their own work for themselves, but have been searching for another or others who would do this for them.

"By the time they come to you, my brothers, they will be very tired. They will have used much of their energies in traveling along empty corridors only to find them blocked when they arrived at the end of them.

"They will look at you through eyes that will show the weight of continual disappointment and hurt from all they have done. And they will hear you through ears that have become used to hearing others tell them what to do rather than listening to themselves.

"All who come before you in this time, my brothers, will be look-ing for many answers in those things you have to share. When they hear from you these things we have been willing to share with you, they will be filled with surprise, a surprise to hear the simplicity of truth and the direction they need to travel to find their own answers.

"When you have many of the two-legs come in search of their answers, share with them what they have been searching for has been with them all this time, that there is no thing they hold a need to know that is not within them, only they have forgotten to remember this.

"Many have forgotten to remember how to listen to their spirit within, this same spirit that holds all of the knowing and under-standing for all that has happened, and will happen, to them.

"Because they do not remember the way, they will attempt to make it a journey of unbelievable proportions, one that will have become so complicated that by the time they seek you out, there will be no one, including themselves, who can find anything that will make sense for their efforts.

"When you share with them that all they seek resides within them, they will look on you with a face of tiredness. This will come over them because of all the long and endless journeys they have traveled before, those journeys that did not reveal anything to them, other than a false path.

"So when these two-legs come before you, my brothers, share with them the path to hearing the calling voice of their own spirit, this same spirit who will share the reason and path they have come to travel.

"Have them recall the times in their seasons past when they heard or felt something from within tell them that they should leave where they were. Then have them look at the times they did not listen to this feeling that was coming from within them.

"When they will be truthful to themselves, they will remember that something bad had happened to them because they did not leave. They did not hold a believing in themselves so there was no reason for them to listen to what they had to say. And because of this unwillingness to listen to what their own spirit was telling them, they ended up in a bad situation.

"Next, have them look to another situation, one where they did listen to what this small feeling from within them was telling them to do, this feeling that had been coming to them from their within place that was telling them to leave where they were at the time.

"And when they are truthful to themselves, they will see that nothing happened to them—nothing that could be considered bad—for they had listened to what their spirit was sharing with them.

"Share with them how the times when they either heard something tell them to leave, or felt an urge from within to leave, that this was the calling voice of their spirit. This was the time when spirit, who is them, was speaking to them, and they listened.

"Have them sit in a quiet place that is close to the Earth Mother's children, and review all of those times from their past seasons when this had happen to them. Rest assured, everyone will have had this happen to them at least once, but many of them will have forgotten about it.

"So it is important for them to review as many of these times as they can remember.

"When they have come up with at least one situation where they heard the calling voice of their spirit, have them think on it long enough to make a picture of it, a picture they can place in the front of their thinking minds.

"Then have them keep this picture long enough to make it real, long enough for them to make it come alive in the three dimensions, just as they are used to seeing things before them in their walking time.

"When they do this, there will be a life that will return to this time they are remembering. And once this life fills their thinking mind's picture, they will be able to follow the next step.

"Have them lie in a quiet place where they will not be bothered by anyone. Then have them walk into this picture they have formed.

"Next, have them see themselves walk into this picture that has all of the events that had come to them when they remembered hearing the calling voice of their own spirit.

"Once they are successful in walking into this picture, tell them to listen carefully to the sound and feeling that told them to leave this place they were in. When they will do this, my brothers, they will once again be reminded of the sounds and feelings that came to them, and it will be the calling voice of their own spirit they will hear.

"Then remind them to repeat this process again and again. This will allow them to learn to hear the calling of their spirit. Once they can recognize this calling voice within them, they will have begun the path that leads them to listen to what is being shared, this sharing of all that is needed by them from their own spirit.

"This whole process will take a short time, my brothers, but when one is not willing to do their own work, it becomes an impossible task. Only the ones who are willing to do their own work will find the way. Those who will not be willing to do their own work will only find another's way, a way that is not theirs and does not assist them.

"When they have come to complete this process, my brothers, they will have become successful in completing their needed understanding of the second face of healing their own spirit. And they will be allowed passage into the third step—but not before this one has been completed."

CHAPTER 49

❀

Step 3

Two Clues To Healing Your Own Sickness, Disease, And Illness (Mental, Physical, And Spiritual) —From An Elder in the South

"During The Season of the Long Shadow, many of the two-legs will find themselves filled with sickness, disease, and illnesses they have not heard of. And they will come to those who have not yet learned the process of healing themselves for what they carry with them," began the speaking words from the Elder in the South position.

"The body that carries our spirit was not made to be sick or ill, my brothers, but there is a great reason that it has become so plagued with many of these things, and those reasons cause it to look tired and feel worn out.

"The reason is the freedom of making one's own choice for all that will be presented to them while they are in this domain of the Earth Mother, the choice that is theirs to make for all of the lessons that will be presented to them. It is this choice that will allow them to either look at the lessons being offered to them and learn to understand what is being presented, or to look away and carry another layer of emotion on them.

"For the ones who will choose to turn away from their lessons, there will not only be another layer of emotion tacked onto them, but they will find no escaping for what they have set themselves to learn from. If they turn away from one situation, they will find the same lesson return to them in another face—and another time. And each time it will return, the emotion will be stronger than it was before.

"As you enter The Season of the Long Shadow, all life will be given the opportunities of paying off all these old bills, all of these lessons they have been turning away from. As this takes place, there will be a great acceleration of emotion that will come to them as well, an acceleration of emotion that has always been with them, but will not be content to reside behind them any longer. For that time they all once knew will be over, and it is time to see what is needed.

"This will cause many of the two-legs to create sickness, disease, and illness on themselves. And it will not be limited to the body parts, but will include the mental as well as the spiritual parts of themselves. For there will be many lessons that will confront all of them when it is time to pay off these very old debts they owe to themselves.

"And this will cause many to travel holding their bodies in a place of great sickness. They will come to you looking for a cure or a healing. But this is something they must do for themselves. If you were to do their work for them, there would be nothing permanent about it, and they would find themselves returning to the same place very soon.

"Until the two-legs come to know how to heal themselves, there will be no thing permanent for them. All they will find will be fleeting for them and will not remain with them longer than the passing of one moon.

"So when they come to you looking for healing of their illnesses, sicknesses, and diseases, share with them this third step to healing themselves. It is not a complicated process and will be understood by those who have eyes to see and ears to hear with.

"When they come to you seeking your assistance, have them look at what is bothering them. Have them look at those things that have manifested on each of them from the beginning.

"They must first see what caused this problem to come to them, my brothers. Have them look carefully at the last time they can remember when they were not ill or sick. And within this time, there will be a great clue for them to see.

"However, for those who have come only seeking assistance, they will not be able to see this clue that will allow them to heal themselves, so you will have to share with them in another way, one that is even less complicated than this one I have been speaking of.

"Share with them that this illness or sickness is allowing them to either do something they need to do, or not to do something another is telling them to do. And this being sick is an excuse for them to act as they wish without feeling guilty about it.

"However, as it is with all things that reside within the great illusion, this is something they cannot see. If they allow this sickness to continue its path in this direction, there will surely fall on them an even greater disease, one that will completely rot the body away from them, and once this has taken place, there will be no turning back for them. Once this has taken place, all that will be available for them to see is that sickness, disease, and illness is a way out for them, a way out for them to do those things they wish to do without feeling guilty while doing them.

"However, there will be many of the two-legs who will wish to relieve themselves of this burden that has caused them to feel sick and diseased for many of their seasons. And these will be the ones who will benefit from these speaking words we have been willing to share with all of you on this day.

"Have them look at what they can do more freely now that they are sick. And have them remember there are certain things they have to do, with or without the permission of another, this need may not be seen by them yet, but it will make itself clear once they have begun this path, for it will allow them to see why it is that they are calling this illness to them.

"Have them look through the pains and discomfort of this sickness so they can see what it is they are doing. In order for them to look through this pain and discomfort, they must first be willing to stop feeling sorry or pity for themselves.

"When they have looked through their own inflicted feelings of discomfort, they will see what it is they are now able to do, or do not have to do, because the illness has given them an excuse. They can do, or not do, that which they have a need for without feeling the weight of guilt over them. And many of those things they need to do, they have wanted to do for a long time.

"Next, have them look at the behavior others put up with from them because they are not well, this behavior that is tolerated by the ones who are near them because they are sick. When they will come to see the reason for it being with them is really an excuse for them to act a certain way without feeling guilty about doing or not doing something, they will be surprised. For they have not realized this as being a cause for themselves to have such a great illness or disease. They will have looked on this behavior they are now able to do as something that is tolerated because they are not well.

"But I tell you this, once they see what they are doing, or what they no longer have to do, have them tell themselves that it is all right to do or not to do this. Share with them they have a great need in doing or not doing this, but as long as they look at themselves through the eyes of others, there will not be any peace for them. As long as they see themselves through the eyes of others, there will always be many things that they have a need to do. But since they are not on their path, they will feel guilty about doing them—and they will go undone.

"As long as they carry these feelings of guilt, there will be sickness, illness, and disease with them. For not until they have come to see through their own eyes will they see these things they wish to do, or those things they do not wish to do, as having good to them at all.

"But I tell you this, the minute they see themselves through their own eyes and understand that it is all right to do or not to do those things they have a need for, they will feel the sicknesses begin to fall away. For they will no longer need the excuse of being sick or ill in order to do or not to do those things that have come to them. They will see the illnesses that had been with them for many seasons leave because they no longer have a need for them. For this path they will see to travel has been set into motion by their own spirit long before they had come to draw the first breath in this domain of the Earth Mother.

"And there is much they have a need to do here, but as long as they will not see those things with their own eyes, they will be made to feel guilty about doing them. And it is guilt that adds an emotional weight to them; an emotional weight that will manifest itself into a sickness, illness, or disease for what they believe it can do for them. There is much work for them to do, my brothers, but until they will be willing to do it, there will be no rest for them.

"Remember, before you can heal another, you must first learn to heal yourself."

❀

Step 4

How To Attract From Within
—From An Elder in the West

"The two-legs have paid great amounts of attention to how they look on the outside or how they will appear to others," began the speaking words from the Elder in the West position. "They have forgotten a great truth, and it is one that is to be found in this fourth step of healing oneself.

"When one is concerned with how they look to another, they are looking away from their own path. When they will be more concerned with how they look to another they will forget how they appear to themselves.

"When they have let this self-seeing fall away, they will attract to them all of those things that are needed by someone else, they will no longer be attracting any of those things they need.

"You see, my brothers, when one will look at their life path through the eyes of another, then they are no longer walking their own path. They are traveling the path of those they are trying to please or gain acceptance from.

"When one will walk a path that is not theirs, then they attract to them what another has a need to learn from. And none of it will make sense to them, for these lessons have been especially tailored for the one who designed them.

"When The Season of the Long Shadow has entered this domain, there will be many two-legs wearing a look of great worry over them come to you. It will be a worried look because there will be an increase in everything that has been coming to them. And they cannot make sense from any of it.

"They will come to you looking for a way out of this rut they are stuck in, and they will initially want you to do their work for them. But this will not work.

"For as it is with all life, one must be willing to do their own work in order for it to have a lasting presence with them.

"When the two-legs come before you and share their worried faces, remind them of the reasons that are behind this. Share with them why they have seen disaster and disappointment come to them is because they have been calling it to them. That it is they, not any other, who is responsible for this.

"Remind them of the places they have traveled before coming to you. Have them look at all they have worked so hard at doing, and how they were not done through their own eyes or direction, but from another's.

"While they will look through the eyes of another, there will not be anything they do that will come up to the standards they have been following. For those standards have been set by another and will only be met by the one who has made them. They will not ever meet another's standards, for they are theirs.

"However, they have traveled long with these efforts they have been making, but have yet to meet the expectations of others, of those who have placed these goals in front of them.

"Because they have not had good success in their earth walk, they have come to expect failure from all they will encounter. They wear a good face while things are going well for them, but as time will pass, they expect to see disaster raise its head. This way of seeing has come from the many habits they have been carrying, those habits that have showed them their failures so many times, so they assume that this failure will come to them for all they will do, say, or think.

"If they wish to do away with all the misery that has been coming to them, to do away with all of the failures they have encountered, then tell them to just let them go. Because what they carry with them, in the front of their thinking minds, is what will be attracted to them.

"When they see good come to them that for them is too good to be true, they will repel the good and draw the bad. What they believe, they will create. And it is creation from our thinking minds that draws things to us.

"In order for one to create, they must first understand what it is they desire. And what they desire is what they have come to expect from the life path they have been traveling.

"When the two-legs come to see themselves for who and what they are in truth, and through their own eyes rather than another's, they will understand the meaning in this kind of creating. And they will understand what we are sharing with you.

"And for the two-legs who will come to you with this face of concern, have them think on all of those failures they have encountered. But have them think in truth to themselves alone, and they will see where they had called this failure to them by thinking something was too good to last and looked for all that was wrong with it. When they did this, they called this failure into creation, which resulted in fulfilling their own prophecies of life.

"When they see the thin line that separates their wants from their needs, they will understand that work on their wants will not ever come to them as they would wish for it.

"However, when they will work on their needs, then all of their wants will be taken care of. When they begin working on their needs, have them see the picture of what it is they are in need of. And have them create this picture in three dimensions in the front of their thinking minds.

"When this picture of need and outcome has formed itself and is just as real as life, have them light sage and cedar then place this picture of theirs into the rising smoke. When the smoke rises into the sky nation, it will go to the North or South or East or West. And this will be the direction the assistance will come from.

"Have them study the directions of the Great Medicine Wheel of Life to understand how these blessings will come to them.

"If the smoke travels to the East, they will need to look through their own eyes of balance from spirit and earth walker, for this is the place of beginnings. If the smoke travels to the South, they will need to look through their own eyes of innocence. If the smoke travels to the West, they will have to look through their own eyes of seclusion in order to glean out what is for them, and what is not. And, if the smoke travels to the North, they will have to look through their own eyes of wisdom, these eyes of wisdom that will be opened for them as they will learn to receive from others, to receive so they will no longer have to give but will understand how to share.

"For the next seven days, have them continue to hold this spirit picture of their needs in the front of their thinking minds. Have them hold it with the same level of life they held from the beginning. Then on the seventh day, repeat the process using the sage and cedar.

"When those who would come to you wearing their faces of concern for what has happened to them and all of the disappointment and failure that has come to them, use this process that is within this fourth step of healing one's spirit, they will see their old habits drop away and begin to see that all is as it should be in order for them to learn from their lessons that have been offered to them.

"You see, my brothers, there will be many who will have much work to do on themselves. This work will be in the process of learning more about themselves than they had previously seen. And those things will come to them in response to what they have been asking for.

"Remind them that lessons must be completed and understood by them before they can receive what they have requested.

"Share with them that all of these lessons will come to them for their own benefit, and not as punishment. As they look through the emotions of these lessons, they will gain more understanding for themselves and all that is with them. They will be on the beginning path to seeing themselves for who and what they are in truth.

"When they have journeyed this path only a few times, they will see that creating from their needs is very simple and will take less and less time for them to accomplish.

"And once they have completed this process, they will be ready to journey into the fifth face of these eleven steps. For they will carry with them a greater understanding of themselves, an understanding that will be needed by them if they are to reach an understanding for the next step of healing."

CHAPTER 51

❀

Step 5

Time Is An Illusion
—From An Elder in the North

"When The Season of the Long Shadow has been born into this domain, many of the two-legs will hold a great sadness to the face they wear. This face will be the result of having turned away from all that had been offered to them. Those people they felt close to did not share with as they wish they would have. And this will bring to them a great sadness. For the ones who lead them in the illusion told them that once a time is over, it is done," began the speaking words from the Elder in the North position.

"I share this with all of you, my brothers, this concept of time, as it has been perceived by the two-legs, is one of the greatest illusions of all.

"Time is an illusion, my brothers, and this brings us to see the face of the fifth step of healing our spirits within.

"Many see time as something that does not stand still, but I tell you this in truth: it does not move. For all the time you have ever known or will know is just as much in the present with you now as it has ever been. When one will see this truth, there will be a great opportunity for them to continue learning from all that has ever been presented.

"Once they understand how to see this, my brothers, there will be a great relief that will come over their faces, one that will allow them to wear a good face for themselves and for what they have been told was no longer available for them to learn from.

"When these who will come to you hear what I am now willing to share, there will be a great gasp of surprise from them. For when they will come to you, there will be many seasons that have passed them by and they will feel the weight of missing over them.

"The nature of the time that is soon to be with all life is one of acceleration to all lessons. And by the time many will find you, they will believe they have already lost much due to this false concept of time. Many will believe those emotions are lost so far in their past, they cannot be reached any longer.

"When they come to you, they will do so out of desperation for they will believe much is no longer available to them. And this will make them sad because they will look on their life path as a series of missed opportunities that can not ever be worked with again.

"This will be the time when you will share with them that time is an illusion. This will be the time when you will share with them that what has been, is still, and they possess the ability of sharing with all that is, has been, or will be.

"For the ones who will sit before you, share this procedure with them. It is a procedure that will allow them to pass through the great veil of illusion and onto the path that has always been theirs to travel.

"For those who will not have the eyes to see or the ears to hear, walk past them. Do not waste your efforts with them, for there will be much to do, and little time, as it is perceived in this domain, left to do it in.

"Do not worry for them, for there will be another messenger who will come behind you, and one behind them. For each life will be given four opportunities of learning to see and hear themselves, four opportunities to return to the place they have been seeking, this place that is within each of them.

"But after they have been offered this for the fourth time and still have not seen or heard, they will be cast adrift to float alone in their sea of illusion. And here they will remain until they will be required to make their great decision.

"During The Season of the Long Shadow, you would do well to keep focused on your path, and yours alone. If you attempt to work on another's path, surely you will fall from the one you have agreed to travel.

"For those who are willing to see and listen to these things you will share, have them follow this simple procedure that will allow them to be in their past and present to learn from all they had been offered but chose to turn away from.

"Within this process they will find answers to many things they have yet to find and will see how illusionary time is, that is, from the definition given to them by others.

"Have them take a few moments and look at the first event that comes to them, this event that has caused them to hold a weight of emotion over themselves for not doing what they needed to do.

"Remind them this event has not left them, but because they have been living within the illusion, they have come to believe it cannot return to them ever again. But all they will have to do is look at this event that resides within them and they will see how real it is in their present time. And how it affects them.

"From the time they have been caught in the sleep of illusion, they have lost the eyes to see this. They have come to the place of believing that once something is gone from them that it is over. But I tell you in truth, it is not. For it is just as real today as it was then. And the confirmation is how it is affecting them now.

"Have them sit in a quiet place where they will not be exposed to any other two-legs. Once they have arrived in such a place, preferably next to one of the standing people, have them place this event from their past into the front of their thinking mind. Have them do this until they can see it take on its own form of life within them. For this is the true meaning of time, my brothers, time is what we carry with us. It is not measured by the passing of a sun or a moon.

"When they have a firm picture of the people, places, and things that were involved with them from long ago, have them to see it for what it is.

"When they do, there will come to them a feeling of being in that time and place once again. But it will be from a more objective perspective because all of this is still living within them. Because it is living within them, it will be their own eyes they see through, and only their ears they will hear with.

"They will discover, once they have completely formed this picture in the front of their thinking minds, there is indeed life within it. For the people who are no longer with them will begin to speak, and the life they once knew will live again.

"At first, they believe this is only in their imagination, but I tell you it is not. For life that has been is still and none of it is ever lost, but much of it has been ignored because many have lost their way to remembering.

"Once this picture has formed within the front of their thinking minds, have them walk into it. Have each of them see themselves walking into this picture of those times that were once with them. When they do, there will be a feeling of belonging that will come to them, and with it, a new strength. This strength will allow them to look on those faces and hear their voices as they begin to relive this time they thought was gone from them.

"When they begin to share in the conversation with those who have returned to them, they will see a great change take place for what they have allowed to form in the front of their thinking minds. They will see the clarity and sharpness of this picture take on more form. This will continue until there will be no separation from what they see as they stand with you and speak to what they are seeing now. That which had once been with them has returned.

"When they begin to carry on a conversation with those who have returned to them, they will find another piece of the great illusion leave. They see that the past is just as real as the present, and how they may see great opportunity come to them. One that allows them to relive those times that had once been with them, those times they often wished they had lived in another way.

"They will see this picture just as real as you see those who stand next to you, and have returned to allow you to revisit all you have been holding as regret or guilt from those actions of their past. And there will be no bad faces worn by them as they look at the time they spent with others, there will be no feelings of guilt or shame either. There will only be the re-living that will make great sense then, and will allow them to alter those things of their past seasons they believed could not be changed.

"As they come to see what they have done, there will be a slight blur take place in the picture they began with. It will appear as a sudden shaking of all that is around them, but soon passes and they see this picture has formed itself into two separate pictures, each moving away from the other.

"One of these pictures will go to the left and represents the way they had done things before, which left them with feelings of guilt and sadness. And the other picture will move to their right, which represents how they have come to do things now.

"Once the picture begins to move to their left, it will only last a short time. For it represents a chain of events that are no longer. And very quickly, it will disappear and there will be no trace of it ever having been.

"Then as the picture on the right comes into focus, there will come a feeling of peace from these feelings of fear, sadness, guilt and all of those other emotions that have been reminding them of a lesson they turned away from.

"From the time they see this picture on the right come to life within them, there will be a one-to three-day period before it will catch up with them in their walking time. And when it does, there will no longer be any of those old feelings that had given them a bad face to wear. For they will have the understanding they have gone into their past seasons and re-lived that which was needed by them, those things that they needed to learn from.

"For those who will have the eyes to see and the ears to hear with, they will see this face of the fifth step in healing one's own spirit from within. And they will have seen a great truth; this truth that time in itself is truly an illusion.

"Once they have completed this fifth step, they would do well to move into the sixth step, my brothers."

CHAPTER 52

❦

Step 6

You Have Something To Offer
—From An Elder in the East

"All who enter this domain of the Earth Mother have something very special to offer, something so special only they will have the ability of sharing it," began the speaking words from the Elder in the East position.

"However, those who only know the illusion, have no clues to see, no clues that have been left from those who have told them what the meaning of their life path should be.

"For it is not in the words or guidance of another that one will find this special offering they have with them. They will only find this when they have come to see themselves through their own eyes and not through the eyes of others who would control and manipulate them into thinking that they are not capable of seeing things for themselves.

"When you are invited to visit someone's house, someone who you hold in a place of great respect, you will not come to them with your hands empty. You will bring a gift that is from your heart, a gift for them to see the level of appreciation you hold for them because they invited you into their home.

"Well, this is the same way all spirits come to the Earth Mother. Each brings a great gift with them, one that will benefit many once they understand what it is.

"Keep in the front of your thinking minds how one is to work from the mirror. How one will look into their eyes each day and ask themselves what do they love about themselves. And how this will allow them to see they have love for themselves that can be shared with another. And when one will listen to all they say, they hear the answers to their questions as they discover their wisest teacher once again. And when one will look into the mirror each morning and ask themselves what it is they like about themselves and answer in truth, this will bring them to find their best friend once again, this friend that will not ever let them down or disappoint them.

"With this in the front of your thinking minds, my brothers, I will share this sixth step of healing the spirit from within. This sixth step that will allow all of the two-legs to find what it is they have brought with them to offer, to find what their special gift is, so they may begin to understand it. And once they understand it, they will be capable of sharing it with all who come to them.

"When The Season of the Long Shadow has been born into this domain, there will be many come to search you out. You must see which path they have been traveling, so you will know how to word things so they will understand.

"Those who come to you and are traveling on the path that leads to the left—this path that is led by the body and fed by the emotion—they will see these accelerated events come to them as catastrophes and will only see confusion and chaos before them.

"But for the ones who have begun to find their way back to the path that leads to the right—this path that is led by their spirit and fed by it as well—they will see these quickened events come to them as blessings that have been presented to them in order for them to grow from their within place, this place where each of their spirits reside.

"When you have seen which path they travel, you will understand how to set this process into speaking words they will understand, this process that is the sixth face to healing one's spirit.

"Have them look into a mirror each morning for at least three of their minutes and ask themselves aloud what it is they like about themselves. Many of them will come to see this three minute time for themselves as almost unbearable to endure, for not many have ever taken so much time to look at themselves in this way and they will come to see it as an eternity in the beginning.

"However, as they repeat this process, they will find themselves doing it more and more because of what they find. They begin to find answers come to them that they like, and this gives to them a good face for themselves. And this is good.

"When they look into the mirror each morning, have them look into their own eyes and not take them away for this entire process. For this is a process that is needed for them to see themselves for who and what they are in truth. As they ask themselves questions and find their own answer, the walls that had been built around them slowly begin to come down, those walls that were originally put up to keep others out but ended up keeping them trapped inside.

"This must be done on a daily basis and all of their questions and answers must be done aloud. For this is the only way they will open their own eyes and ears to see and hear themselves once again. If they do this exercise in silence, there will not be any improvement in them and they will find they have not moved from where they began.

"If they will do this exercise silently, they are not yet ready to do their own work and you must pass them by. Remember that they will be given three more opportunities to awaken from the sleep illusion before they are left behind. Hold onto this knowing, my brothers, for the work that is ahead of you is great and there is no time for you to waste on those who are not willing to do their own work.

"For those who are willing to do their own work, have them look into this mirror each morning and speak of three others whom they admire, three people they hold in a good place.

"Next, have them speak of what they see as good from these three people. And have them picture their faces within their thinking mind.

"The reason for this is simple. Once they have seen the face of this other person and have listed all of those things they admire about them, the list they have begun is not for the other person, but it is for themselves. It will give each of them a clue of what it is they have brought with them that is to be shared among the many.

"Have them repeat this process for eleven days, then on the twelfth-day, have them place their face where they had seen the other three, these faces of the other three people they hold in a good place within themselves.

"As they replace their faces with their own, have them replace the other person's name with their own. They will see those qualities that they have seen in another for what they are, in truth. For the only reason they have seen any of those qualities they like in another is because they are within themselves. But they will not see this until they have completed this process.

"In truth, what we see in another is already within us. And the reason we see this in another is to confirm that each of us is ready to allow this to come to life from within us. But until we believe in ourselves again, and see through our own eyes and not the eyes of others, there will be no path open for us to follow that will show us this truth. For the illusion will be too great and none who are trapped within its sleep will perceive themselves as being good enough to receive anything, anything at all.

"From using this process of looking at another they hold in a good place and listing those things they hold a weight of value to, they begin the process of seeing themselves with their own eyes, especially when they replace their face and qualities with their own.

"Through this process, they are given the first of many clues for what they have to offer others. For they will begin to see all of the qualities they thought only existed in another have been residing within them. And this will assist them to believe in themselves once again, for they will see the many great and good qualities they possess.

"When they will follow this sixth step of healing their own spirit from within, they will be ready to learn the seventh...but not before."

❀

CHAPTER 53

Step 7

*Stand Strong Alone First
—From An Elder in the South*

"When the two-legs have come to understand their way through the sixth step of healing, my brothers, they will see how close the seventh step is," began the speaking words from the Elder in the South position.

"How sad it is to see all that has been done within this domain. And all of this has not stopped with the two-legs, my brothers, but it has affected all of the children of the Earth Mother as well.

"They, too, have a life path to travel just as you do, but since the two-legs have become so locked within the sleep of illusion, they no longer have the eyes to see this. They no longer remember that all life is a part of them and they are a part of all life.

"One can only respect another, to the same level they can respect themselves. So many of the controlling ones have kept this truth from others, and have entered this domain blinded by the illusion and left it in the same way. For them, there was no effort to wake themselves from their sleep and they continued to repeat the same lessons over and over again.

"However, once the two-legs will see that they do have something very special to offer that is particular only to them, they will come to the place of believing in themselves again. And when they do, they are willing to do their own work of healing themselves.

"In truth, my brothers, when you will heal yourself, it is a lasting healing that takes place. However, when you will be healed by another, it can only be temporary. It is temporary because the cause of this sickness or disease has not been addressed. For another cannot know what is behind this sickness; it can only be known by the one who is sick. And until they see themselves for who and what they are in truth, there will only be one temporary healing after the other and none of them will be lasting.

"This seventh step of healing oneself is to learn to stand strong alone. This has not been forgotten entirely by the two-legs, for they are always searching for ways to do this. Only they have been attempting to do this through another, rather than themselves.

"This has resulted in them only finding temporary solutions to those things they have been looking for.

"Look at it this way, my brothers: there are many people in this domain of the Earth Mother who are not eating well—some not at all. And in this domain, there is more than enough for everyone when the two-legs will learn to share. But before they can share, they must first learn to receive. And in order to receive, they must first come to the place of considering themselves worthy of receiving.

"However, when one will live within the illusion, they do not see themselves as being good enough to receive anything for their efforts. This is because all they have done was not ever good enough for another and they will not see themselves as being worthy of receiving anything.

"As we have been willing to share with you, this has come to them from looking at themselves through the eyes of others, and doing things for others rather than themselves. As long as they will look at themselves through the eyes of others, they will not be willing to do anything on their own, for they carry a great fear with them of doing it wrong.

"As we have shared with you, when one carries fear with them, they will be controlled by another or others, those who would not wish for them to understand themselves or the truths they each carry within them. For if they were to see themselves for who and what they were in truth, they would begin to understand. And when one begins to understand, they cannot be controlled. This takes away the illusion of power those controlling ones believe they have over them. Because of this threat, the controlling ones have placed many fears in their way, fears that are in truth false friends and will lead them on many false paths to travel.

"However, this is something that can be done away with when one will learn to stand strong alone. And when they see what is being offered to them is good and they are deserving of it, or otherwise it would not have come to them, they find the beginnings of their own balance and see how to stand strong alone.

"Let us say that one who is not eating well in this domain walks into a food store and begins to eat some of the food that is on the shelves. They are doing this because they are hungry and have no money to pay for this food. They are not doing this because they are greedy and want more of what they have already.

"And let us say that they get caught and are taken to jail. And the ones who have food to eat and money to pay for it hear of this event. They do not look on it with a face of pity, but they say 'Well, they deserve what they got. They walked into a store without any money in their pockets and got caught stealing food.'

"When you hear such things, look at those who would say this and see what they are doing. For they have done the same things, my brothers, but what they have done has been much worse than the hungry one has done. For they have walked to another searching for love and friendship and had nothing of themselves to offer. In other words, they walked to another with their pockets empty as well.

"When they find this friend or lover and they are turned away by them, you will see the hurt that will fall over their faces. And you will see the confusion that will fill their eyes as they wonder why this has happened to them.

"In truth, they had become like the hungry one looking for something to eat but did not have any money to pay for it. They have entered a relationship with another with no means of sharing anything of themselves, and this is their jail, this feeling of being hurt and left all alone.

"When one gives, another takes away. And this is what they have been promoting in their earth walk. This is what they have allowed to happen to them, and they believe all they had has been taken away by another because once they used all they had to offer them, they left them with nothing.

"And this will not change for them until they see there is something they have to offer, something that makes them so different from another they see how truly special they are—but to themselves. For in truth, they must first come to see that it does not matter how another would see them as being, that it is only important how they will come to see themselves. Once they see they have something special to offer, they will stand at the opening of the doorway that allows them to stand strong alone first, before they attempt to stand with another.

"Then they will understand they have something of themselves to share with another, and if the other has something of themselves to share in return, they will grow close and there will no longer be takers, only sharers. And this is good.

"In order for them to reach this place of understanding, they still have another exercise to learn. It will have to follow the same sequence in the sixth step of using the mirror.

"They must look into their eyes in the mirror and begin to speak to themselves. They must ask themselves what they like as well as what they do not like about themselves. This must be done for eleven weeks.

"For those things they like about themselves, have them make a list of them and have them do something special for themselves each day. This will be the needed effort of their returning for what they have allowed themselves to receive.

"And for those things they do not like about themselves, have them write a similar list. Then have them discuss these things with themselves as they are looking into their own eyes in the mirror each day.

"First they will come to ask themselves why they do not feel good about themselves for these things. What they will find is a layer of emotion that has been placed between them and this lesson that had been offered to them. And they will see that this emotion is much like a callus that forms on the hands or feet when a constant irritation is rubbing against it.

"As they look at how those things they do not like about themselves make them feel, have them say aloud to themselves, '*It Is All Right*', that it is all right to feel this way about such things.

"For this will be their passage past the emotions that have been holding them back and have blocked their way for seeing themselves for who and what they are in truth. Those blockages will fall away from them as they will spend more and more time in understanding themselves and seeing that it is all right to feel the way they feel about anything.

"You see, my brothers, as long as we are afraid to look in our own eyes and say all is alright, there will always be pain associated with emotions. But this pain is not as it is perceived while one is trapped within the illusion. For as long as one is trapped within their own illusion, they will be afraid of seeing those things they do not understand. And they will not see that what is needed is to look on the face of this emotion and say to oneself that it is all right to feel this way, that it is all right to feel things as they do.

"What they will be doing is getting past this fear they have been carrying with them, this fear that has been associated with the emotion they have been carrying within themselves. As long as they carry this fear with them, there will not be any understanding come to them. And as long as we will not understand ourselves, there will always be fear that will follow us everywhere we go. And what we do not understand, we fear. And what we fear, we attempt to destroy. And what the two-legs have been doing, in truth, has been destroying themselves.

"When one will have done this exercise daily for eleven weeks, they will have come to understand themselves much better. They will have discovered their best friend has always been within them. They will have come to know their best lover has always been within them. And they will have come to know their best teacher has always been within them as well.

"When they will understand these things, they will see that all they will ever need has been with them all along. Then they will understand the importance of standing strong alone before walking to another. And they will have come to understand the seventh step to healing oneself from within and will be ready to go onto the eighth."

CHAPTER 54

❀

Step 8

The Healing Rainbow
—From An Elder in the West

"And the eighth step to healing oneself is to be found in the rainbow healing, my brothers," picked up the speaking words from the Elder in the West position.

"There will be many who will need this during The Season of the Long Shadow. And the reason will be from all of the emotions and events that are escalated; there will be many forms of illness, sickness, and disease that will be found among the two-legs. There will be many of these ailments that will have not been heard of before, and there will be no one who will know how to heal them.

"All of these ailments will affect the body, mind, and the spirit part of all earth walkers. And still there will not be another who will know the proper way to relieve them, none but the one who has taken them onto themselves.

"It is a great truth that has been given to the two-legs many generations before. But it had been stripped away by the ones who did not want others to know of it. This is the truth that shares with all life if they hold onto a sickness, illness, or disease, then they must first find the path to heal themselves. And once they have done this, they will see the path they have chosen, clearly, so others may see how they too can heal themselves.

"This has been so from all seasons past and from all of the generations before who only remain now as a faint memory of a distant shadow. For they remember this truth, and this truth has come back to reside among all life through these speaking words.

"If you will attempt to heal another, be sure you have found the path of healing yourself first. And this is the truth that we are now willing to share with you.

"Remind the two-legs that what they have gone through, all of the misery and illness of their past seasons, these have come to them for a specific reason. And this reason was to experience such things. For without the experience, they would not understand how to heal. But for the times that are over the two-legs now, they have forgotten this truth and have fallen from their path and into the path of self pity and sorrow.

"For the ones who will come before you in these times we speak of, have them see there has not been, nor will there ever be anything that will come to them in the form of punishment for something they have done. All that has come to them has done so by their own spirit's design, and there is no one better than they to understand the why of it.

"Remind them that for as long as they look on themselves and all of those things they have wrong with them through guilt, they cannot take even one step on the path of the spirit. As long as they carry even the smallest amount of guilt over them for what is wrong with them, they will remain stuck in the same place they are in the present. For it will be this weight of guilt that will prevent them from moving further on this path of theirs. And it will be from this weight of guilt they carry that they will not be allowed to free themselves from whatever is wrong with them.

"When you have shared this with another, they may take the next step that will lead the way to the healing rainbow.

"Remind them of the second great truth that is to be found on the path leading to the rainbow healing. This truth shares with those who would listen, that while one is grateful for what they have with them, there is a doorway, which will remain open. And while this doorway is open, there will be more that will come through it for them.

"However, when one is not grateful for what they have with them, or when they are resentful for what another has that they do not, the doorway will close and not allow anything further to come through. And, they will eventually lose that which they had with them to begin with.

"Now, there are many who will say they have nothing to be grateful for. But I share with you in truth, what they are saying is that they feel so sorry for themselves they want another to tell them what they have to be grateful for, because they are not willing to look for this on their own.

"They will tell you they are ungrateful because they have been born into a certain culture or race, and because of this, there cannot be anything good come to them. Because they have been born into a certain path, all that can come to them will be bad.

"But I tell you what they have been born into has been for a reason. And this reason is to allow their spirit a path to learn and understand from the many lessons that will be presented to them, those lessons that could only be learned by them from the place they are at now.

"If they are attempting to change themselves into something or someone they are not, rest assured they will not be traveling their own path. They will be traveling another's path, one that is not theirs. And for all they have gone through will be from the learning perspective of another. And all the effort they have put forth on this path they have chosen, there will be no benefit to them. For when they come to their journey's end and are standing on the other side in the waiting place, they will hold nothing in their arms, for all of the blessings they could have had while they were in this domain of the Earth Mother were ignored so they could be like someone else, and not themselves.

"When you look on them in the waiting place, you will know them. For they will have great tears falling from their eyes. But for them, it will be too late, and this cannot be corrected until they will be willing to walk another journey, with another Earth Mother. However, this is something we will discuss more with you later.

"For those who do not see what they have to be grateful for, share with them that they have life within them, then walk away.

"For those who will see this, share the process of the rainbow healing with them. They will find a path, which will allow them to heal themselves first, then others who will learn to see and come to them.

"First, have them stand on the earth with their shoes off. Also, this should be a place where they will not be bothered with sounds or people who will distract them.

"Next, have them spread their toes apart until the meaty part of their toes touch the earth beneath them. Then have them hold their hands to their side with the palms open and fingers facing toward the earth beneath them.

"Have them know the life that is within the Earth Mother by feeling the earth that is beneath their feet. And this will allow them to understand that life is in all things, and this includes them as well.

"Have them call to the Earth Mother for her acceptance of them, and they will feel a sense of warmth come to them from their feet. This warmth will not only fill them, but serve as a confirmation that they have been accepted by the one who gives them a great gift each day of their life.

"As they silently feel the acceptance of the Earth Mother, there will be a swaying come over them, this swaying will be in tune with the beating of the Earth Mother's heart and comes to them as a reminder that they are within her womb of life.

"When this state has been reached, have them think of all they are grateful for having with them, such as breathing, walking, seeing, hearing, smelling, feeling, calling, and so on. And for each one of these things they are grateful for, have them feel the warmth come in through their left foot.

"Once their left foot feels the warmth and peace begins to fill it, have them send it all the way up the left side of their body until it reaches the top of their head. Then have it follow the same course down their right side until it reaches the bottom of their right foot.

"When this feeling has reached the bottom of their right foot, allow it to follow its course back into the earth that is beneath them. For when it does, there will be a relief felt by them, a relief that will make way for a peace that is soon to follow.

"When the right foot has released back into the earth, their grounding has been attained. It is through this grounding that the rainbow healing may take place for those who find their way. This rainbow healing will allow them to heal themselves in the most permanent way there is, and that is to heal all that is wrong with them themselves.

"When they have attained this grounding, have them call on all they have with them which they are grateful for; one by one. Have them hold them, one at a time, for the passing of eleven breaths, then go to the next one.

"Have them follow their natural rhythm of breathing, but as they breath in, have them draw from beneath the left foot and as they breath out, have them extend it below the right foot, all the while thinking of what they have with them to be grateful for.

"As they breath in from below the left foot, have this breath, and the picture of what they are grateful for, follow them all the way up to the top of their head and down past the right foot. This process will allow them to draw additional blessings of healing from the

Earth Mother. And, as the blessings pass through their body and return to the Earth Mother, she will see the process they are attaining with her. When she sees this, she will bring to each of them a reminding that all they once held with the weight of sickness, illness, or disease will be dissipated. It will be taken back to her until they are ready to encounter it again. For the illnesses they hold with them are reminders of lessons they have entered this domain to learn from. But when the lessons manifest into an illness, there is a need to take a short break, a break that will allow them to regain their balance and breath before they encounter this lesson again.

"The ones who will come to learn this process of the rainbow healing will need to repeat this process once each day. It is not necessary for them to go through each thing they are grateful for once they understand what those things are. For once they hold an understanding of what the rainbow healing is offering to them, there will only be a need of taking one thing with them. And this will be sufficient to allow them to feel the anchoring of themselves to all life and be reminded of the balance they need to travel their path, without the additional weight of those things that cause them to feel sick, ill, or diseased.

"For there is no thing that can infect any life that cannot be healed by that same life. But many have forgotten to remember this truth.

"When the two-legs have come to understand this eighth step in healing their spirit, they will be ready to begin the ninth step—but not before."

CHAPTER 55

Step 9

Listen To What We Have To Say
—From An Elder in the North

"All earth walkers will receive what they request," came the beginning of the speaking words from the Elder in the North position. "However, it is from what they do not understand of themselves that they are caught up in the illusion of believing they are not worthy, or ready to receive what they are asking for.

"This is nothing more than old habits they still carry with them. As soon as they will allow themselves to see through the illusion of their life path, they will be ready to receive from themselves again. But until that time, they will remain in the place of believing they are not going to get what they asked for. And this limitation comes to them from listening to others tell them they will not ever be good enough to receive anything.

"This is the place we will begin our re-remembering of this ninth step in healing ourselves, this ninth lesson that reminds us to listen to what we have to say.

"We have explained to you about the two paths. How the one that travels to the right is led and fed by spirit and can be attained by those who allow themselves to be. For there is nothing more for them to do, other than to be. And this is the path that allows one to understand the 'I AM' in all things.

"And we have explained to you about the other path that leads to the left, this path that is led by the body and fed by the emotion, and how emotion will always be stronger and longer lasting than the one who is either fighting it or wrestling with it; how this is the path where one will always be found trying, and when one tries, they are always becoming someone or something they are not. This continual state of becoming leads them to frustration and the more frustrated they become, the harder they will try. But more than this, my brothers, this path that leads to the left is one where those who travel on it will always hold the believing that 'I AM NOT', and this is what brings many things that they do not like to see, and things they are not happy with.

"What determines how we arrive on either of these two paths is to be found from the many old habits one will carry with them, these old habits that only serve to remind them they are not worthy or good enough at anything they will do.

"It is from these old habits that we begin our discussion of this ninth step that is greatly needed in healing oneself, my brothers. For as long as these old habits remain with anyone, there can be but one thing come to them. They can only become more sick, more ill, and more diseased in their body, mind, and spirit.

"There will be many who will come to you for healing which not only comes from you or from us, but healing that will come from within themselves so they will know the path to follow, this path that will lead them into a place where they will understand how to heal themselves…and then others as well.

"Remind them that this shell they travel in, this part of themselves they call their body, it was not designed to be sick or to hurt. However, when one realizes they have the freedom of choice for all they will see and do, they will understand only one person has caused this sickness or hurting that is with them. And this one person is himself or herself.

"And when there is only one person who has caused such a thing, only that person will have the ability of keeping it away permanently. What we are now willing to share with you must be applied to those who will come to be healed. They must hear of these things if there is to be any long-lasting healing for them.

"In order for any to reach this ninth step of healing, this step that requires one to listen to what they say, they must first come to the place of seeing themselves in the seasons of their past and how this still affects them.

"When they were short of seasons and still living with their parents, they were told what to do and how to do it. They were told what was good to do and what was not good to do by their parents and the others who would be close to them. There was not time for them to see these things in any other way. And the reason for this is quite simple.

"They were taught this way of seeing by their parents, teachers, and friends because this is how their parents, teachers, and friends were taught.

"None of this was done out of punishment, nor was it done to control them. They did this because there was no other way for them to see. But this time will soon be over and when it is, all of the walls will come down and there will no longer be any place left to hide such things. They will be shown for what they are. When this happens, many will hold others with them by having them believe they can bring back the past, bring back the days when they were not feeling these things that are now with each of them. And they will do this through fear and lack of understanding for oneself.

"This is what causes so many to remain ill for the earth walk they have come to learn from. Until they are willing to see what their truth is rather than another's, they are destined to remain in this place that holds a great sickness and ill health over them.

"Until they come to understand that it is from the way they were raised that has resulted in their finding illness, sickness, and disease, there will be no other way for them to see. Until they will come to see this, my brothers, they will not be willing to do their own work on this step. And for them, it would be better if they had not ever heard of this. For you, it is better to walk away, for there will be many who will be willing to listen and it would be foolish to spend your time on those who are not yet ready.

"Remember, my brothers, all will be given three more opportunities of seeing themselves for who and what they are in truth. And after that, they will be left alone until it is time for them to make their great decision and I share with all of you, this time is not far away. For our arrival with you on this land is a sign that it is very close at hand.

"Share with the ones who are willing to listen and do their own work. Remind all of them of the times they have been told what to do and why, as well as what is good and not good to do.

"Then have each of them hold these things in the front of their thinking minds and look at what has taken place. They will find that for all of their seasons with the Earth Mother, they were not allowed to find their own way or truth. For their time has been spent in listening to others tell them what is their truth. And having heard this many times, they believe it is theirs as well.

"There can only be one truth, my brothers. And this is the truth that is found within each of you. It will be different from another's and if you would attempt to make their truths or standards yours, then you too will fall away from your path as well. When you do, you will fall into the dark places of non-understanding where manifestations will come over you in a wave of sickness, illness, disease, and fear.

"Remind the two-legs of the time they have been living with others' truths and standards. And how all they have done was not ever good enough. No matter how hard they worked to gain pleasing words from another, they would always be asked to do more.

"And for this, they have come to expect that all they do will not be good enough for those they are attempting to gain acceptance from. The reason for this is that they are living to another's standards by doing those things they tell them they should do, or should not do. Whenever anyone will use the truths and standards of another to live by, they will continually meet with failure. This is what caused them to carry old habits with them.

"It is from these old habits that they believe they will not ever be good enough, nor will they ever be deserving of anything good in their life.

"And when there will come to them something that is good, they will stand and look at it. But they will not see it as something they are ready to embrace, and will see it through eyes of fear that tell them this is just too good to be true, and soon the floor beneath them will disappear and they will fall and be hurt once again.

"For those who remain locked within their sleep of illusion, this is their truth, and they will attract to them those who mirror themselves at the time. However, this is not a truth they must remain in. It is only the illusion of truth that causes them to see in this way.

"In truth, my brothers, they are deserving for what comes to them. They are deserving because they have been willing to do the work needed for them to see it. No matter how good it may seem to them, it is theirs to share with them.

"But their old habits tell them they are bound to fail at everything they will do. They will see all things that come to them from these eyes of failure and non-worthiness. If they continue to carry this with them, there will not ever be a time or a place where they may discover their own peace, this peace they were born to that will allow them to find the path of healing themselves.

"Remember, my brothers, all which has ever been and all that will ever be, is with you now. When you look on yourself with the eyes that see a new discovery of your own truth, remember this has always been with you and has not ever left your side. The only reason you will see this with the eyes of a new discovery is because you have been willing to do the work needed by you to open them and no longer look through the mist of illusion.

"The more one will awaken themselves from their sleep of illusion, the more they will come to see they have not ever been alone. They begin to see more and more of their own family around them and will feel no separation between their hearts.

"But this message is for another time and another place. I will now return to the process of healing.

"Remind the two-legs, who wish to receive a healing, of the old habits they have learned. Of all that is holding them back, the most important one is this.

"When they began their earth walk, there was not ever a time when they were not being told what they should do, or not do. And within this process, they were told that it was better to give than it was to receive. But I share with all of you that this is not a truth. For as long as there is even one within this domain who is giving, there will be at least three who will be taking. And as long as there are takers, there will be darkness over them, a darkness that will not allow them to find their way to understanding.

"For as one gives, they force another to take. And this is the one thing that so many do not like in another. When they come across another whom they like, they will sit next to them and share how bad this place is because of all the takers there are in it. And because there are so many takers, there will not be any peace or safety for anyone.

"Then with these words of theirs just out of their mouth, they will look on this other person and tell them that as long as they do not become the taker in this world, they will be their friend. And without hesitation, they reach deep within their own pocket and pull something out that is very special to them. And they give it to this other person who they do not want to be a taker in life. But as they do this, they have made them a taker as well.

"Now, the giver will continue to do this until they run out of things to give to another or others. And when this will take place, they become the thieves who will rob from another so they may continue with their giving.

"This becomes the circle of illusion from which there will be no escape, not until they learn to receive. For as long as they continue to give, they will be so uncomfortable with receiving, they will turn away from it. But when they learn to receive, they will understand, that all which will come to them, does so when they are ready and deserving for what they are being presented. When this takes place, they see there is nothing to feel guilty about when they learn how to receive. For it is in the path of receiving that we are shown one of our most valuable lessons and that is the lesson of not having anything expected or owed for what has been shared.

"When we learn to receive, first from another then from ourselves, we begin the journey of balance in our life. And when this will take place, we begin to see that all is as it should be, for it is already and has always been.

"When we learn to receive, we begin to see that all which is with us has always been with us and it is we who are remembering our way back home. When we travel this homeward path, many will see us and know this is also possible for them, too.

"Once they understand that when something is offered to them, it is time for it to be. They will be in the place of seeing themselves with eyes that are theirs and not another's. They will also be in a place of seeing themselves with more clarity than they ever held with them before.

"When they learn to receive, they will come to know that from that point on, there will no longer be a need to give anything again. For there will only be one thing needed from them and that is to share.

"When one learns this process of sharing, they will understand that only their presence is required of them. It is their presence among others that becomes the greatest gift of all. It is a gift that allows one who will feel their presence to know what they see in you is also possible for them as well. But in order to find this path, they must first learn to receive.

"It is from receiving that they will understand they, too, have something great to share. This greatness comes from within each of them and is present within each living life in this domain that is the Earth Mother.

"When they see this within themselves, there will be no controlling them. For they have found their way back to understanding and seeing themselves for who and what they are in truth. From this moment on, they will only have a good face to wear for themselves and will no longer know the tiredness that is so prevalent among the givers and takers within this domain. For they have allowed another part of this great illusion to fall away from them, and all of this has resulted from your presence among them.

"When those who come to you understand what we have been willing to share, have them look over their past seasons and see all of the times they have been told by another or others what it is they should be doing, as well as what is good to do and what is not good to do.

"Have them see this as a part of their sleep of illusion, this sleep that has been keeping them trapped has also been stopping them from healing themselves.

"For it is their own spirit within that continually speaks to them for what they need to do while they are in this earth walk. But their imbalance has been created by the ones who have been telling them what they must do and what they must not do.

"Have them look at those things they have been told to do, or not to do, as something that has been controlling them and has not allowed them to see themselves. When they do this first step, they will understand why it is not important how another will feel from those actions you must do. It is only important how you feel from all that you will say and do.

"However, in order to go further on this path, one will have to understand all they do and say. They must regard themselves as a part of Creator. Because they hold this perfection and love within them, then those things they feel a need to do as well as all of those things they will have a need to say are for their own ears to hear and understand.

"And from all they will do, they bring a valuable lesson that will later be understood by them for what they are in truth.

"For all that we will do and say in this life path we have been given is for a specific reason that will allow us to understand what resides within each of us, that part of us that so many dream of but do not remember how to touch. And this is the part of us that is Creator.

"But we cannot find our way back until we are willing to listen to the calling voices within each of us, these calling voices that come to all life from the lessons that are being presented, those lessons will only come when we are free to do those things we have a need to do, and say those things we are free to say, free from the controlling efforts of others who would not wish for any to see.

"For when one will see who and what they are in truth, there is but one path for them to follow. And this is the path they have designed for themselves. This understanding will fill them with each breath of their lungs and will allow them to accept that which has always been with them. That is the peace from understanding that nothing ever comes from punishment for what you have or have not done. But there is that which you have a need to do, and when it is understood, there will be a flooding of light within you that will light all of your world. When this light within you is seen by another, it will cause them to seek theirs as well.

"When there is enough light for all to see, my brothers, our hearts will smile. For the time for separateness will be over for you and the path to healing yourself will have begun. For the path of returning has been found and you will find all of us waiting at the end of it to welcome you home once again.

"Those who will see these truths for themselves will see a great change come over them. It is a change that will begin to restore their bodies to a place that was with them all the time, a place where there is no hurting or pain. A place where they are willing to be and this place they are willing to be, is called 'I AM'.

"When they have seen their own truth, my brothers, they will have completed this ninth step of healing. And once they have found understanding in this step, they will be free to heal another or many others by understanding that it is not important how another will see you, it is only important how you will come to see yourself.

"Remind them when they allow themselves to be, they are already. For all that is needed by them has already been done. All that had been required of them to perform has been completed. Their hard work is over, and now is the time for them to be once again. And they will remember, my brothers, they will remember once again."

❈

CHAPTER 56

Step 10

Creating The Cone Of Healing Using The Four Colors From The Medicine Wheel Of Life
—From An Elder in the East

"And when they understand the ninth step of healing themselves, my brothers, they will be prepared to encounter this tenth one," began the speaking words from the Elder in the East position as she placed her left hand on my right shoulder. "There is great abundance in this domain that is the Earth Mother. To think otherwise is to be locked within the great sleep of illusion that allows one to only see things as they would wish for them to be and not as they are in truth.

"Remember to keep in the front of your thinking minds that all that is or will ever be, is now in the present. However, many have closed their eyes to their own truths and have forgotten to remember this. But I share with you this is truth.

"Things which seem new to you have always been with you. And this is the same way you will discover your spirit family when they will greet you. In the beginning, you may only know two or three of them. But as your understanding for yourself and all that is with you increases, you will find there are no strangers among you. All know you; you will remember.

"Now for this tenth step in healing oneself. Share with them what a cone of healing is used for, in the same way I will share with you on this day.

"A cone of healing is what allows us to enter a place that is not seen by many in this domain, but it is a place like any other you had once come to know and understand. It is a place where you allow yourself to enter the field of your own spirit's energy and all you will have need of at that time will be provided to you.

"The two-legs who come to you in The Season of the Long Shadow will be in great need for this kind of healing to be with them because so much of what they will see before them will be dying. And for the life that is not yet ready to leave this domain with their bodies, there will be a great need to restore themselves so they may continue to learn and understand the last parts of those lessons they have come here to walk with.

"The cone of healing may be done from a sitting or standing position. The position does not change the dimensions. However, for this explanation, I will speak to the standing position.

"Take two sticks that are able to touch the face of the Earth Mother when you hold out both of your arms at shoulder height. With your arms fully extended, place the two sticks where they touch the earth. Once this has been done, turn slowly in a clockwise circle.

"When the full circle has been completed, set the two sticks aside and thank them for assisting in opening a doorway for you. Then look at the circle that has been drawn around you.

"This circle you have created is the base for the cone of healing and will serve as a reminder of the limitations for this process. However, this is a limitation only in the beginning. It is possible to expand this circle to encompass the entire Earth Mother when it is a part of your path. And when this is needed to be done, all within its presence will receive a great healing from their own spirits as well.

"We have done this before, my brothers, and so have you. But in this time that is The Season of the Long Shadow, none of you will be allowed to spread this healing across all of the Earth Mother until the Great Messenger has arrived and has taken away those who need to travel into the twelfth Earth Mother. Then you will be allowed to spread the healing cone over all of the Earth Mother, and as you will, there will be a complete restoration to all of this domain. There will be a newness for all life that has chosen to remain here.

"But for now, there will be only a small part of this that will be allowed. And this small part may only be applied to the shell or body each of you travels in. It may be shared with others, but they will have to do this work on themselves by themselves.

"Once they have drawn this circle around them, have them set the sticks down and after thanking them for their assistance, stand in a position that is comfortable to them. Then have them feel a growing from the circle that is around them. This growing will be in an upward motion and will continue above them until they can see it form a point and end. This point will have an ending that will be approximately seven feet above their head and will represent the part of themselves they can see, this is the body part.

"Next have them extend this cone under them. Its point should be about seven feet below their feet and will represent the part of themselves they do not see. This will be their spirit.

"Remind them they do not have to be concerned with the bottom part of the cone. For all that is needed from this point will be taken care of by their own spirit from within. And to think on this part of the cone of healing that is not visible would only confuse them. Later, as they will become more aware of who and what they are in truth, they will see what may be done with the unseen part of themselves. But for the beginning, there is no thing they would understand so it is best to leave this part unsaid.

"Once this double cone of healing has formed, there will be an immediate feeling of life come over them. It will be a feeling of life not many remember.

"For within this feeling, is to be found the unconditional love of creation. And this is what all life was created from.

"Once the top portion of the cone has been connected, they will feel a lightness fill into them. And it will come to them from the above place that is to be found at the top point of the cone itself.

"As they feel those things that are with them, they will see that this is like a gentle waterfall. And it comes to them from the above place of the cone in a manner that is washing them clean. These they will feel, and will later understand the reasons for it being so.

"Soon after they feel the lightness washing over them, there will appear to each of them a weaving. This weaving will cause them to rock back and forth in a very powerful but gentle motion.

"Share with them this is nothing to fear, for it is only the beating of the Earth Mother's heart and is being felt by them to remember the connection we all have to her.

"While the beating or rocking motion is with them, they will see many colors fill this cone they have created. There will be all of the colors of the rainbow of promises and variations of other colors as well.

"These are the colors they will have a need for. Each color holds its own life and vibration rate, and is proceeding with what is needed by you for this healing.

"When these colors fill their cone, they will swirl around you, then find their way into your body. As they enter the body, they do so in an effort of sharing what they have found as their own truth. It is this truth of the colors that will share what is needed in order to heal yourself. And as each of these colors will enter, you will see a picture in the front of your thinking mind for what must be done.

"In some cases, you will receive many pictures. And there will be those times when you will only receive one. But there will not be a time when you will not receive any.

"Take these pictures with you and walk the four-corners of their circle. In each of those four-corners of the circle, understand the purpose of the four directions to the Medicine Wheel of Life. For what will be required next may only be obtained by this process.

"First, face the east point in their circle. This does not have to be the true point, for to think on such things is a great waste of your time. All you need to remember is where you are being led and the rest will take place by itself.

"While you face the east within their cone of healing, look at the one picture you have seen. As you look at it, there will be a relationship form over it. This will not be a kind of seeing you have become used to; rather, it will be a seeing of feeling something more than seeing it with your eyes.

"Remember that while you are looking into the east place of this cone of healing that it is the home of eagle. And eagle reminds us of the need to be balanced between spirit and earth for all things we will endeavor to do. It will be in this yellow point of the east where you will see where this imbalance has occurred and has caused you not to feel well. From what will be presented, you will come to understand what was lacking. Once you see where the imbalance within you was, you will understand how to correct it and allow yourself to be freed from it in this first point of the healing circle.

"Secondly, face the south point in the cone of healing. And as you do, remember this is the place of red as well as the home of child and coyote. The color red from the south point of this circle reminds us that we will be given two choices of attaining the knowing we are in search of, this knowing that is the second step for all.

"From the east, we received a picture of what was needed. In the south, we receive the path that we must travel to understand what we saw in the east.

"The color red reminds us that we will find what we are seeking, my brothers, but how we will do it will be a choice each of us will make for ourselves. For this south, or second, point on the wheel has two faces to it. There is the face of the child and there is the face of coyote.

"The face of the child reminds us we carry only innocence with us, and through this innocence we will come to know that our receiving of all things presented to us may be done with an open heart. From the face of child, we hold the knowing that all things we have done or will do have been done for a great reason. And this has been to allow us to learn our lessons well and this is the home of lesson that we are facing when we are in the south point.

"Now the second face is the coyote. This face teaches us that while we will choose to remain the adult that we will only grow old from all that will come to us. Coyote is called the trickster because of how he will present lessons to you. If you take the path of the adult while seeking your answers, there will be many falls, scrapes, and bruises on you when you reach this journey's end. And the path of coyote will end in the same place the path with child does. The only difference will be that when one will travel with the child, there will not be the falls, scrapes, and bruises that one will encounter with the coyote's path. But both will reach the same place and at the same time. The choice you will be given in this point will be how you would wish to travel.

"Thirdly, face the west point of this wheel. In the west you will find the color black and the home of bear. Black is the place of sleeping and this is what bear will do. Bear will spend its seasons gathering many things, just as the two-legs will gather many things. Then bear will enter the home it has found and sleep on all of these things that have come to it, and will exit from its sleep of silence with an understanding. It is an understanding of its own truths that are within all of those things they know about. When one will find their own truth, there will be a great level of increased understanding over them. For they have found their own truth and no longer have to rely on another's truth that will confuse them and keep them from moving forward on this path they have chosen to travel.

"The fourth point on this wheel is the north. It is here that we find the color white, the buffalo, and the elder.

"But the color white on the north point of the medicine wheel of life is not any one color, it is a combination of all colors.

"The north point is white because one cannot enter here until they have encountered and worked with the other three. The north point of the medicine wheel is one of abundance and prosperity as well as the home of buffalo and elders. But one will not be allowed to experience any of this until they have successfully gone past the east point and understood what has come to them. Nor will they be allowed to enter the north point until they have made their decision of how they will travel this path from the south position, the decision that allows them to walk with coyote or with the child of their innocence. And they will not be allowed to enter this north point until they have been through the west point of the medicine wheel where they will encounter bear and learn to travel into the silence and exit with their own truths.

"When all of this has taken place, they will be welcomed by the north position and will find the wisdom they have been seeking, this wisdom that first came in the vision, the east point, and how it related to them on their earth walk, then found their path to travel, the south point, and decided how they would arrive, then found the understanding for what they were doing, the west point, and saw their own face of truth.

"When this has been accomplished, they are allowed to enter the north point and see their wisdom, this wisdom that will allow them to use their understanding and the clarity of seeing which will find them.

"For each of those things the two-legs will enter the cone of healing with, and take with them through this four step process, they will find a great blessing come to them. It is the blessing of remembering how to heal themselves once again. And for this, there will be a good face worn by each who can understand this process."

CHAPTER 57

❀

Step 11

Giving Stops When Sharing Begins
—From An Elder in the South

"Giving is like trying, my brothers, and you will remember what we have been willing to share with all of you on this," began the speaking words from the Elder in the South position.

"When one will use the word 'try', they are saying 'Will Not'. And when they substitute 'will not' for each time they wish to use the word 'try', they will see more clearly what they are calling to themselves. It is the vibration that is created from the use of this word that stops one from having to take responsibility from anything they will say, and it is this same vibration that will keep them from living in the present.

"Have the two-legs, who will come to you and use this word, remove it from all of their sentences and ask them what they feel. They will feel the responsibility and presence of their own path as their own truths come to life for them.

"And it is the same for giving. For it is from this word, and the actions that accompany it, that one will find them sick, ill, or diseased. And for as long as they will use this process, their sickness will not leave them.

"But this is getting ahead of where we wish to go with this eleventh step in healing. Let me explain some of the younger parts of this and you will not have difficulty in seeing past the confusion.

"There is only one kind of giving that can live in balance while one is in the domain of the Earth Mother, and this is the kind of giving all of us will do at one time or another. For it is a giving up of our robes so another or others may use them for their own needs.

"Think of this: it does not matter what you eat so much as it matters how you eat it. When you have a plate of food before you, do you eat it without consciousness? If you do, I assure you there will be very little benefit from what you consume.

"In truth, you are eating the children of the Earth Mother. And to consume them without giving thanks for what they have offered to you will only cause a growing imbalance within you.

"When you will look at this food that has been placed before you, understand that these children have given up their own life path for this end. So before you consume them, say to yourself:

'Thank You For Giving Up Your Life Path, My Brothers And Sisters, So I May Continue With Mine.'

"When you say this over the ones who are lying before you, there will be such a feeling of gratitude for their gift that all which is needed by your body to continue will be met by whatever you will eat.

"Keep this in the front of your thinking minds, my brothers, that there is not ever a journey that will end before its time, and when it has ended there will have been many lessons that will be understood, these lessons that have been understood by these children who wish to assist you in continuing with your life path. They will share them with you when they feel you understand the balance of life. And you thank them for what they have given up for you so that they will share all they have come to understand from their own life journey.

"Remember what we have shared with you, my brothers, that there are not only the two-legs who have life to them, but there is life in all things that have been created by Creator. And where there is life, there must also be understanding. It is from understanding that we find the wisdom that allows you to see these things we are now willing to share.

"When you will not take the time of giving thanks to these children of the Earth Mother before you consume them, you will only receive their pain and suffering which came to them as they felt their life paths end. For even the fruit on the vine feels the sorrow of loss when it is torn away from its mother.

"But so many of the two-legs hide behind their emotions and call the great illusion over themselves that tells them they are the only life living in this earth walk. But I tell each of you; this is not truth, not truth at all.

"However, for all they do not understand, they jump into the emotional part of their existence, even the feeling they have of loving another.

"But remember, love is not an emotion—it is life itself. And emotion is a friend who is continually reminding you of lessons needed by you to learn from in order to reach the next higher place of spirit, this next higher place that will take you one step closer to home.

"For the two-legs who are stuck in the emotion of their life paths, share with them this saying, for when they will repeat this saying silently to themselves three times for each emotion that will come to them, they will no longer be stuck within its illusion. But they will come to see through the emotion and onto the face of lesson. And when it has been seen and learned by them, they will no longer have a need of it and it will no longer come to them.

"Have them stand before this emotion that has come to them and say: 'Thank You For Coming To Me, My Friend. What Have You Brought For Me To Learn From You Today?'

"When they will have consciously repeated this to themselves for the third time, they will no longer feel that emotion's weight on them. There will be no trace of it, and it will be so complete they will wonder what they had been so worried about in the beginning.

"When they have learned this pathway, they will be ready to encounter the next part of this eleventh step of healing oneself again.

"Next, have them look at those things they have done, or are doing, with their life. They will encounter what this eleventh step of healing speaks of. They will see they have been so used to giving things to others that they have forgotten the truth to it, this truth that shares a great secret, which has been kept from all of the two-legs by those who would wish to control. From the ones who would wish to control, they have led the others into believing that it is better to give than to receive. But I share with all of you, this is not truth. In fact, it is farther from the truth than one could ever be and still have eyes to see anything.

"When one will give, they force at least three among them to become takers, and it is from the takers in this domain that so much greed and imbalance has come to reside in this domain.

"And in addition to this, my brothers, for those who would be the givers in this domain of the Earth Mother, they will soon steal from those who hold even a little of anything. They become the thieves when they run out of things to give others.

"The reason they become the thief is because they have been giving things to others for such a long time, they no longer see any other way of doing this. And this is prevalent when you will sit and listen to them speak with each other.

"You will hear them say there are so many problems in this world is because there are so many takers. And not wanting those close to them to be takers, they tell them that if they will not become takers they will give them something very special. And once again, they have created another taker, one that will be in a continual state of expecting things to be given to them.

"And all the while the giver is giving, they are locked in a continual state of worry. They worry about many things, but the one that bothers them the most is what they can give next and what will be expected of them once they have begun this giving of theirs.

"You see, my brothers, there cannot ever be an alternative for them. Once they begin this giving, it will always be expected from them. Should they ever attempt to stop, there would be a great loss of prestige from those who have been traveling with them, from the ones who have become so used to taking from them that this is the only way they see them and their life together.

"So what has taken place is the givers have come to believe they are doing the right thing for the takers who surround them because they do not believe there is any other way for them to follow. And both of them create a pressure on the other to continue in their role.

"Those who would not be willing to see this for what it is will continue to be locked within the sleep of illusion that will take them no place very fast.

"However for those who would listen to what we have been willing to share with you, tell them this can be changed, but they must be the one to change it.

"Have them look at what their giving has brought on them. It has brought them many feelings of lack and not the abundance that is available to those who would see it. This has brought them a feeling of sadness and limitation for what they are giving or taking from each other. And these feelings, if left to them, result in great sickness, illness, and disease for them. They result in these things because this is what they manifest into.

"Those who are willing to see this will ask you what they can do. And I assure each of you that they will be waiting for a very complicated answer, for they have been locked within their own illusions for such a long time, they have forgotten how simple truth is when it is understood.

"The simple truth for them is this: '*Allow Yourself To Be And You Will See That You Are Already.*' The answer is just that simple. However, there is a process they will need to follow in order to make sense out of it.

"Have them learn to receive from another without feeling they have to return something for it, or justify what they have received from another.

"For receiving from another will show them there is nothing more they need to do, for they have done all that is required of them in order to allow themselves to be, now.

"Unless they are willing to embrace this truth, my brothers, they will always be waiting for all things to be right. They will want to do just one more thing before they are willing to allow themselves to be, and will not see that they are, already.

"For them, there will always be one more thing to do before they can rest. For them, they will not ever be because they cannot see that they are locked within their own circle of illusion and trying.

"But for those who are willing to receive without condition, it will not matter if it is a physical gift or a compliment. The important face to this lesson they are learning is to receive from another without condition. For this allows them to find the way of receiving from themselves. And from all we have seen within this domain of the Earth Mother, this is what we have observed less, rather than more of.

"When one will learn to receive without condition from another, they understand they are ready and deserving of whatever may come to them, for they are beginning to see within themselves that there are true values they hold within them. And from these values, there will be a willingness for them to see it has come to them from all they have done, brought them to this place where they are now, standing with themselves showing a good face.

"It is through this process that they will come to believe in themselves once again. And through this process of believing in themselves they will understand that all they have ever done has been done for the right reason and in the right time, that there has not been anything done in their seasons past they should feel guilty about or carry a great weight of guilt for their actions.

"By believing in themselves again they will open their eyes to see this truth. And when they will, there will be a great sound of relief from them, a relief that they are already who and what they are and have become one who can be believed in by them.

"When there is a willingness to believe in themselves once again, they will find the answers to all they have been looking for.

"You see, my brothers, when one will stop believing in themselves, there is no longer the sounding voice of spirit within us to show us our own way. And when we are without direction, we depend on another to show us our path. But since they are not us, they cannot know our path—they can only know their own. And when we travel any path that is not ours, it is destined to fail for there is nothing on it that we can ever succeed in doing or learning, for ourselves or for them.

"However, when the two-legs will come to you in this time of The Season of the Long Shadow, they will have seen their own path to believing in themselves once again. And they will be the ones who will know this is good.

"They will see how useless it is to give to others, and they will see what this has been creating from all of the generations that have been in this domain. Remember, when one will give, they create three others who will be takers. Understand the path that lies before the giver, and know why they will soon become the thieves.

"When one learns to believe in themselves once again, they find a great freedom to walk with, this freedom they see from looking at all of their past events with an understanding they have all been for a reason, that they have all been so they could be who and what they are today.

"Once this has taken root within them, they will find a freedom come to life from within them. They will find themselves with the freedom to do all they will do, with understanding that they are going to do those things anyway, but when they will understand why they do them, there will not be the need to carry the weight of guilt or doubt with them any longer. For they have come to a place where they can learn from those lessons immediately and will no longer have to pass time in order to feel their weight build. For the weight of lessons not learned will build until they call our attention to them so we may understand them.

"When this has taken place, my brothers, they will have found their own freedom, this same freedom they have been born into, and they will be willing to allow this same freedom come to life for another and will not be tempted at controlling them like those who have not found this.

"Then there will be a great shift in them and it will be seen by all who are around them.

"They will have begun to share, and the greatest gift that any has to offer is their presence. When they will have taken all of these steps we have been willing to share with you, they will have come to the place of discovering their own presence. And when a presence is felt by another, there is no thing further that will ever have to be done, for the giving will have stopped and the takers go away. When sharing has returned to live among life once again, and another is sharing their presence, there is only one thing for them to do. And that is to be who and what they are in truth. For when this happens, those who would look on them will see what they have done. And they will not see this in a way of greed or envy, but they will know that this is possible for them to do as well.

"You see, my brothers, when one will see that a path is possible to find for oneself, they are not going to follow yours, but they are going to be more willing to find their own. And when presence is among any, this is what others will see.

"Presence is the greatest gift of all. And when it is shared, there will be no further giving and taking, for this will be a thing of their past, this past that has been holding them down for as long as they can remember.

"This then is the final step we are willing to share for healing oneself. It would be good to review them many times. As you will, you will continue to grow in understanding why one will choose to carry with them these things called sickness, illness, and disease. As the two-legs come to see their own reasons, they will see they are the only ones who may call on them to drop away. For this is the process that will allow them to drop away and not ever have to return to them again because they will have learned from their lessons and need to move on."

PART IX

❀

THE SEVEN WARNINGS FOR THE SEASON OF THE LONG SHADOW

CHAPTER 58

❀

First Warning

When Thirteen Stars Form A Circle In The West-Southwest Sky
—From An Elder in the West

"There will be warnings for the times that are ahead, my brothers. That is if one will be willing to see what is being presented to them," began the speaking words from the Elder in the West.

"When it is time for the closing of The Season of the Long Shadow, many events will have taken place. Events that will seem very bad to those who have not yet learned to see their own truth.

"However, I will share with you there is not going to be an ending to the Earth Mother herself, only a great change. And it is to be a change that none of the earth walkers may follow, not as they are now. They will only be allowed to enter her fifth world of peace and light when they no longer have need to learn from the lessons that will be from her past.

"For when she has gone through all of her changing and cleansing, these lessons will not be available any longer, for these are the lessons that have made her so heavy and where she is going, there is no place for them.

"Those lessons will have been moved to the twelfth Earth Mother where they will be waiting for the arrival of those who will not be allowed to remain here. And when they will enter this new Earth Mother, they will find all they had been turning away from has followed them. They will have not escaped the process of learning from their own lessons; they have only moved to another schoolhouse.

"When the events signal it is time for the final cleansing to take place, this cleansing that will tear away all life that can no longer be sustained here, warning signs will be given. These warning signs will allow one to see their own face of truth and find the path they need to travel so they will not have to be a part of this great cleansing of the Earth Mother.

"But these warning signs will only be seen by those who have learned to see and hear with their own eyes and ears. All others will not see them and will remain in those places where the pains of this last and final cleansing will be felt the most.

"In the times that are not distant from now, there will be the first of thirteen stars that will make their appearance known to all who are still living in this domain. And its entry will be seen in the night skies and will not be missed by any who can see anything, though there will be those who would wish they had not seen anything.

"For this first star messenger is one of thirteen who will be seen. And when the thirteen stars will find their own place in the west-southwest sky, the flood of their presence will be felt over all this domain we call the Earth Mother. It will be felt by all life, and for the ones who do not understand, they will run and hide in an effort of escaping from what is coming.

"They will not understand what it is, but feel as if they remember what is going to be. For there will be a great awakening over all of them, and this awakening will cause them to feel that all of this is for a reason, a reason they do not wish to participate in.

"The first star messenger will be seen only by a few in the beginning, but as it comes closer to this domain, more and more people will see it. And just as they come to believe that it is going to hit them, this great star body will stop its progress and remain motionless in the night skies and await its other twelve brothers and sisters to join him.

"All that is felt by the presence of this first star body will not go away. And as each additional star messenger will come and join the first, the additional energies will multiply and be felt by all, to a level many times their own numbers.

"As each of these stars enter the night skies of the Earth Mother, they will manifest themselves into a great and brilliant light. This light will become so bright that night will almost cease to exist.

"There will be a pattern these star messengers will follow, for as each of them enter the night skies of the Earth Mother, they will stop at a place that will complement the other. And those complementary positions will share with all that see them that it is forming a great circle of thirteen stars and will remain stationary in the west-south-west sky.

"It is their presence that will allow the Earth Mother to take to herself all of the energies she will need in order to begin her final cleansing. The thirteenth, and last, star body will complete this circle that marks the time for those who have learned to see to leave the lands they are in and head to the safe lands.

"The safe lands will be shown to each of them when the time is right. They will be shown a picture of a place that will offer them all that they will have need of. These pictures will come to them in the front of their thinking minds and they will know them. If they have no current memory for the location of these lands, there will be placed before them a picture from one of their books showing them where this land is.

"When they hear the calling voice showing them the way to those lands, they would be well advised to pack up and leave immediately.

For when the final positioning of the thirteenth star has formed itself into the west-southwest skies above them, there will be a great cry that will come out of the depths of the Earth Mother herself. And this cry will cause all of her lands to open up and take all fuels deep within her and well out of reach of those who have been using them.

"These fuels will be taken to her deep places where they will be used later to ignite her body and burn off all that is no longer needed, to end life as you have come to know it so the new life may enter.

"When the fuel is taken away, the diseases and plagues will begin. And the foods that have been so common among the two-legs will no longer be available. This will cause them to begin eating each other for lack of anything else to consume.

"Only the ones who have found their own path will recognize the pictures of the safe lands and how to get to them. And those who have remained lost within the sleep of illusion, they will remain where they are and will not be allowed to venture more than one hundred miles from their present location. For to travel any further would surely bring an end to their life path.

"Remember, my brothers, to think that one can alter any of these events is to live within the illusion, this illusion that causes them to see things only as they would wish for them to be.

"There is only one thing that can change, and that is themselves. Those who understand themselves for who and what they are in truth will see and hear what they are to do next, for they will not have to go through these great changes that are even now on their way."

CHAPTER 59

❀

Second Warning

Leaving For The Safe Lands
—From An Elder in the North

"During The Season of the Long Shadow, there will be many other great changes that will come," began the speaking words from the Elder in the North. "Changes that will cause one to believe there is an end coming to all living things. However, I tell you this in truth, it is not. But all life as you know it will be changed and only those who have been willing to prepare themselves will be allowed to pass through this time. The others will be torn away from the Earth Mother's breast in the same way an infant is taken away when the mother's milk is no more.

"During this time of the great cleansing, the Spirit Wind will cross over all of these lands in a very unpredictable way. For what had been brought to many from their seasons past will not continue in the same way. For it is during this time of the great cleansing that the Spirit Wind will be charged with hurling himself over places that hold imbalance on them. And he will do this in a very powerful way.

"From out of nowhere he will appear in a mighty blast of his own spirit. And the force of his presence will tear the skin away from any that are unfortunate enough to be standing in his way.

"And from his power that is to be unleashed on this domain, there will be a time of silence to one of incomparable sounds. For he will unleash mighty blasts of air that will cause the iron birds to roll over and fall to the earth below them, sudden blasts that will cause the mighty trucks and buildings to roll and fall to the ground and be destroyed.

"Keep in the front of your thinking minds that none of this is done to punish anyone. It is only with them because it is time for the great cleansing to begin, this cleansing that will only allow those who no longer have need of lessons to remain with this Earth Mother. This cleansing will assist the ones who still need to learn from lesson's journey to the next Earth Mother who is very far away from this one.

"For without this cleansing, my brothers, those who would have nothing left to learn in this domain would not leave. And they would be without progress in their circle of life if they were to remain.

"All things take place when it is time for them to be. And for those who have come to open their eyes and ears of spirit, they will have a great need for these safe lands. And they would do well in seeing them as a place where the impact of the great cleansing will not affect them so strongly.

"The safe lands will be located within tall mountains. And there will be a valley within a valley where they will remain until it is time for the Great Messenger to arrive and call on all life to choose between the two paths, the path that will lead to the left and into the next Earth Mother where all of this will be repeated once again, and the path that leads to the right which will lead into the fifth world of peace and light, this fifth world that will no longer be heavy with the lessons that are currently within it now.

"For it will be in the safe lands that the Spirit Wind will see no need for the great cleanings. And the force from his presence will not be felt as strongly because he will see that there will be a balance to life that has come to live in these valleys within the valleys.

"While he will not ignore them, he will not be as devastating, for there will not be a need for this.

"And within these safe lands, there will be water for drinking and cleaning. This water will come from great distances below the surface and will not be affected by the diseases that will be found in all other water.

"For as the great cleansing takes place, there will be many new and fatal diseases which will be unleashed from below the surface of the Earth Mother. These will be diseases that had been known long before, as well as some that have not. And they will rise from the openings of the cracks, which are created by the earth shakings and will be carried to all four directions by the Spirit Wind.

"This is what makes for a new face to this cleansing, my brothers. All of these diseases will not be located in only one area, but they will reach all areas because they will ride on the back of the great Spirit Wind and fall wherever they will feel their presence is needed. As they fall over the face of all lands, there will be a great covering of them over all living things.

"To some, these diseases will cause a quick end to a life path. But to others, the ending will be long and drawn out. None of this will be pleasant to observe.

"Then the waters will fall from the cloud nation and wash these diseases into the waters below the shallow surface of the earth and into the life that draws its life from them. And as they are touched by the water spirit, these diseases will change in a continual manner. For there will not be the passing of one sun that will shine on the same form of the disease twice. And because of the rapid change, there will be no known cure. For the ones who will contact them, there will be but one certain end. The only variable will be the speed at which it will come.

"But the water provided within the safe lands will not be affected by these diseases. They will not be in the safe lands because the breath of the Earth Mother will continually blow them away from her valleys within the valleys. And all life who is within these safe lands will not know the pains that will be so abundant in the times of the great cleansing.

"However, once these great earth changes begin, there will be no leaving the safe lands. There will be no leaving because of all these diseases that will have been left on all of their surrounding places. If one would attempt to cross over these lands at the outer places, they would fall victim to these diseases. For these diseases will lie on the face of the Earth Mother and will awaken when a living thing will come near them. They will awaken and find their way into that life and end it, for this is their purpose and there is nothing that may stand in their way.

"So when it is time and the two-legs have found their way into the safe lands, remind them of these things we have been willing to share with all of you. Remind them so they will not forget. For if they do, then they will surely have been better off if they had not ever come to know of them.

"Remind them there will not be any who are missed by these great earth changes, my brothers. Remind them that this has come to all life and marks the beginning of a new world for all, a new world that will allow for more growth, clearer seeing, and the attainment of coming one step closer to our home with Creator.

"When they will see things for what they are in truth, my brothers, they will not see them through the eyes of fear. They will see them with an understanding that it is time to move on, to move on to the next place of learning for everyone."

chapter 60

Third Warning

Who Are The Messengers
From An Elder in the East

For those who do not hold an understanding of these times that are soon to be, there will be a great fear fall over them, came the speaking words from the Elder in the East position. Keep in the front of your thinking minds that fear is only seen for those places within themselves they do not yet understand. And while there are places within themselves where there is no understanding, there is fear for what is presented.

Those who have many places within themselves which are not understood will run to another and seek their advice. But it is not their advice they are after, my brothers, it is to have another do their work for them.

And there will come bud calls from the four directions where those who are still locked within their own illusion, the sleeping ones, reside calls that will be heard by all who will listen to them. These calls will request that a great gathering be made, one that will include all of the controllers who have amassed many with them.

"For it will be in these times when you will see many being led by the few. And those few who will be leading are just as lost in their sleep of illusion as the ones they lead.

"But not many will see this taking place in them, not until it is too late for them to make a difference in their own life path.

"For as the song legends of all people have shared with the ones who would listen, they will continue to follow these false leaders until their time has ended. And when their time has ended, there will be a flash of awakening that will come to them, a flash of awakening that will show them what they have done and what has returned to them for their efforts.

"The Season of the Long Shadow is an acceleration of all processes used by the two-legs. There will also be acceleration for the way they will look to another or others for their direction and guidance.

"When one is not willing to do their own work, there will be a great desire to have another do it for them. The reasons will be many, but the major one is because they no longer feel in control of their emotions. And the stronger emotions will come to them, the more lost and out of control they will feel in their life path.

"As The Season of the Long Shadow is born into this domain, my brothers, all of these emotions they had experienced before will get stronger and stronger. And as they will grow in strength, many believe there will be no ending to their being with them.

"As we have shared with you previously, there is only one purpose for emotion to enter anyone's life path. And that is to remind them of a lesson they need to learn.

"For those still sleeping within the illusion, they will either fight or argue with them. And in both cases, emotion will prevail because who they are fighting, is themselves. When one will fight with themselves, there can only be one winner and one loser—it can only be them.

"During The Season of the Long Shadow, there will be many living with a great level of frustration that comes to them from having so many emotions they cannot get away from.

"In this time, there will be many who will call themselves Messenger, but in truth, they will not be what they will claim to be. For they have come to control these others who are living with these high levels of frustration. They have come to control them, not to assist them. And as it is with so many things that are to be found in the great illusion, many will not see this until it is too late for them to do anything about it.

"During this time, there will be many who will wear the false face of illusion over them. At first they will appear to you as those who understand all that you are going through, but they do not.

"For when they come to you, listen to those things they have to say and see if there is truth within them. You see, my brothers, when one will speak truth and understand it, you will not only see their truth in those things they have to share, but you will find yours as well. And there is not anything you will have to change or do to yourself in order to come to a place of understanding.

"However, when one says they are speaking truth to you, they are but repeating something that sounds good to them, because you will have to change many things about yourself in order to get to their place of their seeing, their place of seeing those things they are repeating to you.

"Whenever you are asked to change anything about yourself or the life path you have come to travel, there is no messenger of truth before you, there is only one who does not understand truth at all, and they will be speaking to you from a position of control, a position that will allow them to control you if you will do what they tell you to do.

"These are not the Messengers we have come to speak of, my brothers. They are the ones who continue to live in the great illusion of not seeing, and would wish to do the same to all who would come to them.

"For the Messengers will not ask you to change yourself, they only ask that you understand those things you are doing.

"The Messengers we are speaking of have passed through their long night and succeeded in exiting on the other side of the illusion. These Messengers will have seen much of what they had in their life path fall away, and have come to a place of understanding that had it not fallen away from them, there would not be any room for the new to have come to them, those new things that carried another part of their truth to them, truth that is applicable to all.

"These Messengers have come to know the light and the dark, and will understand that both are from oneself. For when one sees who and what they are in truth, they see a light, this light that has always been within them.

"These Messengers will also know the dark and what it brings with it. For when they will see those who carry the dark with them, they understand they are the ones who still have a great distance to travel, a great distance to go before they will be willing to listen to these truths.

"They will not look on those who travel in the dark as anything but another member of their own spirit family who has need of lesson, a great need to learn and later to understand those lessons they have surrounded themselves with.

"And, they will not attempt to change them. For they hold the understanding that all things are at the right time and the right place of being. They walk away from them because they understand that for each moment they will spend on one who is not ready to listen, one moment is taken away from one who is. And this will be in the front of their thinking minds, my brothers. They do not turn away from these others for any other reason—and this is truth.

"These Messengers will be awakened during The Season of the Long Shadow, and will be seen and felt in a much different way than any others during this time. They will not appear to be different on the outside, but what is felt from them will be different. They will be the ones who have allowed themselves to be. And this will bring disquieting feelings among those who have not yet awakened from their illusion.

"At first, they will feel love for them but this feeling will not last long. For as soon as they find so many of their lessons and emotions come over them from being near one of these Messengers, they will blame them for all that is not right and will come to hate them.

"For those who remain lost within their own sleep of illusion, they will continue to hate these Messengers because they believe all they are going through is the Messengers' fault and has nothing to do with themselves.

"However, for those who take advantage of what is being shared, they will soon fall out of this hating period that is with them and see the Messengers for who they are in truth. They will see them as a good friend and another member of their spirit family. They will understand that all they are going through are those things they need to learn from. And as they find this understanding for what is coming to them, they will be grateful for all they have seen within themselves and for them, this is good.

"You see, my brothers, The Messengers will be those who have understood that all things will be regardless of what you might want. They see that when one is trying to make something happen, they are only getting in their own way. They understand they will end up in the same place but covered with scars and bruises all over themselves. And those scars and bruises will have been caused by their own efforts of trying to make something happen that is going to be anyway.

"Those who continue to try, will be seen as ones who are not willing to make any effort in doing their own work. And they will see the Messengers as weak and not possessing the strength and stamina they do. For if they did, they would surely see how much wrong there is in this earth, and would try to change it.

"Those who would see the Messengers in this way, they will only see things in one way—theirs. For to do something in any other way is to do it wrong, and is bound to fail.

"However, those who would see the Messengers in this way will decrease. As they decrease in their numbers, they will see the Messengers as a great threat to themselves and the life path they have become used to. But there will be sufficient numbers of those who have begun to wake from the sleep of illusion to counter their efforts, and harm will not be allowed to come to them.

"The Messengers will also understand there is but one great gift and this greatest of gifts is one of presence, the presence of one who is within the One of all living life.

"For the Messengers understand that to give creates at least three takers, and from this giving there will always be more takers than the giver can satisfy. So the giver will eventually become the thief who will rob from one who may only have a little and be left with nothing.

"So the Messengers will neither give nor will they take, but they will share, and they will receive. For to share means there will not be any strings attached, and to receive is to believe in one's self. And this is good.

"This then is the path to finding presence with oneself, my brothers, and when you come close to any of these Messengers, you will feel a great many things come into your life path.

"For when you are in their presence, you will feel great peace as well as great uncertainty. The great peace will be from those things you have come to learn and understand. And the great uncertainty will come to you from those things that still need to be worked on, by you.

"It is the presence from the Messengers that will awaken you to this, awaken you to see what is still needed to be done by you in order to learn, awaken within you the path you felt had been lost to you.

"When you will be in close location to any of the Messengers, you will find them walking their life path and teaching the truths that have been shared with them. You will not see any of them calling on others to change or follow them, for the Messengers ask that you follow yourself, and not them. For this will not be the time for following another, not during this time of The Season of the Long Shadow.

"However, the Messengers understand there will be many who will travel close to them. And that is because their life path is close enough to theirs to allow for this. But they will remind them, before others are allowed to do such a thing, they will have to be willing to stand strong alone first. For to stand strong alone first will allow them to find their own truths and see their own path. When they have seen this, they can see if their path is close enough to the Messengers that they may travel close to them. For each path in this domain has its own distinct feature, and those features will be in the form of lessons that are continually being learned by all life.

"The Messengers will not be interested in the numbers of people who will listen to those things they have to share. They will only be interested in staying focused on this path they have been given to travel while they are in this domain of the Earth Mother. Those who do not have an understanding for themselves will see this behavior of the Messengers as one that does not care for any one or anything but themselves. And those who have come to awaken themselves from their illusion will see this behavior from the Messengers as being truth, not only for them, but also for all life.

"These Messengers will be heard and felt for this path they have chosen to travel. But they will not be seen running, for they understand there is no place one can run to.

"It will be those who have not come as a Messenger who will do this, my brothers, those who call themselves by this name but do not understand it.

"They will be the ones calling on all life to change what they are doing in order to right all of the wrongs that have been done. It will be they who will hold everyone they speak to within this great illusion and within their control. And this control will come with the face of fear.

"The Messengers will solicit change in others, my brothers, but this change will come by them looking at themselves and finding their own face of truth.

"However, those who are not Messengers will cause change to come over others by telling them if they will not do as they say, they will surely pay for it. And this change they bring to them only comes through the face of fear, this fear they will hold over all until time for them is ended.

"These are the two kinds of Messengers who will surface during the Season of the Long Shadow. And as it is with all life and all domains, there is always free choice. So take this information we have been willing to share with all of you and know that it will be your choice to pick which path you will be willing to travel."

CHAPTER 61

❀

Fourth Warning

Why Another Would Not Want You To Find Your Own Truth
—From An Elder in the South

"When it is time for The Season of the Long Shadow to enter this domain, my brothers, there will be great efforts to increase the level of control used on others," began the speaking words from the Elder in the South position.

"Many would rather run and hide from the events that will be coming to them. But those events are not meant to harm them, nor are they meant to give them pain or fear. They are only a reminding of the lessons they need to learn so they may find their way to the path they have chosen to travel in this domain of the Earth Mother.

"However, as we have seen from the actions of those who are traveling in this domain, there is very little they wish to understand about themselves. They do not want to understand those things because someone along the way told them that it could be bad. And this has caused them to walk with a great fear for themselves and what they might be.

"So they have found it more comfortable listening to what others tell them rather than listening to themselves, and for them, this has become their accepted way of life. And most of them do not want to change this.

"You see, my brothers, there is a great truth that resides within all that travel their life path with the Earth Mother. And this great truth says that all things happen to you because you have called on them, that only you can understand them, and as long as you will listen to what another or others will tell you their meanings for them are, you will travel within their circle of expression. This circle of expression is more commonly called the great circle of illusion.

"When one is within this circle of illusion, they find themselves only repeating what another has told them. They will not understand those things they will say and do, and when they encounter something that is not like what they have been trained to repeat, they completely immerse themselves within their own emotions. For it is their emotions they have come to find their greatest strength in, but it is a strength of reaction that does not cause them to think of what they will do or say, but only requires them to yell and wrestle with what they do not understand.

"Because their numbers have been so great in the seasons past, they believe that if so many are doing this, they must be right and justified in doing this too. But I tell you this is not truth, for it is very far away from it.

"Only when one will be willing to see through their own eyes will they find their own truth, my brothers. And when they do, they will no longer be lulled into the illusion from what another tells them, from the efforts made by the few who would wish to control them and have them believe their way must be the exact same way as another's, if they are to be correct in what they will do or say.

"However, as long as they are willing to believe what another tells them is right and wrong, good and bad, they will be within their control. This is why so many would not wish for you to find your own way on this earth walk.

"For when you find your own way, there is a great shift in the energies that are within you. And those energies will clash with what many have come to accept as the established way of life. This will cause them to feel changes. And for them, changes are an enemy to be feared, not understood.

"All of this has taken place through the time of the four worlds, my brothers, but it will increase when it is time for The Season of the Long Shadow to arrive.

"It will increase in this way. All of the lessons that have not yet been learned will be returning during this time. This will not be limited to the lessons from this earth walk, but they will be the lessons you have missed from all earth walks as well.

"As it has always been, the number of times you will turn away from lesson, there will be one additional layer of emotion that will be drawn over it, an additional layer of emotion that will make it more difficult to work your way past it in order to see what the lesson is.

"There will be many returning lessons that have been turned away from and it will cause the two-legs to feel as if their whole world is falling apart. And this way of thinking is not far from the truth, for life as they have come to know it will not be for much longer. And change will be a constant companion to those who are within this domain, more so than ever before.

"It will not be long into this time we have come to call The Season of the Long Shadow that the two-legs will believe they are at their limit for emotional turmoil. And this feeling will cause them to feel that just one additional event of an emotional nature would surely break them.

"They will spend great amounts of time and effort in gathering to themselves those who are like-minded. When they will gather into these places, they will be lulled into the illusion that they are in a place where no change will come to them. But they will soon find this is not a truth they hold, and begin to see those who once stood with them and their way of thinking beginning to change.

"Those who have begun to change will have done so by doing their own work of looking past the emotions and into the lesson that had come to them. And when they did this, they say the emotions that had been coming to them were not the enemy they once thought they were. But they see them as reminders of things they need to work on. As they work on those lessons, they see their own way and no longer need direction from the group they once found refuge in and will leave them.

"When the ones who continue to hide within their own fears see this take place, they feel more threatened by these actions others have taken and will call them the enemy, an enemy to a way of life that no longer exists, but a way of life they are holding onto.

"They will take great efforts from all of their tools, talents, and resources in making sure that others would not follow the same path as those who have left them. For them, this is their last line of security of keeping those things they have come to believe in, those things they have been led into believing will keep them from feeling insecure in their own life.

"Their efforts will make it impossible for another to think for themselves at all. For they will create group rules and laws that would prohibit these things and the penalties will be very harsh and in many cases fatal.

"As this process begins, the ones who wish to control others will do so with the resources they believe they have control over, things such as the food they eat and the clothes they wear.

"Those who will not go along with their way of living and thinking will be denied these things. But I tell you in truth that this process will not last long, for soon all of those things will be taken away from these groups and they will find themselves without food or clothing to control others with.

"When this takes place, my brothers, the ones who had left to find their own way will have seen the safe lands, and will find others who have also found their own path to travel as well. And they will have found safe waters to drink and food to eat.

"And once they arrive in the safe lands, they will forget about the others who remained in the large groups. They will have forgotten about them because they understand that they have their path to travel as well, and to interfere with one's learning and lessons being offered, is to alter one's own life path.

"When the two-legs come to you during this time we speak of, share with them that it is better to find their own way early during this season of the great change and cleansing. For the sooner they will see their path, the more quickly they will come to know where these safe lands for them are. And when it will be time for them to leave for the safe lands, they will know where they may go.

"Remind them during this time of their waking from their own sleep of illusion that there will be many times they will feel as if their whole world has been caught on fire, when all they have held onto had left them. But share with them that this has taken place for all who begin to travel their own path, and is only a process they are doing for themselves, a process that reminds them that if they will continue to hold onto these old things that are not in service to them, there will not be room for the new that will soon be with them.

"Also remind them while they are waking from their own illusion, there will be many times when they will feel themselves getting sleepy and begin to wonder if they are sick. But share with them that those things come to all who begin to wake, for the sleep time comes to them so they might be adjusted and altered in order to receive more information, information that is from themselves and their spirit family.

"When these times of sleeping come to them, and they will not allow it to be, they will find themselves in a waking state that is not completely awake and could cause themselves injury or harm. For during these times of adjustment, the old ways of seeing are taken away from them so they can see new. And if they will not follow the sleep that will be placed over them, they will feel as if they are living in a fog. But this is a natural process when one will allow themselves to be adjusted to receive more information. Do not worry about it.

And when they will not fall asleep, they will feel as if they are losing their sense of perception and balance. But share with them that all who begin this path of their own spirit will encounter such things and not to fear them, for they are being called by themselves because it is time."

CHAPTER 62

❀

Fifth Warning

Wicked And Evil Exist When We Look
Through The Eyes Of Others
—From An Elder in the West

"When The Season of the Long Shadow has come into this domain, there will be a great call from many that there is a great wickedness and evil that is spreading over all of the lands. But I tell you this in truth, my brothers, what they will see is only themselves, those parts of them they have forgotten to look at," came the immediate following of the speaking words from the Elder in the West position.

"For during these times there will not be many things left that they can relate to, not in the way they once were. For there will be shortages of the many things the two-legs had once considered to be in abundance. And those shortages will cause them to see that soon there will not be enough of any one to sustain life with. Next, they will look through the eyes of fear at others who are near them, those who might take away something they have.

"During this time, there will be great fears that will confront those who have not yet awakened from the sleep of illusion. And they will grow into a deep—but not understood—hatred for all things that might do them harm.

"This emotion will fuel many at this time to collect themselves together and say that everything they fear and hate must be destroyed and done away with. That is, if life is to continue for them.

"But they do not see life as they have come to know it as being over, or that it is simply time to move on. For those who have remained locked within the sleep of illusion will hold onto the believing that what they are doing will keep their ways alive. That if they will not recognize those things that are being presented to them, then they will have to go away.

"However, they will not go away. They will become more pronounced with the passing of each day. And as they become more prominent in their daily lives, they will find their fears growing.

"Keep in the front of your thinking minds, my brothers, there is no evil or bad. It is only when we do not understand something that we will come to think in this way. And this is the face of truth for this fifth warning we are now willing to share with you.

"This truth of seeing things as bad and evil come to us when we do not understand what is before us. For those things we do not understand, there has always been but one answer throughout the history of the two-legs, and that is to kill and destroy it.

"This takes place when one does not understand what is being presented to them and are not willing to work within themselves to see past the illusion.

"When The Season of the Long Shadow has arrived, there will be many such issues that will confront the two-legs, and they will present themselves in ways that have not yet been seen by any who travel in this domain of the Earth Mother.

"They will come to all very quickly, and just as one of them is understood, another will arrive but a little quicker than the last.

"This will cause the two-legs to lose their perspective on themselves and life that is around them. For they will soon look at all life as something that is out to get them. That is, if they will not act collectively to get it first.

"This, then, is the beginning of where this fifth warning will come to you then. It will be when the two-legs will group together in order to protect themselves from what is taking place for all of them. To group themselves together means that there will be certain ways of looking at things. And all must agree, for there will be rules to govern the way they are to live their life with the group. To them, this is the only way the group can survive these times. But they will not see that this is the beginning of their end.

"By the time these groups will form themselves, most of those who have seen the safe lands will have been gone from those locations. And it will be good for them because they will not be willing to succumb to the conditions these groups will make on its own members.

"Those who will remain in those locations—the ones who are in the process of awakening but have not yet reached their place or their path—they will see with eyes that are not of the group and will move further and further away from their controlling environments. For they will see what the end will be for such endeavors and will not wish to take part in it.

"There will be others who have awakened and learned the path of invisibility and return to these locations to retrieve the ones who are beginning to awaken, from these lands. They will return in very small numbers and will walk unnoticed past these groups, and will call to those who are ready to leave.

"And they will follow them to lands where there will not be control over them, and they will be free to look at their own life paths with their own eyes and not the eyes of others.

"Remember, my brothers, wicked and evil arrive with us when we look through the eyes of others. And the reason for this is very simple.

"When we see through our own eyes, all that comes to us can be understood. There may be many things we might not wish to look at, but still the possibility of understanding them is within us. That is, if we are willing to do our own work and pass ourselves through the emotion that resides just to the front of our own lesson.

"But when we look through the eyes of others for what is presented to us, we use their eyes for explaining things, and ignore our own, and we lose the possibility of understanding anything at all.

"In each of these cities where the groups will have formed, there will always be four groups. And when they will run out of others who are not a member of one of these groups to kill, they will turn on themselves.

"They will turn on themselves until there is only one of these four groups left in the city. Then they will look to the next city and do the same to their four groups.

"This will continue until there are only four great groups left in all the earth. And when they find the final locations of each other, they will mass themselves together and wage a great battle, a battle that will be seen in their eyes as the final one before all of this destruction that has been with them can be ended.

"Since none within these four groups can agree on anything, there will not be any sides taken. And this means that each of them will kill and destroy the other with the same vigor. So there will be no truces among them.

"Since there will not be fuel for them to run their great killing machines, they must all be pulled or pushed by hand. So each of these four groups will form themselves into four armies and will begin to move all of their killing machines to one location. It will be a location each of the four armies will reach without much difficulty. For all four of these armies will end up in a similar location, and they will amass to do their final battle with each other.

"However, just as they form themselves where this final battle is to begin, there will be a great and brilliant white light that will come over everything. This brilliant white light will be the Great Messenger who has returned to the two-legs.

"And in all places where this light of the Great Messenger will shine, illusion is torn away. And where there is no illusion, there can be no control.

"For those who have followed their groups, there will be a fear come to them. It will be a fear of seeing all things for what they are, and they will not know what to do with this.

"They will become frightened and not know where to run or hide, so all of the four armies will turn their guns on themselves and end their life paths. At least, this is what they believe they will do.

"But there will be no place left for them to run and hide. And for those who shoot themselves, they will see their body fall to the earth beneath them but will remain standing as spirit.

"This will cause the others to fall prey to their own fears and turn their guns on themselves as well. And they too will see their bodies fall to the earth but their spirit will be left standing. Standing without a body, but standing just as they had been before.

"Through this process, they will feel the pains of death many times, my brothers. They will feel the pains of death at the time they will have their own bullet enter their body, and they will feel this same pain of death until the Great Messenger will call them to make their choice between the path that will lead to the left and the path that will lead to the right.

"And for all of this time, there will be heard great sounds of pain, and cries of torture from them. For they will be carrying these pains of death until they make this choice, these pains of death they had caused to themselves.

"For those who have not seen wickedness and evil by looking with the eyes of others, their fate will not be the same. For when they see the light of the Great Messenger come, they will feel a great peace and comfort fill them, one that will share with all of them that the time to return home is soon at hand.

"And for all of this, they know is good. And they will be ready, for they have prepared themselves as only they could do.

"This, then, is the face of the fifth warning for The Season of the Long Shadow, my brothers. Remember it well, for there will be a great need of its companionship for the times that are soon to be."

CHAPTER 63

Sixth Warning

Race Is Not A Physical Issue, It Is Spiritual —From An Elder in the North

"During The Season of the Long Shadow, many will continue to see separateness in all things, my brothers. And for as long as they see this separateness among themselves, they will reside within the great illusion that will not allow them to see anything for what it is in truth, but only as they would wish for it to be," came the speaking words from the Elder in the North position.

"As long as those who wish to control others can keep these others in a place of separateness, a place that tells them there are great differences between them and others, they will not fear losing their control over them. They will not fear this because their ego will be fed, and there is nothing in this domain that is easier to feed. That is from all of those things that exist within the illusionary part of a life path.

"Keep in the front of your thinking minds that we have all come from one source. We have all come from the same Creator and to this same Creator we will all return. Some will take longer than others, but nevertheless, we will all return.

"Share with the two-legs who come to you during these times those things we have left with you from long ago, one of them being the song legend of beginnings.

"This is where Creator was sitting within the Oneness which is Him and looking around all parts of Himself, He decided to share yet another level with Himself, this level that would be called understanding.

"So looking to all parts that are of Him, He allowed many pieces to break away, that is, the ones who would be willing to learn to understand from the lessons that would be needed, those lessons that would allow them to return to Creator with a great understanding for all things that are.

"From this beginning place, Creator looked at all of his children, those of the two-legs, the leaf, those of the paws and wings, as well at the ones of the day and the night. And looking at them, He smiled and said:

'Go now and begin this great journey I have designed for each of you, this great adventure that will take you far and wide throughout all of these domains I have created for you. Go now and learn from the lessons we each have spoken of, for when you will do these things, you will each return to me with more understanding of the One within the One...of the place of beginnings...and of the I Am which is you...and of the I Am which is me. When you return to me, we will be One within the One once again. But remember, to travel with fear, is to travel with illusion. For it is fear that will keep you separated from all life and understanding. To travel with understanding for all that will present itself to you is to travel in love. And it is from love that one is reminded of life.'

"And so it has been that in all of the domains our spirit families have traveled through, there have been the four colors of the races.

"However, it would be well to keep in the front of your thinking minds how they began, and we will share this with you at a later time. But for now, remember that all life began as One within the One. And it is not until later that the distinct separations occur.

"They occur for specific reasons, my brothers. And for those who would tell you they only occur to show you who is higher and who is lower, they are as lost as any we have come to find in this or any other domain. For what they speak to you of is not truth at all, it is illusion. And within illusion, there can be no truths residing.

"However, we are getting away from the face of this sixth lesson, this lesson that shares with us that race is not a physical issue but a spiritual one.

"When all of us began this great journey, we had many lessons to learn, lessons that could not be accomplished in just one life path.

"Because of the diversity of those lessons, we became aware of what our own limitations were for finding the understanding that was needed by each of us, this understanding that must encompass the entire circle of our spirit path.

"The circle of our spirit path is much more than the circle of life we have come to travel in this domain of the Earth Mother. For just as the circle of life holds all parts of ourselves for the earth walk, our circle of spirit holds all parts of ourselves in spirit. And spirit is much more complete than this shell of a body you travel in here.

"When we look at lessons that are needed by spirit, we see that each of us holds different needs for our learning. And as we see the differences—what we need to learn—we choose accordingly how we will enter to walk our life path.

"Our choice will determine if we will walk as a member of the red race, the yellow race, the black race, or the white race, for each of these paths will hold something different for us to learn from.

"So when you will see one who is traveling their earth walk as one of the four races, understand that you have traveled with them before—perhaps in another time, another place, and in another race. But understand that they are in truth, related to each of you no matter how they appear to you now.

"And understand that how they appear to you now is a reflection of the lessons they hold a need to learn. Do not look on them with eyes that would either feel sorry for them or envy them. Look on them with eyes that are yours through understanding, eyes that will share with you that all they are going through is what they need to learn from. When you will do this, it will be much easier for you to know that they hold with them all that they need. For when they will come to a place of finishing one of their lessons, they will enter a place of the next one.

"Remember, there is not ever anyone who is without assistance, my brothers, assistance from those who are in a place of helping them to attain those things they need to learn.

"Do not make the mistake of thinking you can change or alter their life paths for them, either. For to think of such things would surely throw you and them away from the path that is needed, this path where only they can find the lessons they need to learn from.

"This is why we have reminded all of you that in order to find your own path in this earth walk, one must be willing to travel within. This is where one will find the understanding that will allow them to see their own face of truth. And where there is understanding, there will be the freedom to doing those things there is a need of doing.

"Think of it in the way we have shared with each of you before. And that was to look at each of the four races as a separate color of a car.

"Let us take only two of these colored cars, the white one and the black one.

"When these two cars are left in the parking lot on a hot and sunny day, you will see that the black car will get much hotter than the white car. Because the color black will receive more of the rays of the sun than the white color will, for the white color tends to reflect more of those rays of the sun than it will receive. This is what causes the two colors that are on the cars to be so different. But this is not the end of this comparison; there is more.

"When you see how each of these two colored cars react to the light rays from the sun, you can see how this affects the level of heat each of them will hold within it. Now, take these rays that are being received and reflected away from them and substitute lessons for rays of the sunlight.

"When you will, you begin to see why each of us have to walk through each of the four colors of the races. For it is within each of these races that we will find certain lessons we will need, but not all of them. For there are only certain ones to be found within one race, and others to be found in others.

"So whatever your spirit needs to learn, that will be the race you will travel in your earth walk. And it is from a spiritual perspective that this is done, my brothers, not from anything that is physical in nature, other than the lessons that will be attracted.

"Once this truth is understood, and you see another walking before you, one that is not within the same race you have chosen for yourself, then you will not see an outsider, but you will see one of your brothers or sisters, one of your own spirit family members who is traveling with those lessons they hold a great need to learn from.

"And when this is seen, you will have reached the place of understanding that there can be no separateness on this path that leads to the spirit, this spirit that resides within each of us. For it is this same spirit who is from Creator—and Creator is within all of us.

"There will be many during this time of The Season of the Long Shadow who would tell you that there is a difference between you and another, a difference that will place you either above them or below them. And if you will listen to those who would speak of these illusions, then you will become as lost and locked into the great illusion as they are. And when the time comes for the Earth Mother to begin cleansing herself, then you will be locked into the places where the groups of controlling will be, and there will not be an awakening for you until it is time for the Great Messenger to arrive.

"Listen well to these speaking words from this sixth warning, my brothers. Listen well and hold them with you at all times. For soon, very soon they will be needed by you and those who will come to you."

CHAPTER 64

❀

Seventh Warning

Who The Great Deceiver Is:
He Will Be The Result Of The Many, Not
The One
—From An Elder in the East

"Many of the two-legs will sit in awe for all the events that will be taking place during The Season of the Long Shadow, my brothers. One of them will be the appearance of The Great Deceiver and, for the most part, the two-legs will not have a clue to why or how this one person has entered as they have," began the speaking words from the Elder in the East position.

"However, let me share this with all of you. When one will keep their thinking minds on those things that are yet to take place, those things that will be when it is their time for them to be, then they will have wasted many of their seasons by concerning themselves with things they do not have any control over.

"And for those who would be willing to continue with such foolishness, they will not have much with them when they will leave this domain of the Earth Mother. They will not have much with them, because they had not taken the time of doing their own work, this work that could have led each of them to find their own truth and discover their own path to travel.

"It is the illusion that tells us we can change the world, my brothers, that we can make things different than they are going to be. But it is through finding one's own truths that they will understand this is not possible nor is it important for any one to change the world or any other.

"For when one will work within themselves, they will find there is only one thing they have any affect on, and that is themselves. For when they will come to see themselves for who and what they are in truth, then they have come to alter their own perception. And this allows them to see that it is not as important to work on changing something as it is to see it for what it is in truth. When this has been accomplished, the two-legs will come to see that all which is within this domain is here for a reason, a reason that may not just include them, but one that is for all life for what these adventures will present.

"Remember to keep in the front of your thinking minds that there is not now nor will there ever be anything which has been created by Creator which is evil or bad. There are only those things that have been created by him because they are needed. And all that has been created is a part of him.

"However, when we will look with the eyes of others and remain locked into the illusion, then we do see things that are evil and bad. For we do not see them as they are, only as others have told us to see them.

"This, then, is why we show you these speaking words of caution, my brothers. It is to remind you that as long as you will remain focused on the path you have been given to travel, there will not be a need for you to see any of these coming events as bad or evil. Rather, you will see them as being necessary in order for life to continue to grow and follow this great journey all of us are on.

"The Great Deceiver has been sought by many in this domain. But they have sought after him in ways that are as far from truth as you are from the farthest star, for they have been seeking him in places other than themselves. But it is from those places that are within each of them that this one will come from. For it has been from those places that have created the necessity of him to come into his place once again.

"And it has been through everyone's efforts that he has been called on to return to this domain to do his work. But until the ones who are calling on him stop these efforts, there will be no thing that will stand in his way of entering. For what so many will be doing during this time of The Season of the Long Shadow will cause everyone to give a part of themselves away, and it is from these small pieces of themselves that his life will be created among them.

"As we continue with this description of who the Great Deceiver is, my brothers, it would be wise to keep in the front of your thinking minds that there is no thing that has ever been created that is bad or evil. However, there are those things that have been called into this domain because of freedom of choice. And those who follow the path of the controlling groups will soon be seen like a snake that is eating itself.

"They will be the ones who will call on the Great Deceiver, they will be the ones who will feel the pains and frustration that have been so prominent in their life paths. But for those who have come to know the path of the spirit—those who have come to find their own truths and follow their own path—they will not be seen nor will they be bothered by the Great Deceiver. They will not be bothered by any of those things he will be allowed to do in this domain, because they have not been a part of his coming to life.

"However, they will still have to work with all of the earth changes and cleansings that will be prevalent during this time. And they will have their path filled with their own lessons as well. But they will not have the additional lessons given to those who have called the Great

Deceiver to return. For them, there will be many things happen to them. And as it is with all things, they will be filled with lessons for them to learn from, lessons that will show each of them what they have done by not learning from them.

"Remember what we have shared with you before, that when lesson is turned away from, there will be another layer of emotion that will cover it?

"Well, the result of all these emotions will be in the returning to life this one we have come to call the Great Deceiver.

"For he will be the manifestation of all those unanswered or unworked lessons and as he will feed on them, his strength returns to him once again. For his nurturing is one of emotion and his domain is the illusion.

"Wherever emotion and fear will travel, you will find the manifestation of the Great Deceiver. But in the times that are just ahead of all life, his form will enter one who will be walking a life path with the Earth Mother. And his path will require him to tear away all living things who had followed him, to tear them away and toss them into the next Earth Mother, this next place where all of this will have to be done once again by those who had not been willing to work through their own lessons this time.

"For when the time of the great choice will come over these lands, my brothers, there will be no place available for those who still need to learn from the lessons that are making this domain so heavy now. There will be no place for them because this Earth Mother is preparing herself to enter her fifth world of peace and light. And the lessons needed by the ones who will call the Great Deceiver back to life, will be in another time and in another place, and they will no longer be allowed here.

"But when they see what this Earth Mother's fifth world is like, they will not want to leave. And this would cause great problems for the ones who will remain.

"So in effect, the Great Deceiver will be the one who will call to those who can hear him. And when they will go to him, he will lead them away from this life...at first one by one, then in great numbers.

"The Great Deceiver feeds from those who live through control and greed. For this is his food, and they are his meal.

"But what has caused this Deceiver to live among the two-legs? It has been their path, this path that has allowed so few to control so many for such a long time, this same path that has allowed them to keep things that were meant to be shared to themselves, this path that many have followed and by doing so, have ignored their own lessons for the sake of the ones who have been telling them how to live, what is right and wrong, what is acceptable, and how much better they are than the ones who do not agree with them.

"From their actions, there has been a great amount of food available for the Great Deceiver, and he has always been in this domain. Only now, he will manifest himself within a shell and walk among those who have called on him.

"And he will call on them in order to have more food to eat, for his food is created by emotions that are not understood. And what is not understood is seen as fear, hate, and greed to oneself.

"These are things that he will need to consume if he is to continue with his body during this time for The Season of the Long Shadow, my brothers. The difference from the past is that now those emotions have become so strong, he has to enter this domain just to keep them from taking over all life.

"For he will only eat those things we have been speaking of, and those he will influence and have dominion over will be the ones who will have caused him to enter this domain.

"The others will not be recognized by him, and they will not be influenced by him either.

"Think of this, my brothers: in the seasons of the past has there not always been at least one person who has called many to his side so that he could make war or kill others who did not agree with him?

"This has been a small result of what happens when so many think in the ways we have been speaking of, those who carry with them fear, hatred, greed and so on.

"And when there was one among them who told them all of their wants would be satisfied if they would follow their lead, did they not follow?

"For this has always been the way of the lost, the path of those who remain lost within the great illusion, who have always been led by another, and who have always lost more of what they once had after the battles were over.

"But those are from the seasons of the past, my brothers. In the season that is just ahead of you, there will be an increase in feelings and emotional issues that will not be understood by all of the two-legs. There will be a perception that everything is going very fast and for the most part, they will be correct.

"For in The Season of the Long Shadow, all life will be in an accelerating review of all lessons they had turned away from, those lessons that were to be found on the present earth walk as well as from those in their past.

"For the most part, these lessons from this earth walk could be understood, but many will continue to turn away from them.

"But the lessons that will be coming to them from their previous earth walks, will not be as easy to understand. For the reference to those lessons has been left in a time and a place that is no longer with this earth walk of theirs. This will add to their confusion, my brothers, and the more confused the lesson learners become, the harder they will try to hide from their lessons. For there will continue to grow within each of them a feeling of helplessness, one that will cause them to run to those things they once held onto for their own security, those things they once felt secure with.

"It is to be during this time when all of the wealth you have gathered to yourselves will hardly be enough to buy food to eat or a safe place to rest. For those who do not have enough, will steal from others and there will be no one who will be there to stop them from doing this. For those who once enforced the laws that were made to protect them will be gone, and there will be no one who will be willing to replace them.

"All through this time, there will be an increasing level of want for material things, those material things that will bring them to places they consider safe, as well as those places where they will find safe food to eat and water to drink. You see, during these times, and after the food and water have been so contaminated, there will not be enough for everyone. And there will be great competition for what remains.

"This in itself will cause the emotions of hate, greed, fear, and uncertainty to grow among the two-legs, those same things that feed the Great Deceiver. But there will be more.

"The fighting within the four groups will also add to the levels of these non-understood emotions. And as these levels of emotion increase and manifest into their lives, this will add to the food that will be calling the Great Deceiver into his own life once again.

"And he will come—and he will answer all of their demands.

"For he will have come from a place that is greatly endowed with all those things that had once been of value to the two-legs. And for certain items, he will have more than many had ever dreamed of having.

"They will have forgotten there is any real meaning to living in this domain of the Earth Mother by this time, and they will believe that the only measure for their own existence will be the amount of wealth they have attained, even at the expense of the ones who are the closest to them.

"The Great Deceiver will come to them from his place on a high mountain where he will have spent most of his time away from the troubles and turmoil that others have been living with.

"He will come down from his high place with two others who will also be feeding from those who have called to them, two others who will be very close to the Great Deceiver. They will tell those who have called them into life, that there is a fourth place with them, one that may be filled by the one most deserving among the two-legs.

"For the one who will be called to walk with them, there will be no more hunger or pain. And they will show them all of their great wealth. For those who will see this, they will look into themselves and drop away those things that had kept them fighting among themselves. They will do this and follow the Great Deceiver and his two assistants to a place where their final journey will have been prepared for them, this final journey that will lead them to a place that will be remembered for many generations.

"It is a place where all of them will be gathered and discover they have been fooled into believing that this Great Deceiver could ever have enough wealth to give to all of them.

"But when this awakening will come to them, their time in this domain will be over, and they will look to the skies and see the arrival of the Great Messenger, the Great Messenger who will cause the Great Deceiver to leave this domain and come to reside in the next Earth, the twelfth Earth.

"However, as the Great Deceiver leaves, those who have followed him will feel that great hooks have been inserted in each of them, hooks that will tear at their skins and bodies and will cause their insides to fall out before them.

"And as the Great Deceiver leaves this domain, he will make a great movement of his arm and all who have been attached by these hooks will be torn away from their life here, torn away, but heard screaming and crying for anyone to let them remain. But it will be too late, for their lessons are many, and can no longer be found here but only in another time and in another place, another time and another place that the Great Deceiver will lead them to.

"All of this that we have been willing to share with you, my brothers, is to be. None of it can be changed, for the ones who would be so foolish to think they could change an entire domain are only to be found with the illusion.

"However, while it is not possible for them to change this earth, it is possible for them to understand themselves. And by doing so, they will not be affected by many of those things that are soon to be.

"For those who would wish to follow their own path and learn from their own lessons, we will leave with them a great truth, one that will assist them greatly for those times that are ahead of them: *'You Are Who And What You Attract To You.'*

"For those who have eyes and ears to see and hear with, this will be seen as a great blessing. And for those who cannot see or hear this, they, too, are on their own path, one that will have to be traveled to its own end."

PART X

❀

You Are The Stars Who Fell To This Land

CHAPTER 65

❀

This Is The Eleventh Earth We Have Passed Through

—From An Elder in the South

"There are not many of the two-legs who remember how all of this began, my brothers, how it came to be that the Earth Mother is greatly blessed with all she has now," came the speaking words from the Elder in the South position as she was looking deep within each of us sitting next to the warming fire.

"For when the Earth Mother was given this domain, there were no things that were available to her, not in the beginning. And because of the lack of life in this domain, none could travel with her, not even her own children.

"So there was a great cry for assistance to the Old Ones of all spirit families, a great cry for their assistance to unlock the many blessings that had been left with her, but could not get out.

"As the song legend goes, my brothers, Creator gave her all that she would need. But none of those blessings could be released until there would be those who would succeed in walking a life path with her.

"For each one who would successfully walk their path with her, there would be released to her one rain drop in memory of their success, this success that results from one doing those things they need to learn from and then move on to other lessons.

"However, there was quite a problem for the Earth Mother. Without the blessings of the water spirit over her lands, she could not release any of the life that was needed to support the ones who would eventually travel with her. For without the blessings of the water spirit, there can be no life sustained in this domain.

"As she would look over her domain, all she could see was barren land and great places within her that could not hold life to them.

"As she would look above her, she could see many spirits who were coming to her domain so they could learn from lessons only she could make available to them.

"For those who had come to her to learn, they had no other place left to go. The domain they once traveled in was no longer available to them, and in order to continue the great journey back to Creator—this journey that all of us are on—they would have to learn from their lessons that which would allow them to reach a needed level of understanding for themselves and all life that was with them.

"So it was that the Earth Mother was stuck. She could not release any of the blessings of the water spirit to begin the cycle of life in her domain until there had been successful life paths traveled with her. And no one could travel their life paths with her until she would be allowed to release the blessings of the water spirit.

"This then was her call to the Old Ones of all nations, my brothers. She was calling on those who would be willing to manifest themselves into one of her shells and travel a life path with her. But there were only a few who held this ability of doing such a difficult task, and these are the ones she called on to come to her in this time of need.

"From the four corners of all creation they came, my brothers. They came to do this request for the Earth Mother you now travel with. And they came with their hearts in a good place, for they knew the hardships that would be encountered by doing such a thing.

"Even the Old Ones would have to travel in a shell while they were in this domain. But because they had been blessed with having left their own domains with their bodies when the time was right, there were many things they would be allowed to do in this domain that the others would not be allowed. Those things would be in the path of creating for themselves those things they would need.

"For they had come to a place of understanding that all is available for those who could be willing to ask. And this is what they would do while they traveled in this domain. They began to create those things that would be needed by them and others who were soon to follow.

"As they sat in council with the Earth Mother, they told her what they would be willing to do while they were here. And they shared with her that before they began their earth walk with her, they would create a great garden, one where there would be no ending for any that would eat from its bounty.

"Then rising to enter this domain, they were each given a shell that would be used to carry their spirit. And they all traveled together crossing many places in all of the lands. They were looking for the place they would plant this garden of theirs, this garden that would be the beginning of all life as you have come to know it now.

"Having found the place where the garden would grow well, they released the waters from within their shells to feed it. And the waters that each of them carried with them were so rich in life and understanding, that the plant children grew very quickly and returned many blessings.

"As they tended this garden, there appeared many fruits, vegetables, and other blessings that could be eaten by those who would come into this garden of beginnings, this place that would allow all life to enter once again to learn the many lessons that were still needed by them to understand.

"And the Old Ones of all the nations looked over these lands and said this was good and the beginning has begun.

"Next, they called to the Earth Mother and told her they were ready to begin populating her domain. This populating would allow those spirits who were seeking to learn of their lessons to enter and begin their path.

"However, before they would be allowed to enter, each of them had to take one seed that had been grown in this great garden and hold it within them, to hold it within themselves as a reminder of what could be when all life is traveled in balance.

"For the Old Ones and the Earth Mother knew that once these spirits would enter this domain that the garden would have to be taken away. For its presence would preclude any of them learning from their own lessons because it would be too tempting for them to remain within its presence and ignore those things they needed to learn from.

"However, by having each of these new arriving spirits hold one seed with them, they would always be reminded of the times when they could be forever. The times that had once been living in this domain of the Earth Mother could return again, but only when all of the two-legs would gather unto themselves and each plant their own seed from the garden into the Earth Mother...together...and as one.

"They were told that until they would come to the place of seeing an ending of separation from themselves and all things, this seed would only remind them of a time and a place that is no longer with them, a time and a place that could be for all of them, but not for only a few.

"And so it was that as each of these spirits would near the garden, the Old Ones would give them one seed, then would return to the waiting place where they would wait to be called on when there was a shell ready for them to travel in.

"For several generations, the Old Ones would walk with all life. And as they would do this, they would also assist with the populating of this domain of the Earth Mother.

"Then those spirits who held a great need to learn from their own lessons began to enter this domain in greater numbers. But as they entered, the lessons they needed to learn from were not there, for those lessons had not yet been given permission to enter. For as long as the Old Ones would be traveling in this domain, those lessons would have to wait, to wait until the Old Ones had left.

"However, these lessons were waiting to enter in the skies above all living things. And they were seen as a great umbrella that completely enclosed all of the Earth Mother.

"For they were, in these times we are willing to share with you, a great canopy, one that did not allow the cold or heat to change, and one that did not allow the sun, the stars, or the moon to be seen by any who were walking here.

"However, as the Old Ones of all nations began to leave, there was a sudden change in this canopy of lessons that had been living in the high places in the sky nation. It was a change that was seen by all that held life within them.

"As the Old Ones began to leave, the canopy of lessons came closer to the Earth Mother. And the closer it would come, the more its presence and heaviness would be felt by all.

"When the last of the Old Ones left, there was a great reminding that was shared with everyone, a reminding that each of them held the great boat within them and they should run for its protection, for soon a great flood would fill all of the lands, a great flood that would not be of water, but of emotion. And this emotion would be the carrier of all lessons that would soon be presented to everyone.

"For it would be from the onset of this great flood that life could begin to do those things it needed. It would offer an opportunity of growing through understanding lessons that were needed by all.

"And this great boat they each held within themselves would allow them to float on the top of the flood of emotions—or, they would not use their great boat and would sink to the lower places where emotion would be felt the most.

"The Old Ones reminded the two-legs that for the remainder of their time, they would always be free to make their own choices. And one of these choices would be to remain in the great boat, or to sink to the deeper parts of emotions. But in either case, they would have opportunities of learning from their own lessons.

"As the Old Ones left this domain we call the Earth Mother, they reminded the two-legs that each of them carried a seed within them, that they each held within them one seed that was given when the great garden had been with them.

"And when they would all come together as one family, they would be allowed to plant this seed into the Earth Mother, and she would allow all pain and suffering to stop, for when one is within the great garden, there is no illusion and the lessons that are needed may be seen without the confusion of emotion or separateness among any.

"This was the beginning of this beginning, my brothers. And this is how we have come to say that you are the stars, who fell from the sky, for in truth, you are.

"And when it is time to travel further on this great journey, we will return and you will know us once again."

CHAPTER 66

❀

What Is Waiting For Those Who Remain

—From An Elder In The West

"During this long journey back to Creator, no one will be lost or forgotten along the way, even those who may not remain with this Earth
Mother because their lessons are located in another place and with
another time," began the speaking words from the Elder in the West
position.

"It would be well to keep in the front of your thinking minds there
will always be the slow ones, and there will be those who will journey
faster. But this is not to say any are greater or lesser than the other is,
it is only to say that they have different paths to follow. And on each
of their paths, they will gain in their own levels of understanding,
those same levels of understanding that will allow them to see their
own face of truth through lessons.

"When the great fire of cleansing will come over the Earth
Mother, the Star Nation will see many of its children impact with the
face of the Earth Mother. And when they will enter this domain, they
will ignite all of the fuels that will have returned to the top of all
lands.

"And this will set into motion the last cleansing. For it is to be a cleansing that will be complete for all living things in this domain. And from this cleansing, there will be a final farewell to all life that may no longer remain in this domain. For the change that will come to this Earth Mother is one of lightness and light. This is because there will no longer be the weight of lessons that have been with her for such a long time.

"But without lessons, there can be no continued learning. And those who still have a need to learn must be taken to the next Earth Mother where all of this will be done once again. All of those lessons they choose not to learn from will be offered to them again, but when they will come to them in the next domain, they will have added weight. For each time a lesson is turned away from, it will take onto itself another layer of emotion. And as the layers of emotion add up, so does the weight of the lesson, and its intensity.

"So each of these domains become more intense than the last and this is a truth that will continue until the journey is over.

"For the ones who remain in this domain, my brothers, will no longer have a need for those lessons that will be taken away. And the fire that is to perform the final cleansing will do so because there will be so many who will face a great fear of what is to come to them next. And they will not be willing to leave this Earth Mother willingly.

"It is for them that these final fires of cleansing will be placed on all lands. For this is the means of having those who need to leave do so. It is the final tearing away of the life that many no longer have.

"As the final places of the Earth Mother have been ignited and cleansed, the Great Star Nation will see that all that has been needed has been done, and they will send one great star relative to fall into the great waters.

"When this last act is performed, there will be great waves of water that will cover the Earth Mother. And from those waves of water, there will be fires no longer, only a white mist that will rise from her surface and into the sky nation.

"It is this white mist that will signal the Old Ones that the time has arrived to allow the return of the new earth walkers. It will be those who have been willing to do their own work and have attained the levels of understanding that were needed to take their bodies with them who will be returning at this time.

"For they will be the ones who will cause the many blessings of this Earth Mother to return. They will be the cause of opening the doorways that allow the flowing of the waters of life to once again bless all of the lands that will be left within this domain. And it will be from the flowing waters of life that all life will be restored, but not in the way that you can imagine now, for the changes in this domain will be great, greater than any can now imagine.

"The differences can be compared to living in the bottom of a deep, dark, and cold lake of water. As you reside there, you can feel the weight of the waters all around you. And while you reside there, there is no light that will be shown, no light that will resemble any light of truth.

"This, then, is the way we perceive the Earth Mother now.

"But the way we see life walkers after the great cleansing is comparable to leaving these dark and cold waters and returning to the skies above them. As one does this, there will be an appearance of a small tunnel of light as they emerge from their dark, cold, and heavy places. But as they strive to reach the surface of the waters, they see that this light is not a tunnel at all, but only a signal that there is light ahead of them.

"As they leave the waters that had been their home for such a long time, and break free of the holding waters of emotion and lesson to enter the freedom of the sky above them, they feel the warming of the light of life and peace and will know this is where they belong.

"They will have with them the freedom of Eagle and no longer have to reside in the mud that is found on the bottom of the lake of emotion and lesson.

"For when they re-enter this domain of the fifth world of the Earth Mother, they will do so as the life walkers they were meant to be. They will no longer have with them sickness or disease, nor will they see an ending of their shells they travel in. For all will have been returned to the One within the One. And from this place there will come many blessings, for they will have been returned to a place on their journey that will bring them closer to being with the Creator once again.

"And all of this they will know as good, for it is a signal their journey is coming closer to an end and soon, they will be home."

There was a silence that filled the air in this stone sheltering place with the Ancient Ones, a silence that was being born new to our council of five that something else was building, something I did not hold an understanding for.

"Our time with you is over now," came the speaking words from the Elder in the North position.

"We have shared with you what was needed to be heard. Now, it is time for us to return to those places where our presence is required.

"Night Hawk, are you ready to come with us, our brother?"

PART XI

❀

THE JOURNEY BEGINS

CHAPTER 67

❀

The Journey Begins

Looking over to the place where Night Hawk had been sitting, there were many questions that had quickly come over the faces of all of us, the faces of Grandfather, Two Bears, Cheeway, as well as myself.

For our seeing this one called Night Hawk only as an old friend of Grandfather and Two Bears had just been proven wrong. Even though he was still their friend, there was now something more about him none of us had seen before. And it was these same feelings I had about him all through this time of sharing with the Old Ones.

Seeing this look that had come over all of our faces, Night Hawk turned to face Grandfather and Two Bears, the ones who had spent so many of their seasons traveling with him.

"Do not be concerned, my brothers," began the speaking words from Night Hawk. "For I have not come among you to say good-bye. Rather, I have come among you to say hello."

These speaking words of his set many new questions into the front of all of our thinking minds, and from the face that Night Hawk was sharing with all of us, he knew this as well.

"The questions you hold for me can now be asked, my brothers. Use this time we have been given to share, for while we do not have much of it left, there is enough for what needs to be answered," Night Hawk said.

"Night Hawk," came the beginning of the speaking words from Two Bears. "Why is it that I did not see this thing in you, my brother? It concerns me that I did not notice."

"Do not be concerned, Two Bears, for this is no longer a rare occurrence among the ones who have been allowed to leave with their body and return. Not any longer," Night Hawk returned with the voice of a great understanding in the tone of his speaking words.

"You see, you know me as brother and friend, for this is how I have always appeared to you. So when it was time for my return into this domain, you did not see any great change around me because to you, this is how I have always been.

"When the times we are soon to be in arrive, there will be many such as I who will be walking among all of you. And to them, we will only be someone who will feel like an old friend, as someone who is very familiar to them, but they do not know why.

"However, many will feel our presence among them in this way. They will be pondering a problem that has found its way to them, and will have gone through many emotions to find their way through it. Then, just as they are no longer thinking of it, an answer will come to them. This answer will come to them with great clarity and they will see how simple the answer is, and that it had been with them all the time. Then, just as they will wonder why they did not see this answer before, they will look up and see one person walking away from them. They will see this one person, whether they are in a crowd of other people or all alone, walking away from them but also looking over their left shoulder smiling at them.

"They will sense there is a connection to this other person they have seen and the problem they have just found their way out of, but they are not sure.

"And by the time they have reached any conclusions as to our origin, we will be gone. For this is the path all of us who return must take, at least for the beginning parts that is. Later, we will have our identities known to all who are still walking their life paths in this domain."

"There have not been many who have been allowed this in the seasons past, Night Hawk. Is this not so?" came the questioning from Grandfather.

"Yes, my brother, this is truth. But the seasons that have been with us were for much different reasons. They were with all life in a way of allowing them to understand their own freedom of choice for that which would come to them. But in those seasons that are past, they had time enough to make them," Night Hawk returned. "The times that are ahead of us will not be filled with this time. For this time that had once been so abundant in the seasons past will almost be nonexistent."

"And what of the preparing, my brother, will this not affect all of the two-legs as they will pass through this Season of the Long Shadow? Without preparing for the energies that are from them-selves, there will not be the understanding for what has been offered," came the speaking words from Two Bears.

"This is true, my brother, for as each of the two-legs will move ahead in their life paths, they will encounter new energies that are from themselves. These energies are of themselves, but when they are not understood by them, they will experience great anxieties and explosions of consciousness," Night Hawk returned.

"And these are the same energies they need in order to accomplish what they said they would do while they journeyed with the Earth Mother," Grandfather returned.

"How will they reach their own levels of understanding and not fall into the path of the illusion, this path that would only show them fear for all they are encountering, if there is not the proper time for them to adjust to these new parts of themselves?

"We have seen what this had done to many in the past, my brother. For when these energies are encountered on any ones life path, and there is no understanding for it, the emotion and confusion is so strong it creates a void and many fall into it. And this void is filled with alcohol, drugs, and giving up for the two-legs. Is this to increase as well during these times that are soon to be with us?" Grandfather asked.

"Yes, Grandfather, they too will increase," came the return from Night Hawk. "They will increase because the opportunities of paying off all old debts will have increased for them as well.

"The Season of the Long Shadow is not only for the Earth Mother to cleanse herself, but it is the time for all life that is with her to do the same. That is, if they will take this great opportunity that is being presented to them.

"It is during this time when all of the old debts from this earth walk as well as those of the past are brought to these earth walkers. And it is done through the emotions that shroud their lessons even now.

"As they encounter these great changes that are soon to be with them, they will also feel the added weight of their emotions come to them. And those emotions will bring all of those things they had not understood, the lessons they continue to carry with them as a weight of guilt and confusion and pain within each of them.

"They will carry these lessons with them as they enter this domain of the Earth Mother so they may have the opportunity of finally learning from them. This process allows them the opportunity of clearing away all of these old debts, this karma, and be able to finish with all of their old business, to finish with the old and begin with the new, as they continue the great journey back to Creator.

"But there is a great price for this opportunity, my brothers, and that price is for each person to choose if they will run away from their lessons, or work with them.

"For the ones who will run from them, you will see an increase of the drug users, the drinkers of alcohol, the ones who will take life and property that is not theirs, and the ones who give up on themselves and look to blame others for all that has come into their life.

"For them, there will be no turning back, and the path they have begun must be completed. But for those who are willing to work their way past these lessons and emotions that are presented to them, they will see great hope before them.

"For those who choose to clean up all of their debts with life, we will be with them. And it will be from our presence among them that they will find the peace they need in order to continue the process of cleansing themselves.

"They will see us as someone they feel comfortable with, as someone who is not familiar to them, but someone nonetheless they will be willing to confide in.

"And they will find when they are near us, they will be relieved from many of their fears that have come to them from all of these new energies and emotions that will be with them.

"For it is through these new energies, and emotions of lessons, that they will be capable of doing what they said they would do in this domain of the Earth Mother.

"Remember, my brothers, it will be during this final time for cleansing that much will need to be done. For those who will be willing to do this work, we will be seen and felt among them. We will appear to them as messengers of light and bringers of peace.

"But they will only encounter us for brief moments of time, for if this were not so, they would not be willing to do their own work or remain long in this domain so they could learn.

"And this is why we will only be seen among the two-legs for short periods of time—but we will be seen, my brothers. And there will be no mistaking us for who and what we are. We are now where they may all be soon; that is, for those who will undertake this great adventure of returning to themselves while they are in this domain and in this great time of opportunity.

"It would be well to keep in the front of your thinking minds that for each one of you who now travels in a shell or a body, there were millions who were not given permission to enter during this time. And this makes it even more special for you to do those things you said you would do. For it was by your word of doing these things that allowed you entry into this domain instead of another. And it is from our presence among you that you will be shown a small light that will allow you to see what it is you must do next.

"Remember, there is no thing that will ever come to any of you by chance, for all that will be presented to any earth walker is done when it is time for it to be.

"And for those who would travel on the path that leads to the left, this path that is led by the body and fed by the emotion, they will see all events that will come to them during these times as one catastrophe after the other. And for them, there will not be any peace, there will only be one fight after the other and to them, rest will not come until their journey is over. For at the end of their journey, they will enter the place of the great sadness because they will see what they could have done, but did not. And they will understand that it was they who chose not to do it.

"For those who will travel on the path that leads to the right, this path that is led and fed by the spirit within each of us, they will see all of these events that will be presented to them as one blessing after the other. For it will be they who will have their eyes and ears of spirit opened for them. And they will be the ones who will not only see and feel our presence among them, but they will know us for who we are."

"And for you, Night Hawk, how was this process delivered? Was it as the song legends of our Old Ones told us it would be?" came the questioning from Grandfather.

"Yes, my brother. It was that and much more," Night Hawk returned. "More than I can relate to any of you at this time we have been given to share. However, for the parts I can relate to, I will do so now.

"It is true as the song legends say. There are two choices that are given.

"The first choice is given when one will finally complete all of the lessons they have set forth for themselves to learn from. They are taken to a place where there is seen before them only one person. And this person is holding a great book, which they begin to read from.

"Within this great book they shared with me all of the events that had come to me during my earth walk, and told me that I had succeeded in learning from my immediate lessons.

"They gave me the choice of leaving with them, or to return to the Earth Mother where I could work through all of the other lessons I still carried with me.

"And when this first choice was made to me, I did not see anyone come to get me. Rather, I was taken by hands that I did not see and we traveled down a very long and dark hallway that was made out of the night skies in every direction I could see.

"When I made my decision to return and finish up with all of my other lessons, I was returned. I did not remember any of the return journey or the conversations that were shared with me from the tine I made this decision. All I can remember was there had been many voices in the night skies around me and they were making great sounds of happiness for this choice I had made.

"When I had completed the tasks I had set before me, these tasks of working my way through all of the other lessons, that was the time that I remembered. For I was sitting on the spirit caller's ledge of the lands of the mesa when they came to me once again, those same ones I had felt before but could not see.

"As I saw them approach me and the sitting position I was in, I felt myself getting lighter and lighter until I was no longer sitting on the earth herself.

"They shared with me all I had accomplished and told me that if I would so desire, I could leave this domain and take my body with me. That was when they told me if I were to do this, I would be allowed to reenter this domain any time I would see a need to, and I would no longer have to go through the pains associated with the birthing and dying process that all of us must live with.

"I was told that for each of the other domains I had traveled through, I held another shell with me. And this shell or body was a vehicle that I had earned, just as we earn the right to wear the feather of Eagle. And for each of the domains we would travel through, we would hold a body to enter them with.

"Next, they shared with me the four steps of leaving, my brothers. The four steps needed in order to accomplish the final parts of this preparing.

"And as I would perform each of these steps, I would see many great changes come over me, changes that were washing away all of my old and worn out parts and renewing or replacing them altogether.

"For as I was going through this last stage of cleansing, I was told that this shell or body we travel in was not ever meant to wear out, hurt, or to end, not in the ways it has done for the two-legs of this domain. But as long as we fight with ourselves, we will continue to injure ourselves to the point that the outer self wears out or breaks down completely.

"Once the last step had been completed, I was taken to all of the domains that have ever been created as well as the new one where those still in need of lessons are soon to travel. As they shared all of this with me, I was told what was to be in the seasons that were ahead.

"I was also shown the four of you entering this valley, and that you would be sitting with the Ancient Ones of our people. It was the thought of being with you once again that I found myself standing at the opening of this great stone sheltering place and sharing your warming fire.

"But now, my brothers, I must be on my way. Rest assured that our paths will cross again, and when they do, they will have time to share our stories of life together as we sit around the council fires of old. And when we will do this, we will know it is good."

"Be well, my brother, Night Hawk," came the speaking words from both Grandfather and Two Bears in unison.

"Be well and travel in balance and understanding for all life that is living," came the final return from Night Hawk to all four of us.

"The journey has begun, my brothers," came the immediate response from the Elder of the East.

"Travel in wisdom and understanding. For as you will, with every moment of your earth walk, you will hold the understanding that you are not ever alone, for we are with you, as we have always been with you."

About the Author

❀

Patrick "Speaking Wind" Quirk, a Native American author, lecturer, and publisher, was raised by Grandfather, Two Bears, and White Eagle of the Pueblo People. He knew them as Spirit Callers, but in today's terms we would call them "SHAMAN". He, and his brothers, Cheeway and Nahe, were raised in the mountains of northern New Mexico by Grandfather and Two Bears for almost twenty years of their early life. This is where they were introduced to the ways of the spirit.

However, these teachings were to be put asleep for a time, and were not to be remembered until the time was right. But before the time was right, Grandfather, Two Bears, and White Eagle left, with their bodies, and several years later, Cheeway, and Nahe, ended their journey with the Earth Mother as well. That left Speaking Wind alone, to sort and process, what he had been given to share.

When Speaking Wind, Cheeway, and Nahe were very young, they were placed in a boarding school for several years. And this became the first of their experiences from having the control of others attempt to bury their spiritual beliefs. During their boarding school experience, they were not allowed to speak their peoples language, or practice their spirituality. And there were placed on them many scars of abuse for breaking these rules.

During the boarding school years, they, as well as others who were either mixed, or full blooded Native Americans, were not taught to read or write. Instead, they were marched to the back of the school and picked up by residents, then taken to their private homes, and farms, where they would work, for no pay. They would be returned to the boarding school, only, when it was time for them to learn of its religion.

However, they had asked too many questions from the teachings of Grandfather, Two Bears and White Eagle. Questions the teachers could not answer. So, they were labeled as "Spawns Of Satan" and forced to leave so they would not influence the children who were not following the "devil's evil ways".

When Speaking Wind, Nahe, and Cheeway entered the public school system, they could not read or write. They had not been taught. So not only the teachers, but the students, called them dumb Indians.

That left a mark on them, and gave them the determination to pursue their academic goals. Cheeway completed his doctorate and worked as one of the lead archeologists in the Yucatan Peninsula uncovering many of the ancient writings and civilizations that related to the sacred writings of the Pueblo People.

Nahe pursued a career in law enforcement, then went on to become Sheriff in a small town in New Mexico.

Speaking Wind attained two undergraduate degrees, two graduate degrees, and completed one half of his doctorate. He taught in the school of business, at the University Of Phoenix, then worked as a consultant in Asia, and for almost sixteen years, as a consultant in Europe.

However, for Speaking Wind, all of this was to end in 1993 when he died and was taken to the lands of The Ancient Ones. This is where he was not only reunited with Grandfather, Two Bears, White Eagle, Cheeway and Nahe, but also the "GREAT MESSENGER". This was when the "GREAT MESSENGER" gave Speaking Wind a message to bring back...a message that was to be shared with all who had the eyes to see, the ears to hear, the heart to feel, and the willingness of spirit to understand. It is a message of love, a message of hope, but most of all, it is a message that can replace fear, with understanding, for everyone.

It was at this time, when Speaking Wind was told it was time to begin his work, and return to Turtle Island (The Continental United States) with his son, White Raven. Speaking Wind, and his son, have traveled together since White Raven was six.

For the next five years, Speaking Wind and White Raven toured the United States holding seminars and lectures. In these, Speaking Wind presented Native American spiritual practices and performed healing ceremonies to all those who were ready to receive them. One of the most compelling of the ceremonies Patrick performed were the spirit drummings. During some of these, a dimensional "portal" would open and people looking into the eye of a stranger would be able to see an aspect of their own spirit as they truly were. Many times this image would be something that needed to be worked on.

But it was the drumming at Kinlock, one of the sacred areas in the land now known as Bankhead National Forest, which always resulted in different manifestations. Many times, people heard native flute music playing. And on more than one occasion, several people admitted to actually seeing images of the Old Ones.

Times were very fast paced for Patrick during the 1990's. Years of a grueling seminar schedule and many overnight hours of working on his latest manuscripts finally took their toll. On December 22nd, 1998, Speaking Wind crossed over. Or, as Patrick would say, he allowed his robes to fall away and leave the Earth Mother.

Since his departure, his physical presence has been greatly missed. But his spirit has visited many of us. And while his teachings are carried forward in the form of his books, manuscripts, and tapes, it is his personal impact on a small circle of friends and seminar acquaintances that will remain with us for the rest of our lives.

Washte Speaking Wind.

www.ingramcontent.com/pod-product-compliance
Lightning Source LLC
Chambersburg PA
CBHW020651270326
41928CB00005B/69